Skills for Helping Professionals

This book is dedicated to all of the children, families, and students that I have worked with over the years and to Kevin, Monica, Curtis, Yuol, and Griffin. All of you have graciously trusted me to help you in times of need, and all of you have taught me more than you ever will know about helping.

SAGE was founded in 1965 by Sara Miller McCune to support the dissemination of usable knowledge by publishing innovative and high-quality research and teaching content. Today, we publish over 900 journals, including those of more than 400 learned societies, more than 800 new books per year, and a growing range of library products including archives, data, case studies, reports, and video. SAGE remains majority-owned by our founder, and after Sara's lifetime will become owned by a charitable trust that secures our continued independence.

Los Angeles | London | New Delhi | Singapore | Washington DC

Skills for Helping Professionals

Anne M. Geroski
University of Vermont

Los Angeles | London | New Delhi
Singapore | Washington DC

Los Angeles | London | New Delhi
Singapore | Washington DC

FOR INFORMATION:

SAGE Publications, Inc.
2455 Teller Road
Thousand Oaks, California 91320
E-mail: order@sagepub.com

SAGE Publications Ltd.
1 Oliver's Yard
55 City Road
London, EC1Y 1SP
United Kingdom

SAGE Publications India Pvt. Ltd.
B 1/I 1 Mohan Cooperative Industrial Area
Mathura Road, New Delhi 110 044
India

SAGE Publications Asia-Pacific Pte. Ltd.
3 Church Street
#10–04 Samsung Hub
Singapore 049483

Acquisitions Editor: Kassie Graves
Editorial Assistant: Carrie Montoya
Production Editor: Bennie Clark Allen
Copy Editor: Lana Todorovic-Arndt
Typesetter: Hurix Systems Pvt. Ltd.
Proofreader: Annie Lubinsky
Indexer: Julie Grayson
Cover Designer: Scott Van Atta
Marketing Manager: Shari Countryman
eLearning Editor: Lucy Berbeo

Copyright © 2017 by SAGE Publications, Inc.

Printed in the United States of America

Library of Congress Cataloging-in-Publication Data

Names: Geroski, Anne M., author.

Title: Skills for helping professionals / Anne M. Geroski.
Description: Los Angeles : SAGE, [2017] | Includes bibliographical references and index.

Identifiers: LCCN 2015040234 | ISBN 9781483365107 (pbk. : alk. paper)

Subjects: LCSH: Helping behavior. | Interpersonal relations. | Social service. | Counseling.

Classification: LCC BF637.H4 G47 2017 | DDC 158.3—dc23 LC record available at http://lccn .loc.gov/2015040234

This book is printed on acid-free paper.

16 17 18 19 20 10 9 8 7 6 5 4 3 2 1

Brief Contents

DETAILED CONTENTS

The SAGE edge companion site at **edge.sagepub.com/geroski** provides password-protected instructor resources including a test bank, PowerPoint® slides, ideas for class assignments, access to the original videos created for the text, and more, as well as mobile-friendly web quizzes and flashcards for students.

Note: PowerPoint is a registered trademark of Microsoft Corporation in the United States and/or other countries.

PREFACE

I confess that after my initial training as a counselor, I was proud to think that I had joined the club of special individuals who exclusively possessed the seemingly magical and potentially powerful skills of helping. This idea helped bolster my developing and naïve professional identity and all of its concealed insecurities by allowing me to believe that as a trained therapist, I was unique—that I had skills others did not have.

However, as I moved out into the world of work, I began to notice that many of the ideas and skills that I had learned in my clinical training also guided my work in other domains. These same skills (when I used them well, of course) made me a better teacher. And, as I became a parent, I found that these skills and ideas were the ones that I used when I was parenting at my best. These skills also appeared in my healthiest interpersonal relationships; they were the tools that I was using to forge connections and to navigate challenges.

When I looked around, I noticed that professionals in other fields also used many of these "special" skills. The most competent social workers, nurses, doctors, early childhood interventionists, and lawyers that I knew seemed to have these skills that I thought were unique only to therapists. In fact, much to my surprise, I saw that the most helpful and effective grocery clerks, bus drivers, airline flight attendants, receptionists, and other service providers that I encountered in everyday life also seemed to possess some of these very same skills! Hmm.

These skills of helping, I began to see, cut across a variety of contexts. They are not owned solely by any one helping or service profession. This is not to say that the work of counselors, teachers, parents, doctors, lawyers, grocery clerks, and customer service representatives is the same; intention is what guides the ways in which we engage with others in the various venues of our lives. All of these helpers have different jobs to do, and they also have unique and uniquely different sets of knowledge and perspectives that dictate the ways in which they engage with others. But when it comes down to interacting with others, those who seem to be most successful use many of the helping skills outlined in this book.

This, it turns out, is true. One of the most important findings that has informed the professional training and practice of helping across a broad scope of settings is that the ability to form meaningful relationships and being intentional in those relationships are critical to effective helping. This ability to form meaningful relationships happens in a multitude of settings and is facilitated by a variety of professional and lay helpers, not just clinical therapists. Relationship and intentionality do not guarantee change, of course, but we do know that helping is less likely to be beneficial without either of these.

The intent of this book, then, is to introduce important helping relationship skills that we know are useful in supporting and promoting positive growth and development in others. My hope is that you will come away at the end of the semester with a strong foundation of knowledge and communication skills, as well as a solid commitment to provide careful, intentional, respectful, and beneficial service to others. I hope that you will also commit yourself to engage in continued learning and practice so that your helping work will develop over time and be sensitive and flexible enough to meet the diverse needs of helpees from a variety of backgrounds and situations.

This book begins with an overview of the broad field of helping. We will see that while professional helping practice comes in a wide variety of forms, there are some specific factors that are common to most helping professions and that have been shown to be effective in promoting therapeutic growth and change. These common factors are reviewed in Chapter 1. The next two chapters in this text focus on theoretical ideas about people and helping. The discussion introduced in Chapter 2 outlines key normative concepts in psychology, human development, and neurobiology that orient us in terms of how we think about people and the challenges they face. This chapter also calls attention to the ways in which unique aspects of culture and social experiences shape how people perceive the world and how they are perceived and treated by others. These experiences shape human development and influence needs of those being helped. Chapter 3 focuses on the theories that guide the ways in which helpers do the work of helping. The intent here is to illustrate that how you intervene as a helper is tied to how you understand human development and the etiology (cause) of problems. The major takeaway from these two chapters is that helpers need to examine the assumptions that are operating behind the interventions they use in the lives of others. Our ideas about human nature and what causes difficulties in people's lives influence how we offer help; what we think really does matter.

Chapter 4 introduces the ethical and legal principles that guide helping practices. Readers are advised to seek the codes of ethics and relevant state and national laws that monitor, shape, and regulate their particular area of practice. Appendixes A and B list a number of helping professions and include website addresses for their related helping organizations. Many organizations of helping professionals have their own codes of ethics that their members are expected to follow. Chapter 5 discusses the importance of helper self-awareness. Here the focus is on the importance of being cognizant about how our experiences in the world shape how we interact with others. Helpers are encouraged to develop insight into their own personal values, beliefs, understandings, experiences, cultural background, and social class identities because these shape how we think about and interact with others. Beyond self-awareness, helpers are also called upon to develop awareness about the cultures and social identities of those with whom they work. Embedded here is the important point that understanding self and others must include recognition of the detrimental effects of social discourses that confer privilege upon members of some social groups over others. These dynamics of privilege and power affect helpees and helpers, and, of course, the ways in which help is delivered and received. The discussion of positioning theory, which is reviewed in the following chapter, offers a road map for navigating these challenging social issues. Finally, Chapter 5 addresses helpers' abilities to regulate their own emotional reactivity and emphasizes the importance of engaging in self-care so as to avoid burnout, vicarious traumatization, and impairment of competence.

Chapter 6 initiates the skills section of this book. This chapter focuses on assessment, which is the clinical term for collecting information about the helpee and the challenges that are to be addressed in the helping relationship. The more relevant the information you have about the helpee, the type of assistance that is being requested, and the helpee's level of investment in change, the better able you will be to put into place an effective plan for your work. In this chapter as well, helpers are shown how to set goals for their work, and they are asked to think about the position they will assume in helping. The emphasis in this chapter and in the others that follow is for helpers develop a style of helping that is more in line with the concept of doing *with*, respecting, and promoting agency, rather than doing *for* or *to* the helpee.

Chapters 7 and 8 identify and describe a series of skills that are used for listening, responding, and promoting change in helping conversations. These are the skills that are the foundation of training for most clinical helpers, and they also are used across a multitude of helping situations to form relationships and encourage change. Brief video illustrations of these skills are included on the companion website. These videos were created to help you see how these skills may be put into practice and are indicated by a margin icon. No doubt you will see imperfections in these clips, and hopefully, your critical analysis of them will inspire you to perform the skills in your own creative and, perhaps, more useful or productive ways.

The skills identified in Chapters 7 and 8 are also used to assist others when they are in crisis, which is the topic of Chapter 9. The experience of being in crisis can result from a variety of circumstances, including natural or human-made disasters, situational challenges such as the death of a loved one or employment changes, or psychiatric conditions. It is important for us to remember that when we work with people who are in crisis, we are seeing them at their most vulnerable moments. For this reason, particular attention to assessment and protection are underscored in this chapter. We will also review basic warning signs and protocols for responding to people who are in danger of harming themselves or others.

The final chapter in this book, Chapter 10, is about working in groups. This chapter builds on the knowledge and skills outlined in all of the earlier chapters, but it introduces the additional complexity of working with multiple people at the same time. Whether you are called upon to lead counseling or therapy groups, teach skills groups, or conduct meetings, this chapter offers basic insights into group processes and outlines specific skills that can be used across all of these group types to promote learning and positive change.

This book is intended as introductory, to initiate undergraduate and graduate level students into a career in professional helping. Each chapter within its covers could easily be an outline for a whole text on that particular topic itself. Indeed, there are entire books that have been written on each of the theories that I mention just briefly in the early chapters in this text, and those authors offer countless details and nuances that I have not had space to detail here. There are semester-long classes on group work, crisis intervention, and ethics, all of which offer important depth that is not possible in an introductory text like this. And a more thorough investigation into theories, issues, and challenges related to working with individuals who identify or are positioned in a variety of social and cultural groups is critical for all helpers. I want to be clear that reading this book is an introduction that I hope will stimulate you to further your study of human development, neurobiology, psychology, sociology, culture, and the various theories of helping that are mentioned within these pages. And the skills that I outline in the various chapters in this book are offered as basic instructions for a practice that will take years to develop. I, for one, after all these years, am still working to refine my interpersonal communication and counseling skills, and I continue to study new methods of helping practice. It is a dangerous assumption to think that one has learned it all.

It has been said that when you give to others, you get back double in return. This speaks, I believe, to the ways in which reaching out to and helping others nurtures one's own soul. Of course most helpers are not looking for what they will get in return when they enter into a helping profession, but it is true that there is something very fulfilling about working with others. This book is intended to assist in shaping your helping practices so that they are fulfilling to you and so that they are beneficial to the people who entrust you with their vulnerabilities and have faith in your ability to help. I encourage you to work diligently under the careful tutelage of the professor or supervisor who is working with you in your study of human relationships so that your work will enable you to reach these goals of professional satisfaction and making a difference in the lives of others.

ACKNOWLEDGMENTS

Kassie Graves, Associate Director and Publisher at SAGE Publications, is the strong woman behind this book. Without her firm and supportive encouragement, gentle guidance, bottomless reserve of knowledge, warmth, and sense of humor, this book would never have been coaxed into existence. Thank you, Kassie. I can't find the words to express how much you and this project have meant to me.

I also owe an appreciation to Carrie Montoya, senior editorial assistant at SAGE, who was always available to answer all of my silly questions with endless patience. And thanks to Bennie Clark Allen, SAGE project editor, and Lana Arndt, copy editor, who had the tough job of making sure that all of the t's in this book were appropriately crossed and the i's dotted correctly, and for taking this book through production. A special thanks also goes to all of those involved in the production of the videos that accompany this book, especially Bryan Fishman and Lauren Habib, who demonstrated endless patience and stellar camera competence and creativity. All of these people have worked tirelessly with the SAGE approachability and professionalism that has made this book possible. Thanks to all of you at SAGE for your generosity in knowledge and gracious spirit.

A big thank you also goes to all of the readers who offered thoughtful comments and excellent suggestions on earlier versions of this book:

Gregg Amore, DeSales University

James Boyd, Walla Walla University

Kathleen Lynch Conway, Wayne State College

Barbara J. Crowe, Arizona State University

Paige E. Dickinson, Eckerd College

John L. Garland, Alabama State University

DeAnna Henderson, Alabama State University

Mary-Anne M. Joseph, Alabama State University

John Jurowicz, Lewis University

Judith Kuppersmith, City University of New York

Christopher T. H. Liang, Lehigh University

Jodi McAdams-Radzin, The University of Arkansas-Little Rock

Maxine L. Rawlins, Bridgewater State University

Sara Satham, Bunker Hill Community College

Elaine M. Sharpe, Rockford University

Amy L. Skinner, University of Tennessee

Barbara N. Vesely, St. Cloud State University

Eric G. Waldon, University of the Pacific

Ed Watkins, University of North Texas

And also to David Hutchinson, who shared a parallel path with me from the start of this project, and whose friendship has nurtured me through the ebbs and flows of life over the past 20 years. Thanks, too, to Kim Murton, my childhood friend who created the wonderful helping relationship donkey-van illustration for this book. And finally, I continue to be indebted to my colleagues and friends at the University of Waikato, Hamilton, New Zealand, especially Kathie Crockett, John Winslade, Lorraine Smith, and Wally McKenzie, who taught me to see the world in new ways—an influence that is clearly present throughout this text.

My appreciations would not be complete without acknowledgement of others who have been with me and offered me much during this writing process. To start, I am very thankful for the University of Vermont field house upper track where I spent many days these past two very chilly Vermont winters mapping out many sections of this book in my head while running circles. This circumstance, I believe, explains any inappropriate circular arguments and flighty ideas that may appear in the text. For those errors, I do apologize and also blame on bad weather. I also want to thank Dean Miller of the College of Education and Social Services at UVM for her support that allowed me to work on this project. Dean Miller's support enabled me to enlist a UVM Counseling graduate student (who has now graduated), Cori Chandler, to read over every single sentence in every chapter of this text, offering me thoughtful comments and appropriate edits. Thanks a million, Cori, for your edits, questions, suggestions, your work on the supplemental materials, and most of all, for your cheerleading. Without you, this book would have been just a jumble of words on paper. Thanks, too, to graduate student Laura Engstrom for your careful checking of all of the references in the final stages of my writing.

And last but never least is a huge appreciation for my partner, Kevin Rodgers, who endured and supported me at each and every stage of this writing process. Kevin and our children, Monica, Curtis, Yuol, and Griffin, offered applause, encouragement, caring, patience, and millions of "learning opportunities" that are embedded within the covers of this text. Being in relationship with the people that I love the most has brought knowledge, nuance, and creativity to my professional clinical training in helping. Wisdom grows in the most unexpected places.

A single-authored book is never created by that one author alone. A project like this is always built upon the ideas, support, lessons, and enthusiasm of a large group of others who stand behind the scenes contributing in ways they may never realize. To all of you mentioned here and to those who have been unintentionally omitted, thank you!

About the Author

Anne M. Geroski, EdD, is associate professor in the Graduate Counseling Program at the University of Vermont. She has served as Counseling Program Coordinator and School Counseling Track Coordinator and has taught a variety of courses in the Counseling Program over the past 19 years, including an undergraduate Helping Relationships course, for which this book was originally conceived. She has a number of scholarly publications on issues relevant to school counseling, social and emotional development, and human development. She also is the coauthor of a book on group work in schools. Anne has worked as a school counselor, mental health counselor, school teacher, and school administrator, and in nonclinical helper roles in a variety of settings across the United States and abroad. Anne and her partner, Kevin, live in Burlington, Vermont, and they are the parents of Monica, Curtis, Yuol, and Griffin.

CHAPTER 1
HELPING PROCESSES

LEARNING OBJECTIVES

1. Learn about various professional helping roles

2. Understand the differences between helping, counseling, therapy, and advocacy

3. Understand, very generally, what is helpful when working with others

INTRODUCTION

Welcome to the world of professional helpers!

If you are reading this book, it is probably because you have an interest in working with others, even if you are not sure exactly what that might look like in the future. In this chapter, we will discuss various types of helping professions and review what the literature teaches us about what is helpful in working with others.

HELPING TERMS: HELPING, COUNSELING, PSYCHOTHERAPY, THERAPY, AND ADVOCACY

Helping

When we use the word *helping* as a noun, one definition is "a portion or serving of food." Of course, in this book, we are not really interested in talking about food! Here we are looking to understand the word *helping* used as a verb, when it is used as an action that is aimed toward others. Permit me to borrow the reference to food as a metaphor for what helping is, though, because ironically, the food metaphor is oddly fitting here, too. Food is the substance that enables us to grow. And helping is that which we give to others so that they may grow. Helping is the effort that we make to offer strength and support to people who want to learn, change, and grow, or who need something when times are hard. Helping is the plate of food that we lay before others to fortify them, offer nourishment, and help them feel cared for.

Counseling, Psychotherapy, and Therapy

Within the category of "helpers" exists an expansive array of clinical and nonclinical roles and professions. **Clinical** helpers are those who have received advanced level training (master's or doctoral degrees), typically including extensive supervised clinical practice experience, to offer therapeutic interventions for people who struggle with personal or interpersonal difficulties or mental health challenges. Examples of clinical helpers include mental health counselors, marriage and family therapists, psychologists, psychiatrists, and clinical social workers. While **nonclinical** helpers may also work in the area of mental health providing adjunct care, support, or instruction, they typically have a bachelor's level educational degree, and their work is under the close supervision of a clinical mental health professional. Job titles for these nonclinical positions include counselor, advocate, and therapy assistant. Nonclinical helpers may work in a variety of other settings, too, providing, for example, career guidance, nutrition counseling, exercise coaching, education, assisting with a multitude of daily living tasks, etc. Nonclinical helpers also occupy a vast variety of roles in the medical field. These latter positions may require advanced-level educational training or degrees. A list of many of these varied roles is included in Appendix A.

There is much confusion regarding the terms *counseling* and *psychotherapy*. You may notice that in some settings, they are used somewhat interchangeably, yet in other settings they have clear and distinct meanings. For example, a lawyer provides legal counsel, which is obviously very different from the counseling services provided by a mental health counselor. Most of us know not to go to a lawyer for therapeutic intervention regarding our mental health concerns, and not to seek mental health counseling for legal advice. Lawyers, then, are nonclinical professional helpers, and they have advanced degrees and training in the law and legal practice.

In this text, we will use the term **counseling** in reference to a helping practice that it conducted by clinical and nonclinical helpers and is aimed at assisting others with personal, social, or psychological issues or concerns. As mentioned, the distinction between clinical and nonclinical counseling has to do with training level and scope of practice. **Psychotherapy** typically refers to a mental health clinical practice, and **therapy** is just a shorted version of the word psychotherapy. So, clinical counseling and psychotherapy are two terms with virtually the same meaning and are often used interchangeably (Sommers-Flanagan & Sommers-Flanagan, 2004).

The work of counselors and psychotherapists has to do with symptom remission and improved everyday functioning (Lambert, 2013). They help people cope with interpersonal and mental health difficulties such as those posed by addictions, trauma, mental illness, experiences of stress, and difficulties in adjustment. They also help people develop healthy interpersonal relationships, which sometimes includes thinking about situations differently, developing better communication skills, or behaving in different ways. Additionally, counselors and psychotherapists work with individuals in decision-making for the present and future or developing healthy lifestyles, and they provide support for people experiencing crisis or challenges in their lives. The work of counselors and psychotherapists is based on training in psychology and human development theories, such as those discussed in Chapter 2, and also on practice theories such as those reviewed in Chapter 3. A list and descriptions of various clinical and nonclinical helping positions is included in Appendix A.

Advocacy

When we are witness to the adverse effects of social forces such as prejudice and discrimination (in all of their overt and subtle forms) that lead to problematic institutional practices and barriers in the lives of the people we serve, intervention should focus on those sources of problems rather than on the individual. What sets advocacy apart from counseling and psychotherapy, then, is that advocacy attempts to change variables that sit outside the individual—systems and institutions that hamper people in various ways (Funk, Minoletti, Drew, Taylor, & Saraceno, 2005; Lewis, Lewis, Daniels, and D'Andrea, 1998). Advocates are helpers who work *with* and/or *on behalf* of people or groups for a particular cause or policy, and the implicit goal of most advocacy efforts is to increase peoples' sense of personal power or agency. Of course, advocacy is not limited to issues related to mental health. It is relevant in many other fields as well. There are patient advocates in hospitals, child advocates in court systems, advocates for individuals who have disabilities, etc. More about advocacy as a helping intervention is included in Chapter 8.

HELPING RELATIONSHIPS

Being helpful generally refers to doing something for others. Synonyms for helping relationships might include being accessible, supportive, benevolent, useful, and working for the benefit of others.

Illustration 1.1 is interesting, but you are probably wondering what it has to do with helpfulness. I would like to propose that it captures the essence of professional helping relationships. Really! Notice in this illustration that despite their obvious differences, the donkey and the van are traveling together. They are traveling in the same direction, side by side. If we were to think of the van as the helper, we can imagine that it has the potential to offer shade to the donkey if the journey becomes too hot or bright. Also, the van looks like it might be used for camping, with a mini fridge, stove, and storage capacity, and thus we can imagine that it might have a cache of food and water inside. So, this helper van is in the position to offer nourishment and sustainability to the

Illustration 1.1   The Helping Relationship

Kim Murton

donkey, if needed. We are also aware that while the van could probably travel much quicker than the donkey, it doesn't. They travel side by side. The van doesn't stir up a lot of dust, doesn't run the donkey off the road, and doesn't hurt the donkey by running it over—it travels respectfully at the pace of the donkey. As a metaphor for the helping relationship, then, we see a journey among two who are very different. Yet the journey is shared, with one in the position of walking forward toward the goal and the other, of offering comfort and nourishment as needed along the way.

The Contract

It is important to distinguish helping relationships from the other types of relationships that we all have in our lives. The journey of helping is not the same journey as friendship, even though many of the qualities of being a good friend are also qualities of being a good helper. The helping relationship is best thought of as a contractual relationship where one is in the role of providing

Illustration 1.2 A Contractual Relationship

©iStockphoto.com/

goods to someone who has requested them. In fact, in many professional helping relationships, helpees are called *clients*—the person for whom professional services are rendered. This term emphasizes the idea that the recipient of services is a consumer who receives services in exchange for some kind of payment. An important marker of helping relationships, then, is the helping contract. This alone makes it different from the other relationships we have in our lives. All of the components of the helping contract discussed here are outlined in Table 1.1.

Like contracts in other settings, helping contracts contain agreements about the exchange of **services and compensation** that will be a part of the helping relationship. As Illustration 1.2 suggests, these may be formal or informal, and explicit or implicit. For example, if you are working as a residence hall advisor, you have been hired to supervise students in the dorm—that is the contract you are working under. As part of this contract, your role is to be available to help students when they have questions, are in trouble, or seem to be struggling with something. Your role is also to protect the premises and enforce the residence hall rules. You will probably be required to post hours so the students will know when you are available, talk to all of the residents about the dorm rules, and maybe also plan a certain number of social activities throughout the year. Also part of this contract is the compensation you will receive for your work. This may be in the form of a tuition waiver, a salary stipend, or perhaps it includes a meal plan and a nice room to live in. All of these agreements are made explicitly and in advance so that everyone is clear about your role within this helping relationship. They form an explicit helping contract. For another example, let us say that you have offered to be a volunteer "friend" for a new refugee family in the community. This helping relationship is far more informal, with the details of the support you will provide to be worked out with the family, depending on their changing needs over time. This latter helping relationship has an implied helping contract, however informal it may be, because your contact and role with the family is to provide services or assistance that they may need. Because of this, it is not the same as a friendship, even if it grows and feels like one, even if you call yourself a "family friend."

A defining component of the helping contract that is evident in the above examples is the concept of **nonmutuality**. Unlike other relationships, the focus of the helping relationship is always on the needs of the helpee. This is not to say that you, personally, do not have any needs. Nor is it to say that you may not benefit from the relationship in some way (such as payment or satisfaction). What nonmutuality does mean is that the sole focus of the work and all of decision-making must be based on the interests and needs of the helpee. And this, then, is the substance of the helping contract. For example, as a victim advocate in a rape crisis phone hot line, you will not be talking to callers about your own trauma experiences. A customer service representative in a department store will not be talking on his personal phone when a customer is present. A counselor sitting in the room with a client is not daydreaming about what she will be doing after work. And none of these helpers should be engaged in making plans with the helpee to go to a coffee shop to further discuss the issue at hand. The helping relationship is not a mutual relationship.

While it is important for helpers to have a professional level of emotional investment in the helping relationship, this investment comes with **restrictions**. These restrictions include prohibitions against intimacy, mutual friendship, and physical contact. These will be discussed in more detail in Chapter 4 in the discussion of helping ethics, and alluded to again in Chapter 5, where the discussion focuses on helper self awareness and competence. What is most important here is that the conditions of the helping contract outline the parameters of the helping relationship; helping must be focused on the decided upon goals of the work together.

It might be helpful here to talk a little about **liking**. One of the rewards of working as helpers has to do with the emotional investment we make in the helping relationship. For example, an assistant day care teacher I know really enjoys her work, and she clearly likes all of the children in her care. In fact, it is probably accurate to say that her fondness for the children is part of the informal compensation she receives for her work—and it is probably why she is so good at what she does. However, with her, like with all helping professionals, liking should never get in the way of doing what is necessary and appropriate to help achieve the goals of the helping contract. In the preschool, for example, liking should not prevent my friend from disciplining a child when it is needed. Also, liking should obviously not yield unfair treatment of one child over another. But notice how subtle this piece about liking can be. Liking is important to what we do, but it also can have a way of working itself into our helping relationships and influencing them in ways that we do not always clearly see. A professional level of liking means that we are invested in the best interests of the helpee, and that investment compels us to work with intentionality, even when that requires us to do things that are uncomfortable.

A second component of liking worth mention here is the need to be liked. Wanting to be liked by others is by no means a bad thing. Social interest develops because we want to be part of community, and to do so, we act in ways that are accepted and favored in that community—we become likeable. For example, lending money to a friend is a nice thing to do, and it probably will cause that friend to like you. We all like the student in our dorm who shares the home-cooked treats that he has just received in the mail. But when we work hard to be liked in helping relationships, the focus shifts from the helpee and back on to us. Suddenly the direction of our actions is on being liked rather than on what is best for the helpee. Worse yet, it may be hard for us to enter into difficult conversations, provide feedback, or take action that may be needed but not favored by the helpee, if we are concerned about being liked. So, remember that the helping contract is what defines the helping relationship. *Liking* and *being liked* are nice, but they should never get in the way of the work that needs to get done in the helping relationship.

Related to these thoughts on liking, **truth and honesty** are critical to helping relationships, but they can also be tricky. Just as we navigate difficult decisions about being honest and truthful in our personal lives, we also must be careful about these in helping relationships as well. For example, in some friendships, you may feel completely comfortable talking about politics and revealing who you will be voting for in the upcoming election. However, if a helpee wants to know if you like a particular political candidate, responding with this information may have the potential to compromise your relationship. Similarly, if a helpee asks, "Do you like me?" then you are faced with a dilemma about honesty. What if you really don't like many things about the helpee? Is it appropriate to say that? Or if you do like the helpee very much, might your saying so lead to misinterpretations or to behaviors that are aimed at nurturing your liking rather than the goals of the helping contract? Many of us have worked with individuals struggling with substance use who have asked us if we, ourselves, drink or use. Helpees often want to know if we have had the problems that they are grappling with. All of these situations are very complicated, and they are easily complicated when one has a strong need to be liked by others.

The implications of responding with truth and honesty can be deceptively larger than we are aware of in the moment. For example, might the helpee above who asked about your substance use then tell others about your history? Might she then minimize her own use because she thinks that clearly you had substance use problems and got over them? And, as seems most evident in all of these scenarios, notice how easily truth and honesty can shift helping conversations from the helpee to the helper. So, keep in mind that being honest and truthful in a helping relationship is structured by the contract of the relationship. It might be appropriate for helpers to provide truthful feedback or information to helpees on issues related to their work together. If the helpee is asking for your honest opinion about something that is unrelated to the topic of your work together, however, or if you think that there is even the slight possibility that answering a question could possibly compromise your work, you may need to refrain from being completely honest.

Photo 1.1 Truth and Honesty

©iStockphoto.com/Diosmirnov

Investment is another important aspect of the helping contract. Meeting the goals of the helping relationship, being present through the challenges as well as the joys, and working until the final goal is met, all have to do with investment in the helping relationship. You should not enter into a helping relationship that you are not able to commit to, and you should always honor the commitments you have made.

Another aspect of investment that is important for helpers to be aware of has to do with the relative balance of investment in the helping relationship. Here we are talking about the extent to which a helper is invested in the helping relationship and the work that is part of the helping contract, in comparison to the level of investment of the helpee. Clearly, your level of investment in the work of helping should not exceed that of your helpee. If you are more invested in the achievement of the goals than the helpee, you may find yourself working harder and doing more of the work that needs to be done. Remember: Reaching the goals of the helping contract is the responsibility of the helpee. Your job is to help her do this. Investment in the relationship should always be to do what is appropriate and within your power to help the helpee reach the

Table 1.1   The Helping Contract

Key Components of the Helping Contract
• Services and compensation
• Nonmutuality
• Relationship restrictions
• Liking
• Truth and honesty
• Investment

goals that are important to him or her. Helpers should not do *for*, they should do *with*. The discussions on stages of change and motivating change in Chapters 6 and 8 is relevant to this conversation about helpee investment in the helping goals.

WHAT WE KNOW ABOUT BEING HELPFUL

Change happens in helping relationships as a result of a complex mix of a variety of factors including the type and enormity of the issue or concern, the helpee's style and motivation, and the ways in which the helper intervenes. Research in the field of clinical helping provides insight into some critical components of helping relationships and helper behaviors that have been shown to be effective across helping situations (this is called "evidence-based practice"). Below we will discuss the important helping conditions of competence, intentionality and integrity, empathy, attunement and alliance, and the ability to inspire and empower. All of these are also outlined in Table 1.2.

Competence

Being an effective helper requires extensive **knowledge** in the area that is the focus of the helping contract (Hubble, Duncan, Miller, & Wampold, 2010). For example, career counselors need to have knowledge about career trends, application information, resume writing, and interview practices. Childcare workers must know about child development and have knowledge about effective teaching and discipline strategies. Teachers working with children to develop social skills need to know something about interpersonal effectiveness. College residential counselors need to know about the workings of their particular institution as well as common developmental issues that are present in the population of students in their dormatories.

It is not enough to just have knowledge about the subject area that is the focus of your helping relationship: Helpers also need to be able to communicate that knowledge. So here we are talking about the importance of basic **communication skills** in helping. We all know of teachers who are brilliant in their subject area, but unable to articulate that information to their students. Having a big heart is nice, but if one can't communicate that caring, it hardly matters how warm the helper is feeling inside. To be effective, then, helpers must have basic communication skill competence; they must be able to communicate what they know and must have the skills necessary for engaging in an appropriate helping relationship (Hubble et al., 2010). The skills discussed in Chapters 7 and 8 are critical helping intervention and communication skills.

Helper competence also has to do with engaging in **ethical and responsible behavior.** While specific codes of ethics vary across various domains of helping and related helping professional organizations, there are common key ethical principles (which we will review in Chapter 4) that cut across most helping professions (Francis, 2002). These should guide the work of helpers. There are several good reasons for being ethical, but perhaps most important is that acting ethically ensures the best service is provided to the helpee. Codes of ethics protect you and your helpee by assuring adherence to best practice; they enable helpers to make intentional and appropriate decisions in their work.

Helper competence also speaks to your duty to be professional in your work as a helper. **Professionalism** refers to behaviors that communicate competence and respect for others and that adhere to the helping contract. These include being clear about the services you are able to offer, not providing services for which you are not trained, being fair and consistent in compensation arrangements (i.e., payment for services), being respectful in all communications, and overall, adhering to ethical practice guidelines. It also includes being on time for meetings, maintaining confidentiality, being fully present during the time together, and attending to paperwork, phone calls and any other situations that require follow-through. Finally, as will be discussed in more detail in Chapter 5, professionalism has to do with having a level of self-awareness and self-regulation so as to be able to manage yourself when you are helping others. Self-management is about being sure that you are not overly triggered by what is being said or done by the helpee and that you are not confusing your own issues, concerns, challenges, situations, and abilities with those of the helpee.

Cultural competence is another critical component of helper competence. Definitions of what it means to be culturally competent vary across and within helping professions (Fields, 2010). However, Arredondo et al. (1996) make a strong case that such competence, however defined, entails having an awareness of one's own attitudes and beliefs; having an understanding of the racial or cultural heritage, beliefs, values, lifestyles, and worldviews of self and others; and engaging in culturally appropriate interventions that are aligned with the specific beliefs, values, and needs of your helpees. As will be discussed in Chapter 2, cultural competence also requires an understanding of the cultural context of power and privilege in our lives, and particularly, an awareness of how individuals in various social groups are treated by others in their communities and in larger society. Helping requires an understanding of these important issues as well as an ability to manage oneself and be engaged in a relationship that is truly beneficial to the helpee. Cultural competence in helping will also be discussed in more detail in Chapter 5, and some specific skills for working across differences will be introduced in Chapter 8.

Research shows that almost 80% of individuals who need therapeutic intervention do not seek it because they do not have confidence that it will help (Hubble et al., 2010). Interestingly, these authors also suggest that when a therapist is using an approach that is consistent with his or her beliefs and values (allegiance to method), that approach is likely to be helpful because it arouses the helpee's hope or expectation that it will work. These findings speak to another important component of helper competence: **confidence**. When a helper is confident in the approach that he or she is using, that confidence sets in place an expectation on the part of the helpee, which, it turns out, can have a strong influence on the helping outcome. Believing in what you are doing, then, is an important component of helper competence.

A caveat is needed here. Wampold (2010) suggests that if the help that is offered does not seem to be working well, helpers often respond by continuing to deliver the same type of help, sometimes even with more vehemence, even if it isn't working. And this, of course, furthers the likelihood of failure. This brings us to the next important point: While helpers must be knowledgeable, capable, and confident, they also must be **flexible**. When things are not going as planned or when a particular approach to helping is not working, it is time for the helper to stop what he or she is doing, talk with the helpee about the goals of the work together, and make appropriate adjustments.

Intentionality and Integrity

Intentionality derives from the Latin word *intention* and verb *intendere*, which means being directed toward some goal or accomplishment. In the context of helping relationships, *intentionality* refers to working in a careful and thoughtful manner toward the desired outcome of the helping contract. Integrity, similarly, refers to a commitment to follow through as promised. It means doing the right thing. Taken together in the context of helping relationships, intentionality and integrity refer to making a commitment to help and, as a part of that commitment, being knowledgeable and thoughtful in carrying out that commitment. We will review these important ideas about remaining true to the commitment we make in helping relationships when we discuss the moral principle of fidelity in Chapter 4.

In a review of 25 therapy outcome studies, Norcross (2010) found that positive outcomes in therapy were related to **goal consensus** in 68% of the studies reviewed. That is, negotiation and agreement on the goals of the work together leads to successful outcomes in helping relationships (Anderson, Lunnen, & Ogles, 2010). Intuitively, this makes sense; the process of discussing and agreeing on goals provides clarity in the work. It also assures "buy-in." Additionally, we know that goal consensus strengthens the therapeutic alliance (Gaston, 1990; Norcross, 2010), which, as will be discussed shortly, is an important condition for change (Lambert, 2013). So, intentionality and integrity have to do with being committed, being thoughtful in how the work will unfold, and being in agreement with the helpee on how the work together will be carried out.

Hubble et al. (2010) found that a lack of structure and focus is a strong predictor of *negative outcomes* in helping relationships. Better stated: When the work of helping is **structured and focused** on the agreed-upon goals, success is more likely. These authors also point out that **monitoring the progress** of the work toward the intended goals helps ensure that the goals will be reached. The research is loud and clear: It is our responsibility when helping others to be intentional in what we do.

Empathy

Empathy refers to the capacity to recognize and understand the emotions and experiences of another person. The term originally comes from the German concept of *einfuhlung*, which means *feeling into* (Frankel, 2009; Neumann et al., 2009). It refers to the ability to enter into the world of the other to understand the helpee from his or her own perspective (Rogers, 1951). It is an affective reaction that stems from a deep understanding of someone else's emotional state, current condition or situation (Neumann et al., 2009). Rogers is famously quoted as describing empathy in this way: "To perceive the internal frame of reference of another with accuracy and with the emotional components and meanings which pertain thereto *as if one were the person, but without ever losing the 'as if' condition*" (as quoted in Rogers, 1975, p. 3, italics in original). It is about making a connection (Brown, 2013).

Most agree that empathy is critical to helping relationships (Wiseman, 1996). In studies of the effectiveness of therapy, for example, empathy has an effect size of .32, meaning that it accounts for one-third of change that is associated with therapy (Norcross, 2010). Norcross explains that this is because empathy fosters a "corrective emotional experience" (p. 119) for the helpee. A corrective emotional experience is a clinical term that refers to a therapeutic process where the helpee learns new patterns of thinking and behaving by reexperiencing earlier unresolved feelings and needs in a current supportive context. Empathy creates this condition and thus promotes insight and understanding; it supports the process of healing. It is this type of connection, Brown (2010) proposes, that gives purpose to people's lives.

Let us take a minute, then, to explore what empathy might look like in helping. First, it refers to **understanding the helpee's feelings** (Wiseman, 1996), in all of their complexities. When you understand that a helpee feels sad in addition to the obvious anger that she is expressing, for example, you are understanding some of the complexities in her internal emotional experience. Empathy also refers to having a **nonjudgmental presence** (Rogers, 1957). That is, when you communicate that even though you may not be happy that the helpee has not been able to follow through on the agreed-upon actions discussed in your last meeting, you are able to withhold judgment and condemnation. You are able to remain present and nonreactive. Finally, empathy entails an ability to **communicate** that understanding to the helpee (Wiseman, 1996; Wynn & Bergvik, 2010). This is an important point. Feeling connected to the helpee and truly understanding her does not equal empathy; that understanding and connection must be *felt by the helpee* in order for empathy to exist. In fact, Wynn and Bergvik (2010) describe empathy as a three-part process that includes (1) an initial expression or story from the helpee, (2) the empathic response that is first felt by the helper and then communicated to the helpee, and then, (3) the full-circle feedback loop where the helpee then communicates back to the helper that the empathy was felt. Interestingly, studies show that helpers are inadequate judges of empathy—that is, they are not able to accurately determine if their helpees actually feel their empathic communications. The primary way to determine if empathy has been communicated in a helping relationship is to ask the helpee (Frankel, 2009; Norcross, 2010). So, this reminds us that it isn't enough to just feel empathic to our helpees; empathy doesn't happen unless the helpee feels it too.

Finally, it should be mentioned that prerequisite to being able to engage in empathic communications is the ability to step out of one's own experience, current situation, and frame of reference. This refers to an ability to have an **awareness of self** (Wiseman, 1996). Similarly, the ability to engage in an empathic connection also requires helpers to be able to **regulate** their own internal experiences, so as to be fully present with their helpees (Neumann et al., 2009). These two concepts of self-awareness and self-regulation are discussed in more detail in Chapter 5.

Relationship Attunement and Alliance

Of all of the things that therapists do in helping, Hubble et al. (2010) assert that the creation of a strong therapeutic relationship is the most critical. In fact, Lambert (2013) estimates that the therapeutic alliance is more highly related to therapeutic outcomes than any specific therapeutic treatment modality. The importance of a therapeutic alliance is not limited to clinical helping relationships—all helping relationships require a strong helper–helpee bond.

A therapeutic alliance has to do with the creation of a **strong relationship** and **therapeutic space** where the individual feels supported, understood, accepted, and heard (Bohart & Tallman, 2010; Norcross, 2010). **Attunement** is a term that is sometimes used in the counseling literature to describe this kind of bond that is critical to the attachment relationship: the ability to accurately read one's cognitive, emotional, physiological, and behavioral cues and respond accordingly (Blaustein & Kinniburgh, 2010). When the helper is accurately attuned to the helpee, she is able to create the necessary therapeutic alliance necessary for supporting change.

Bohart and Tallman (2010) report that feeling understood, accepted, and being heard; being able to explore and try out new feelings, thoughts, and behaviors; feeling support when in crisis; and receiving advice when needed are identified by clients as essential components of therapeutic helping relationships. Additionally, the Rogerian concept of **unconditional positive regard** (Rogers, 1951) and what Norcross calls a "**warm acceptance** of the client's experience without conditions," (Norcross, 2010, p. 123, bold added) are key components of therapeutic relationships that effect positive change outcomes. Similarly, Lambert (2013) concluded, after an extensive review of psychotherapy outcome literature, that effective therapeutic relationships are formed when the helper demonstrates understanding, acceptance, **kindness, warmth,** and **compassion**. For Noddings (2002), this is an **ethic of care**—centering a commitment of caring for the other in the helping relationship. In the words of Eliot (2013), helpees "want more from clinicians than 'reasons' and 'evidence,' or exercise of competence; they want connection, communication, and caring, or evidence of compassion" (p. 629).

Ability to Inspire and Empower

While some helpees grow and change even without the benefit of helping relationships (Bohart & Tallman, 2010), we also know that helping relationships do help many people change in positive ways (Lambert, 2013). How does

Photo 1.2   Kindness, Warmth, Compassion, and Caring in Relationships

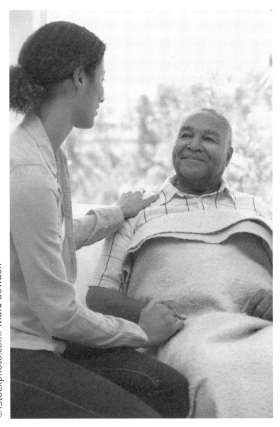

©iStockphoto.com/Mark Bowden

that happen? In his seminal work *Client Centered Therapy*, Carl Rogers (1951) proposed that allowing the client to determine the direction of the work in therapy communicates a true **belief in the client's capacity to grow and change.** And indeed, research has shown that hope and positive expectations are always a critical factor in promoting positive change in others (Hubble et al., 2010). So, the emphasis here on inspiring and empowering as a critical component of helping is based on indications that bringing out the best in others is very helpful. This is a sentiment that is the foundation of positive psychology, which is discussed in Chapters 2 and 3.

Psychiatrist Victor Frankl (1963) deemed **hope** to be essential for the existence of life and humanity, and positive psychologists identify hope as a crucial ingredient for change (Larsen & Stege, 2010). Hope is powerful, Eliot (2013)

Table 1.2 What We Know Is Helpful

Competence	Intentionality and Integrity	Empathy	Relationship Attunement and Alliance	Inspiration
Knowledge	Goal Consensus	Perception of the Person's Emotional State	Therapeutic Space	Belief in the Helpee's Capacity to Change
Communication Skills	Structure and Focus	Nonjudgmental Presence	Attunement	Hope
Ethical and Responsible Behavior	Monitoring Progress	Communication of Understanding	Unconditional Positive Regard	Promote Agency
Professionalism		Self-Awareness	Warmth and Kindness	Uncovering the Helpee's Strengths and Abilities
Cultural Competence		Self-Regulation	Compassion	
Helper Confidence			Ethic of Care	
Flexibility				

suggests, because when one has hope, he will act in ways that will realize his expectations. It "leaves the window open for unanticipated solutions" (Larsen & Stege, 2010, p. 296). Hope, according to Eliot, is "the reason patients keep doing whatever their treatment entails, however arduous" (p. 630).

Another component of inspiration and empowerment is to **promote agency** in the helpee. Agency refers to one's ability to make choices and to act on one's own will. Agency is a key component of contemporary strength-based, solution-focused, and narrative therapies that have at their very foundation the practice of **uncovering individuals' strengths and abilities,** and this important focus has been found to be a critical component of successful therapeutic change (Bohart & Tallman, 2010). When individuals are empowered to see what they are capable of, they are better able to live their lives in ways that are in line with their hopes and expectations. Underscoring the critical role that helpees themselves play in creating change—even when in helping relationships, Bohart and Tallman recommend that helpers should actively work to uncover and promote client strengths and abilities and that they should also promote client agency.

CHAPTER SUMMARY

Helping professionals work in a variety of clinical and nonclinical roles and practice settings. Terms such as counseling, psychotherapy, and advocacy are defined, and various helping professions are described here and in Appendix A. A number of factors implicit to the helping contract, such as services and compensation, nonmutuality, and restrictions and conditions of the relationship, distinguish professional helping relationships from other kinds of relationships in people's lives. Research has revealed a number of variables in helping relationships that promote positive growth and change. These include helper competence, working with intentionality and integrity, demonstrating empathy, relationship attunement and therapeutic alliance, and the ability to inspire and empower others.

DISCUSSION QUESTIONS

1. *Helping, counseling, therapy, psychotherapy,* and *advocacy* are all terms used to describe various ways in which helpers orient in their work with others. Describe how these terms differ.

2. What are the differences between professional helpers, clinical helpers, and nonclinical helpers?

3. What is advocacy? What are two types of advocacy?

4. Name five factors known to be important to helping relationships and discuss why they are helpful.

CHAPTER 2

UNDERSTANDING DEVELOPMENT: THEORIES, SOCIAL CONTEXT, AND NEUROSCIENCE

LEARNING OBJECTIVES

1. Describe how various developmental and related theories influence how helpers think about growth and change

2. Describe two major ways in which social and cultural factors influence development and well-being

3. Describe how neurosynaptic connections and brain structures interpret and transmit sensory information, and how these processes regulate meaning-making systems and behaviors

INTRODUCTION

This chapter begins with a discussion about theory, that is, what a theory is. Then, what follows is a brief review of some of the more commonly used human development and related theories that underlie the thinking and direction of individuals in the helping professions. The purpose of discussing these theories is to expose some of the ways in which helpers think about people, conceptualize problems, and how these ideas then influence how they approach their work of helping. While many theories of development talk about the ways in which social and cultural factors influence development, I will also highlight additional perspectives related to social issues, culture, and people's experiences in the world. This latter discussion is intended to emphasize the point that what we do, where we live, what we think, what we value, and also the ways in which we are treated by others all influence who we are and our experiences in the world. The chapter concludes with a review of neuroscience research that offers another lens into developmental processes and helping practices. Many of the ideas presented here will be referenced in subsequent chapters, as they all inform and shape the important work that happens in helping relationships.

Finally, I conclude this introduction with a disclaimer. The theories reviewed in this and the following chapter are presented as brief summaries of important and complex ideas. Thousands of books have been written on the various perspectives included in this text; my summaries only capture a minuscule portion of what has been said and written about these theories. Also, these theories and their related practice components, for the most part, outline methods of intervention that are intended for use in clinical settings—work that goes beyond the scope of practice of entry-level helpers. So, my disclaimer here is twofold: (1) The summaries included here and in Chapter 3 do not capture the entirety nor the nuanced complexities of the theories described, and (2) I have attempted to highlight, both in this chapter and the one that follows, the portions of these theories that are most relevant for nonclinical helpers.

THE PURPOSE OF A THEORY

What do we mean by *theory*? Is theory an idea? Or is it a fact? Does it tell us what to do? What to think? Where do theories come from? Why do we have theories? These are the questions I hope to address in this chapter.

The definition of theory, according to Dictorary.com, is "1. a coherent group of tested general propositions, commonly regarded as correct, that can be used as principles of explanation . . ." and "2. a proposed explanation whose status is still conjectural and subject to experimentation" ("theory," n.d.). In short, a theory is a set of ideas that *may* or *may not* be true. Theories of human development, then, are ideas, often very good ideas, which offer explanation and serve as a basis for understanding the complexities around how we develop—what makes us "tick." Most theories of development also offer ideas about what can go wrong in development—what causes problems for people. Even if spoken as certainties, however, it is important to remember that theories are propositions and hypotheses. They are not truths.

In our discussion of theories, I want to draw attention to the difference between a *theory of human development* and a *theory of helping*. Theories of human development are models for understanding how individuals develop, grow, and change over time. As mentioned, they help us make sense of the ways in which individuals think, the decisions that people make, the conditions that best promote change, and what can go wrong in development to cause problems. Theories of helping, on the other hand, are oriented to the helper and the helping process. They direct what helpers do; they map out how helpers can intervene to promote change in others and how to intervene when an individual is experiencing a problem. This chapter offers a brief review of major theories of human development (defined quite broadly). In Chapter 3, we will then talk about how these theories influence helping practices—theories of helping.

It is important for us to have some knowledge about the various theories of human development because how we think about growth and change influences how we will intervene to help others. But theories introduce bias: They offer only one perspective. And while bias isn't necessarily bad, we do need to be aware of how our thinking biases our work. Thus, it is important for us to be clear about the ideas and belief systems that underlie the work we will be doing with others.

THEORIES OF DEVELOPMENT

While the multitude of different human development theories all share the goal of describing how individuals develop, they differ in their explanatory processes around the etiology (root) of development, they call upon different metaphors for describing developmental processes and trajectories, and they attend to different influences on development. In this chapter, I have included theories that are commonly referenced today in the fields of human development and psychology, that cover a variety of perspectives on development, and that have particular application to the work of helpers. This review is organized into the categories of psychodynamic, ethological, humanistic, behavioral/learning, and contemporary theories. However, you will notice as you read through the chapter that there is much overlap among the conceptual ideas across these categories. Theories typically are developed in relation to and in response to earlier ideas—theorists learn from what others have suggested and then add to or shape those ideas with their own experiences and ideas. These larger categories that I am using, then, are not mutually exclusive. It is also important to be aware that there are, of course, many other theories related to development and change that I have not included in this discussion. Theories that are not included in the discussion here also offer excellent frameworks for understanding specific components of development. For instance, there are theories about cognition and moral reasoning, and theories that describe racial, sexual, and gender identity developmental processes. All of these are very informative, but they fall beyond the scope of this text, so they are not included in our discussion here. I highly recommend that theories in these specific areas be thoroughly explored by those who will be entering into helping relationships.

Psychodynamic Theories

Some of the earliest theories of human development are based on the psychoanalytic principles first articulated by Sigmund Freud in the late 19th century. **Psychoanalytic theory** is based on the idea that psychological and unconscious forces—forces that are outside of one's awareness—motivate human behavior, feelings, and emotions (Boyd & Bee, 2011; Goldhaber, 2000; Luborsky, O'Reilly-Landry, & Arlow, 2008; Miller, 2002). A key aspect of Freud's theory is that these unconscious, biological, instinctual, and what he identified to be sexual drives push for discharge within the psyche. When these drives are socially inappropriate, however, the individual works to control them through conscious and unconscious actions. This classic conflict between the conscious and unconscious plays out among the well-known psychoanalytic concepts of the id, ego, and superego (Luborsky et al., 2008). The *id* is the term used for the unconscious (sexual) drives that the psyche works so hard to control. The *superego* is the portion of the ego that maintains focus on moral principles—the part of the ego that stands for the right thing to do. It might be considered the Ethics Master of the psyche. The *ego* is what orients the individual to the external world; it plays the role of mediating between the internal experiences of the id and the social expectations in the real world. It is considered the go-between the id and the superego.

Frued's psychoanalytic theory also includes the concept of *defense mechanisms,* which are used by individuals to protect against the potentially destructive and socially inappropriate expressions of unconscious (id) impulses (Weiner & Bornstein, 2009). Also considered to function out of our awareness (i.e., unconscious forces), defense mechanisms diffuse the anxiety that results from id impulses that are seeking release. While defense mechanisms protect us from uncomfortable id-related feelings and experiences, they also can cause difficulties because they are primarily reactive forces that shape behaviors and experiences in ways that are not always desirable or productive. For example, if someone is experiencing extreme sadness after the loss of a loved one, but carries himself or herself as if all is well, the denial of this sadness is likely to impede his or her ability to authentically engage in relationships with others.

Freud is also known for his model of psychosexual development, which proposes that healthy child development occurs through a series of stages that are informed by specific unconscious sexual drives or instincts (Boyd & Bee, 2011; Goldhaber, 2000; Miller, 2002). Most texts in human development outline the various stages of development in this model, so I will not present them here, but it is important to point out that this model of development has had a profound influence on thinking about the developmental processes of children both in professional human development circles and in the lay public. For example, the concept of having an "oral fixation," which is used colloquially in reference to someone who likes to persistently suck on candy, is a referent to Freud's concept of the oral stage of development.

Freud's theoretical ideas have evolved over time. A range of other theories that derived from and share many of these basic psychoanalytic premises are called psychodynamic theories (Day, 2004). More contemporary psychodynamic theorists have challenged the patriarchal underpinnings of traditional psychoanalytic perspectives, taken issue with the unequal power differentials in psychoanalytic therapeutic relationships, reformulated the original ideas about gender, and are less reliant on universal principles and the concept of objective reality (Safran, 2012). With this in mind, Safran points out that contemporary psychodynamic thought still focuses on the idea that humans are motivated, at least in part, by unconscious experiences including wishes, fantasies, and knowledge, and psychodynamic helping orientations continue to focus on increasing the helpee's awareness of these unconscious experiences so as to reveal motivations and increase choice.

Adlerian theory, also called **individual psychology**, is a psychodynamic theory that shares many contemporary applications, particularly in the field of education. Alfred Adler studied with Freud early in his career but disagreed with Freud's overemphasis on sexuality and the rigid focus on intrapersonal processes; he was eventually jettisoned from Freud's inner circle of psychoanalytic thinkers (Prochaska & Norcross, 2007). Adler was most interested in the social aspects of development, and his ideas continue to inform education and parenting practices in the U.S. today. Adler emphasized that humans are born social, and he believed that healthy development requires *social interest*—a sense of being part of and contributing to one's social community (Mosak & Maniacci, 2008; Prochaska & Norcross, 2007). Adler was interested in the prominent role that early childhood experiences play in development, suggesting that these experiences inform *lifestyle* beliefs—the ideas that people use to organize and make sense of their experiences in the world. Lifestyle beliefs, according to Adler, are the foundation for *goal-directed behaviors* (Mosak & Maniacci, 2008; Prochaska & Norcross, 2007). In short, Adler believed that people develop perceptions about the world based on their early experiences in family, and those perceptions drive their later actions. According to Alder, having social interest as well as a sense of competence or *superiority* are markers of healthy development (Prochaska & Norcross, 2007). So, while Adler, like Freud, still emphasized the role of unconscious processes in development, his theory focused more on conscious processes and environmental influences, particularly *family atmosphere*, on development.

Harry Stack Sullivan was another major psychodynamic thinker worth mention in this discussion. Sullivan attempted to shift the psychoanalytic focus on internal unconscious biological, sexual, and instinctual drives to ideas about interpersonal relatedness (Levenson, 2010). Sullivan, like Adler, proposed that children develop from the interpersonal patterns and styles that they are exposed to in their childhood interactions with their parents—an important concept that is at the heart of attachment theory, which we will discuss shortly. Going on to create the **interpersonal theory of psychotherapy**, Sullivan believed that all behaviors, including dysfunction or psychopathology, are interpersonal in nature (Purkey & Stanley, 2002). In fact, Sullivan proposed that the self does not exist as an individual entity; it is always in relationship with others (Purkey & Stanley, 2002).

Erik Erikson's **theory of psychosocial development** was influenced by Freud's model of psychosexual development as well as these new additions in psychodynamic circles, particularly those of Sullivan (Levenson, 2010). While Erikson followed Freud's lead in characterizing development to be ruled by unconscious forces, he also recognized the important influence of the social environment on development (Miller, 2002). Erikson's model of development lays out as a series of critical tasks that people face across the lifespan. According to Erikson, development is impeded by an inability to successfully negotiate the challenge at each of these stages in the developmental process (Goldhaber, 2000). Erikson's model, too, still holds contemporary interest, and it is outlined in most texts on human development. The commonly referenced concept of a "midlife crisis," for example, is a colloquial expression referring to changes that occur in midlife, particularly with men, that is loosely based on Erikson's model of development.

In summary, psychodynamic theories promote a deterministic model of development, meaning that much of development is based on variables and experiences over which we have little control. These ideas about development have had a sustained prominence in our colloquial understandings about personality for decades. We hear references to Freudian ideas such as "oral fixation," "Freudian slip," and "Oedipus complex" in everyday conversations, for example. It is not uncommon for many of us to refer to the culpability of the unconscious in motivating our actions—many of us have heard others proclaim, "I'm not sure why I did it—it must have been unconscious." All of these are a testament to the voracity of psychodynamic ideas about human nature and development.

Ethological Theories

Ethological theories of human development look at the evolutionary significance of behavior as an explanation for human growth and change (Miller, 2002). They approach the study of human development through the same lens that attempts to understand animal behavior, and thus, focus on instinctual and evolutionary survival behaviors that have evolved over time (Boyd & Bee, 2011; Crain, 2011). **Attachment theory** is arguably the most well-known human development theory in this category, largely because of its resurgent popularity spawned by some of the new developments in neuroscience that will be discussed later in this chapter. Based on his observations and concerns regarding the development of children growing up in orphanages that lacked emotional interaction between children and caregivers, attachment theorist John Bowlby proposed that the bond between young infants and their primary caregivers is the critical ingredient for nurturing healthy emotional development (Crain, 2011). Bowlby's work has had a significant impact on the field of human development with its detailed focus on parental care-taking practices.

Bowlby (1969; 1988) proposed that caregiver responsiveness (Bowlby wrote about the "mother" rather than a "caregiver") during infancy and early childhood (from about 6 months to 2 years of age) creates attachment bonds, and these bonds become what he called *working models* for future relationships. This idea of attachment is firmly routed in the ethological observation that young animals have an instinctual *imprinting* tendency to form an attachment to the first object they are exposed to in early critical periods of development. The young animal follows and imitates this attachment figure in order to learn how to function in its environment (Crain, 2011). Similarly, then, Bowlby proposed that an attachment mechanism serves human development by creating a context of safety and species-appropriate learning. Although emphasized as critical for the developing child, Bowlby suggested that attachment is important throughout the life cycle as evidenced in the ways in which people of all ages seek social relationships and support (Crain, 2011).

Attachment theorists propose that early attachment behaviors inform the perceptions, emotions, thoughts, and expectations that individuals carry into later relationships, through *working models* (Crain, 2011). Attachment theorist Mary Ainsworth (Ainsworth, 1973), and her colleagues (Ainsworth, Blehar, Waters, & Wall, 1978) studied the ways in which infants and young children instinctually signal and maintain proximity to their caregivers. These behaviors, they proposed, center the parent–child relationship as the *secure base* necessary for survival. For example, when a young baby cries because he is hungry, he is cuing the caregiver to feed him. When he gurgles, giggles, and makes cooing noises, or when a toddler engages playfully with his parent, as seen in Photo 2.1, this is a signaling behavior that engages the caregiver to attend to and care for him. Ainsworth and her colleagues found that when young children experience caregiving that is responsive to their needs, they develop a sense—a working model—that people are trustworthy and the world is a safe place.

As infants become children, the caregiver becomes a secure base for exploration into the world. Running (or toddling) back and forth between a caregiver and something new and exciting in a toddler's environment is an example of maintaining proximity to a secure base. Ainsworth (1973), Ainsworth et al. (1978), and other subsequent researchers found that children who consistently experienced a secure base (that is, they had secure attachments and were able to accept comfort from their caregivers after brief experiences of stress or separation) felt safe to explore their environment. Conversely, children who regularly experienced inaccessible or unresponsive caregiving did not seek comfort from their caregivers when they were fearful, and they often appeared ambivalent to their caregivers. These children also responded to new experiences and separations with stress, fear, and anxiety.

Photo 2.1   Parent–Child Attachment

©Can Stock Photo Inc./Paha_L

Subsequent research (e.g., Blaustein & Kinniburgh, 2010; Thompson, 2008; Weinfield, Sroufe, Egeland, & Carlson, 2008) seems to confirm the notion that early attachment bonds—whether they are appropriately safe and secure or not—become the template for later behavioral and emotional adaptation, self-esteem, self-efficacy, and future interpersonal relationships. This extensive body of research makes a strong case for the importance of a strong attachment bond for later healthy growth and development.

Humanistic Theories

While humanistic perspectives were originally rooted in psychodynamic theory, they offer a decidedly different perspective on developmental trajectories and they move far from the psychodynamic foundations when it comes to the application of theory into practice, which will be described in more detail in Chapter 3. The theories in the humanistic category all share the important fundamental idea that people have an innate self-actualizing tendency (Cain, 2002). This shift to self-actualization is a move away from the psychodynamic idea that development is predetermined and largely related to unconscious processes and impulses. Humanistic-oriented theorists believe that healthy development occurs in a context of being supported to develop one's own inner resources, when one is self-aware, and when people are given responsibility to make appropriate choices (Cain, 2002).

Perhaps best known in this category are the ideas of Carl Rodgers, articulated in his **client-centered theory**, published in the mid-20th century. Based on his research, Rogers came to the conclusion that children will normally grow in functional and adaptive ways when they are nurtured in an environment that meets their emotional, intellectual, and social needs (Rogers, 1951). From this, Rogers proposed that people have an innate ability to grow, develop, change, and to live their lives effectively—it is an idea that is typically referred to as the *self-actualizing* principle (Rogers, 1951; Rogers actually attributes this term to Kurt Goldstein, who used it in reference to a striving to be more advanced). Using these conclusions to inform his work as a therapist, Rogers developed his client-centered approach to therapy, which will be explored a bit more in the next chapter as it is a theory of helping rather than development.

Like the Rogerian ideas just mentioned, **gestalt therapy**, which is a helping theory rather than a theory of development, rests on the idea that people have an innate potential to become self-regulated and growth-oriented (Yontef & Jacobs, 2008). Relevant to our discussion about human development, is the gestalt concept of *contact*, which refers to awareness and connection, that is considered necessary for healthy human growth and development. It is from having an awareness of self and boundaries between self and others (appropriate contact and contract boundaries) that one develops a sense of who one is and how to be in relationship with others (Strumpfel & Goldman, 2002; Yontef & Jacobs, 2008). That is, people discover and create themselves through connecting with and differentiating from others (Yontef, 1993).

The therapeutic practice of gestalt therapy is to help people develop insight and awareness into their styles of contact (awareness and connection). They are encouraged to develop authentic and meaningful relationships but also to be able to regulate themselves in order to establish functional and healthy boundaries. From this awareness, people are able to make choices for how to live their lives in a healthy balance between self and surroundings (Yontef, 1993). When we are aware in the present moment and in contact with our affective, sensory, and cognitive intrapersonal and interpersonal experiences, we are able to live authentically, and we are able to be an agent in the decisions we make. On the other hand, when contact is disrupted—when we lack awareness of our internal and interpersonal experiences or when we choose to ignore these sensations—problems develop. A core gestalt philosophical position, then, is that individuals cannot be seen as existing apart from others; we always are one with our environment (Yontef & Jacobs, 2008).

Existentialism is another paradigm for understanding human behavior that sits within the circle of humanistic theories. While not attempting to offer a comprehensive or generalizable theory of the human psyche, existentialists grapple with philosophical notions of meaning in human existence (Walsh & McElwain, 2002). They suggest that our processes of engagement in the business of living our lives and our efforts to make meaning from our experiences give rise to growth and development. Existentialists are particularly interested in the ways in which humans negotiate the key philosophical themes of freedom, meaning, and death. The constant exploration of and tension between these themes color our choices and the decisions that we make.

While humanistic ideologists view people as social beings who are self-aware, engaged in a process of meaning-making or constructing their own reality, and actively making choices about how they will live their lives (Cain, 2002), existentialists remind us that that freedom comes with certain responsibilities and limitations (Walsh & McElwain, 2002). Freedom, they remind us, is limited by the responsibilities we carry when we live in relationship with others. But perhaps even more importantly, existentialists point out that personal freedom is also largely restricted by the limitations that we impose on ourselves. When individuals experience "existential anxiety" around death, freedom, responsibility, isolation, or meaninglessness, this anxiety can restrict how they live their lives (Walsh & McElwain, 2002). For example, Yalom (1980) proposed that awareness of one's mortality offers a powerful motivation for living—an opportunity to live life in an authentic manner (Medelowitz & Schneider, 2008). But a generalized preoccupation with death can cause anxiety, and some people develop a complex system of defenses against death, leading to maladaptive clinical symptoms. Similarly, the existential issues related to freedom, isolation, and meaninglessness can also give rise to anxiety and tension (Cain, 2002; Yalom, 1980). In the existentialist paradigm, *authenticity* entails taking responsibility for one's life, with all of its possibilities and limitations. It also means being fully self aware, which happens through engagement despite existential tensions around death, isolation, freedom and a search for meaning (Yalom, 1980). Authenticity, Yalom asserted, is how "one can grasp the power to change oneself" (p. 31).

The **positive psychology** movement, while considered a relatively new movement in the field of psychology based largely on the work of Martin Seligman and his colleagues, has its roots in humanistic psychology (Joseph & Linley, 2006) as well as other disciplines of thought (Seligman & Csikszentmihalyi, 2001). A major premise of positive psychology is that all human beings have an innate motivation and the potential to live a good life when they are in an environment that fosters such development (Joseph & Linley, 2006).

In positive psychology circles, the concept of leading a good life generally refers to Seligman's notions of happiness and well-being (Seligman & Csikszentmihalyi, 2000; Seligman, Linley, Joseph, & Boniwell, 2003). These are described as the subjective experience of "contentment and satisfaction (in the past); hope and optimism (for the future); and flow and happiness (in the present)" (Seligman & Csikszentmihalyi, 2000, p. 5). Happiness refers to being satisfied with life, attaining affective balance (i.e., experiencing a balance between positive and negative affect), and being oriented toward growth and fulfillment (Joseph & Linley, 2006).

Seligman's concept of well-being reminds us of Roger's concept of self-actualization (an idea which was also championed by other developmental theorists and psychologists such as Horney, Adler, Jung, and Maslow), discussed earlier. It is the idea that human beings will naturally gravitate toward healthy growth when they are nurtured in social and emotional conditions that foster such growth. While some may discount the seemingly superficial notion that just being happy promotes health, Salovey, Rothman, Detweiler, and Steward (2000) show that this notion is supported by research findings. They report that negative emotions and moods are associated with unhealthy physiological functioning and, conversely, positive emotions are linked to healthy cardiovascular functioning, stronger immune system functioning, and other positive health outcomes. In explanation of these findings, Salovey, Rothman, Detweiler, and Steward (2000) propose that people assess information about themselves (and their health) through emotional responses—that is, through positive or negative emotional states—and they alter their behavior accordingly. So, positive emotional experiences may influence people to actually feel better because they believe in their ability to be healthy and behave in healthy ways. In other words, people conform to the expectations that they have for themselves.

A second important foundation of positive psychology is the valuing of one's subjective experience. Like the person in Illustration 2.1, who sees himself as a superhero, positive psychologists value the idea that people are the experts of their own lives, and they emphasize that what people believe about themselves, their experiences in the world, and more generally, about human nature, has a profound influence on their identity, how they live their lives, and their attitudes toward others (Joseph & Linley, 2006). They might argue, for example, that a crocodile who sees himself as a sheep might live a life of being gentle to others (although we still might worry about his well-being if he strays too far from water and what he might eat if he is living on a farm). Humor aside,

Illustration 2.1   We Are Who We Want to Be

©iStockphoto.com/tintin75

Seligman and other positive psychologists argue that people are motivated by positive tendencies for growth and development, and when helpers shift the focus away from pathology, and on to facilitating healthy development and developing positive qualities, they are able to promote the development of these qualities (Seligman & Csikszentmihalyi, 2000). In nurturing one's strengths, we can build buffers against challenge and pain, and we can bring forward the best in people's lives. These ideas rooted in positive psychology carry over into many of the contemporary theories we will discuss shortly.

In summary, humanistic theories propose that people are complex and always engaged in the process of living. They suggest that we have the potential to be self-aware, to make changes, and to be responsible for the choices we make and the direction of our lives (Cain, 2002). Humanistic theorists reject deterministic ideas about development that suggest that individuals grow in linear and universal ways, emphasizing instead self-actualizing principles, cognitive processes of meaning-making, and responsibility. An important implication of these theories for helping relationships, as we will see in the next chapter, is that they all emphasize the importance of creating a particular kind of therapeutic environment for promoting growth and facilitating change.

Behavioral/Learning Theories

The theories we will review here are linked by their common emphasis on behavior and learning rather than innate personality as a key developmental process. They have no interest in the psychodynamic concept of the unconscious nor are they concerned with existential questions or self-actualization. Instead, they are based on the idea that all we can know about an individual comes from what we can see: behavior. Some behavior and learning theories focus almost exclusively on how behavior is shaped by various antecedents and consequences in the environment, whereas others consider how behavior is mediated by thinking processes. But all of these theories see humans as being relatively passive recipients of environmental stimulation, and all focus on behavior as the unit of analysis for understanding humans. The discussion in this chapter will focus primarily on behavioral and social learning theories. Cognitive behavioral theory, which is directly linked to the theories mentioned here, will be discussed in Chapter 3 because it is more of a theory about helping than it is about development.

Classical conditioning is based on the experimental work of Pavlov in the early 1900s. Pavlov proposed that learning results from a stimulus-response system that is typically initiated by biological impulses or reflexes (Boyd & Bee, 2011).

Pavlov is best known for his experiments on dogs where he showed the ability to shape animal behavior by pairing an unconditioned stimulus (a prompt that exists in the environment) with a conditioned stimulus (a prompt that has been taught) to produce a particular response (Goldhaber, 2000). Watson applied these ideas to human behavior in his famous "Little Albert" experiment (Miller, 2002). By pairing a loud noise with exposure to an otherwise gentle rat that Albert enjoyed playing with, Watson was able to condition Albert to have a fear response to the rat. This human example of classical conditioning promoted the idea that individuals learn through establishing associations between various external events or stimuli (Miller, 2002). A more contemporary example of this might be found in an elementary classroom where children learn from repeated exposure that recess occurs after the mid-morning prompt "quietly put your books away, tidy your desks, and put their heads on your desks when you are ready."

While classical conditioning principles focus largely on what prompts individuals to behave in various ways, Skinner's concept of **operant conditioning** addresses the ways in which consequences shape behavior and learning as well (Boyd & Bee, 2011). According to operant conditioning principles, reinforcement and punishment—those things that happen *after* a behavior occurs—shape and maintain behaviors, thus creating a learned response (Skinner, 1971). Simply put, behaviors that are followed by satisfying consequences tend to be repeated and behaviors that are followed by unpleasant consequences are less likely to be repeated. For example, when a child is told that she will get dessert after finishing her dinner, the dessert serves as a reinforcement for finishing every last morsel of food on the plate. If the child who does not finish her dinner is punished by not being allowed to eat the delicious dessert that lies waiting, this child, too, has learned—this time through a punishment—the important lesson of finishing dinner so she can have dessert. Classical and operant conditioning theories are about human behavior rather than personality development, but the implication is that human development can be explained, or at least is largely explained, by events in the immediate environment.

At about the same time that Skinner was experimenting with the shaping effects of reinforcements and punishments on behavior, Bandura was examining the ways in which learning occurs as a result of observing someone else perform a particular task (Boyd & Bee, 2011). Bandura's **social learning theory** focuses on how modeling, observational learning, reinforcement, and motivation influence learning and behavior (Bandura, 1965; Boyd & Bee, 2011; Goldhaber, 2000). This theory proposes that when individuals witness another person engaging in a particular behavior, they will vicariously learn to engage in that behavior as well (Bandura, 1977).

Photo 2.2   The First Ball Determines What Happens Next

©iStockphoto.com/3dalia

The principles of social learning theory come from Bandura's early experiments in which he would have a child watch a person engage in aggressive behavior. What Bandura found was that when the child witnessed the model perform the aggressive behavior, the child would engage in the same aggressive behavior. But if the initial role model was punished for engaging in the aggressive behavior, the child would be less likely to repeat it (Bandura, 1965). Thus, Bandura found that vicarious reinforcement (i.e., the punishment that went to the model for being aggressive) shapes observational learning (i.e., what the child does).

Bandura's conclusion was that individuals make decisions about their behaviors based on a number of variables including their predictions of whether or not it will be reinforced (Bandura, 1977). Thus, he proposed that behavior is mediated by cognitive or thinking processes—which is a key concept in the helping approach called cognitive behavioral therapy (CBT). As another example, one could argue that television commercials work on social learning principles. When we witness an attractive woman driving a car being noticed by an attractive man, the expectation, at some level, is that buying that particular car will make one worthy enough to attract the attention of desirable others. At least this is the vicarious reinforcement the car company sponsoring the advertisement is hoping for. Conversely, we should wonder about the vicarious reinforcement effects of violent movies where heroes are showered with adoration after particularly violent episodes of behavior.

Contemporary Theories

Contextual, feminist, and ecological theories emphasize the ways in which human development and behavior is constructed from historical, social, and cultural influences. These theories are often not considered to be developmental theories because they do not offer comprehensive explanatory systems for development. Also, they are often omitted from discussions about human development, I believe, because they do not offer concrete and linear models that easily describe developmental trajectories. Instead, they address different components of development, pointing a finger, we might say, to aspects of development that are not adequately explained in the more traditional models. Here I will spend a bit more time discussing these theories because it is possible that these ideas are new to many of you.

Lev Vygotsky, who was a Russian psychologist working in the early 1900s, had a strong influence on social constructionist thinking. He proposed that human behavior and mental processes (psychological processes) cannot be separated from their cultural context, and that personality develops from interaction with others (Douthit, 2008; Miller, 2002), largely through the medium of language. For example, as a developing child begins to understand the symbols of communication in his native language, he uses language to engage with others. Through this, he develops ideas about how he should behave, what is right and wrong, etc. These are messages of cultural practices, Vygotsky proposed, that then guide his psychological as well as his cognitive development (Douthit, 2008, Miller, 2002; for more on Vygotsky see Vygotsky, 1997).

Vygotsky's notion of the *zone of proximal development* (ZPD) has also had a tremendous influence on educational communities and is an undercurrent in contemporary educational practices across the United States. The ZPD describes the conditions that are most ripe for learning: when an individual is working at a level that is between where he or she can work independently and where he or she needs help or assistance (Douthit, 2008; Goldhaber, 2000). The ZPD highlights how challenge and scaffolding (i.e., structured support) are critical components of learning—an important point for those who are engaged in helping others.

Social constructionism, largely articulated in the 1980s and 1990s, stems from Vygotsky's work as well as that of more contemporary critical psychologists such as Burman, Walkerdine, and Gergen and Gergen (for more on the work of these critical psychologists, see Winslade & Geroski, 2008). Social constructionists propose that development is not a product of naturally occurring stages, nor is it shaped by random experiences in the environment. Instead, they assert that development is constructed and socialized in interpersonal, cultural, historical, and political contexts (Burman, 1994; Burr, 1995).

Social constructionists were influenced by Vygotsky's attention to language as a key in the process of socializing development. Language—the meaning of words that are articulated—represents contemporary ideas in society that are communicated as expectations in families, schools, and communities. Normative ideas about social practices are also articulated socially through the images and languaging of music, TV, and, for example, the Internet. All of these avenues of language transmission, according to social constructionists, form the basis of socialization and development (Winslade & Geroski, 2008). We might consider the multimillion dollar industry of wedding planning as an example of this. Ideas in society about what weddings should look like, what brides and grooms should wear, and the social practices around the send-off of bachelor- and bachelorettehood abound. While these ideas don't mandate how young couples in contemporary society should tie the knot, and most would argue that there is nothing inherently wrong with them, they certainly do paint a picture of what most of us commonly think of when we think about weddings. Whether we like these ideas or not, they certainly add color and context to the question "Will you get married?"

Social constructionists point out that language is also rooted generationally, and as such, language is an important conduit for the transmission of past ideas into present (Winslade & Geroski, 2008). As an example of how common and subtle this process sometimes can be, remember back to the earlier point that Erikson's notion of an identity crisis, which was formulated in the early 1900s, continues to be a contemporary metaphor for adolescence. This notion of identity crisis describes adolescence as a tumultuous period in one's life from which one emerges with a clear sense of who one is. This idea persists even when many of us experience young adults in this age group as calm, centered, and not seeming to be in any type of crisis. And it persists even when we know that few individuals at the age of 18 (adolescents in the Erikson's phase of identity) have a clear sense of who they are.

Narrative theory, not to be confused with *narrative therapy,* uses the metaphor of a *story* to describe how experiences and ideas that are transmitted socially (and generationally) have structuring influences on people's lives (Bruner, 1986; 1990). (Narrative therapy is a helping theory described in the next chapter that relies on a foundation of narrative theory and social constructionism.) Brunner suggests that individuals are interpretive beings and that we use stories to narrate our experiences in a meaning-making process. For example, let's say that your friend just broke up with her boyfriend. The next day you overhear the ex-boyfriend in a store making a rude comment to the cashier.

"He must be very angry about that break-up," you tell yourself, "otherwise he would never act that way. Poor guy, he must be hurting." This story is based on your interpretation of the boyfriend's rudeness based on the prior knowledge about the young man. It is a story that you use to make meaning of the behavior you witnessed.

Narrative theorists also suggest that stories are a foundation of identity development (Winslade & Geroski, 2008). They propose that the stories that we tell about ourselves and the stories that are told to and about us become the foundation for how we see ourselves and how we understand others. In this last example, if your friend had told you a story about how her ex-boyfriend was mean to her and just not a very nice person, your perception of his behavior in the store might be less generous. For example, the storyline might change from "poor guy" to "Yes, he is a very angry man. Even here in this store he is mean. I can see why Leila broke up with him. He is horrible." Another example of how this process works can be seen when individuals make statements about their own identity. Consider what one is saying about his identity when he tells others, "I am a shy person." According to narrative theory, identity conclusions are typically buttressed by a series of stories that contain the named identity as their plot. So, for example, this person might offer more evidence of the validity of the shy person identity story by adding these additional pieces of information: "When I was 3 years old, I got lost. And then, of course, I was the youngest of 5 children, so everyone in my family always talked over me. My family always talked about me as the shy one."

Offering an identity conclusion supported by stories that attest to its factual nature alerts others to what they might expect from you. But notice how a story such as this sets one up to be perceived in a particular way by others. More vividly, what identity conclusions are being made when one is described in stories about being a "victim" or "disabled"? It is as if that one descriptor tells the complete story of identity. But it doesn't; social constructionists assert that individuals have multiple ways of being. Rather than adopting the concept of a single, static personality, social constructionists propose that individuals have multiple identities or multiple ways of being that are called forth in various contexts (Winslade & Geroski, 2008). For example, one might be shy in some situations but not in others. One might have a disability when it comes to sight, but not with intellect. One might have been a victim to a horrific crime, but he also has had other experiences where he has been in control of what has happened in his life.

Social constructionists are particularly concerned by the ways in which historic and current events including politics, social and cultural ideas, and systems of power and privilege influence identity development (Winslade & Geroski, 2008).

This seems esoteric, so grounding it in an example might be helpful here. Let us think about the ways in which identity ideas that are communicated to young White girls through mass media are very different from those communicated to young African-American boys.

Photo 2.3   The Pink Little Girl

©iStockphoto.com/Peopleimages

In both cases, social constructionists are likely to argue, the unique aspects of subjugation experienced historically by women and African-Americans have lasting and different influences on identity possibilities. With even just a super-ficial look at popular media, we see communications about how women can continue to *serve* dominant culture through dress, behavior, and even career choices. The example illustrated in Photo 2.3 portrays the little girl in a "sugar

Photo 2.4   The Guy in the Hoodie

Digital Vision/Photodisc/Thinkstock

and spice and everything nice" storyline, leaving some of us wondering if that little girl could ever really be taken seriously. Similarly, African-American boys and men still carry the legacy of being seen as a force to be dominated, and this is communicated through media images, such as the one in Photo 2.4, and stories of African-American men being dangerous and scary. Clearly, media offers a multitude of communications, and it is not the only source of identity options. But it would require a large number of alterative images, stories, and lived experiences about White girls or African-American boys to counterbalance the powerful force these particular messages have on the development of young boys and girls.

Moving from these ideas to, perhaps, a more familiar contemporary theory of human development is Bronfenbrenner's **ecological theory** (Bronfenbrenner, 1979). Ecological theory proposes that development occurs within complex social systems that project unique spheres of influence on peoples' lives (Hess & Schultz, 2008). According to the theory, these spheres of influence contain roles, norms, and rules that inform psychological development (Bronfenbrenner, 1979). The theory unfolds as a kind of mapping of these social systems and their spheres of influence, offering a concept of development that is not universal across individuals and proposing that development occurs as a lifelong process.

The five social systems that shape Bronfenbrenner's concept of development are the microsystem, mesosystem, exosystem, macrosystem, and chronosystem. The *microsystem* refers to the multiple places or settings where an individual interacts in everyday life. For example, family, school, and work are some of the various microsystems that are the contexts of our lives. The unique influences of these various microsystems shape us in a variety of ways, thus having significant developmental impact. The *mesosystem* refers to the interactions across the microsystems of our lives. For example, Renata is in law school (one microsystem), and she lives with her mother at home (another microsystem). We can see that when she does her homework at home, the home environment then comes into interaction with law school. Certainly doing homework affects her progress at school and conversely, spending countless hours in her bedroom studying is surely exerting an impact on the home environment. The *exosystem* refers to linkages between various settings that do not directly include the individual. As an example, let's say that one day when Renata is doing her homework, her mother comes home from work with the news that she has lost her job. The consequence is that she can no longer pay for Renata's law school. In this example, it is easy to see how Renata is affected by an event that occurred in her mother's microsystem. The *macrosystem* refers to the overall cultural patterns and behaviors in a system. Here the reference is to how beliefs, values, norms, and expectations in one's cultural context affect development. We might imagine that if in Renata's macrosystem, higher education is hugely valued, this sudden loss of her mother's employment would have grave effects on Renata's own identity and how she might be perceived by others if she did not complete law school. The *chronosystem* level refers to the cumulative experiences that one has had over one's lifetime. This may include major life events such as the birth of a sibling, the death of a parent, or a move to a new country. It may also include historic events such as the Civil Rights Act that paved the way for school integration, from which Renata would have likely benefitted if she was a student of color (of course, the benefits of integration are felt by all students, not just those of color). Environmental events such as a hurricane or an earthquake are other examples of chronosystem level events that affect people's lives.

In Bronfenbrenner's model, as in the social constructionist perspective mentioned earlier, development is linked to the complex interplay of experiences that occur within the multiple contexts of one's social system and which converge to influence individual growth and development. Rather than identifying specific stages, states, or even processes of development, ecological theory invites us "to discover what is most salient to the client" (Hess & Schultz, 2008, p. 63) in our conceptualization of who one is and how one has developed.

Feminist theories inhabit another category of contemporary theories of development. Feminist theories tend to be more commonly referenced as helping theories rather than theories of development, but I have included them here, because they, too, speak to the ways in which development is influenced by social experiences and historical context. Also, it should be noted that there is not one feminist theory, but rather there are numerous different feminist perspectives on development. As Mareck (2002) says, feminist personality theory is "an arena for vibrant, sometimes fierce, critical interchange and rigorous debate" (p. 6). Common to most feminist theories, though, is the concern for and attention to gender equity—that is, the extension of equal opportunities for women, across political, social, and economic domains (Sommers-Flanagan & Sommers-Flanagan, 2004) and a focus on the uniqueness of women's development, particularly in regard to the centrality of connection in women's lives (Jordan, 2004; Jordan & Walker, 2004; Surrey, 1991).

In terms of developmental theory, most feminists take issue with Western developmental theories that privilege ideas of masculinity as the standard for normal (Conarton & Silverman, 1996; Sommers-Flanagan & Sommers-Flanagan, 2004). Feminists claim that contemporary theories of human development implicitly value the concepts of a separate self—the extent to which an individual is independent and autonomous—and the ability to use thought to manage emotion, as defining characteristics of normal and healthy development. As a result, they argue, women tend to be pathologized for their normal expressions of emotion, dependence, and for needing connection (Jordan & Walker, 2004).

Conarton and Silverman (1996) point out that while separation and individuation is an important process for all children, boys and girls go through this process in different ways. They report that males appear to begin the process of separation in infancy, whereas females move into separation and individuation much later in life. These differences, they suggest, account for the relational differences seen in men and women. And these differences are important because most feminist psychologists believe that a sense of self develops from interpersonal experiences and in relationships. Speaking of the importance of relationship in development, Jordan (2004) says:

When we cannot represent ourselves authentically in relationships, when our real experience is not heard or responded to by the other person, then we must falsify, detach from, or suppress our response. Under such circumstances we learn that we cannot have an impact on other people in the relationships that matter to us. A sense of isolation, immobilization, self-blame, and relational incompetence develops. These meaning systems and relational images of incompetence and depletion interfere with our capacity to be productive, as well as to be in a creative relationship. They inhibit our engagement with life and our capacity to love and to move with a sense of awareness to meet others, to contribute to their growth, and to grow ourselves. (p. 11)

Relational competence, which develops from connection, has to do with the ability to attend to others and engage in "growth-fostering" (Jordan, 2004, p. 15) relationships. Jordan says that this has to do with the ability to engage in mutuality, anticipatory empathy, allowing oneself to be influenced by the other, being vulnerable, and focusing on connection with rather than power over the other. These are the experiences that girls are primed for when they develop in a relational context, feminists argue. Rather than seeing this emphasis on connection as pathological, Conarton and Silverman (1996) argue that these critical components of women's ways of being in the world "enhance the quality of life for everyone" (p. 47). With relatedness being central to women's needs and experiences in the world, feminists argue, developmental models must acknowledge this as a critical aspect of identity development for women.

Feminists are concerned with the ways in which relational competence are denigrated or resisted in society. This, Jordan (2004) points out, is particularly salient in the social norms that tend to value masculinity and expressions of certainty, competition, and power, over connection. These values and expressions, according to feminist theorists, don't represent the normal and healthy experiences of women in society. Pointing out that the concept of striving for individuality is not accurate to women's experiences, nor is it reflective of women's preferred identities, Miller (1991) and her colleagues introduced a model of identity development that describes relational development as the norm for women (this model is called relational cultural theory [RCT]). They recognize that women's sense of identity and esteem are based on their participation in meaningful and caring relationships with others (Jordan, 2010). In fact, Jordan and others argue that experiences of interconnectedness and interdependence foster healthy development for *boys and men* as well (Bergman, 1995; Jordan, 2004). Dooley and Fedele (2004) propose that when boys have relational skills and emotional awareness, they subsequently have higher capacity of engagement in responsible and collaborative relationships. These authors propose that the result of the valuing of relational development for

Table 2.1 Summary of Human Development Theories

Category	Theory	Familiar Names	Key Concepts
Psychodynamic	Psychoanalytic	Freud	• Development influenced by unconscious drives • Id, ego, superego • Defense mechanisms • Childhood stages of development
	Individual Psychology	Adler	• Social interest • Early environment • Private logic • Goal-directed behavior
	Interpersonal Theory of Psychology	Sullivan	• Self as interpersonal
	Psychosocial Development	Erikson	• Development influenced by unconscious drives • Development influenced by cultural factors • Identified lifespan stages of development
Ethological	Attachment	Bowlby	• Development influenced by caregiver–child attachments
Humanistic	Client-Centered Gestalt Existential Positive Psychology	Rogers Perls Otto/May/Yalom Seligman	• Self-actualization • Contact • Authenticity • Subjective meaning

Behavioral and Learning	Classical Conditioning	Pavlov/Watson	• Behavior conditioned by pairing stimulus to response
	Operant Conditioning	Skinner	• Behavior shaped by reinforcements
	Social Learning	Bandura	• Behavior mediated by learning processes • Observational learning
Contemporary	Feminist	multiple	• Development is influenced by the socio-cultural and political factors that oppress women
	Cultural-Historical	Vygotsky	• Mental functions develop socially and are part of history and culture • Zone of Proximal Development
	Social Constructionist	multiple	• Development is constructed in interpersonal, cultural, historical, and political contexts
	Narrative Theory	Brunner	• Story metaphor used to describe identity construction
	Ecological	Bronfenbrenner	• Development occurs within complex social systems that project unique spheres of influence on peoples' lives

boys will be a higher level of respect for women in society, which has the potential of altering our "pervasive societal problem of violence" (Dooley & Fedele, 2004, p. 224). In Chapter 3, we will explore some of the ways in which helping relationships may be framed using these ideas from the feminist perspective.

CULTURAL AND SOCIAL FACTORS IN DEVELOPMENT

Communities across the United States are vastly different from one another and the people who live in these communities have different life experiences, ways of thinking, and different values and belief systems. All of these factors are, of course, hugely influential to behavior, development, and helping relationships. In this section, I will begin with some basic definitions and then discuss two important ways in which values, beliefs, cultures, and diverse experiences "frame people's lives" (Anderson & Collins, 2004, p. 1). In the next few chapters, we will pick up on this discussion again to talk about how helpers can work with these concepts in their helping relationships.

The term *race* typically refers to the distinguishing group characteristics that are considered to be natural or genetic in origin (Monk, Winslade, & Sinclair, 2008). *Culture* refers to the values, beliefs, norms, and lifestyles of a particular social group that are transmitted generationally and which give meaning to the social group members' experiences and behaviors (Hogan-Garcia, 1999; Monk et al., 2008; Sue & Sue, 2003). Collins and Arthur (2010a) point out that a working definition of culture for helpers must go beyond mention of race and ethnicity, as we know that factors such as age, ability status, sexual orientation, gender identity, religion, language, and socioeconomic status are additional identity characteristics that are assumed within one's sense of cultural being. We often encounter the term *diversity* in reference to the variety of racial and cultural groups in the United States, and particularly, the term is used colloquially in reference to non-dominant or minority group status. Diversity is also used to identify social initiatives that are aimed at identifying and celebrating racial, class, and gender differences and to acquire multicultural awareness (Anderson & Collins, 2004).

While there is debate about whether age, gender, socioeconomic status, sexual orientation, gender identity, and individuals who congregate around common spiritual or religious beliefs constitute distinct cultural groups (Collins & Arthur, 2010a), we do know that the experiences of individuals within these categories shape how they understand and act in the world, in much the same way that racial and ethnic identities shape individuals' experiences and ways of being in the world. We also know that all of these group identities shape how individuals who identify in these groups are viewed by others (Sue & Sue,

2003). *Social location* is a term that attempts to capture the systems of social stratification that are inherent to membership in various social groups (Kubiak 2005; Pearlin 1989), and it opens our discussion about social and cultural identities to include these other identity characteristics. Individuals who occupy social locations such as elderly, disabled, poor, gay, lesbian, and transgender, to name a few, experience marginalization in society in much the same way as those from martinalized racial and ethnic groups, and thus the reference to social stratification is fitting. The term social location reminds us that the categories that foster diverse experiences in life are situated in social contexts of power, privilege, and inequality.

Discussions about cultural and social factors related to helping relationships inevitably become intertwined with discussions about values. *Values* are our fundamental beliefs about the importance or worth of a social principle or ideology. They might be comparable to Freud's concept of the superego as one's moral principles that guide the direction and daily practices of living. It is important to mention here that when helpers are working with individuals who are culturally, socially, racially, and otherwise different than themselves, they need not change their own personal values. However, as will be discussed later in Chapter 4, helpers do have a moral obligation to respect the beliefs and decisions of others. As we will see when we speak more about ethical practice in Chapter 4, helpers are asked, in a sense, to bracket their own values in order to be present for others. This ability to step out of one's own belief system and honor that of others is part of the helping contract, and it is a component of helper competence. Otherwise the helper is impaired.

Social Group Factors That Influence Identity

Most of us can intuitively understand how the differing experiences of race, class, gender, religion, spirituality, and even geography influence development. For example, a child living in a large urban center experiences life differently than a child who is raised on a farm. Consider how males and females are raised, from a very young age, to think and act. Think about how identifying as Muslim, Christian, or Jewish shapes one's values, beliefs, and the rituals of everyday life. We are aware that growing up with wealth offers more privilege, material, and educational options than growing up in poverty. All of these factors form the context of people's lives—they influence individual's everyday experiences, their values, their beliefs, and their hopes and dreams for the future. This is the important first point that we need to understand when working with diverse populations: social and cultural context influences development.

Sue and Sue (2003) argue that most models of human development neglect the hugely important ways in which social and cultural group experiences influence development. In their tripartite framework, identity is constructed from three components: *individual* (unique biological, genetic, family, and personal experiences that vary by the individual), *universal* (biological and physical characteristics and experiences that are common to all humans), and *group* experiences. Group level experiences refer to the ways in which the beliefs, values, and social practices of one's social or cultural group shape identity. Sue and Sue (2003) emphasize that the experiences of being in a particular social/ cultural group shape how one thinks, what one values, the experiences that one will have, and self-perceptions.

But exactly how do these aspects of group identity shape development? Some writers use the term *worldview* to talk about the ways in which individuals in various social groups interpret and function in the world around them (Diller, 2007; Ivey, Ivey, & Zalaquett, 2010). Worldviews are described in terms of how different groups perceive nature and the environment, how they are oriented in regard to time, and the values individuals hold regarding the role of family and work (Diller, 2007). Worldviews also describe the relative focus in some groups on individual versus community needs and the very essence of human nature (Diller, 2007). Racial, ethnic, gender, and other social group experiences shape individuals' worldviews (Sue & Sue, 2003), and group beliefs are typically communicated and passed down through generations.

Of course, not all individuals within particular social or cultural group act or think the same. Also, many individuals hold membership in multiple and overlapping social groups. For example, while a person of Hispanic dissent may hold certain values about family that are generational and common to his ethnic group membership, he may also identify as an upper middle class male and hold values and beliefs that are unique to that group as well. As Sue and Sue's (2003) model suggests, every individual has a unique make-up that comes from the various social groups to which they belong, as well as unique experiences related to biology, genetics, family, and community (Sue & Sue, 2003). All of these inform development.

External Factors Related to Social Location That Influence Identity

All of the factors mentioned above—where one grows up, one's culture, ethnicity, religion, and gender, and many others including age, sexual orientation, ability status, gender identity, and socioeconomic status—also influence the ways in which individuals are perceived and treated by others (Pieterse, Lee, Ritmeester, & Collins, 2013; Sue & Sue, 2003). As Monk et al. (2008) remind us: "It's not enough to just celebrate the rainbow of colors of diversity without taking seriously the ways in which cultural divisions lead to differential opportunities in life" (p. 49). This, then, is the second important point that needs to be emphasized when working with others: who one *is* is influenced by how she is perceived and treated by others.

The concept of *discourse,* introduced by Foucault (1972), helps us understand these shaping processes. Discourses are the structuring ideas that are taken for granted in a given culture—the ideas that shape everyday understandings of just about everything. Discourses may best be thought of as cultural stereotypes or "generalized expectations about how others are motivated, behave, feel, etc." (Van Langenhove & Harre, 1994, p. 360). They are the assumptions that become the backdrop for how we understand self and others (Winslade & Geroski, 2008). Discourses that become popular or that are ascribed cultural capital in a community at a given time become the norms that are used to see, understand, and evaluate self and others. For example, we have discourses about gender—these play out in ideas about how girls and boys should dress and behave. And current notions about acceptable gender-specific behaviors are different today than they were a century ago. Parenting discourses define "good parenting" and are influential to how we raise children. These, too, have changed over the past few decades. There are discourses related to, for example, what it means to have a mental illness, to be gay, or poor. And these ideas structure the ways that individuals in these various groups are perceived by others; they define what we consider to be right and wrong, weird or strange, good and bad. They have a norming influence in society.

As Monk et al. (2008) state, "it would be nice if all the social groups to which people belonged were equally valued in our communities. . . . A moment's reflection on life in the United States at the moment, however, is enough to see that this situation does not exist" (p. 141). Discourses are not neutral. Discourses are formulated in complex and unequal societies where some groups are privileged over others; they develop from and are nurtured by systems of power (Drewery, 2005). For example, we know that with identical resumes, White job applicants are twice as likely as applicants of color to receive a callback for a job interview (Bertrand & Mullainthan, 2004) and that young Black college graduates earn on average 11% less than their White counterparts (Roth, 2012). These experiences are not due to cultural identity or worldview; they are due to the ways in which people of color are viewed and treated by others. They are a reflection of inequities in our society that are based on social location.

So, "understanding diversity" must go beyond understanding the unique influences of culture on one's worldview; understanding diversity must also recognize the influence of existing systems of power and privilege that benefit individuals from various social locations unequally (Anderson & Collins, 2004; Pieterse et al., 2013). Understanding diversity must also include the understanding that individuals who identify in marginalized social locations, such as those who identify as women, poor, gay, transgender, people of color, etc., are affected by the discourses about these social locations in society. And as helpers, then, we need to be curious not only about how culture shapes development, but also how social discourses influence the very lives of others. As helpers, we also need to be aware of, think about, and, as we will discuss later in Chapter 8, open up discussions about how our helpees' lives are positioned by discourses. These conversations must also address the important understanding that discourses also influence the work we do in helping relationships.

CONTRIBUTIONS FROM NEUROSCIENCE

The fields of neuroscience, psychology, and human development have long sought to understand the connections between brain functioning, developmental processes, and psychopathology (i.e., mental health difficulties). Fortunately, new methods of studying brain processes have illuminated important research findings that identify the connection between brain functioning and human interactions. To help us wade through this complicated body of research, we will begin with a definition of the mind and then move into some brain basics. From there, I will highlight some important findings in the field of interpersonal neurobiology that are relevant to our discussion about human development.

The *mind* is a word and a concept that is commonly used in everyday language. But what do we mean, really, when we talk about the mind? What exactly are we talking about when we comment that someone "has lost his mind" or when we refer to "the good minds" that help us understand something? As these comments suggest, the mind typically refers to some kind of brain activity or psychological phenomenon. Author and clinical psychiatrist Daniel J. Siegel (2012) offers this definition of the mind: "an embodied and relational process that regulates the flow of energy and information" (p. 2). More simply, we might think of the mind as the "software" (Walsh, 2004, p. 27) of the brain machine. These definitions capture the critical idea that the mind is a process rather than a thing.

Siegel (2012) points out that the flow of energy and information that encompasses the mind is located in the central nervous system, extends throughout the brain and the rest of the body, and includes communication patterns that emerge within relationships. This description of the mind underscores a very important point: Brain structure and functioning, neural connections, and the expression of emotions are shaped, at the neurological level, by a variety of *external* processes, including interpersonal relationships (Coan, 2008). So, while we know that brain functions influence individual behaviors, researchers are now beginning to understand how interpersonal relationships affect brain functioning at the neurological level. This line of inquiry is referred to as interpersonal neurobiology (Siegel, 2012) and is what we will be exploring here.

The Central Nervous System and Synaptic Functions

Let's back up a bit and talk about what is meant by neural connections and how that relates to energy and information flow. It may take a leap of faith to realize that instead of being a hard, dense structure, the brain is actually a complex interwoven web of billions of neurons that are best known as the central nervous system (Siegel, 2012). Each neuron is a cell that is elongated to reach out to other neurons, and each neuron has *synapses* and *dendrites* at its ends. The synapses and dendrites facilitate the connection of a neuron to tens of thousands of other neurons within the nervous system, looking something like what is illustrated in Photo 2.5.

Neurons send out electrical impulses, which in turn release chemical *neurotransmitters*. Neurotransmitters are emitted through neural synapses and received through dendrites. This system of communication between the synapses and dendrites of neurons is typically referred to as *synaptic connections*. Synaptic connections are best thought of as the functional connection between neurons, and these connections make up the foundation of the brain. So, the image here is of a web of cells that are sending out and receiving chemical messages in a complex and extremely large web of cross-communications. It may be helpful to consider Walsh's (2004) metaphor of the brain as a busy complex electrical system.

The synaptic connections between neurons are the processes of the mind at work. To better understand how this all works, let us now go back to the definition mentioned earlier that the mind regulates the flow of energy and information within and outside of the brain. Sensory systems of the brain respond to external input—sensations that are perceived through the five senses. This sensory material sets off a pattern of neurotransmitter flow between the synapses of neurons. In this process, "mental symbols" (Seigel, 2012, p. 8) or

Photo 2.5 Synapses, Dendrites, and Synaptic Connections

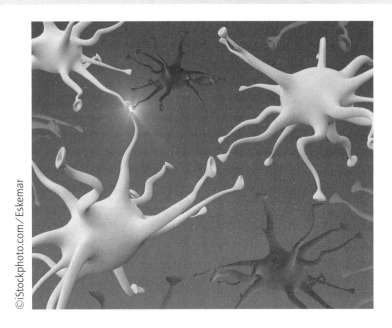

©iStockphoto.com/Eskemar

representations of information, are transmitted. Over time, repeated patterns of neurotransmission give rise to meaning. Patterns of neurons that fire together are known as a *neural net profile* (Siegel, 2012), and it is these neural net profiles that form a concept representation. For example, seeing a salivating dog drooling and walking slowly toward you on a street during the day might set off a series of neurotransmitter firings that come together in a neural net profile to form the concept of a dangerous rabid dog. This concept is stimulated by the visual input of seeing the dog (not just any dog—it is a salivating dog that is coming toward you) and moves into an electro-chemical meaning-making process between neurons within the complicated web of the central nervous system. What is important to remember here about this process is the necessary link between the neural activity within the brain and the environmental input that stimulated the synaptic firings in the first place.

As will be discussed shortly, interpersonal relationships also yield sensory information that stimulates or inhibits the neural-level functions within the brain (Coan, 2008). Neurologists have found that there are certain times in the development of the brain when particular neurons fire and result in specific patterns of representation or understandings (Johnson, 2005; Walsh, 2004). In early development—infancy and young childhood—brains are particularly vulnerable to experiences in the environment, and these experiences influence neuron firing and concept development. These neuron development time periods are called *sensitive periods* (Johnson, 2005). We might think of them as windows of opportunity for certain connections to be made. When these windows are closed, the opportunities are largely lost. Research has shown that neural systems are unusually responsive to experiences during these sensitive periods, they are particularly affected by stress, and that sensitive periods in brain development primarily occur in early childhood (Johnson, 2005; Siegel, 2012). Research looking at the long-term effects of stress during sensitive periods of brain development has shown that that if children experience stress at a young age, they are vulnerable to stress response system deregulation (i.e., difficulties in managing their responses to stress), particularly when they again experience stress at a later age (for more on this, see Kindsvatter & Geroski, 2014). Conversely, social behaviors such as maternal grooming or physical contact (holding a child) are known to attenuate or calm stress-related activity in the brain (Coan, 2008).

Brain Structures

Now we will wade through the passages of brain architecture to lay the foundation for another important aspect of interpersonal neurobiology. This discussion will be limited to those aspects of brain structure that are commonly known to affect behavior.

Neurons within the brain are organized according to various levels of complexity, and neuroscientists categorize neural clusters according to where they are localized in the human brain (Siegel, 2012). With the help of Figure 2.1, we will take a brief tour of the basic brain structures, remembering of course that the term *structure* in this context actually refers to closely intertwined neural connections.

The **lower brain structure**, more commonly known as the *brain stem*, is home to neuron clusters that tend to regulate energy flow, arousal, and physiological states of the body, such as body temperature and breathing. One important cluster in this section of the brain is the *thalamus,* which is thought to regulate incoming sensory information and also to mediate conscious awareness (Siegel, 2012). This is the part of the brain that regulates the flow from body senses to the meaning-making structures of the mind.

Also located in this lower brain region are the *hypothalamus* and *pituitary,* which are critical components of the *stress response system* (SRS). The SRS is a process of neural firings that release hormones enabling what is called *flight or fight* reactions to stress. They also help the body maintain or return to

Figure 2.1 Brain Structures

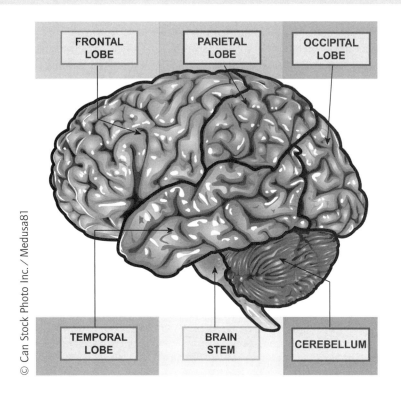

equilibrium after an experience of stress. The stress response system occurs through what is called the *hypothalamic-pituitary-adrenocortical (HPA) axis* (for more on this, see Kindsvatter & Geroski, 2014). Here is an example of how this works: Let's say that you are driving behind a car that slides on icy road conditions and crashes into a tree. Your initial physiological response is likely to be a fast heartbeat and a triggered sense of fear—preparing you to move away to safety or hold on to your own steering wheel tightly so as to avoid the same fate of running off the road. Slowly, as you navigate past the scene (and perhaps stop to offer assistance), you notice your heartbeat slows down a bit and your mind talks you through what to do next. After a few hours, you are back to normal, going about your day with only, perhaps, a storied recollection to your friends about what happened earlier in the day. In this example of a normal stress reaction, an initial sensory input triggers a flight-or-fight response that is then regulated back to equilibrium over a period of time.

The **central brain**, also known as the *limbic region* of the brain, holds the neuron clusters that are called the *hippocampus* and *amygdala*. These two clusters are known for their roles in regulating memory (hippocampus) and emotion (amygdala). Working closely with the sensory input funneled through the brain stem, they have the important work of coordinating functions within various parts of the brain, and particularly in mediating emotion and motivation. Because memory is so important to the process of making meaning of sensory input, these neural clusters play a key role in how social cues are interpreted and also in emotional activation (Siegel, 2012). The amygdala, too, is highly sensitive to social cues and our ability to make sense of the emotional expressions of others (Coan, 2008). For example, when a child encounters someone who is smiling at her, the child registers the expression of emotion that is being witnessed, and it is the memory of the meaning of a smile that enables her to understand the gesture as a friendly communication. If the person who smiled at the child is someone familiar (again, the memory helps make this connection), this connection likely prompts a feeling of warmth or care.

The **upper brain structures**, also known as the *cerebral cortex*, are related to complex information processing systems such as perception, thinking, and reasoning. These neural clusters mature in what look like columns that develop from back to front and over a long period of time—developing well into young adulthood (Seigel, 2012; Walsh, 2004). Communication between the various neuron columns in the cerebral cortex is critical to advanced-level information processing that includes being able to navigate advanced perceptual and abstract representations. These are the kinds of mental processes that are required to understand complex ideas, such as those offered in college classrooms or in dense textbooks that you might be reading (or even, perhaps, these ideas from neuroscience that I am talking about right now). Knowing that the maturation process of the cerebral cortex extends well into adulthood helps us understand the limited cognitive complexity in the thinking processes of children and teenagers (Walsh, 2004). It also explains why the level of learning tasks in college is more demanding than earlier levels of education—college students are expected to have more mature development in their cerebral cortex.

The portion of the cerebral cortex that is located in the front part of the brain (behind the forehead) is known as the *prefrontal cortex* and is related to working memory and attention. Another important role of the prefrontal cortex is to bridge the cerebral cortex thinking functions to the limbic systems, which, you will remember, control emotion. So as an example here, let's go back to when you witnessed the car accident. Let us say that after witnessing the car crash, you were having a difficult time regulating back to normal, so you decided to return back home right after the accident, still a bit shaken, although not in tears. As you walk in the door, your roommate says, "Wow, it looks like you've had a rough time. How can I help?" You tell him what happened, and after hearing the story, your roommate says, "Wow, that must have been really scary." This comforting response by your roommate comes from a place of cognitive complexity. First, your roommate was probably "reading" your body language, which indicated that something was wrong or different about you when you first walked in the door. Second, knowing that witnessing an accident can be jarring, your roommate was able take this information and offer an appropriate response. Cognitive complexity informed your roommate's appropriate empathic response of caring. Studies show that this cluster of neurons, located in the middle section of the prefrontal cortex, are critical to self-awareness, empathy, memory, emotional regulation, and attachment feelings and cues (Siegel, 2012).

As mentioned and critical here is that the cerebral cortex is known to mature slowly over time, not reaching optimal development until early adulthood. Remember that this portion of the brain mediates complex and abstract thinking as well as attention processes. It also links cognitive processes to the emotional centers of activity in the limbic system. Given that these portions of the brain do not reach maturity until well into young adulthood, we can begin to understand why self-regulation (managing impulses and reactions, making sense of feelings, and being able to maintain attention) is a developmental challenge in childhood and adolescence (Walsh, 2004).

One final point here has to do with the concepts of neural *blossoming* and *pruning*. Recall the metaphor of the brain as an electrical system. As with all electrical systems, new wirings create new connections and old circuits eventually die out. Similarly, neural connections within the brain that are consistently stimulated grow stronger with use—they blossom. Those that are not stimulated cease to function—which is a process referred to as pruning. These processes of blossoming and pruning occur largely during childhood and adolescence (Walsh, 2004). That is, the connections between neural synapses develop with use and fade with neglect, and although the brain appears to have the capacity to modify neural connections throughout the lifetime (Doidge, 2007), interpersonal neurobiologists emphasize that childhood is a critical period of synaptic development. It is best to strengthen adaptive neural connections early on and over time rather than try to reshape faulty developmental processes at a later date.

Brain Development and Human Development

Due to advances in neuroscience, there have been advances in understandings regarding the role that emotions play in behaviors and change processes (Levenson, 2010). Here I will highlight some important aspects of interpersonal neurobiology that have ramifications on human development:

1. There is a link between what happens outside the individual (one's experiences with things and persons in the environment) and the electro-chemical transmission process that happens within the brain. In short, the mind creates cognitive understandings that come from sensory experiences and interpersonal relationships.

2. The ability to use complex mental cognitive functions develops slowly and is not completed before young adulthood. The abilities to make meaning of social cues, regulate emotional responses, and sustain focused attention are processes that are affected by this slow rate of maturation.

3. Research indicates that there are critical sensitive periods of neurodevelopment that occur during childhood. One's ability to self-regulate, particularly in response to stress, is largely influenced by experiences and neurodevelopment that occurred in early childhood.

4. The processes of neural blossoming and pruning mean that repeated experiences are likely to form lasting neuron connections within the mind, and a lack of certain experiences may result in closed neuro-circuitry.

There are a number of important "takeaways" from these findings. First is that consistent patterns of healthy parent–child interactions, particularly during sensitive periods of development, structure better integrated neural functioning and create a blueprint for future relational development (Coan, 2008; Seigel, 2012). Repeated exposure to stress, particularly during sensitive periods of development, can have lasting effects on later emotional regulation abilities, cognitive functioning, and behavior (for more on this, see Siegel, 2012, Kindsvatter & Geroski, 2014; Johnson, 2005; Perry & Szalavitz, 2006). Also, due to the process of blossoming and pruning, well-developed neural pathways can be very difficult, although not impossible, to restructure in later life (Perry & Szalavitz, 2006). Higher-level thinking abilities, which reign the regulation and meaning-making processes of emotion, do not form until young adulthood, making it difficult (but not impossible) for children and adolescents to understand their feelings and be able to control their emotions, thoughts, and impulses. As Walsh (2004) laments, "adolescence is a heck of a time for the impulse control center—the prefrontal cortex—to be under construction" (p. 65). He likens this precarious developmental process to a new car with a high-powered engine taking off with no brakes to stop it. Helpers working with children and adolescents need to adjust their interventions accordingly.

CHAPTER SUMMARY

As this brief review of some of the major movements in the conceptualization of human growth and development suggests, the processes of human development are puzzling and complex. Some theories point to critical components of early caregiver–child attachment bonds as predictive of later human functioning. Others identify unconscious desires and impulses to be the motivating forces of development.

Some theories describe development in a predictable series of stages that occur across a wide scope of social and cultural groups. Others reject the notion that development is the same for everyone, and point to developmental differences based on gender, culture, and location of birth. Learning and behavioral theories point to immediate experiences in the environment as catalysts for learning, growth, and change. Contemporary theories add to the mix a focus on historical and social conditions that shape paths of growth and development. In addition to these theories about how individuals develop, we can see that cultural and social context influence how individuals understand and experience the world. We also examined how discourses about culture and social location shape the ways in which individuals are seen and treated by others. These contributions help us understand development as more than a process that happens internally, but instead as a process that is formidably shaped by external forces. Research in neuroscience support this claim showing that events that happen at the neural level inside the brain are shaped by events and even relationships in our everyday lives.

Each of these theories capture our attention and invite us to think about the people with whom we work in very different ways. And, as mentioned, all of these ideas offer very different pathways to helper actions, which will be explored in more detail in the next chapter. It is important to remember that the ways in which we think about human development, the etiology of problems, and the processes of change influence the ways in which we intervene in the lives of others. It really does matter how we think.

DISCUSSION QUESTIONS

1. How are the human development theories discussed in this chapter relevant to helpers who are working in nonclinical helping roles?

2. The author mentions two important threads in understanding social and cultural influences on development: (1) systems of meaning-making and

experiences within one's family, social, and cultural group, and (2) the experiences of individuals in marginalized social locations that affect their systems of meaning-making and experiences in the world. How are these two threads different, and how are they relevant to our work with individuals who are different than us?

3. How is understanding neurobiology relevant since these are things that can't be altered?

CHAPTER 3

HELPING THEORIES FOR WORKING WITH OTHERS

LEARNING OBJECTIVE

1. Understand how the various conceptualizations of human development discussed in the previous chapter promote different orientations toward helping

INTRODUCTION

In this chapter, we will be discussing helping theories. Again, helping theories are slightly different than human development theories because they are ideas about action—they direct what helpers do. So, in this chapter, we will explore how the ideas discussed in Chapter 2 inform the work of professional helpers. We will begin with two case examples that will be used throughout the chapter to illustrate the various helping theories presented. It is important to reiterate that the purpose of this chapter is to identify some of the helping approaches that are theoretically connected to the ways in which we think about others and the problems they encounter. That is, these theories describe the ways in which human development theories structure helping practice. The point is that how you think about others informs how you will intervene in helping.

CASE STUDIES

The case studies below are offered to illustrate how the various helping theories might look in a nonclinical practice setting. The intent is to show how a nonclinical helper using each orientation might be thinking about his or her work from that particular framework. They omit details in some places, suppose circumstances in others, and they do not offer a thorough analysis of the problems or offer detail regarding specific skills that would be used to carry out the suggestions. They offer a glimpse; further in-depth study of each of these helping approaches is recommended.

Case Study 1

Jorge is a teaching assistant in a preschool classroom for 4-year-olds, much like the one pictured in Photo 3.1. Mia is a child in his classroom who has been having difficulties, particularly around rest time. While it is now 3 months into the start of the school year, Mia is still refusing to nap during rest time. Most recently, her rest time behavior has included singing loudly and running out of the classroom, saying that she "wants to play outside," which has been somewhat disruptive to other children trying to sleep. Mia is the younger of two children in her family, and both of her parents are college professors at the local university. This rest time behavior is particularly problematic for Mia's parents as she arrives home from preschool exhausted and has difficulties staying awake in the evening. If she sleeps in the evening when she gets home

Photo 3.1   A Preschool Classroom

©iStockphoto.com/Christopher Futcher

from preschool, she misses out on important family time, and she then has disrupted night sleep habits.

Case Study 2

Emma is a care attendant working at a local senior living community, and she is also the case manager for Mrs. Morrison, who might look something like the woman in Photo 3.2. In the case manager role, Emma is assigned to oversee the care for Mrs. Morrison and to be the "point person" for communications with Mrs. Morrison's family members. Mrs. Morrison is a new resident in the living community and has aroused concern among staff because she appears depressed and unengaged in community activities.

THEORIES OF HELPING

Before moving ahead, I should point out that the review of the ideas offered here is no substitute for more substantial training in these theoretically based helping practices. My summaries do not capture the entirety or the nuanced complexities

Photo 3.2 Mrs. Morrison in Her New Residential Living Community

©iStockphoto.com/bjones2

of the theories that are presented. Also, while most of the theories presented here are oriented toward clinical helping, we will focus on the aspects of these theories and related practices that are most relevant for nonclinical helpers. Finally, the case study application examples offered in each section here do not presume to outline all components of the various helping theories or all of the approaches within each category; they offer only a small window into how the theory might influence helper action. My intent is to invite front-line nonclinical helpers to be aware of how their actions are based on underlying assumptions that are informed by theories of development and related helping theories. This awareness invites helpers to be thoughtful about the direction of their helping relationships.

It is also important to point out that while meta-analytic studies indicate that clinical therapy does indeed help individuals with mental health difficulties (Wampold, 2010), this research is inconclusive regarding the effectiveness of one theoretical approach over another. In other words, no one theoretical formulation of helping is more effective than another. What we do know, however, is that when a helper believes in the approach that he is using, when the helper and helpee are in agreement about the goals they are trying to accomplish, and when there is a strong working relationship between the helper and helpee, clinical success is likely (Wampold, 2010). Two additional important take-home messages in this chapter, then, are to work with intentionality and to never underestimate the importance of developing a strong and collaborative helping relationship.

PSYCHODYNAMIC APPROACHES TO HELPING

As you will recall from Chapter 2, psychodynamic theories about human development and psychopathology (i.e., difficulties in psychological functioning) are based on the idea that psychological and unconscious forces motivate human behavior and emotions, and form one's personality. Most psychodynamic thinkers also emphasize the influence of early childhood experiences, particularly the family, on individual functioning and developmental trajectories. Many also speak to the importance of social experiences on human development and personality development. It is probably fair to say that most, if not all, approaches to helping have been influenced in some way by psychodynamic theories—either in alignment with or in response to these theories. A quick digression here offers a visual testimony of the power of psychoanalytic ideas even in lay person notions about therapy. If you do a search of online images for the term *therapy*, you will find multiple images of a patient passively lying on a couch (see Illustration 3.1) while a Freud-like therapist is apparently attempting to exorcise some hidden disturbance from his unconscious. This classic psychoanalytic image of therapy still shapes current ideas about the meaning of therapy.

Illustration 3.1   A Classic Visual Definition of Therapy

Dynamic Graphics/liquidlibrary/Thinkstock

Psychodynamic-oriented clinical work focuses largely on enabling insight into unresolved conflicts and difficulties with the intent of freeing clients from the effects of these past conflicts on their present behaviors and relationships. Classical psychoanalytic- and psychodynamic-oriented clinical therapists typically focus on creating a therapeutic alliance that sets the stage for the processes for insight development and for what is typically called a *corrective emotional experience* (Levenson, 2010). A therapeutic corrective emotional experience is when a therapist creates a safe environment that allows the client to revisit a conflict or traumatic emotional experience from the past while currently being held in the safety of therapeutic relationship and environment. As a result, the client is uncoupled or freed from the past experience.

An example of a corrective emotional experience might be when a client has a male therapist whom she trusts, and within this therapeutic relationship over time, she has been able to talk about and move away from the crippling effects of an abusive relationship she had at the hands of a step-father far back in her past. So, here, being in a healthy therapeutic relationship with the male therapist might be considered a corrective emotional experience for this client, giving her the opportunity to experience healthy cross-gender relationships and allowing her to develop insight into the ways in which earlier relationships restricted her. Psychodynamic therapists also use the techniques of interpretation, free association, examining transference and counter-transference, analysis of resistance and defense mechanisms, and dream interpretation (Luborsky, O'Reilly-Landry & Arlow, 2008; Prochaska & Norcross, 2007; Safran, 2012; Sommers-Flanagan & Sommers-Flanagan, 2004). The goals of psychodynamic helping theories tend to include fostering insight, enabling the unconscious to become conscious, facilitating the articulation of feelings and wishes, and establishing meaning-making and agency (Safran, 2012).

So far, I have mentioned psychodynamic and particularly psychoanalytic helping strategies used by clinical mental health practitioners. Psychodynamic ideas are relevant to and visible in the work of nonclinical helpers as well. Two of the most obvious and perhaps the most significant ways in which psychodynamic ideas are used by nonclinical helpers are outlined in Figure 3.1 and discussed below.

Relationship

Most nonclinical helpers work to establish strong and supportive relationships with their helpees. As mentioned in Chapter 1, research indicates that of all the things that helpers do, the creation of a strong therapeutic relationship is the most critical (Hubble, Duncan, Miller & Wampold, 2010), and this is key in psychoanalytic helping (Safran, 2012). Through processes such as the corrective emotional experience, the helping relationship has the potential to offer a unique opportunity for the helpee to feel safe enough to try out new behaviors, feel supported, and grow. And this growth can and does happen in helping relationships for many, even without deep therapeutic conversations about the specifics of past trauma, unhealthy relationships, dream analysis, etc. Providing a space for change, regardless of the specific content that is addressed within that space, is what helpers do. The helping relationship is what creates therapeutic space for change.

Insight

A second important way in which psychodynamic ideas influence nonclinical helping can be seen in the ways in which helpers work to promote awareness or insight as a key component of their work (Safran, 2012). For example, Janie is rude to her teacher and threatens to kick another child in class. As the paraprofessional in the room, you are asked to walk Janie to the "quiet room" and sit with her until she is calm. When she is calm, you ask Janie why she acted in that way. Then you suggest that her outburst may be related to the fact that earlier in the day she was told that she would not be able to go on the walking field trip after school. As evidence, you may point out that you noticed her angry behavior started shortly after that. You also point out that when she loses control like that in the classroom, it sends the message that she is not able to go out on walking field trips because she is not in control of herself. This perspective is intended to offer her insight into the ways in which her behavior influences the decisions that are made about her. Here the idea is that such insight will facilitate change.

Another way in which the psychodynamic idea that insight effects change is demonstrated in multiple nonclinical helping venues where helpees are provided with information and discussion related to their helping goals. For example, a career counselor working with high school students in a workshop setting had them complete a self-awareness inventory and personality style assessment. The point of using these tools was to promote insight into who one is (identity), and what type of learning input is most productive for helpees (learning style). The underlying intent of this intervention was to help the participants develop self-insight and then use that to help them determine an appropriate career path. In both of these examples, the psychodynamic undercurrent is present—it is the idea that if we understand *why*, that awareness can lead to change (Safran, 2012).

Figure 3.1   Psychoanalytic/Psychodynamic Theories

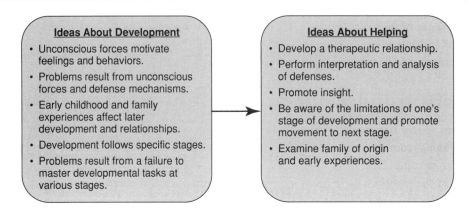

Ideas About Development
- Unconscious forces motivate feelings and behaviors.
- Problems result from unconscious forces and defense mechanisms.
- Early childhood and family experiences affect later development and relationships.
- Development follows specific stages.
- Problems result from a failure to master developmental tasks at various stages.

Ideas About Helping
- Develop a therapeutic relationship.
- Perform interpretation and analysis of defenses.
- Promote insight.
- Be aware of the limitations of one's stage of development and promote movement to next stage.
- Examine family of origin and early experiences.

Case Studies Illustrating a Psychodynamic Approach to Helping

Case Study 1

Recall that 4-year-old Mia is having difficulties during rest time. Jorge, the teaching assistant in the classroom, seeks guidance from his supervisor on how to intervene. His supervisor suggests the problem may be related to insufficient ego development, prohibiting little Mia from being able to control herself. Another teacher suggests, instead, that Mia is unconsciously angry at her parents for leaving her in daycare all day and acting out on this anger during rest time. Having been schooled in Erikson's ideas about psychosocial development, a third teacher believes that Mia has not sufficiently mastered the stage of basic trust (i.e., Erikson's stage of *trust* versus *mistrust*) and thus is not able to relax enough to sleep. With these ideas in mind, the teachers recommend the following:

1. Jorge and the other teachers will work hard to establish a relationship with Mia so that she can begin to trust the preschool teachers and feel safe in the preschool environment.

2. Jorge or another teacher may want to speak to the parents to learn more about any potential anger Mia may be experiencing related to attending preschool. This exploration may yield some suggestions for how to ameliorate any anger, if that is motivating the difficulties experienced at the preschool.

3. Jorge or another teacher may want to suggest to Mia's parents that she go to the university-sponsored child guidance clinic. There Mia can engage in nondirective play therapy to help her develop ego strength and a sense of personal competence, which will then transfer into her ability to feel more personally safe and participate more constructively in the preschool.

Case Study 2

Emma raises her concerns about Mrs. Morrison in a staff meeting at the senior living community. She asks for help to determine the best course of action regarding Mrs. Morrison's increased isolation and overall mental heath. At the meeting, one staff member suggests that Mrs. Morrison is likely surveying her life and feeling despair (i.e., Erikson's stage of *ego integrity* versus *despair*). Another suggests that Mrs. Morrison is feeling anxious and unsettled in her new setting and that her avoidant behavior is a defense mechanism. A third wonders if this is a pattern of behaviour for Mrs. Morrison, related to her level of ego development. Staff recommend the following:

1. Mrs. Morrison is referred for therapy with the staff mental health clinician to assess and possibly work through issues of despair about aging. In this meeting, the clinician may also be able to assess for the possibility that she has an anxiety disorder.

2. Emma works to establish a relationship with Mrs. Morrison by visiting her every day she is on duty. Emma should also assign a care assistant in each shift to check in with Mrs. Morrison and spend a short time with her each day. Increasing personnel to support Mrs. Morrison is expected to offer comfort regarding any feelings of loneliness she may have. It is also expected that giving Mrs. Morrison a time to talk about her life and her experiences in her new home may also give her the opportunity to work through any feelings of despair she may be experiencing and to develop insight around her depression.

3. During Emma's time with Mrs. Morrison, it is suggested that Emma talk to her about her transition and try to determine if there is anything in her past that would help explain her difficult transition. It was also suggested that Emma contact Mrs. Morrison's sons to see if they have any information that will help them understand what is happening for Mrs. Morrison.

ETHOLOGICAL APPROACHES TO HELPING

As discussed in Chapter 2, attachment theory rests on the idea that caregiver responsiveness during infancy and early childhood creates attachment bonds that become working models for future relationships. This theory proposes that understandings of self, others, and self-in-relationship-with-others grow in the context of a strong parent–child (caregiver–child) attachment relationship (Ainsworth, 1973; Ainsworth, Blehar, Waters & Wall, 1978; Bowlby, 1969; 1988). Research suggests that secure caregiver–child attachment relationships affect later social functioning and the physiological processes that support emotional self-regulation (Calkins & Hill, 2007). These ideas position helpers to be concerned about the emotional climate of early childhood and to hold early attachment patterns culpable for later challenges that individuals may face. The extension of these ideas into both clinical and nonclinical helping relationships calls on helpers to work with parents and caregivers to strengthen attachment bonds and to work directly with children and caregivers in the development of self and self-in-relationship with others (Levenson, 2010). These ideas are summarized in Figure 3.2.

The Attachment, Self-Regulation, Competence (ARC) Model of Intervention

The ARC model (Attachment, Self-Regulation, Competence) is a therapeutic intervention framework that uses attachment theory principles for working with children and families who have experienced trauma (Blaustein & Kinniburgh, 2010). This model orients helpers to promote strong attachments between children and their parents/caregivers, to strengthen children's self-regulation abilities, and help promote children's competencies. While the ARC model focuses primarily on working with children who have experienced trauma, it is applicable to a variety of children and families and can also be used by nonclinical helpers in their work directly with children. The framework instructs helpers to become attuned to children's needs and offers strategies for promoting emotional self-regulation and competence. These strategies can be used directly with children or taught by helpers to parents to promote healthy development.

Attunement

Attachment theory emphasizes the important ways in which parents and caregivers are responsive to the signaling and proximity-seeking behaviors of their infants and young children, suggesting that the parent–child relationship is a *secure base* necessary for survival (Ainsworth, 1973; Ainsworth et al., 1978). Infants and children who experienced sensitive responsiveness to their early cues develop a sense of the world as a place where their needs will be met and they learn that they are able to influence the world around them—a sense of competency (Weinfield, Sroufe, Egeland, & Carlson, 2008). Another function of the attachment relationship is to assist the infant or child in regulating emotional arousal, which leads to the child's ability to become competent in emotional understanding and self-regulation (Thompson, 2008). It also fosters a capacity to be empathic, navigate relationships with others, and develop a personal sense of personal competence (Thompson, 2008; Wienfield et al., 2008). At the heart of all of these important developmental processes, according to attachment theory, is the ability of caregivers to accurately read and respond to the infant or child's cues—this is what is meant by attunement (Blaustein & Kinniburgh, 2010).

According to Blaustein and Kinniburgh (2010), caregiver attunement can happen at the physiological, cognitive, behavioral, and emotional levels. For example, being attuned to a child's signals of being hungry or cold is to be attuned to the physiological needs of that child. Being attuned to a child's cognitive needs can look like answering questions, providing explanations, and helping him make sense of what he encounters in his environment. When a

Photo 3.3 Mother–Child Attunement

©Can Stock Photo Inc./Paha_L

caregiver is watching a child's behavior and responding accordingly, we might conclude that he is attuned at the behavioral level. For example, upon watching her child dip and almost spill off the two-wheel bicycle she is learning to ride, a sufficiently attuned parent can see that her daughter needs help balancing the bike, and she will respond accordingly. At the emotional level, attunement refers to understanding and consistently responding in a comforting and respectful way to children's fears, expressions of anger, etc. So, if the daughter falls off the bike and cuts her knee on the sidewalk, the parent would, perhaps, embrace her, acknowledge that her knee hurts, perhaps wiping it and putting on a Band-Aid.

Self-Regulation

The second part of the ARC model focuses on promoting children's self-regulation abilities (Blaustein & Kinniburgh, 2010). Self-regulation refers to the processes that we use to influence the expression of emotion, which is specifically called *emotional regulation* (Gross, 1998; Westphal & Bonanno, 2004). It also refers to the ability to manage one's physical behaviors, such as we see when a basketball player holds off on shooting a basket until the player guarding her is not in the way, and cognitive behaviors, such as, for example, paying attention when someone is talking.

There is ample evidence that children's abilities to regulate emotional responses to external stimuli are developed through attachment relationships, meaning that self-regulation is taught by caregivers (Calkins & Hill, 2007). Also, evidence suggests that children continue to develop self-regulation abilities even into late childhood and adolescence (Thompson, 2008). According to Blaustein and Kinniburgh (2010), helpers can promote emotional self-regulation by working directly with children or working with their caregivers. The ARC model focuses on these components of emotional self-regulation: being aware of one's internal emotional state, being able to tolerate emotional arousal, and being able to modulate emotional arousal appropriately. These abilities require a child to understand the connections between a stimulus (emotional trigger), feeling, thought, and behavior, as well as being able to effectively communicate her emotional experience with others (Blaustein & Kinniburgh, 2010). To this end, helpers teach children to identify the sensations that are indicators of emotional arousal and they teach cognitive skills (i.e., thinking and language practices) that can be used to mediate overarousal states. They also help children develop increasing tolerance to stimulation (i.e., become more able to sit with uncomfortable feelings or experiences), and they work with children to use effective communication skills to alert others to what they are feeling. Examples of these processes are offered below in the first case study (Mia).

Competence

Finally, in the third part of the ARC model, the focus is on building children's competencies (Blaustein & Kinniburgh, 2010). A sense of competence has to do with the perception of adequacy—having the necessary skills and appropriate self-judgment to be able to carry out a task. Personal self-competence, particularly in regard to seeing oneself as being loved and loveable, develops from consistent secure caregiver–parent relationships (Thompson, 2008). As an example of how competence may be promoted, let us look back on the example above with the girl who fell off her bicycle. The mother's response was attuned to the child's fall, and she appropriately offered emotional and physical comfort. Promoting competence would likely be reflected in an additional response, after comforting her, of gently suggesting to the daughter that falling off the bike is part of the process of learning,

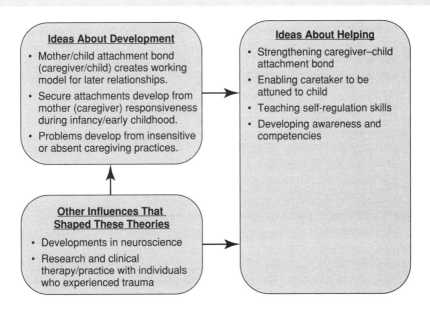

Figure 3.2   Ethological/Attachment Theories

Ideas About Development
- Mother/child attachment bond (caregiver/child) creates working model for later relationships.
- Secure attachments develop from mother (caregiver) responsiveness during infancy/early childhood.
- Problems develop from insensitive or absent caregiving practices.

Ideas About Helping
- Strengthening caregiver–child attachment bond
- Enabling caretaker to be attuned to child
- Teaching self-regulation skills
- Developing awareness and competencies

Other Influences That Shaped These Theories
- Developments in neuroscience
- Research and clinical therapy/practice with individuals who experienced trauma

albeit not fun, and by emphasizing her confidence in the daughter's ability to learn to ride the bike, offering encouragement that she should try again.

Blaustein and Kinniburgh (2010) argue that when children have not been able to develop expected developmental personal cognitive and emotional competence, and when they lack interpersonal effectiveness, helpers can intervene to promote development in these areas. In the ARC model, teaching and coaching *executive function skills* can promote competence. These executive function skills include the ability to delay or inhibit responses and to engage in active decision-making that includes contemplating consequences, evaluating outcomes, and intentional action. Again, here, helpers can work directly with helpees to promote competence, or they can work with parents/caregivers by coaching them to interact in these ways with their children.

Case Studies Illustrating an Attachment Approach to Helping

Case Study 1

Jorge seeks guidance on what to do with Mia's rest time behavior. His supervisor, who is oriented in attachment theory, believes that Mia's behavior suggests separation anxiety—perhaps due to insecure attachments—exacerbated by the stress Mia experiences in the hectic family life of a busy family with two working parents. The supervisor believes that Mia needs to develop the skills to regulate her emotional states so that she can properly calm herself enough to sleep during rest time. To this end, the supervisor recommends:

1. Jorge will spend time each day teaching Mia self-regulation skills. This will happen in the larger group during instruction time since all of the children in the center could use assistance in this area. These skills include developing an emotional vocabulary and awareness of physical signs of emotional states, understanding external signs of others' emotions (i.e., what we look like when we are angry), appropriate responses we can make to the emotional expressions of others, and self soothing techniques (e.g., breathing exercises).

2. Jorge also will provide individual coaching to Mia when she appears unable to manage her emotional states and prior to nap time. He will coach her, using the self-soothing techniques that were instructed in the class.

3. Mia's parents will be referred to the university-sponsored child guidance clinic where they can learn attunement strategies and develop skills in order for them to be able to coach Mia in emotional regulation.

Case Study 2

Emma calls a staff meeting at the senior living community to discuss the concerns about Mrs. Morrison's mental heath. It is decided that Mrs. Morrison has not been able to develop new attachments at the center and that she is likely mourning the separation from her familiar home, community, and surroundings. Staff suggest that transitions seem particularly hard for Mrs. Morrison and speculate that she may always have had difficulties with change, probably related to her own early attachment history. Staff notes that it appears that Mrs. Morrison is having difficulty regulating her sadness, and they wonder if she also may have some anxiety around meeting others and feeling safe in this community. The following recommendations are made:

1. Emma is assigned to be an initial attachment figure for Mrs. Morrison. She will check in with Mrs. Morrison at the start of her shift, spend additional time with Mrs. Morrison during the day, and accompany her in various center activities.

2. Emma will contact Mrs. Morrison's family and friends and invite them to come to the center to spend time with her to help with the transfer of attachments from her former community to her present residential community. Emma will also ask family members to bring some additional objects such as pictures, photo albums, bedding, etc., from Mrs. Morrison's home to her apartment in the center to help facilitate the transition.

3. The staff mental health therapist will meet with Mrs. Morrison to assess her level of depression and determine if she is also experiencing anxiety. If it is determined that Mrs. Morrison is experiencing difficulties regulating her emotional states, Emma and other staff members will help Mrs. Morrison develop self-regulation skills.

4. Emma and other staff members will help Mrs. Morrison develop a routine of self-care that includes healthy eating habits, age-appropriate exercise, and engagement in activities. They will initiate this by inviting Mrs. Morrison to participate in center activities each morning and arranging for someone to accompany her to the dining room at meal times.

HUMANISTIC APPROACHES TO HELPING

Humanistic-oriented helping approaches, such as those mentioned in Chapter 2 including client-centered, existential, gestalt, and positive psychology, are based on the concept that all humans have an inherent self-actualizing tendency or drive toward healthy growth and development (Cain, 2002). Humanists see people holistically—they believe that individuals are connected to their immediate environment, and they emphasize the connections between physical, emotional, and social processes and experiences. Humanists also emphasize people's capacity to make rational choices and develop to their maximum potential. The helping practices in this orientation diverge significantly from models of helping that humanists believe focus too much on "advice-giving, persuasion, exhortation, and interpretation" (Cain, 2002, p. 3). Instead, humanistic approaches are oriented toward supporting the development of self-actualization and are geared toward exploration of one's emotional experiences within the context of a therapeutic relationship. In fact, with current advances in research and knowledge in the area of brain chemistry, memory processes, and self-regulation, a resurgent interest the emotion-based approaches has emerged in the field of clinical helping (Levenson, 2010). Here we will briefly review a number of helping practices that stem from these humanistic orientations and that are commonly used by both clinical and nonclinical helpers in their work with others to promote change. These are summarized at the end of this section in Figure 3.3.

Client-Centered Orientation

Client-centered therapy, based on the work of Carl Rogers, rejects the idea of helpers being the authorities on experiences of others. Instead, helpers oriented in this way promote change by creating a helping relationship that centers on unconditional positive regard, congruence, and communicating empathy (Cain, 2010; Raskin, Rogers, & Witty, 2008). They assume a nondirective stance, allowing the helpee to direct and take charge of the process of change. Client-centered helpers encourage helpees to rely on their own inner strengths and knowledge rather than those of the helper. This is an approach that lends itself easily to the work of nonclinical helpers as well. For example, a nurse working with a patient in a hospital who is recovering from surgery asks the patient what kinds of things he needs so as to facilitate his recovery. A teacher in a classroom offers a variety of learning activities and asks students to develop research projects that reflect their own interests. The focus is always on creating the conditions to bring forward the best of what the helpee has or can develop.

Mindfulness

Gestalt therapy, which was mentioned in Chapter 2, is largely a clinical practice, so I will limit our discussion here to the gestalt concept of *contact*, which is relevant to helping relationships in a variety of contexts. From the gestalt perspective, you will recall, contact has the unique meaning being aware of one's affective, sensory, cognitive, and behavioral experiences in the moment and an ability to manage self and other boundaries effectively (Yontef & Jacobs, 2008). Gestalt practitioners believe that with awareness of self and others, people then have choices and self-directed abilities to make changes in their lives. So, with regard to helping, this concept of contact emphasizes the importance of helping individuals develop awareness about their experiences in the moment. One contemporary and popular application of this notion of contact is at the center of what is known as *mindfulness* practice. Mindfulness is a practice of attunement or awareness (Siegel, 2010), with roots in a variety of spiritual, cultural, philosophical, and healing traditions beyond humanistic psychology. However, due to its core focus on awareness, it is relevant to our discussion here.

Mindfulness is practiced in a wide variety of ways, but all have a meditative component as their base (Melbourne Academic Mindfulness Interest Group, 2006). As a helping practice, mindfulness typically entails guiding the helpee to develop awareness of sensory input and bodily sensations in the present, refraining from thinking about the past and present when in the moment, and to practice unconditional self-acceptance. Research suggests that mindfulness may be particularly helpful when working with people who experience anxiety and stress, chronic pain, and other health conditions, and for some individuals with eating and affective disorders (Melbourne Academic Mindfulness Interest Group, 2006), and for emotional awareness and regulation, and general well-being (Brown & Ryan, 2003). For example, a nursing assistant noticed that a patient waiting to see a physician appeared extremely nervous as he waited to learn about his diagnosis. Knowing that the physician was running late and the wait time would feel excruciatingly long, the assistant said to the patient, "I know that it's hard to wait, especially when you are waiting to hear the test results. Sometimes it can be helpful to take some deep breaths and relax at these times. Would you be willing to let me coach you through a very brief mindfulness breathing exercise that might help you relax?" With the permission of the patient, the assistant led him through a 2-minute breathing exercise that focused on awareness and emotional self-regulation.

Existential Conversations

Existentialists, as you may remember from Chapter 2, see humans as self-determining beings who are bound by the responsibilities inherent to and limitations imposed by their personal contexts, social relationships, and personal struggles. Existentialists are largely interested in the existential themes of death, freedom, responsibility, isolation, meaninglessness, and the choices that we make as a result of these themes. Fundamental to helping orientations grounded in existentialism is the idea that people are capable of growth and change—we are always in the process of becoming (Walsh & McElwain, 2002). Many existentially oriented clinical helpers try to expose the ways in which we become immobilized by "existential anxiety" (around the existential themes) as it is thought that this anxiety manifests in rigid patterns of defensiveness or self-restrictions that prevent us from living our lives to their fullest. Interventions typically include creating a therapeutic relationship centered on understanding the subjective experience of the helpee and within which the existential themes can be explored. The focus is on developing awareness, choice, and motivating personal responsibility for one's choices (Walsh & McElwain, 2002). Existential helpers stay focused on the subjective experience of the helpee—what is meaningful for the helpee. They encourage the helpee to become meaningfully engaged in life, which includes an orientation to and connection with others outside of and bigger than one's self (Yalom, 1980). How these ideas might be put into practice in nonclinical helping relationships is demonstrated below in Case Study 2.

Positive Psychology Orientation

Helpers working from a positive psychology perspective are largely focused on promoting helpees' overall well-being and fulfillment (Joseph & Linley, 2006) rather than on addressing specific problems. In the words of Seligman, "treatment is not just fixing what is broken; it is nurturing what is best"

(Seligman & Csikszentmihalyi, 2000, p. 7). Focusing on the strengths of helpees and maximizing the conditions for self-actualization are key components of most humanistic orientations to helping. Specifically to positive psychology, Seligman (2002) promotes a model of helping that encourages the helpee to experience pleasure and positive emotions, to be engaged in life, and to find meaning in life (Seligman, 2002). To these ends, Seligman, Rashid, and Parks (2006) recommend that helpers engage helpees in gratitude and forgiveness exercises, teach helpees to savor experiences rather than rushing through life, and identify and find opportunities for helpees to use their strengths and talents. They also recommend that helpers work with helpees to structure their lives in ways that enhance agency, to find meaning in life, and to use their strengths and talents to "belong to and serve something that one believes is bigger than the self" (p. 777). This idea about engagement in something bigger than the individual may entail promoting engagement in a religious or political institution, for example, or in family or community.

Figure 3.3 Humanistic Theories

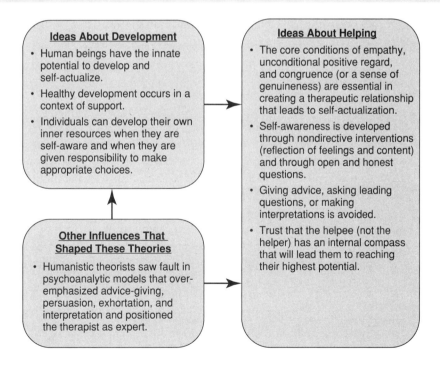

Case Studies Illustrating a Humanistic Approach to Helping

Case Study 1

Jorge seeks guidance on what to do with Mia's rest time behavior. Oriented firmly in a humanistic orientation at the childcare center, Jorge and the other teachers believe that providing a nurturing and stimulating environment is key to promoting children's healthy growth and development. He and his supervisors interpret Mia's behaviors as systematic of a problem in the environment that inhibits optimal behavior. As a result, they:

1. Evaluate the classroom environment, particularly at naptime, and brainstorm ways to optimize the conditions so that Mia (and the others) can feel relaxed enough to sleep.

2. Institute a mindfulness calming practice at the start of naptime for all of the children where they are guided through a body scan and breathing exercise while resting on their mats.

3. Consider that Mia does not need to sleep during rest time and offer an alternative quiet activity for her so that she does not bother the other children.

Case Study 2

Emma calls a staff meeting at the senior living community to discuss the concerns about Mrs. Morrison's mental heath. The staff at this senior living residence is influenced by the existential notion that people are always engaged in meaning-making, and they are aware that their elder population, particularly, often grapples with issues around mortality. With this in mind, their suggestions to Emma include the following:

1. Emma should make time daily to spend time with Mrs. Morrison, allowing her to dictate the topic and tenor of their conversations. With time, comfort, and Emma's appropriate receptivity, they believe that the existential themes of existence will soon appear in Mrs. Morrison's conversations. They believe that talking about anxiety around life and death in the context of an accepting relationship will help release its restricting hold on Mrs. Morrison, and free her to be more engaged with her life at the senior living community.

2. Emma and other staff should encourage Mrs. Morrison to try the book-reading group that is regularly held at the center. Existential topics of freedom, choice, and mortality are often the undercurrent in the book discussions, and the staff believe that Mrs. Morrison would benefit from engaging in these conversations with her peers, who are much older, of course, than the staff at the center.

3. Noting what Mrs. Morrison's son had told them that she really enjoys children, Emma and other staff should encourage Mrs. Morrison to volunteer in the center's Foster Grandparent program. They believe that being around young children, which she apparently enjoys, will coax Mrs. Morrison into connections and relationships with others and will offer her an opportunity to develop a sense of meaning in her new life in the senior community.

BEHAVIORAL AND LEARNING APPROACHES TO HELPING

In Chapter 2, there were a number of theories about development that focused on behavior rather than personality. These behavior theories looked at how behavior is shaped by antecedents and reinforcements in the environment. The social learning theories in Chapter 2 focused on how behavior is mediated by thinking (cognitive) processes. Here we will talk about how these ideas influence helping practices. These approaches to helping are reviewed in Figure 3.4.

Behavioral Interventions

The process of change in behavioural approaches does not extend far beyond the immediate environment, and insight, as it is conceived in psychodynamic theories, is irrelevant. Instead, the focus for change is on shaping the conditions that initiate, maintain, or reinforce behaviors. The term *applied behavioral analysis* is given to helping interventions that are based on operant conditioning principles of stimulus control, reinforcement, and punishment (Sommers-Flanagan & Sommers-Flanagan, 2004); it is the study of the significance of a particular behavior in a particular setting (Gresham, Watson, & Skinner, 2001). Behaviors, these latter authors assert, typically serve these functions: for social communication or attention, to enable access to tangibles or preferences (i.e., to help someone get what they want), to avoid or delay aversive or undesired tasks or activities, to avoid contact with specific individuals, or for internal stimulation. The idea is that positive change happens by manipulating the conditions that allow undesirable behaviors to meet their desired functions, and by setting into place conditions that stimulate and reinforce more positive behaviors. This is the aim of applied behavioral analysis.

Most behaviorists initiate their work with a careful assessment of the conditions that stimulate and reinforce a problematic behavior—a *functional behavioral analysis* (FBA) is often used to this end (Gresham et al., 2001). One of the primary tools used in conducting an FBA is to observe behavior in its natural setting so as to determine the immediate antecedents and consequences that condition or reinforce it. Interviews, records, rating scales, and checklists can also be used to assess behaviors. Once the function and conditions eliciting and supporting problematic behavior are identified, helpers working from a behavioral perspective can establish an intervention plan to change unwanted behaviors and simulate more functional, adaptive, or desirable behaviors.

There are numerous behavioral strategies readily available to helping professionals that move away from the careful assessment and treatment processes of applied behavioral analysis. *Progressive relaxation*, which originated in the early 1900s, is one such helping strategy that is based on behavioral and learning principles and neurophysiology. In progressive relaxation, individuals are taught to develop awareness of their tense muscle states and apply tension-reducing strategies to become more relaxed. It is often used to address anxiety or tension (Bernstein & Borkovec, 1973) and is not too dissimilar from some of the mindfulness practices described above. In fact, there are a variety of awareness and relaxation strategies (not just progressive relaxation) that are used in helping individuals who struggle with anxiety, anger, chronic pain, and migraine headaches (Poppen, 1998). These include autogenic training, behavioral relaxation, electro-myography and thermal biofeedback, hypnosis, breathing exercises, yoga, imagery, and meditation (for more on these, see Smith, 2001).

Cognitive Behavioral Interventions

The interventions already mentioned in this section of behavioral and learning theories have focused on behavior as the major conduit for creating change. Another group of strategies within this category are those that focus on cognitive processes as the avenue for facilitating change. We will start with skills training or instruction. Teaching new skills through information and practice is one of the major ways in which helpers of all kinds promote growth, development, and change. *Skills training* interventions, sometimes called psychoeducation, may focus on whatever area of learning is assessed to be needed. Skills training is used to teach assertiveness, basic communication skills, emotional self-regulation, problem solving, decision-making skills, etc. In skills training, specific behavioral and/or cognitive skills are typically introduced in an instructional sequence, and they are often taught in a group or classroom setting. Typically, skills training interventions include a practice component where trainees receive feedback on how they executed the specific skill and instructions for improvement. I encourage helpers working with individuals on intrapersonal and interpersonal challenges to learn more about and explore the numerous and varied skills-training manuals published for promoting behavioral, cognitive, and emotional skills across a wide range of areas and with a broad scope of populations.

Cognitive behavioral approaches to helping, typically referred to as CBT, focus on the ways in which cognitions (i.e., thoughts) specifically shape emotional experiences and behaviors (Creed, Reisweber, & Beck, 2011). While CBT is most commonly known as a clinical intervention, the principles behind this approach are used in a variety of settings and also by nonclinical helpers.

Illustration 3.2 Skills Training

©Can Stock Photo Inc./thebp8

CBT is based on the notion that individuals are constantly thinking about and interpreting their everyday experiences in the world, and these thoughts influence how they feel and behave (Creed et al., 2011; Leahy, 2003; Sommers-Flanagan & Sommers-Flanagan, 2004). For example, Jack arrives home late after work. If his partner, Maria, thinks that he is late due to a traffic jam, then she may be annoyed at his lateness, but likely not hold him culpable and thus not be angry at him. But if, while waiting for Jack to arrive home, Maria convinces herself that Jack is late because he stopped at the bar for a few drinks with a buddy on his way home, her response would likely be very different. In this case, she might greet him at the door with anger. Or, if her thoughts really got carried away and she interpreted his behavior as a reflection of herself—that he stopped at the bar to have drinks because he was falling out of love with her and maybe that was because she just isn't good enough—her response might be different again. In this latter scenario, you might see anger, tears, self-criticism, or some other response that reflects her self-critical interpretations. The point is, of course, that how Maria makes meaning of or interprets Jacks behavior (i.e., her cognitive processes) affects her emotional state and ensuing behavior.

CBT, then, is based on the idea that an event triggers a cycle where thoughts lead to particular feelings and behaviors. These feelings and behaviors are based on the interpretations or appraisals of the triggering event. Linehan combines the application of CBT skills with mindfulness practice in the therapeutic practice of *dialectical behavior therapy* (DBT) that she developed for working with individuals with chronic and severe mental health challenges that typically include suicidal or para-suicidal behaviors (for more on DBT, see Linehan, 1993; Linehan, Armstrong, Suarez, Allmon, & Heard, 1991; Linehan, Heard, & Armstrong, 1993; Shearin & Linehan, 1994).

As mentioned, cognitive behavioral approaches to helping are not solely within the domain of the work of clinical therapists. When helpers conceptualize difficulties as learned, reinforced, or to be a product of one's meaning-making cognitive processes, than the helping interventions will likely be aimed at changing behaviors by focusing on automatic thoughts (i.e., cognitions). Nonclinical helpers may use a cognitive behavioral orientation in helping relationships to illuminate thinking processes that lead to reactive or unhealthy feelings and behaviors. This will be illustrated in our Case Study 2. As with all of the strategies mentioned in this book, helpers using behavioral and cognitive behavioral interventions should acquire more specific training in these approaches to be most effective in their practical applications.

Figure 3.4   Learning/Behavioral Theories

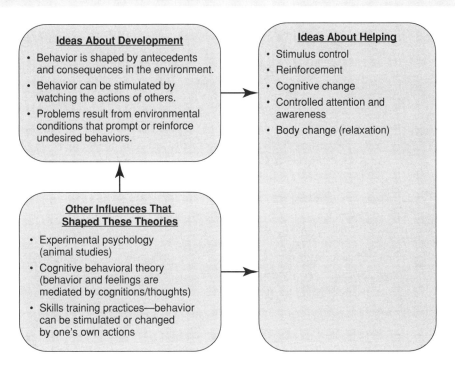

Case Studies Illustrating Behavioral or Learning Approaches to Helping

Case Study 1

Working from a behavioral orientation, Jorge and his supervisor use the following interventions to address Mia's problematic rest time behavior:

1. First they will examine the classroom routines that happen prior to rest time in order to determine what evokes the problematic behaviors. Logging observations of Mia's behavior in a *functional behavioral assessment* (FBA), they determine that eating just prior to rest time causes Mia to become very energetic. They also observe that Mia settles into a quiet space more easily when music is not playing and when she is not able to see other children in the classroom. The functional behavioral analysis

also examines the conditions that reinforce Mia's inappropriate rest time behaviors. They find that when Mia makes noise in the room, other children giggle and seem interested in what she is doing, and this then seems to encourage Mia to continue "misbehaving." The analysis also reveals that when Mia runs out of the room at rest time, she is quickly (and appropriately) pursued by a staff member. Her giggling at that moment of being caught seems to suggest that she enjoys the chase activity.

2. Working from a behavioral perspective, Jorge and his supervisor intervene by manipulating some of what occurs before and during the rest time period. They decide to institute a 15-minute quiet play time for all of the children before rest time. This gives Mia and the other children time to settle down after the noon meal. Also, Jorge develops a ritual that cues the children to settle down and facilitates the transition from lunch to rest time. This ritual includes some of relaxation strategies, including mindfulness and progressive relaxation.

3. Jorge also finds a "special place" for Mia to rest that is slightly removed from the other children. He also informs her that she is allowed to play quietly if she is not tired (thus removing the "naughty" component of her former behavior).

4. Finally, staff agrees on a consistent mode of responding to Mia if she runs out of the room during rest time. This response will include redirection and minimal attention. Their last resort, they agree, will be to use an adapted token economy of reinforcements and punishments if the former interventions do not work.

Case Study 2

Emma has called a staff meeting for consultation regarding Mrs. Morrison in the senior living center. Center staff suggest that the root of Mrs. Morrison's difficulty is that she is beginning to believe that because she is old and now living in the senior center, she is entering the final stages of life and unable to enjoy life as she once did. They believe that these thoughts on aging lead her to feeling depressed and becoming inactive. Their recommendations include:

1. Emma will have a discussion with Mrs. Morrison about her experience at the center so far to determine if she is feeling depressed and what her thoughts are about aging and her life here in the center. If it is apparent that Mrs. Morrison has some thoughts about aging that prevent her from

engaging in center activities and relationships or that appear to be causing sadness, she will invite Mrs. Morris to the Thursday Afternoon Conversation group, led by the center's mental health clinician. This group focuses on exploring the concept of aging and encouraging residents to make active choices about how they want to live their lives in the center. An explicit goal of this group is to help residents consider their residential placement at the center as an opportunity to meet new people and engage in new activities rather than think of it as a place to grow older.

2. Emma will spend time with Mrs. Morrison to introduce her to the various activities at the center. On Monday mornings, she will explain all of the week's activities in detail and leave a written daily activity guide for Mrs. Morrison with the times and locations of the various events at the center so as to stimulate engagement in some activity.

3. Emma will offer to take Mrs. Morrison to an activity that she seems to be interested in (stimulation) and, knowing that Mrs. Morrison enjoys walking in the garden, will offer to go for a walk with her at the end of the activity time (reinforcement).

CONTEMPORARY APPROACHES TO HELPING

The contemporary theories describing development discussed in Chapter 2 included feminist theories, constructionism and related theories, and Bronfenbrenner's ecological theory. Across these approaches are the common themes of valuing the subjective experience of the helpee and understanding how social context, including social norms, culture, and history, are key shaping experiences in development. There are numerous contemporary approaches and strategies for helping—far too many to describe here, given how broad this category is, so I apologetically limit this discussion to narrative and feminist practices. The reader is encouraged to explore the narrative and feminist practices introduced here in more depth, and to delve into a more extended study of the many other contemporary practices of helping that are available. Figure 3.5 at the end of this section summarizes the ways in which contemporary theories influence helping.

Feminist Approaches to Helping

As mentioned in Chapter 2, there is no one feminist theory of development. Nor is there just one feminist approach to helping. But, in general, a *feminist ideology* appropriate to helping relationships will likely acknowledge women's (and men's) relational development and competence, discuss issues related to independence and autonomy, and attend to the debilitating effects of living in an invalidating and oppressive society (Sturdivant, 1980). It should be pointed out that feminist approaches to helping are not limited to work with women; fostering relational development and generating understandings about the oppressive nature of social norms defining masculinity and feminity are also important foci for working with boys and men (Bergman, 1995; Dooley & Fedele, 2004).

Many feminist helpers focus on systems change—public education and advocacy, rather than change at the individual level. This focus is based on the idea that the many problems facing women (and men) are related to the oppressive conditions that shape women's (and men's) lives and rigid socially normative ideas that restrict identity development (for men and women), rather than something that is inherently wrong with any one individual (Conarton & Silverman, 1996; Marecek, 2002). In line with these principles, feminist helpers who work directly with women endeavor to establish egalitarian relationships, may serve as role models, are transparent about their goals and the helping processes, and focus on strengthening the helpee's sense of self. Feminist helpers actively validate women's lived experiences of oppression, they encourage competence and autonomy, and they encourage women to be engaged in a community of support. For example, Conarton and Silverman (1996) suggest that helping women develop a true and congruent sense of self involves "re-examining the self; trusting one's intuitive knowledge to sort through the myriad of demands and determine what is really important to oneself; mobilizing the will to implement the necessary changes; developing spiritual awareness; and integrating these aspects of self" (p. 56).

Demonstrating empathy and authenticity and offering help that empowers helpees are critical components of feminist-oriented helping relationships (Jordan 1991; Jordan, 2010; Surrey, 1991). Feminist helpers endeavor to establish egalitarian relationships with their helpees, they respect their helpee's experiences and perceptions, and they also recognize that women's (and men's) difficulties largely have social (i.e., a reflection of subjugated lives) rather than just personal causes. They may take social action on behalf of or with their clients, they sometimes work in a consultative role by sharing their own knowledge and experiences, and feminist therapists typically support women to make their own choices. They often do this by encouraging helpees to be aware of their options (Cammaert & Larsen, 1996). Finally, feminists resist the habits of labeling and pathologizing women's experiences into diagnostic categories, and they focus, instead, on listening to and honoring the unique experiences of their helpees (Merecek, 2002).

Narrative Conversations

Based on the social constructionist ideas discussed in Chapter 2 and similar to feminist approaches, narrative practitioners work with helpees to uncover their own strengths, resources, and abilities to solve problems, and they focus on bringing forward one's preferred ways of living (Monk, 1997). Narrative-oriented helpers position helpees to be agents in a collaborative helping process, and they engage in deconstructing conversations (discussed in more detail in Chapter 8) to understand the meanings that helpees have regarding their challenges and situations. They orient from the concerns expressed by the helpee, rather than those identified by others about the helpee, and they attempt to uncover the substance of the helpee's abilities, skills, thoughts, hopes, and desires as the basis for change. That is, helpers want to know how the helpee understands his challenges, what he already knows that has worked for him in the past, and, importantly, what direction or hopes the helpee has for his future.

The term *narrative* in this approach names its focus on the ways in which individuals use stories to make sense of or interpret their lived experiences—an orientation that is based largely on the work of Bruner (1990), discussed in the narrative theory section in Chapter 2. For example, I used to tell students at the start of a course in which I would be offering them extensive feedback on a regular basis that I "was directive." Then I went on to tell a story about my childhood that served to explain, I believed, why I came to be so directive in my interpersonal interactions. Notice that the idea of being directive (i.e., I said that I *was* directive) locates directiveness inside of me, suggesting a personality characteristic—it is a statement about who I am. This is what narrative therapists refer to as an *identity claim*. From a narrative perspective, stories are used to explain or reveal who one is and to support identity claims. (Narrative therapists do not believe, however, that identity exists within someone, as the idea of an identity claim suggests. They are firmly rooted in social constructionist ideologies, which promote the idea that identity is constructed socially. So narrative helpers would see an identity claim as a construction of self in a particular situation or relationship.)

According to narrative theory, it is not only our own stories about self that lay claims to who we are, but stories that are told to and around us by others.

These, too, have identity-shaping effects on people's lives. I can recall how we used to call our son a "mathematician" when he was just a small child because he loved to talk about numbers and learned to add at a very young age. This label, and the accompanying tales of the mathematical tasks he was able to solve at such a young age, offered him an identity claim of being a smart little guy, particularly with numbers. I am also reminded of the ways in which children are sometimes labeled in less favorable ways, and stories of their behaviors are offered as evidence of their failure-themed identities. I worked in a school, for example, where I learned which children were likely to be mischievous or misbehave, or who were "not very smart" long before I ever met them. It is not difficult to imagine how such labels shaped my perceptions of these children. If they behaved in ways that fit with these labels, for example, no one would have been surprised. If they defied them, however, their unexpected goodness was sometimes treated as an aberration. The point is that labels, typically accompanied by a supporting story, influence how we see ourselves, how we see others, and how others come to know us. I often wondered how it would be for these children if I shared their stories of successes rather than their challenges with future teachers—how that would have shaped the welcome they would receive and the expectations teachers had for them?

Narrative helpers also are concerned about the ways in which individuals are positioned by discourses and other experiences within the social context (Winslade, Crocket, & Monk, 1997). For example, could it be that my son easily became a mathematician in my eyes because my perceptions of my oldest son were influenced by discourses that emphasized boys' abilities in the mathematical realm? Why was it that my daughter, equally smart and almost 2 years older, did not become storied for her academic prowess at that young age as well?

The concept of positioning theory—the ways in which we are influenced by social discourses and how these influences affect our work as helpers—is discussed in more detail in Chapter 6. The premise of narrative theory is that stories of identity are influenced by historic, social, political, and cultural understandings and experiences that are transferred through the language of stories—stories told by, to, around, and about us. Narrative helping practices work to deconstruct these ideas and work to promote helpee agency. They inquire about the ways in which people want to live their lives and work to reveal stories and experiences that support these ideas about preferred identities. Deconstructing conversations, discussed in Chapter 8, is one of the major forms of interventions used by feminist and narrative helpers.

Re-membering Conversations

The concept of re-membering is an important narrative practice identified by White and based on the work of anthropologist Myerhoff (Russell & Carey, 2002; for more on re-membering, also see White, 1989; and for more on Myerhoff's study of re-membering practices, see Myerhoff, 1979). Re-membering refers to actively engaging others into the "club of significant others in a person's life" (Hedtke & Winslade, 2004, p. 7). That is, it is a way of extending or retaining community with those who are important to us because those important people validate our sense of self and they help us make meaning of the events in our lives. It is a concept that refers to actively calling upon another person–dead or alive—to be present in one's life.

Individuals who we re-member into our lives typically are individuals who have been significant to us in the past but are no longer, for some reason, physically present to us. A re-membering conversation purposefully calls forth the presence of this important individual in a meaningful way (Hedtke & Winslade, 2004). For example, as a young adult experiencing the trials and tribulations of parenthood after the birth of my first child, I found myself re-membering my mother into my life. My mother had died when I was a child, yet when I was not sure what to do as a parent, I would have silent conversations with her, asking advice and recalling her mothering style. I also re-membered my mother into my joys—when I had a sense of accomplishment I silently shared that with her too. It was something I would have done, perhaps, in a phone call to her if she had been alive. These acts of re-membering connected me with my mother when I needed her. A re-membering conversation is illustrated in the second case study below.

Case Studies Illustrating Contemporary Approaches to Helping

Case Study 1

In Case Study 1, Jorge was concerned about staff comments suggesting that Mia's behavior is due to inadequate parenting and insufficient attachment bonds. In his assessment, Mia demonstrated appropriate attachments to her parents—he saw this when they dropped her off in the morning, and she clearly was eager to see them at the end of the day. He thought that while Mia's behavior was energetic, it was not beyond the bounds of what he would expect from children her age, except, perhaps, at rest time. And, he always found her parents appropriate and attentive to Mia. He was concerned about ideas that faulted Mia's parents as he understood that parents are always working against discourses that position them as not being good enough, and working parents' discourses, he knew, were particularly harsh. Here is what he did:

1. Working from a more contemporary perspective that centers helpees as experts in their own lives, Jorge decided to invite Mia and Mia's parents to discuss the rest time difficulties. He expected that their knowledge would be most helpful in constructing an appropriate solution. Speaking first to Mia's parents, Jorge was transparent about the behavior problems of concern and he asked them for their perspective on the problem. He also asked them for advice on what sleep routines work well at home and how they thought he should motivate Mia to be more cooperative during rest time at school. Jorge learned that Mia's parents engaged in nighttime rituals at home that included reading a story to both children together and talking about the day, but then they had a strict policy of turning off the light, and the children always stayed in bed at night after that. Both parents agreed that Mia was very active and may need a "downshifting time" at school before being able to relax enough to go to sleep, but they also expressed confidence in Mia's ability to follow rules when they are clearly articulated and enforced.

2. Next speaking directly to Mia just before rest time, Jorge asked, "What needs to happen so that you can have a quiet body at rest time, Mia?" She responded, "I need a book. Come sit with me, Jorge." That helped Jorge understand her difficulties, and he told her that he would read her "just one story" at rest time. He emphasized that after reading the story, it would be time for her to "respect the rule of quiet" and lie on her mat to rest. He also assured her that he was confident that after the story, she would be able to calm her body and rest, "just like nighttime at home. I think you can do that. Right, Mia?" he asked. "Okay," Mia agreed. Even if she would not be able to follow though on her end of the plan immediately, Jorge wanted to communicate respect by honoring Mia's suggestion about reading a book and communicating confidence that she would be able to follow through. He realized that he might have to continue to have this conversation with Mia in the future, linking what she knows about calming herself and following rules with the expectation that she has the competence to do these things at school. (The major focus of these suggestions are grounded in contemporary

practices of honoring one's subjective knowledge and promoting agency in determining the most appropriate solution. Notice that this recommendation also included a behavioral intervention of setting limits by allowing only one book at rest time and reminding her of the quiet time rule.)

Case Study 2

Recall that there were concerns about Mrs. Morrison's mental heath and engagement with others at the senior living community. Emma understood Mrs. Morrison's symptoms to be normal reactions to the upheaval she experienced as a result of the move to the residential community. Working from a feminist perspective, she immediately recognized the need for Mrs. Morrison to be connected to community, as relationships were likely critical to her sense of self. Emma also recognized the importance of promoting Mrs. Morrison's sense of personal agency. Finally, understanding that her role of being a helper did not make her an expert about Mrs. Morrison's life, and that offering help too quickly can sometimes rob helpees of their own autonomy and power in decision-making, Emma knew that transparency needed to be a key aspect of her approach to this situation. These were her interventions:

1. First, Emma asked Mrs. Morrison how the transition to the new living community was going, and she also shared her concern that Mrs. Morrison seemed to be isolating herself. Mrs. Morrison said that she thought that the transition was going reasonably well, and she was surprised to hear Emma's concern that she was isolating herself. "I don't know about that," she said, "but I sure appreciate that you care."

2. Emma asked Mrs. Morrison what she had enjoyed doing before coming to the center, who was important to her, and how she could bring those important parts of her life into the center. Emma learned that Mrs. Morrison was very knowledgeable about and enjoyed gardening, and that she had abandoned the hope of ever gardening again when she came to the center. Gardening, Emma learned, was something that Mrs. Morrison had done with her own grandmother while growing up. Mrs. Morrison also told Emma about her dear friend, Teva, who recently passed away.

3. Emma told Mrs. Morrison about the garden plots that residents had in the yard at the center, and a few weeks later they arranged for

Mrs. Morrison to acquire a garden plot. Mrs. Morrison called her son and asked him to bring her old garden tools.

4. Using the narrative practice of re-membering, Emma asked Mrs. Morrison what advice her grandmother might give to her for starting a new garden there at the center. Finding that Mrs. Morrison eagerly engaged in a conversation about her grandmother's advice for new gardens, Emma later asked Mrs. Morrison what she would be doing if Teva was here at the center with her. Mrs. Morrison responded that the two had planned to come to the senior center together, and they were particularly excited about the book club and speakers series but, she added, "now that I'm here alone, I just am not as excited about the book club." These conversations were the start of Emma's helping conversations with Mrs. Morrison that progressed over time. Emma hoped these conversations would help Mrs. Morrison become agent in creating a meaningful life for herself in this new residential community.

Figure 3.5 Contemporary Theories

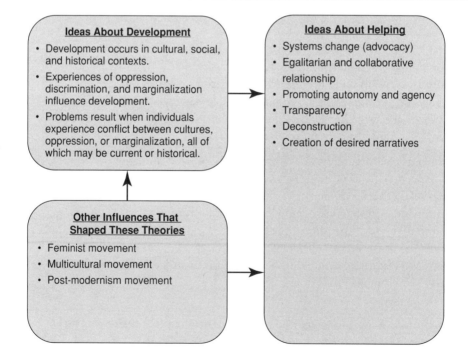

Ideas About Development
- Development occurs in cultural, social, and historical contexts.
- Experiences of oppression, discrimination, and marginalization influence development.
- Problems result when individuals experience conflict between cultures, oppression, or marginalization, all of which may be current or historical.

Other Influences That Shaped These Theories
- Feminist movement
- Multicultural movement
- Post-modernism movement

Ideas About Helping
- Systems change (advocacy)
- Egalitarian and collaborative relationship
- Promoting autonomy and agency
- Transparency
- Deconstruction
- Creation of desired narratives

CHAPTER SUMMARY

This chapter reviewed helping approaches associated with psychodynamic, ethological, humanistic, behavioral/learning, and contemporary helping approaches. The point was to underscore how the ways in which we intervene in the lives of others is tied to our ideas about development and our conceptualizations about the etiology (cause) of problems. Helpers must be aware that even their most basic ideas about helping are based on theoretical constructs; they are not truths. Helping relationships are never neutral; the important work of helping requires us to be clear about what we think, what it causes us to do, and whether or not it is truly appropriate and helpful in each specific situation of helping.

DISCUSSION QUESTIONS

1. How are the helping theories discussed in this chapter relevant to helpers who are working in clinical helping roles?

2. Identify the major tenets or directions of interventions that are consistent with psychodynamic, ethological, learning, and contemporary approaches to helping relationships.

3. Discuss with a partner how you think each of the responses to the case studies (from each theoretical orientation) would have worked in those situations. Ground your responses in your own ideas about development.

4. What new ways of thinking about how you might approach a difficult situation in a helping relationship are you now considering, given these alternative viewpoints? What theories are your ideas related to?

CHAPTER 4

ETHICAL PRINCIPLES FOR HELPING RELATIONSHIPS

LEARNING OBJECTIVES

1. Explain the meanings and definitions of ethical language used in the helping professions

2. Explain the underlying moral principles for codes of ethics in the helping professions

3. Offer a model of ethical decision-making that can be used by helping professionals

INTRODUCTION

What could possibly go wrong, one might think, when we have a well-intended helper working in a helping relationship? Yet, with the review in Chapter 1 of all of the major components of the helping contract and the mix of job and helper dynamics that can complicate the helping process, which will be discussed in Chapter 5, we would be naïve to think that good will and skills alone make for good helping. At the end of the day, one thing we know is that helping relationships are complicated. They can be messy. They don't always go as planned. And, unfortunately, there are many things that could possibly go wrong in helping relationships.

This is largely why most professional helping organizations have created codes of ethics that are intended to guide the practice of helping. Professional codes of ethics are very important tools for minimizing the messiness in complex helping relationships—they might be thought of as a mapping of philosophical ideologies, directives, and suggestions to guide the helping process. Professional codes of ethics underlie professional standards and offer assurance to the consumer that certain principles will be respected within the helping relationship.

While most helping professions have specific codes of ethics related to their particular aspect or focus of work, we will limit our discussion in this chapter to a review of major conceptual themes that cut across these various ethical guidelines. A list of the websites for a variety of helping professions are included in Appendix B, and within those websites, you will see that most of these organizations have their own set of ethical guidelines for professionals working in their particular specialty area. We will conclude our discussion with an ethical decision-making model that can be used for resolving ethical concerns when they arise in your work.

DEFINITIONS

To start our conversation about professional ethics, let's first define a few relevant terms: *morals, values, ethics, laws,* and *policies.* These definitions are summarized in Table 4.1.

Morals come from the concept of morality, referring to ideas and standards that are valued by society or within a particular social or cultural group (such as a particular culture or religion). These ideas are generally accepted as the norm of "appropriateness" by members of that particular group (Gert, 2012).

Values are reflective of an individual's fundamental beliefs about the importance or relative worth of something ("Values," n.d.). They are what you might call deep beliefs about certain ideals. But they are not mandated by society; instead they reflect individual choice and beliefs. While values influence behavior, they are more of an articulation beliefs and ideals rather than statements about expected conduct.

The concept of **ethics** has to do with the parceling out of what is considered right or wrong. Ethics are the moral principles that are adopted by an individual values or a profession that provide rules or standards of conduct (Corey, Corey, & Callanan, 2003). They might be thought of as the action arm of one's individual values or a group's values. A **code of ethics** is an articulated set of principles established by a particular group that structures behavioral expectations for members within that group (Kitchener, 1984). For example, the Ethical Standards of Human Service Professionals (National Organization for Human Services, 1996) is an articulation of the set of standards that should be used among human service professionals to guide professional behavior.

Finally, and slightly different from ethical guidelines, are laws and policies. These refer to rules that are established by a governing power or agency.

Table 4.1 Ethical Concept Definitions

Concept	Definition
Morals	Ideas regarding what is generally accepted as "appropriate" within a particular society or group. They are a set of beliefs that guide behavior, but they are not, typically, specific rules of conduct.
Values	An individual's fundamental beliefs about the importance or relative worth of something. Values typically refer to those ideas and beliefs that are held individually—they are individual ideals.
Ethics	Guidelines or standards of practice or behavior that are related to the moral principles of a particular group or organization. Ethics are ideas regarding right or wrong.
Code of Ethics	An articulated set of principles established by a particular group that structures behavioral standards for members within that group. Codes of ethics outline standards of behaviors that are consistent with an individual's or organization's values.
Laws	Rules about behavior that have been established by courts or legislative processes. They carry legal consequences if violated.
Policies	Articulated rules of conduct established by agencies, businesses, or organizations. The consequences for rule infractions are governed by the agency (business or organization).

Laws are rules about behavior that have been established by courts or legislative processes. They are intended to maintain order in society. **Policies** are principles, protocols, or guidelines that guide practice in a particular agency, organization, or business.

Of course, all of these ethical and legal concepts are interrelated. So, let us go back now with a little more detailed discussion about their interrelatedness.

Morals, like values, refer to a set of beliefs that guide behavior, but they are not, typically, specific rules of conduct. Morals reflect the beliefs that are covenant in a particular society (or in a social or cultural group to which one holds membership). I sometimes think of them as *the ideals promoted by the elders*. Values, on the other hand, typically refer to those ideas and beliefs that are held individually. So, values are individual ideals whereas morals are situated in larger social groups.

Ethics might best be thought of as guidelines or standards of practice or behavior that are related to the moral principles of a particular group or organization. A personal code of ethics is similar in that it reflects standards of behaviors, but is held by an individual rather than a group. Codes of ethics, theoretically, are consistent with an individual's or an organization's system of values. For example, a helper might hold on to moral principles of the Ten Commandments, which are a part of the biblical principles of her faith tradition. She may also have a personal value in the importance of working hard to achieve her goals. While both likely guide her behavior, neither has a specifically defined code of conduct.

Laws are similar to codes of ethics in that they are articulated guidelines for behavior. However, laws are created though legal or judicial branches of government, and they carry legal consequences if violated. Some think of laws as rules for what one *must* do or what one *can't* do, while ethics focus more on what one *should* do. For example, cheating on an exam is unethical, but not illegal. Armed robbery is both unethical and illegal. It would be a rare case for something to be ethical but against the law. However, some might argue that it is perfectly ethical for a patient who is struggling with pain related to a medical issue to smoke marijuana although this behavior is illegal in the majority of states in the United States.

Policies are rules of agencies. Like laws, particular agencies might institute consequences for policy infractions, but those consequences are governed by the agency, not the legal and judicial system. For example, in a particular organization, it may be a policy that helpers adhere to a particular code of dress. And, if that stipulation is written into a contract for employment, it is possible that an employee who fails to dress appropriately could lose his job. However, dress codes are rarely a matter of legal precedence in the United States, so while that individual may be dismissed from a job due to failure to follow a prescribed policy, he has not broken a law.

ETHICS AND PROFESSIONAL PRACTICE

As mentioned, professional organizations associated with most helping professions have established codes of ethics that are designed to guide the behavior of professionals in that particular area of helping. Helping professionals are typically required by licensing bodies and/or employers to follow the ethical codes of their particular area of practice or profession, and enforcement typically occurs through those professional organizations, employers, and laws and/or according to legal precedent, if litigation is involved.

As a helper, you will be responsible for knowing and upholding general rules of personal conduct required of you as a citizen of the nation and of the particular state of your employment. For example, many helping professions do not license and many employers do not hire helpers who have a criminal record. While there are some laws and codes of conduct that also cut across most helping professions in the United States (these are reviewed later in this chapter), it is important to be aware that laws that govern helping practices vary considerably between specific helping roles and between various states. So, it will be your responsibility as a professional helper to become familiar with all of the local, state, and national laws that govern your work. You will also need to continually update this information as you work in the field, because these laws often evolve and change with time. Similarly, you will need to be familiar with the various policies of your agency, business, or organization, as polices affecting the work of helpers vary considerably across agencies as well.

MORAL PRINCIPLES FOR HELPERS

Kitchener (1984) discussed five key moral principles, outlined also in Table 4.2, that serve as the fundamental basis for ethical decision-making in helping professions. According to Kitchener, these principles reflect early efforts by Beauchamp and Childress and others to codify ethical decision-making in the field of biomedical ethics, and they have been adopted as a foundation of codes of ethics in many helping professions, including counseling and psychology. The concept of moral principle used here refers to a "standard of conduct on which many other moral claims and judgments depend" (Beauchamp, 2007, p. 3). In other words, these principles are the norms upon which ethical codes of conduct for helpers are based.

The first of these is the principle of **autonomy**, which speaks to respecting the capacity of a rational individual to make an informed, uncoerced decision (Kitchener, 1984). This means that helpers should respect the right of helpees to make their own choices, even if the helper does not agree with those choices. This respect for autonomy, Kitchener (1984) points out, extends to respecting one's privacy as well. Note that upholding the principle of autonomy is restricted to situations where individuals are competent to make their own decisions and to situations in which they are not infringing on the rights and well-being of others. So, there are some situations where helpers may need to break confidentiality or intervene despite the helpee's objections. These will be pointed out later in this discussion and also addressed in Chapter 9.

The second principle is **nonmaleficence**, which refers to the helper's commitment to do no harm (Kitchener, 1984). The intent of this principle is that the helping relationship should not inflict damage or undue duress on the helpee. In helping relationships, this includes not providing services that are ineffective; that is, not offering services that you know won't help or that will make a situation worse. This principle also speaks to the importance of helper competence. Helpers must refrain from engaging in practices for which they are not fully trained.

Beneficence is action done for the benefit of others. As an ethical principle, it refers to engaging in actions that contribute to the welfare and are in the best interests of the helpee (Kitchener, 1984). This incudes, again, being sure to only engage in practices for which you are trained (competence). Beneficence takes precedence over helpee autonomy in instances of harm to self or others. In other words, if the helpee is engaging in actions that are a clear threat to self or others, you must intervene to protect the welfare of the helpee. This will be discussed more in Chapter 9.

The principle of **justice** refers to a commitment to fairness. In the context of helping relationships, Kitchener (1984) defers to Aristotle's perspective on fairness, which is "treating equals equally and unequals unequally, but in proportion to their relevant differences" (p. 49). So while the moral obligation here is to be fair, we are reminded that fair does not always mean equal. For example, people who identify as gay or lesbian experience discrimination in everyday society due to the sole fact of their sexual orientation. Because of this, many states have named sexual orientation to be a legally protected category, meaning that it is specifically against the law to discriminate against individuals who identity as gay or lesbian. Not every social location is afforded protection by law, but because people who identify as gay or lesbian are not treated fairly in society, their rights are specifically protected by law. Kitchener points out that many issues related to justice are regulated at a societal level through national or state laws.

Fidelity is the final moral principle key to helping ethics. This refers to being honest and trustworthy, and honoring the commitment of the helping relationship. Kitchener's (1984) notion of fidelity is demonstrated by respecting helpee autonomy, providing accurate information, and following through on the commitments of the helping contract.

KEY ETHICAL CONCEPTS FOR HELPING PROFESSIONALS

The ethical codes of the various helping professions all loosely follow Kitchener's moral principles (Kitchener, 1984), even if they differ on specifics related to their particular scope of practice. We will now move into a discussion of a number of specific critical ethical and legal concepts that are especially

Table 4.2 Moral Principles for Helping Ethics

Moral Principles	Description
Autonomy	Respecting the capacity of a rational individual to make an informed, uncoerced decision.
Nonmaleficence	The helper's commitment to do no harm.
Beneficence	Engaging in actions that contribute to the welfare and are in the best interests of the helpee.
Justice	A commitment to be fair, which does not always mean equal.
Fidelity	Honoring the commitment of the helping relationship—being honest and trustworthy.

Adapted from: Kitchener, K. S. (1984). Intuition, critical evaluation and ethical principles: The foundation for ethical decisions in counseling psychology. *The Counseling Psychologist, 12*(3), 43–55. doi:10.1177/0011000084123005

relevant to the work of helpers across most helping professions. These are also outlined in Table 4.3.

Competence

Helper competence, relevant to the moral principles of beneficence and non-maleficence, refers to the importance of working only within the area in which you have been trained. That is, helpers must not offer or attempt to provide services for which they have not been properly trained.

To be true to this principle, many helpers engage in a process of **informed consent,** which really is the essence of the helping contract, as discussed in Chapter 1. Informed consent is an agreement and/or outline of what the helpee can expect from the helper—the provision of helping services that will be provided. An important reminder is due here: You must be sure not to commit to providing services or engage in actions that are not requested or not asked for by the helpee. And, of course, you must not commit to providing services that you are not trained to provide, that are unethical or illegal, or that in some other way breach the ethical principles mentioned above or that are in violation of your professional code of ethical conduct. Documents of informed consent typically identify the specific focus of the helping relationship (goals), reimbursement for services (fees), and they may include other stipulations related to the specific helping relationship or services being provided. For counselors, the informed consent documents typically also include the helper's philosophical orientation and a statement about confidentiality and information privacy, which are discussed below.

Confidentiality

Another important ethical principle that cuts across most clinical and non-clinical helping situations is the commitment to maintaining and protecting helpee privacy. Requirements regarding confidentiality pertain to written records and communications as well as all verbal communications between or otherwise related to the helpee and the helping relationship. Respecting confidentiality means not sharing information communicated in the context of the helping relationship with others outside of that relationship, unless you have the explicit (and typically written) consent of the helpee. In many if not all helping situations, respecting confidentiality also means that you should not acknowledge the helpee in public unless you are approached by her first, as doing so would have the effect of identifying her as a recipient of services that she might not want others to know about.

Photo 4.1   Informed Consent

©Can Stock Photo Inc. /sjenner13

As will be discussed shortly, all helping professionals have an ethical mandate to break confidentiality in order to protect the safety of the helpee. This stipulation is relevant in cases of suspected harm to self or others, and for most professional helpers, this mandate is also a legal mandate. That is, not only *should* helpers breach confidentiality in situations of harm, but they *must* do so. A second situation that may warrant breaking confidentiality is when the helper receives a court subpoena (although there are a very limited number of professional helpers in some states who are immune from prosecution in this area). It is always best practice to seek legal or professional consultation or supervision when you suspect harm and when you receive a legal subpoena regarding your work as a helper. Seeking supervision or consultation from a qualified professional is not considered a breach of confidentiality in helping professional codes of ethics.

The ethics around confidentiality reflect a commitment to the moral principles of autonomy, nonmaleficence, and fidelity. Protecting helpee confidentiality is also a legal mandate that governs many helping situations. Helpers working in the areas of education and health care must ascribe to two laws

Illustration 4.1   Maintaining Confidentiality

©iStockphoto.com/VasjaKoman

related to the confidentiality. The Family Educational Rights and Privacy Act of 1974 (**FERPA**) is a federal law that protects the privacy of student educational records. The Health Insurance Portability and Accountability Act of 1996 (**HIPAA**) is a related federal law that protects the privacy of individual's health information. Both laws protect confidentiality of written records, and helpers are required to align their practice with agency policies that are developed to safeguard the helpee's rights in line with these laws.

Protection From Harm and Duty to Warn

The principle of **protection from harm** refers to the responsibility of a helper to secure the safety of helpees who pose a threat to themselves or who articulate a serious intent to harm someone else. It speaks to the moral principles of beneficence and nonmaleficence, and it is also a legal obligation in most helping professions. The related **duty-to-warn** concept extends helper responsibilities to inform third parties and authorities if a helpee poses a threat to another identifiable individual. In fact, the *Tarasoff v. Regents of the University of Califorina* lawsuit that occurred in 1976 is the legal precedent for this concept of duty to warn. This particular mandate compels clinical helpers not only to notify police or others who are in the capacity to act to protect victims in cases of harm to others, but also to notify potential victims themselves if they are identified to be in danger of being harmed by the helpee (Corey et al., 2003; Costa & Altekruse, 1994; Davis & Richie, 2003; Isaacs, 2003). It is important, then, to understand that malpractice around these notions of protection from harm and duty to warn is referred and adjudicated in state and federal courts. So, helpers have both an ethical and legal mandate to be competent in conducting an appropriate assessment of harm and acting to protect, depending on the level and scope of their practice.

There are two additional legal concepts related to confidentiality and the duty to warn that are specific to working with youth: mandated reporting and the legal age of majority. Professional helpers are considered to be **mandated reporters**. This means that they are required by law to inform appropriate authorities—the state social service agency or local police—if they have any suspicions of child abuse and neglect. The legal status of being a mandated reporter is also relevant for helpers working with vulnerable adults, such as people who are elderly and people with serious disabilities. While the specific reporting procedures for suspicions of child abuse and neglect vary by state, it is important to know that it is your duty to report any suspicions of harm or neglect, even if you are not sure that those suspicions are valid. It is the job of state social service agency personnel to investigate child abuse and neglect concerns, not the helper who has made the report. In every state of the union, legal consequences result when mandated reporters fail to report their concerns around child or vulnerable adult abuse and neglect.

Legal age of majority is a legal concept that refers to the chronological age when minors cease to be considered children (in the eye of the law). This is the age when youth are able to assume control over their persons, actions, and decisions. In other words, the legal age of majority is when the legal control and responsibilities of an individual no longer belong to her parents or guardians. Most countries (including the United States) set majority at age 18. The legal age of majority should not be confused with the legal age of drinking, voting, driving, marriageability, or sexual consent, as these are sometimes independent of and are set at a different age than the age of majority. Laws governing these other issues vary from state to state, and it is important for helpers working with young adults to be aware of these related laws in their state of practice.

Dual or Multiple Relationships

A final important consideration for helpers is to avoid engagement in dual or multiple relationships. While the specifics around this ethical standard vary across helping professions, the basic idea is that it is the helper's responsibility to avoid overlapping duties, roles, or relationships with their helpees. This concept, then, asserts that helpers must do what they can to avoid being in some other kind of relationship with their helpees while they are providing professional helping services. For example, counselors should not provide therapy to their friends, teachers should not socialize with their students, and doctors should not go out for drinks with their patients.

The reason for this caution largely has to do with the fact that, as discussed in Chapter 1, helping relationships are not mutual and equal relationships. The helping contract itself, whether it is an explicit or an implicit contract, positions helpers in a role that has some degree of power over the helpee. This means that it compromises helpee autonomy. For example, a patient sitting in a dental chair with a dentist hovering over her with a drill in his hand is probably not going to feel comfortable denying a request for a date—at least not at that moment. So, even if a helpee is not aware of it, dual relationships put him in a compromised or vulnerable position because the helping relationship itself is not one of equals. Helping relationships, by their very definition, afford helpers an advantage of

Photo 4.2   Friendships Versus Helping Relationships

©iStockphoto.com/monkeybusinessimages

power. Speaking directly about this issue of dual relationships, the Code of Ethics of the American Counseling Association (American Counseling Association, 2014) specifically states that romantic relationships between a counselor and a client or any member of the client's family are prohibited for a period of 5 years after the last professional contact. For psychologists, the same ethical standard exists, although the prohibited period is only 2 years (American Psychological Association, 2002).

The concern about dual relationships also extends to more seemingly benign situations where the helper and helpee may find themselves interacting in roles together that are outside of their helping relationship. For example, when a truant officer at a school also serves as an afterschool tutor, or when a school administrator coaches an afterschool varsity sport, students are potentially compromised because their behavior in one situation may affect their ability to receive fair services in the other. It is not hard to see that dual relationships like these make helpees vulnerable to what the helper may or may not know about them, and how information from one setting may affect the helpee in the other. And all of these ambiguities are significant because they exist in a context where the helper has power over the helpee. Again, this unequal distribution of power is why all helpers must be vigilant about avoiding dual relationships with their helpees, even when helpees are unaware of the potential threat that exists as a result of dual relationships.

Table 4.3 Key Ethical and Legal Concepts for Helpers

Key Ethical/Legal Concepts	Descriptions
Competence	The helper's commitment to work only in his or her area of competence. Helpers must not offer or attempt to provide services for which they have not been trained.
Informed Consent	The helping contract—an agreement regarding the services to be provided in the helping relationship. The helper must not provide services or engage in actions as a helper that are not requested or asked for by the helpee.
Confidentiality	The helper must not share information (verbally or in writing) with others outside of the helping relationship without (written) consent from the helpee.
FERPA	The Family Educational Rights and Privacy Act of 1974 (FERPA) is a federal law that protects the privacy of student educational records.
HIPAA	The Health Insurance Portability and Accountability Act of 1996 (HIPAA) is a federal law that protects the privacy of personal health information.
Protection From Harm	Helpers have a responsibility to get appropriate help for a helpee who poses a threat to himself or herself, or who articulates a desire to engage in serious intent to harm someone else.
Duty to Warn	Helpers have a responsibility to inform third parties and authorities if a helpee poses a threat to another identifiable individual.
Mandated Reporter	Helpers are required by law to inform appropriate authorities—the state social service agency—if they have any suspicions of child abuse and neglect.
Legal Age of Majority	This is the age, according to law, when minors cease to be considered children. Youth are able to assume control over their persons, actions, and decisions at the legal age of majority.
Dual or Multiple Relationships	It is the responsibility of helpers to avoid overlapping duties, roles, or relationships with their helpees.

ETHICAL DECISION-MAKING

With these various moral principles, applicable laws, and must-do ethical considerations, it is easy to see how complex ethical decision-making can be. Many helping professions have developed models that practitioners can use to guide their decision-making process when potential ethical and legal issues arise in their work. In fact, the counseling profession has in its ethical standards that counseling practitioners must follow and document having used an appropriate decision-making model when they encounter potential ethical dilemmas (American Counseling Association, 2014). Online and journal informational outlets across the helping professions abound with such models, and there is much uniformity among them. Here I will present a simple model that includes the basic components of ethical decision-making presented in the ACA code of ethics (American Counseling Association, 2014) and incorporates the work of Forester-Miller and Davis (1995) and Corey et al. (2003). These steps are listed in Table 4.4.

1. **Identify the problem.**
   The first step in ethical decision-making is to gather as much information regarding the situation as possible. It is important to look at the situation from multiple perspectives and consider the history of the situation as well as relevant contextual information. This information will help you clarify the specific concern or problem, understand who is affected by the problem, and determine why it is problematic (including ethical, legal, or other considerations). Documenting your thinking in a clear outline will help provide clarity as you proceed to the next steps in the decision-making process.

2. **Consult the professional code of ethics.**
   Because the various disciplines within the field of human services have their own specific codes of ethics, it is important to consult the specific code that is pertinent to your role within the helping relationship in this particular situation. Here you will want to look for specific aspects of the ethical code that dictate the best-fit course of action. Also keep in mind the moral principles of autonomy, nonmaleficence, beneficence, justice, and fidelity. Be careful to clearly document the specific ethical code that you are using to guide your practice.

3. **Consider relevant legal statutes, agency policies, and best practice mandates.**
   As mentioned earlier, it is critical that all helping professionals keep up to date on legal statutes that are relevant to their work as helpers.

Most states have legal mandates related to confidentiality, mandated reporting, duty to warn, informed consent, record-keeping, and licensure; many of these are mandated by federal law as well. Remember that you are also responsible for following the policies at the agency of your employment, so be aware of these as well. As a general practice, it is also important to always keep updated on the professional literature in your specific helping profession and to keep informed of laws and changes in these laws that are most relevant to your work. If there are legal statutes that relate to the problem you are facing, it is important to learn about those laws, and it may be appropriate to seek legal council. You should always include relevant legal and policy considerations in your documentation of the decision-making process as well.

4. **Obtain consultation.**

It is always best practice to seek consultation or guidance from a supervisor or competent colleague when faced with a potential ethical dilemma. And, as mentioned, if the problem is related to a law, seeking legal counsel is also appropriate. Likewise, if the concern is related to agency policy, consulting with a supervisor who works within the agency is advised. Seeking consultation will allow you to gain additional perspective and possibly uncover information or nuances that you may have missed; it also conveys a sense of professional competence if the issue of concern ends up being adjudicated in a court of law. Be sure to document each consultation, including the name of consultant, date, the gist of the consultation, and the recommended courses of action.

5. **Generate potential decisions.**

After clarifying the problem and reviewing relevant codes, principles, laws, and policies, and after receiving professional consultation, you should be in a position to create a list of potential courses of action. This list should be created in written form. For each item on the list, include a comment on the potential risks and benefits. It also may be wise at this point, if appropriate, to discuss the dilemma or concern with your helpee. When speaking to the helpee, be sure to be concrete, specific, and clear about what the problem is, why it is a problem, and the potential courses of action. All of this information will allow the helpee to understand the problem and participate in the decision-making from an informed perspective. Be sure to document in writing the list of potential actions as well as the conversation you had with the helpee.

6. **Make a decision.**

Carefully evaluate the information yielded from the decision-making process and decide on the most appropriate response to the situation or concern. You should feel okay about your decision, but also be willing to make changes if new information becomes available or the situation changes. Recycling through the decision-making process again at a later date is sometimes appropriate in situations with changing information or in evolving circumstances. Be sure to document your decision and include your rationale.

7. **Secure written documentation regarding your decision-making process in an appropriate confidential file.**

Table 4.4 Steps for Ethical Decision-Making

1. Identify the problem.
2. Consult the professional code of ethics.
3. Consider relevant legal statutes, agency policies and best practice mandates.
4. Obtain consultation.
5. Generate potential decisions.
6. Make a decision.
7. Secure written documentation regarding your decision-making process in an appropriate confidential file.

Adapted from: Forester-Miller, H., & Davis, T. E. (1995). *A practitioner's guide to ethical decision making.* Retrieved from American Counseling Association website: http://www.counseling.org/docs/default-source/ethics/practioner's-guide-to-ethical-decision-making.pdf?sfvrsn=0

CHAPTER SUMMARY

In this chapter, moral principles that underlie codes of ethics in helping professions were reviewed. Additionally, laws related to confidentiality, duty to warn, and mandated reporting were presented. The chapter ended with a model that can be used by helping professionals to guide ethical decision-making.

DISCUSSION QUESTIONS

1. How are morals, values, ethics, laws and policies related, and what are some of the key differences between these concepts?

2. Provide an example of how each of Kitchener's (1984) five key moral principles that serve as the fundamental basis for ethical decision-making in helping professions might play out in a helping scenario.

3. Describe the meaning and importance of confidentiality in helping relationships, and identify standard limits to confidentiality that guide helping practice.

4. Why is it important to avoid dual relationships with a helpee?

CHAPTER 5

SELF-AWARENESS, CULTURAL AWARENESS, AND HELPER COMPETENCE

LEARNING OBJECTIVES

1. Describe how helpers' personal experiences, emotional reactions, assumptions, beliefs, and values affect their work as helpers

2. Describe how social location affects the lived experiences of individuals and why it is important for helpers to be aware of their own social location

3. Describe how social position and cultural capital related to social location affect helping relationships

INTRODUCTION

In this chapter, we will continue to focus on the ways in which the beliefs, experiences, and behaviors of helpers can have a profound impact on their helping relationships. The overarching theme here is the importance of helper self-awareness when working with others. In this chapter, we will focus on these important components of self-awareness: first, being aware of and being able to manage our own personal life and emotional reactivity. Second, being clear about our own system of beliefs, values, and cultural assumptions and how they may differ from those with whom we work. Third, understanding how culture and social location are shaped by systems of power and privilege, in general, and also in helping relationships. The point is that self-awareness and self-management are critical in order for the helper to be fully present and focused on the needs of the helpee, and this awareness requires knowledge about the ways in which people's lives are influenced by social inequities related to power and privilege.

HELPER SELF-AWARENESS

The profession of caring for others is a vocation of giving. And, as Skovholt (2001) says, "caring for others is a precious commodity" (p. 1). Being able to give to others in a helping role, however, demands much of professional helpers. Helping requires a highly nuanced ability to understand someone else's perspective, having a vision anchored in someone else's goals, and the ability to maintain a strong sense of navigation where you are able to point out the direction but resist grabbing the helm. It is a profession that requires constant attention and focus on the other.

Ironically, to be available to help others requires extensive attention to what is happening for the helper. In fact, a cardinal tenet in the clinical training of counseling professionals is that the most effective counselors are those who are mentally fit and able to manage their own personal lives effectively (Donati & Watts, 2005; Kottler, 1991). As Pieterse, Lee, Ritmeester, and Collins (2013) indicate, the importance of helper self-awareness for providing appropriate care to others is "critical and indispensable" (p. 191).

In fact, self-awareness and self-management are highlighted as important in a wide variety of helping professions. For example, Borrell-Carrio and Epstein (2004) call for infusing clinician insight and self-awareness into physician training, and Baum and King (2006) speak to the importance of developing self-awareness in early childhood teacher training. In just about every helping profession, the need to be aware of what one is doing as a helper, how one is doing it, and why one particular intervention should be used over another are critical for assuring that the help being offered is appropriate—appropriate, that is, to the needs of the helpee (rather than the needs of the helper).

Given the general acknowledgement that the use of self in helping is predicated on having sufficient self-awareness, what, exactly, *self-awareness* means is somewhat elusive (Pieterse et al., 2013). These authors define self-awareness as "a state of being conscious of one's thoughts, feelings, beliefs, behaviours and attitudes, and knowing how these factors are shaped by important aspects of one's developmental and social history" (p. 191). Pieterse et al. (2013) suggest that self-awareness should include these facets of awareness: *personal preference*—the ways in which one engages, psychologically, with others and in the environment; *family of origin*—awareness of relationship and engagement patterns in one's formative development; *relationship style*—the ways in which one engages with others including the ability to be emotionally engaged, warm, friendly, and empathic; *racial and ethnic identity*—the values, beliefs, attitudes, and experiences associated with one's heritage and the social position of one's racial or ethic group (and how one is treated because of their social location); and *social class*, *gender identity*, *sexual orientation*, and *religious or spiritual orientation* (and the related experiences of how one is treated because of their membership in these social locations).

Self-awareness, self-management, and general mental health, then, are critical for helpers. But perfection, in terms of knowing who one is and one's ability to function socially, is not the expectation for helpers here. In a seminal article regarding the training of therapists, Loganbill, Hardy, and Delworth (1982) assert, "it is our belief that people who are really effective [as helpers] generally go through a process of letting go of the belief that everything is all right with them" (p. 7). That is, helpers are not perfect; they live with daily challenges and confusions and are not immune from making mistakes in their own lives. However, if a helper is unable to regulate the effects of the challenges in his or her own life, his or her work helping others will be affected.

PERSONALIZATION ISSUES, VICARIOUS TRAUMA, AND BURNOUT

Here we will speak briefly about a number of ways in which a helper's personal life as well as the challenges of being in the role of professional helper can impede one's work with others. As will be evident in this discussion, self-awareness is a critical first step in avoiding the pitfalls of personalization issues, vicarious traumatization, and burnout.

Personalization Issues

Personalization is a term used by Bernard (Bernard, 1979; Bernard & Goodyear, 1998) in reference to the ways in which one's work as a helper becomes contaminated by one's own personal issues. This notion of contamination is based on an assumption, commonly held in the counseling and psychology professions, that a helper is not able to help another person resolve an issue that the helper, himself or herself, has not been able to resolve in his or her own life. While we may rightly argue with this point—that helpers do not need to have had experienced the exact challenges facing their helpees, the point is that helpers do need to have an appropriate level of resolve and functioning in the areas in which they are helping others.

For example, a teacher who is not able to control her own anger is not likely to be in a position to help children develop anger management skills.

A substance abuse counselor is not fully in the position of helping someone grappling with substance abuse issues if he, too, is actively struggling with misuse. Acknowledging the human condition of imperfection, Loganbill et al. (1982) assert that helpers who are aware of the complexities and challenges in their own lives are in a better position to separate these personal challenges from those of their helpees. So, an important first step in managing personalization issues is for the helper to be aware of when she is having an emotional reaction to her helpee or the helpee's situation. That is, helpers need to be aware of what situations are personally challenging and may pose as triggers in their work with others. We will come back to these ideas of self-management and triggers when we review the literature on emotional self-regulation below.

Vicarious Traumatization

The term *vicarious trauma* refers to the traumatic reactions that helpers sometimes have when they are exposed to others' stories of trauma, pain, and suffering (Courtois & Ford, 2013; Skovholt, 2001). Other terms used for having an emotional reaction to hearing stories or witnessing someone else's trauma are *compassion fatigue*, *secondary trauma*, and *empathic strain*. Situations that may lead to vicarious traumatization include being witness to helpees' accounts of sexual assault, abuse, accidents, violence, etc., particularly when these stories are vivid or extreme. Being repeatedly exposed to trauma stories and exposure to these stories when the helper already feels personally or emotionally vulnerable or is under a great deal of personal stress make helpers particularly susceptible to secondary trauma reactions.

The effects of helper trauma responses may include tension or overpreoccupation with the helpee's stories or experiences, a perpetual oversensitive or hyperarousal state, and an avoidance of conversations and topics related to the helpee's trauma experience (American Counseling Association, n.d.-a). Trippany, White Kress, and Wilcoxon (2004) report that helpers who experience vicarious trauma may feel vulnerable, inadequate, mistrustful (of self and others), and empty, and they may be unable to feel interpersonal or intimate connections with others. They also may experience invasive thoughts and images (typically of the trauma stories of their helpees), and their attempts to control these intrusions may include numbing, denial, or avoidance. Helpers who experience vicarious traumatization are very likely to become compromised in their ability to be fully present and functional in their work as helpers, and the effects mentioned above are also likely to appear in their personal lives as well.

Photo 5.1 A Stressed Helper

©iStockphoto.com/~tetmc

Trippany et al. (2004) suggest that helpers can manage or avoid these trauma reactions by working with their supervisors to adjust their caseload (so they are not working with large numbers of trauma victims), participating in peer supervision and support groups, and receiving training that is specifically designed for helpers working with victims of trauma. They advocate that helpers develop systems of wellness that include a balance of play, work, and rest. Because vicarious traumatization can fracture a helper's sense of meaning and worldview, they also recommend engaging in some type of spiritual practice that enables a renewed sense of meaning, connection, and hope.

Burnout

Burnout is another occupational hazard for helpers (Skovholt, 2001). Burnout is slightly different than vicarious traumatization in that it results from feeling overloaded by working with chronic and complex problems, rather than being affected by a specific trauma experience or story of a helpee (Trippany et al., 2004). Skovholt (2001) describes burnout as a "slow erosion" (p. 106) of motivation and competence. It also may include fatigue, frustration, stress, a sense of hopelessness, and emotional drain. It is a "profound weariness and hemorrhaging of the self" (Skovholt, 2001, p. 107); a sense of emotional exhaustion. James and Gilliland (2001) describe burnout as occurring in a progressive series of stages, initiating with depersonalization—a separation of one's feelings and experiences from oneself, moving to feeling a lack of personal accomplishment, and then, emotional exhaustion.

Not only does burnout have implications on helper well-being, we can also see that burnout has the potential to impede one's ability to offer appropriate helping services to others. Recalling the moral principles of nonmaleficence, beneficence, justice, and fidelity in Chapter 4, we can easily see how burnout can potentially lead to unethical helping practices. To avoid this, James and Gilliland (2001) offer a number of suggestions for preventing burnout. First, they point to the importance of orientation and training for helpers, particularly those working in the area of crisis work. This training, they suggest, should include teaching helpers how to effectively manage the demands of their job and to have insight into their personalization issues (their own unresolved issues and conflicts), and they emphasize the importance of helpers developing professional boundaries, so as to avoid overinvolvement with helpees who struggle with multiple challenges. Second, they believe some level of therapeutic detachment and an ability to modulate idealism is critical for helpers. These authors point out that not all helping positions or jobs are appropriate for every helper—particularly in the area of crisis work. Finally, James and Gilliland underscore that helping service agencies should provide professional development to helpers, particularly regarding the topic of burnout, and they should offer support and appropriate intervention to helpers if they are impaired by experiences of burnout. This help may include promoting wellness routines and making adjustments in work demands and routines.

EMOTIONAL SELF-REGULATION

While the term *emotion* is used in common everyday language, emotions are rather difficult to accurately define and describe (Gross & Thompson, 2007; Westphal & Bonanno, 2004). The expression of emotion involves complex layers of neurological processes at the endocrine, autonomic, and cardiovascular levels (Siegel, 2012). According to Siegel (2012), the initial *trigger* for an emotional response is a signal of heightened activity in the brain. It is an internal sensation of cognitive alertness—as if the brain is saying "pay attention to this!" This activation, which typically occurs out of conscious awareness, then triggers a system of cognitive appraisal where the brain determines an appropriate response. The cognitive appraisal may determine if a situation is good, bad, dangerous, happy, etc., and based on this, the brain makes a determination of how to respond. Responses may entail movement to or away from the stimulus, deciding that one is in need of protection, ignoring the stimulus, etc. As Gross and Thompson's (2007) point out, emotions don't just "make us feel something, they make us feel like *doing* something" (p. 5, italics added for emphasis). It is important to remember, then, for the purposes of our discussion, that the expression of emotion entails **attention**, **appraisal**, and **response**.

Studies of individuals who have experienced damage to the brain have taught us that the frontal lobe is an important component of emotional expression. Recall from Chapter 2 that the frontal lobe is the part of the brain associated with executive function. Basically, it is the part of the brain that is responsible for directing attention, motor behavior, expressive language, and abstract reasoning (Cozolino, 2010). This executive function center is where emotions are appraised and actions are decided (Beer & Lombardo, 2007). The idea that emotions are evoked in response to an appraisal of a situation (Beer & Lombardo, 2007; Gross & Thompson, 2007; Siegel, 2012) is significant because, as we will see shortly, thoughts that stimulate emotions are potentially alterable.

A second important neurological process related to emotional sensation and expression is found in the amygdala, which, as mentioned in Chapter 2, is located in the limbic region of the brain (Cozolino, 2010). Developing parallel to the cerebral cortex or executive function center of the brain, the amygdala plays a role in the assessment of social cues—danger in one's immediate environment, for example. The amygdala works in close association with the hippocampus, which is also located in the central brain. The hippocampus regulates memory functions. Memories associated with emotional experiences, often called *emotional memories*, are thought to be stored in the amygdala, and play a "behind the scenes role" (Cozolino, 2010, p. 81) in meaning-making cognitive appraisal processes. When the hippocampus is not effectively imposing logical order and structure on information processing systems within the brain, emotional memories that become triggered in the amygdala can cause emotional dysregulation.

Emotional Regulation

The trio components of emotion—attention, appraisal, and response—lead us to the concept of emotional regulation. *Emotional regulation* refers to the processes that influence the expression of emotion (Gross, 1998; Westphal & Bonanno, 2004). Emotional regulation is a complex process, particularly at the neurological level. It entails "manipulating when, where, how, and which emotions we experience and express" (Beer & Lombardo, 2007, p. 69).

The concept of emotional regulation is as relevant for helpers as it is for helpees, of course. So, while the discussion here focuses on how helpers need to be attuned to and aware of their emotional reactions in helping relationships, recall how these same ideas were discussed in the ARC model (Blaustein & Kinniburgh, 2010) of helping closely associated with attachment theory in Chapter 3. The work of many professional helpers entails helping others develop emotional regulation skills.

Individuals have different thresholds of tolerance for emotional arousal, and while we may all agree that there is nothing inherently wrong with emotions, their free expression is not always appropriate in every setting. This is why the concept of emotional regulation is so important. Well-regulated individuals, according to Eisenberg, Hofer, & Vaughan (2007), are able to respond to the varying demands of their emotional experiences with flexibility. They are not overcontrolled or undercontrolled; they are able to initiate or inhibit their responses to emotional stimuli as needed.

Remember that the expression of emotion is a neurophysiological process initiating from a stimulus that is interpreted in a way that generates a particular response. When a stimulus is appraised as a threat, the stress response system (SRS) sets off a chain of neural firings that prepare the individual to respond accordingly. This is often referred to as a "flight-or-fight" reaction (Siegel, 2012). This response can entail hyperarousal or hypo- or underarousal (Courtois & Ford, 2013). Hyperarousal, often occurring in response to fear, is

Illustration 5.1   Emotional Expressions Depicted in Feeling Faces

©iStockphoto.com/MarynaYakovchuk

when an individual mobilizes at the neurobiological level to defend against an attack or threat. Hypoarousal can be thought of as the opposite—when an individual becomes immobilized, often in response to anxiety. This can take the behavioral form of numbing, shutting down, or disassociation. Here we are talking about reactions to threats, but emotional triggers that are less extreme also lead to similar dysregulated emotional responses (i.e., hyper- or hypoarousal), and a difficulty returning to homeostasis.

Emotional reactivity, then, is the experience of emotion from initial stimulus until discharge. At the end of the process, the goal of emotional regulation is for the system to recalibrate to homeostasis (Westphal & Bonanno, 2004). **Emotional homeostasis** might best be thought of as the ideal balance in the frequency, intensity, and duration of an emotional experience. What is ideal, though, varies according to a number of factors including the type of emotion, and the individual, cultural, and situational variables. But most agree that appropriate emotional self-regulation is essential for personal/individual health and interpersonal functioning (Gross, 1998; Gross & Thompson, 2007) and is particularly important for those who are working in helping roles (Courtois & Ford, 2013).

Emotional self-regulation requires recognition of being triggered to an emotional state, containment of intense emotionality, and the ability to recover, as appropriate (Courtois & Ford, 2013). For example, Lucinda, who works in a rape crisis center, was followed home by a stalker one night after returning from her friend's house. The incident, fortunately, did not escalate to violence, but that was only because of police intervention. She found that for the few weeks after the stalker incident, her own experience of fear was triggered while listening to victim's stories of trauma. Initially, in fact, she experienced some physiological symptoms of fear—her heart was racing, her breaths became short, and she noticed that her palms were sweating—symptoms of the stress response system, which would need to be regulated in order to return to calm. After working with her supervisor, they decided that it would be a good idea for her to assume a more mundane role in the office for a while rather than her usual role of victim advocate. This she did for a few weeks until the emotional intensity of her own experience could be contained using some of the emotional regulation strategies mentioned below.

Most researchers agree that emotional regulation abilities are largely determined by internal and external influences (Westphal & Bonanno, 2004). Internally, neural networks associated with emotional regulation develop rapidly in the brain during the first few years of life, making this developmental period particularly critical to the development of emotional regulation abilities (Cozolino, 2010). They are learned through a process of internalization of adult commands and actions (Eisenberg et al., 2007; Stegge & Terwogt, 2007). Adults tend to regulate the conditions of emotional stimulation in their children by soothing their infant when stimulated, for example, or distracting their child who is upset about something. Young children soon learn these calming habits of self-soothing and shifting attention from these earlier experiences with their caretakers. Although these skills are developed at a young age, particularly in the context of parent–child relationships, experts in the field of trauma have found that instruction in self-regulation strategies can be helpful for children and adults who chronically display emotional dysregulation (Blaustein & Kinniburgh, 2010; Linehan, 1993; Shearin & Linehan, 1994).

Emotional Self-Regulation Strategies

So, what exactly can a helper do to calm himself or herself when he or she is feeling dysregulated, perhaps triggered by something spoken by the helpee, or trying to center after a difficult personal situation? There is an abundance of resources aimed at teaching self-regulation skills to children, teens, and adults who lack the ability to modulate their emotions appropriately. There is less information available, however, that is aimed at enabling helpers to regulate their own emotionality in the moment of trigger when working with others. The recent work of Champe, Okech, and Rubel (2013) is a notable exception as they consider the relevance of helpers' self-regulation abilities to the practice of counseling group work. These authors suggest that the Gross model of emotional-regulation described below (see Gross, 2008; Gross & Thompson, 2007) is an appropriate model for helpers to use when they lack self-regulation.

The Gross model, summarized in Table 5.1, identifies five specific places along a sequence of emotional expression where people are able to intervene to alter their own emotional reactivity. The first entry point is called **situation selection** (Gross, 2008; Gross & Thompson, 2007). Situation selection has to do with *avoiding* a situation that triggers an emotional response. This requires, of course, being aware of what situations or particular issues might trigger an emotional response. The emphasis is on making a decision about entering into a situation (or not) that will likely generate emotional reactivity. Let us return to the example above of Lucinda who worked in a rape response agency and had her own traumatic experience of being stalked. Lucinda was aware of her own fear response when she listened to victim's stories of trauma, so she and her supervisor decided to have her work temporarily in another role in the agency. This is an example of situation selection. As shown in Illustration 5.2, this requires making an active decision about whether or not you should put yourself in a potentially triggering situation.

The next strategy in the Gross model is **situation modification** (Gross, 2008; Gross & Thompson, 2007). This refers to one's efforts to *manage* or *alter* a situation in order to regulate the emotional response that is triggered. So, while situation selection has to do with deciding not to enter into a triggering situation, this has to do with intentionally modifying the situation so as to avoid the specific trigger. In the example above, Lucinda found that her own reactivity became more regulated when she was able to slowly return to victim advocacy by working first as a consultant and then moving into part time work with victims (and then she worked part time in another role in the agency). In the role of consultant, she was not serving as a first responder to victims, directly interacting with them and hearing their stories of trauma, but instead she was available to offer assistance and training to newer workers at the agency. When she noticed that her level of emotional reactivity subsided, she slowly moved to part time work as a first responder. In this way, she modified her situation by being one step removed from the stories that triggered her own emotional

Illustration 5.2   Active Decision-Making

©iStockphoto.com/alphaspirit

reactivity and then later moved back into her former role starting with limited exposure.

Attention deployment (Gross, 2008; Gross & Thompson, 2007) is another point of entry into managing one's emotional reactivity in the Gross model. Gross (1998) identified concentration, rumination, and distraction as three attention deployment strategies. Distraction is to focus on another nonemotional aspect of a situation so as to detract from the more intense emotion that is present. Concentration is to maintain focus in an intentional way—concentration on something that is nontriggering, for example. Rumination refers to a repeated willful concentration on a nonreactive target. Examples of these attention deployment strategies with Lucinda include her intentional redirection of her thoughts to something else when she noticed that she was emotionally activated. At times, she would also intentionally ruminate on a detail in her immediate environment for a brief period—the clock or picture behind her client, so as to distract her from the emotional trigger, if it surfaced when she was with a victim. Finally, she found that stopping in the offices of a few coworkers periodically throughout the day to socialize briefly offered a good distraction as well. This latter strategy helped her relax a little during the day in her emotionally intense work environment.

The next step in Gross's model of emotional regulation is **cognitive change** (Gross, 2008; Gross & Thompson, 2007). This process has to do with intervention at the cognitive appraisal level of emotional stimulation—altering the way in which an individual makes meaning of a situation or emotional trigger, so as to manage subsequent emotional reactivity. For example, Mohammad immediately became anxious when he was assigned to work with a helpee who was known in his agency to be "very difficult." With the help of his supervisor and using strategies of cognitive change, Mohammad recalled other "difficult" clients he had worked with in the past and the strategies he used to work with those individuals. With those experiences in the forefront of his memory, Mohammad was able to tell himself that while it was going to be a challenge to work with this particular helpee, he would be able to do it because he had successfully worked with challenging situations before. This strategy is related to the CBT principles discussed in Chapter 3; using cognitive processes to shape emotional responses.

Not outlined in Gross's model but also considered an important component of emotional self-regualtion is **distress tolerance.** This is an emotion regulation strategy that focuses on being able to manage one's reactivity to emotional triggers in the moment (Stasiewicz et al., 2013). It is an ability to tolerate aversive emotional or physical experiences or discomfort (Bardeen, Fergus, & Orcutt, 2013) without having to act impulsively on them (Rathus & Miller, 2015).

Distress tolerance is a skill component in Linehan's dialectical behavior therapy [DBT], which is a therapeutic cognitive-behavioral treatment aimed at facilitating emotional self-regulation (for more on DBT see Linehan, Armstrong, Suarez, Allmon, & Heard, 1991; Linehan, 1993; Linehan, 2015; Miller, Rathus, Linehan, Wetzler, & Leigh, 1997; Rathus & Miller, 2015). Distress tolerance skills include some of the strategies mentioned in the Gross model, such as distraction and cognitive change, as well as self-soothing, making pro-tolerance decisions based on an examination of the pros and cons, and mindfulness practice (Miller et al., 1997; Rathus & Miller, 2015). These authors highlight that acceptance is a critical component of distress tolerance. Acceptance in this context has to do with the recognition that pain and discomfort are a natural part of life; acknowledging and accepting this frees us to cope with stress, discomfort and aversive experiences. In short, distress tolerance is about accepting discomfort in the moment, knowing that it will soon go away.

The distress tolerance strategies mentioned above require some level of intentional cognitive information processing; distress tolerance requires us to reshape our thinking so as to better tolerate waves of emotion and, ultimately, to avoid responding in unhelpful or destructive ways. For example, Maria, who was grappling with a recent loss of her sister, noticed her own emotional reactivity when she sat with patients in her hospice job. She prepared herself for work by using comfort (self-soothing) strategies such as dressing in her favorite comfortable clothes and bringing a few of her favorite pictures of her children to her office. Also, when sitting with patients, Maria found that physically moving her seat or her position in her seat helped her better manage the growing intensity of sadness when it was triggered. She also was able to coach herself to "notice and not fight" her own sadness when it appeared. This comes from the mindfulness practice of being aware of our sensations and accepting rather than fighting or trying to change them. Paradoxically, developing awareness and self-acceptance enables us to better tolerate distress and manage our reactions to difficult situations. Finally, Maria also found that intentionally coaching herself to smile for her sister rather than cry (cognitive change strategy) also helped her manage high-intensity emotions when they appeared in situations that required management. All of these distress tolerance skills allowed her to manage her own sadness while sitting with others in pain.

Finally, Gross's concept of **response modulation** (Gross, 2008; Gross & Thompson, 2007) refers to strategies that can be put in place *before or after* physiological, experiential, behavioral or emotional responses are triggered. These might best be thought of as ongoing self-care and healthy lifestyle initiatives.

Illustration 5.3 Self-Care

©iStockphoto.com/ohnnylemonseed

Response modulation strategies may include, for example, maintaining a healthy diet, using medication as appropriate and if needed, modulating the consumption of other substances, and engaging in relaxation exercises and therapy, if needed. Linehan (1993) points out that we are more vulnerable to emotional reactivity when we are under stress, so reducing that vulnerability by taking care of ourselves is an obvious conclusion. She emphasizes good diet, exercise, sleep, and engagement in activities that build self-efficacy and competence. As Skovholt (2001) says, helpers "need to be assertive about their own wellness" (p. 162), and to him, wellness refers to physical, emotional and social, spiritual, and intellectual health.

Table 5.1 Emotional Self-Regulation Strategies

Strategy	Description
Situation Selection	Avoiding a situation that triggers an emotional response
Situation Modification	Manipulating or altering a situation so as to regulate the emotionality that is present
Attentional Deployment	Refocusing on a nonemotional aspect of a situation. This may include concentration, rumination (repeated concentration), or distraction.

Table 5.1

Strategy	Description
Cognitive Change	Altering one's cognitive appraisal of a situation or of the emotional trigger. This may include thinking about a situation differently or thinking about one's capacity to manage a situation differently.
Distress Tolerance	Developing the ability to tolerate troublesome emotions without having to act impulsively on them. May include distraction, self-soothing, relaxing, and acceptance.
Response Modulation	Adjusting one's lifestyle to avoid adverse responses to triggers in the future. Strategies may include medication, relaxation strategies, diet, modulating the consumption of substances, and therapy.

Adapted from:

Gross, J. J. (2008). Emotion regulation. In M. Lewis, J. M. Haviland-Jones, & L. F. Barrett (Eds.), *Handbook of emotions* (3rd ed., pp. 497–512). New York, NY: The Guilford Press.

Gross, J. J., & Thompson, R. A. (2007). Emotion regulation: Conceptual foundations. In J. J. Gross (Ed.), *Handbook of emotion regulation* (pp. 3–24). New York, NY: The Guilford Press.

ASSUMPTIONS, VALUES, AND BELIEFS

We have discussed how personalization issues, vicarious traumatization, and burnout can affect our ability to be present and intentional when helping others. We also reviewed the literature on emotional expression and strategies that helpers can use to manage their own reactivity to the stories and experiences of their helpees. (These are the same strategies that helpers may teach helpees to use when they, too, are having difficulties regulating their emotional responses.) Here we turn our attention to the ways in which our own values, beliefs, and assumptions can have adverse effects on our work as well. This discussion will begin with a review of the neurobiology of memory processes.

Memory Processes

Our assumptions, beliefs, and values, stored in memory, are the tools we use to make meaning of our experiences in social contexts (Nelson & Neufeldt, 1998). That is, we access information stored in memory to comprehend current situations. To better understand how this works, we will start with a basic overview of memory processes.

Research suggests that there are multiple memory systems within the brain; the two broadest categories are called explicit and implicit memory (Cozolino, 2010). **Explicit memory** contains information acquired from semantic (language), sensory (from the senses), or motor (movement) input—stored information that was initially acquired as a result of conscious experiences and learning processes. Most of us are able to recall information in the explicit memory easily, and we use it to make sense of everyday experiences. For example, you see a photo of a polar bear and remember that these bears live in the Arctic. Then you shiver to think about what it would be like in the cold Arctic. Explicit memory requires conscious thought for recall. As this example illustrates, memories are linked together to facilitate recollection. Seeing a photo of a bear reminds us of its habitat and that becomes associated with the experience of cold. According to Cozolino (2010), explicit memory is important for emotional regulation, identity development, and the transmission of culture.

Implicit memory, on the other hand, contains "unconscious patterns of learning stored in hidden layers of neural processing, largely inaccessible to conscious awareness" (Cozolino, 2010, p. 77). Memories stored in the implicit memory, then, are acquired largely out of our awareness, and they are recalled unconsciously. That is, we are sensing information all the time in our everyday experiences and storing that information in implicit memory without even realizing it. Information stored in implicit memory also influences our thinking processes. For example, if you encounter a food that at one time made you sick, you may suddenly have an uneasy feeling that is triggered by an olfactory memory of that particular food. The memory of the earlier encounter with that particular food was stored in implicit memory and resurrected at the familiar sight and smell of that same food at a later date. Sometimes we have these kinds of experiences of discomfort without even realizing the connection to earlier experiences.

Information accumulated from repeated experiences or exposure over time are particularly influential to recall, and that information is stored in both memory systems (Boysen, 2010). It has been found that the specific location of each memory system influences what is encoded and retrieved (Cozolino, 2010). The implicit memory actually begins storing information before birth, and it is hosted in primitive brain structures such as the amygdala, thalamus, and the mid-frontal cortex. According to Cozolino (2010), the amygdala "plays a 'behind the screens' role in creating emotional bias in conscious processing" (p. 81). That is, the amygdala is key in processing emotional and somatic (feeling) perceptual experiences, and it enables appraisals of safety and danger by connecting those sensations to meaning. The amygdala is largely responsible for triggering flight-or-fight reactions, among other things. As discussed in Chapter 2, you will recall that the processing of emotional and perceptual experiences happens in coordination with other parts of the brain, particularly the frontal cortex.

The explicit memory develops later as the cerebral cortex and hippocampus mature. Given its location near the hippocampus, explicit memory is more generally ruled by spatial and temporal information processing systems (Cozolino, 2010). This portion of the brain allows for more sophisticated cognitive processing; it is responsible for conscious and logical thought processing and allows for social functioning. Thus, in comparison, explicit memory processing is more logical, cognitive, and conscious.

The interaction between these different memory systems and related sections of the brain is important. Together, they create a broad-based cognitive appraisal system. Boysen (2010) uses the term *dual processing systems* to talk about the interaction between the explicit memory (which he refers to as the *rule-based* memory) and implicit memory (which he calls the *associative* memory). He is particularly concerned with the ways in which assumptions, values, and beliefs stored in implicit memory unconsciously influence the practice of helping.

Implicit Bias

Recall that ideas and concepts that are stored in memory are accumulated from repeated experiences or exposure over time. Also recall that information stored in the implicit memory system is typically associated with somatic and emotional content and that in this system, concept formation happens out of the awareness of the individual. It does not require intentional thought. This helps us understand how repeated experiences over time, and particularly those associated with emotion, lie dormant and then seem to suddenly come out of nowhere and influence one's experience. As an example, consider a family with religious practices of regularly attending a church, temple, or mosque. These kinds of repeated experiences over time, according to Boysen (2010), form *implicit biases*. Implicit biases are unquestioned ideas that are established from repeated experiences. They are what we come to know as normal or as a truth.

Implicit bias, Boysen (2010) points out, plays a key role in how we interpret new experiences. Going back to the example above, it does not take a leap of imagination to understand that the faith experiences of a family shape the way in which family members make meaning of their everyday experiences. This likely happens even out of conscious awareness and without much effort. Because implicit memory processes occur at a level that is out of one's awareness, Boysen's point is that memories stored in implicit memory bias the ways in which meanings are interpreted without our knowledge. As an example here,

I would speculate that repeated exposure to media images, particularly those that are mixed with strong emotions, are stored in implicit memory. Meaning-making systems, then, are influenced by these implicit biases as we encounter these objects in our everyday lives. These likely include the unconscious (and conscious) messages are that girls should be sexy; men should be super strong and, of course, not cry; and love and marriage is between a man and a woman.

It is also important to note that the way in which information is initially stored in memory—the way in which sensory input was initially activated—will determine how particular memories are activated in the future (Siegel, 2012). The example given by Siegel (2012) is that if someone sees the Eiffel Tower on a trip to Paris, the memory of the Eiffel Tower may well be encoded or stored visually in that person's memory. Later when that person tries to recall the trip to Paris, the visual image of the Eiffel Tower will likely surface. This is because, Siegel explains, a neural net profile similar to the one activated at the initial sighting of the Eiffel Tower is reactivated at recall. However, if the Paris visitor was bitten by a dog during the vacation, her recall of the Eiffel Tower may likely also include the sense of anxiety or fear, which is related to the traumatic biting incident. This is because traumatic memories are often stored in the amygdala-related memory systems and recalled unintentionally.

Implicit Bias and Assumptions, Values, and Beliefs

Going back to Boysen's (2010) concept of implicit bias, assume for a moment that an individual has been raised in a social group with particular values, and these values have been articulated and illustrated to that individual in a variety of ways over time. These values are stored in memory and activated in and out of conscious awareness to inform cognitive appraisals of new experiences. If these memories are paired with an emotional experience, that emotion will also be a part of the implicit bias.

For example, an individual who experiences a warm family and community in the context of his religious practices is likely to have that sense of warmth as part of his implicit memory of his religious experiences. Let us say, however, that that individual experienced frustration and turmoil around his early religious experiences and, as a result, eventually ended up leaving the church. It is possible that at a later time when he enters into a church, even if it is not the same church he once attended, those memories associated with turmoil would resurface, giving him an uneasy feeling, possibly even triggering a panic attack or causing other physiological symptoms. It is in this way that repeated exposure to images and semantics that trigger emotion are stored in memory and later activated.

Figure 5.2 Dual Processing Systems of Memory

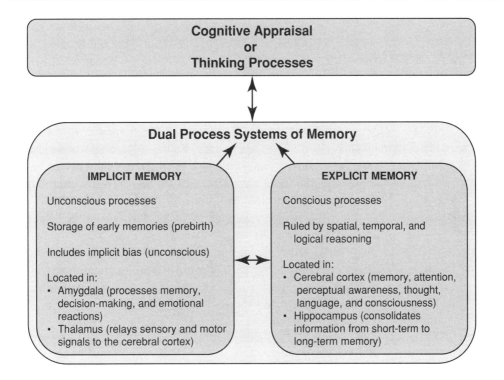

Keep in mind that our values and beliefs are processed from both implicit and explicit memory functions. However, Boysen (2010) reminds us that explicit memory processes are not as quick and automatic as implicit memory systems. That is, the images and visceral messages that are stored in the implicit memory systems are triggered quickly. For helpers, an implication of this lag in recall related to explicit memory is that thought processes associated with explicit memory are not as readily available to us as are implicit memory processes and bias. If our own personal values and beliefs that we have learned from experiences over time are stored in implicit memory, it is these that will initially and more effortlessly inform the cognitive meaning-making processes that we use in our helping relationships. And, all of this happens in a process that is almost entirely out of our awareness.

This is to say that without even being aware of it, our own personal values and beliefs shape what we think about our helpees, how we interpret their experiences, and our initial helping reflexes. This underscores the importance of developing conscious awareness of our assumptions, beliefs, and values, and being intentional about countering the biases that inform how we understand the experiences and expressions of others.

CULTURAL COMPETENCE

Two salient points were made in Chapter 2 with regard to diversity competence. The first was that social and cultural contexts influence development. That is, social group affiliation—experiences of race, ethnicity, socioeconomic status, gender identity, religion, spirituality, sexual orientation, ability status, and even geography—shape our everyday experiences, values, beliefs, and hopes and dreams for the future. We have just learned how this shaping happens through memory and meaning-making neurological systems. All of these variables also affect the helping relationship, particularly when the helper and helpee are situated in different social identities.

Mistrust, conflict, and a reluctance to engage in helping relationships often result when helpees perceive that their helpers are insensitive to their unique cultural and personal experiences (Day-Vines et al., 2007; Sue & Sue, 2008). These perceptions may be in response to the helpee's direct experience with the helper (i.e., helper behaviors—whether or not the helper is aware of such behaviors) or anticipatory, as these perceptions may be primed from repeated and often unacknowledged experiences of discrimination and marginalization. This brings us to the second point raised in Chapter 2: Helpers must understand how experiences of marginalization affect helping relationships.

Systems of power and privilege related to race and social group affiliation are learned at an early age (Van Ausdale & Feagin, 2001) and exert subtle and overt influences on the perceptions and experiences of those who identify in nondominant or marginalized social groups (Monk, Winslade, & Sinclair, 2008; Prochaska & Norcross, 2007). As discussed in Chapter 2, when individuals identify in social groups that are marginalized by dominant society, the resultant experiences of racism (or any of the other "isms") and discrimination have the potential to affect everything from job outlook and educational attainment to everyday encounters with others, including helping relationships. As helpers, we must be vigilant about not replicating these experiences of marginalization in our helping relationships. And this, as we have just pointed out in the discussion about implicit memory and bias, is sometimes very difficult to do. It requires work.

Definitions of what it means to be culturally competent vary across and within helping professions (Fields, 2010). In fact, the whole notion of having competence regarding multiculturalism is misleading as it suggests that competence is a definable stage or level of achievement. Competence is simply not that concrete. Cultures are not clearly defined categories, they are ever-changing subjective creations that defy clear boundaries and definitions (Prochaska & Norcross, 2007), and definitions and understandings about race, culture, and other social groups can be rather confusing. Added to this, a wide variation of individual differences exists even within categorical social group identities. That is, general descriptions and understandings about people who identify in a particular social group may not apply to all individuals in that group (Monk et al., 2008).

We frequently use the term *social location* when speaking about these categories of racial, cultural, gender, and other types of social affiliation. Social location is defined as one's position or place of identity among various social groups—"one's place in society" (Kubiak, 2005, p. 451). It captures a broad array of possible social group affiliations that one may identify with, including race, ethnicity, socioeconomic status, gender identity, religion, spirituality, sexual orientation, ability status, etc., and it also captures this idea of social stratification and social capital. So, social location is perhaps best articulated as "one's position within intersecting systems of stratification" (Kennedy et al., 2012, p. 217). It captures the idea that there are a number of identity categories (in addition to race) that are marginalized in dominant society.

Because of these ambiguities and complexities around the concept of social location and a lack of clarity around what, exactly, is meant by *cultural competence*, it is difficult to imagine that cultural competence could be described as a set of interventions and techniques that are specific to different social groups. For most writers and researchers, cultural competence has more to do with having awareness (self- and other-awareness), and certain attitudes and knowledge, than it has to do with a specific skill set (Arredondo et al., 1996; Collins and Arthur, 2010a; Hogan-Garcia, 1999; Sue, Arredondo, & McDavis, 1992; Sue & Sue, 2003). As a guide for helping practices, cultural competence compels us to think and act with awareness and intentionality. We will review each of these components of cultural competence—*awareness*, *knowledge*, and *skills*—here, but it is important for all helpers to receive more extensive training in these areas so as to be able to provide ethical helping services in their work with others.

This first component of cultural competence—**awareness**—refers to awareness about cultural identity. This refers to helpers needing to be aware of their own *and* their helpee's cultural identities (Arredondo et al., 1996; Collins & Arthur, 2010b). Collins and Arthur (2010b) emphasize that awareness of cultural identity should include being cognizant about the unique factors that shape and define our lives (and the lives of our helpees). These include social location, personal characteristics and experiences, and contextual variables such as experiences of oppression and discrimination. Collins and Arthur also point out that there are some universal factors that are common to all people—the ability to be self-aware, the use of symbols such as language, and biology, for example—that should also inform our understanding of others. All of these variables, however, are fluid and dynamic; individuals express identity in unique ways. Also, people are typically situated in multiple social identity groups at any given time. So, social or cultural group affiliation is never a clearly defined entity, and its influence on development varies considerably across individuals within social groups.

A key component of helper self-awareness, articulated in the work of Arredondo et al. (1996), has to do with the importance of helpers being engaged in a continual process of questioning and challenging their own biases, negative reactions, and preconceived notions about others. The presence of bias is often signaled by a feeling of discomfort around others who are different, so exploring discomfort is a key entry point into this work. Arredondo et al. point out that cultural awareness also extends to recognizing our own limitations in working with others. When we don't know how to help, we are not able to be effective. Working with people from diverse social locations requires us to be uncomfortable, to explore that discomfort, and to seek consultation and supervision at all times.

This last point leads us to a second component of cultural competence identified by these researchers and authors (e.g., Arredondo et al., 1996, Collins & Arthur, 2010a; Hogan-Garcia, 1999; Sue et al., 1992; Sue & Sue, 2003): **knowledge.** Having appropriate multicultural knowledge refers to learning about one's own and the helpee's racial or cultural heritage, beliefs, values, lifestyles, and worldviews (Arredondo et al., 1996). Helpers must constantly update their knowledge base with relevant research and contemporary trends and information. They must also seek consultation and training to improve their understanding and effectiveness in working with individuals in various social locations. Having knowledge about others, particularly those who hold membership in marginalized social locations, requires helpers to be informed about sociopolitical factors that operate in people's lives. That is, helpers must understand how oppression, racism, and discrimination operate in the lives of those who identify in marginalized social locations and also how these factors affect the helping relationship and helper bias. Finally, helpers also need to know about differences in communication patterns across social groups and how their own communication style may affect the helping process.

Having the requisite **skills** for working with individuals from other cultures is the third component of cultural competence in the Arredondo et al. (1996) model. This begins with being engaged in a process of understanding one's own cultural identity or social group membership (Arredondo et al., 1996; Collins & Arthur, 2010b). It then goes one more step by compelling helpers to also know what to do—how to interact with and how to help people who are culturally different than themselves. Collins and Arthur (2010b) emphasize that the "skills" for working with diverse cultures (beyond developing awareness) begin with having the ability to develop and maintain a working alliance with helpees. This type of working alliance, they propose, has collaboration as its guiding principle. In other words, both the helper and the helpee are agent in determining the goals for the work together as well as the tasks and practices that will be used to reach those goals. At the heart of effective cross-cultural helping relationships, Collins and Arthur (2010b) remind us, must be a foundation of mutual trust and respect.

Importantly, Arredondo et al. (1996) assert that cultural competence is strengthened when we become regularly engaged with individuals from various social locations. That is, we can develop competence in working with helpees from different social locations when we have our own personal experiences in meaningful relationships with people who are culturally different than ourselves. This is an important suggestion as it compels us to take personal action to broaden ourselves culturally by stepping out of our own comfort zone and into the lives of people who hold membership in a variety of social locations.

CHAPTER SUMMARY

This chapter focused on the ways in which our personal experiences, emotional reactions, assumptions, beliefs, and values affect our work in helping relationships. First we discussed how personalization issues, vicarious traumatization, and burnout affect helpers' ability to be emotionally present with others. This discussion led to information about emotion—what emotions are, how they are expressed, and ways of regulating emotion. In order to be most effective in their work, helpers need to be able to use emotional self-regulation skills when they are triggered by what their helpees have said or experienced, or by how they act. Self-awareness, self-regulation, and self-care are necessary components of being an effective helper.

The chapter also focused on the ways in which helpers' beliefs and values influence their work as helpers. This discussion led to an exploration of memory systems, and underscored the ways in which implicit bias affects helping. In terms of diversity competence, helpers were reminded of the importance of having awareness and knowledge about self as well as about others. Such awareness will protect the helper from being affected by implicit bias. Cultural competence, it was noted, also must include developing skills for working with individuals who identify in social groups that are different than those of the helper. Again, as in earlier chapters, the point is that we must be aware of the effects of our own personal experiences as well as social context when we are engaged in the complex work of helping others.

DISCUSSION QUESTIONS

1. What are personalization issues, and how might a helper manage these issues as they arise in the helping relationship?

2. List two occupational hazards in the helping profession and how one might cope with these hazards.

3. Describe emotional regulation strategies and give examples of how you use these strategies in your own life to manage triggers or stress.

4. When working with individuals from nondominant social locations, how might a helper avoid replicating experiences of marginalization in the helping relationship?

CHAPTER 6

SETTING THE STAGE FOR HELPING

LEARNING OBJECTIVES

1. Understand key components of helping contracts

2. Describe aspects of initial assessment that will help identify helping goals and strategies

3. Describe stages of change and the implication of these ideas for helping relationships

4. Explain positioning theory and its implications on helping relationships

---

INTRODUCTION

It seems redundant to state that helpees enter into helping relationships when things are not going well in their lives. But, I say this again to remind us that when people seek our help, they often are not bringing their "best self" into the helping relationship. Remember the feelings of vulnerability, frustration, confusion, or perhaps, hopelessness that you have felt when you were struggling with a problem that seemed insurmountable. Think about your own ambivalence at seeking help in times when you probably needed it. Many of us want to figure things out on our own, and we do not want others to see us in a compromised or vulnerable state. These are some of the worries and fears that helpees bring into their relationships with us.

In this chapter, we will discuss the first steps to take when you meet a new helpee and how to establish an appropriate contract for your work together. This important early step in the helping process defines the understandings that must be in place for the work to be relevant. Next we will move into a discussion about assessment, highlighting areas for exploration when getting to know a new helpee. We also will review the theory of change, as it can help us identify the most appropriate starting place for our work in different helping

Table 6.1 Map of Helping Relationships

Getting Started	Helping Contract	Assessment	Goal Setting	Action Plans and Expectations
Respectful Welcoming	Formal versus Informal	Understanding the Helper	Identifying the Problem	Articulation of Goal
Orientation and Explanation	Clarity: Problem/Issue Intent of Work Commitments Expectations Action Plan	Understanding the Problem	Moving From Problem to Goal	Articulation of Strategy
Request for Services	Boundaries	Gathering Information	Clear Articulation of the Goal	
Compassion and Professionalism		Determining Motivation to Change		

relationships. These ideas are mapped out in Table 6.1. Finally, positioning theory will also be discussed in this chapter as it helps us think about how to establish ourselves in our helping relationships so that they are respectful and promote helpee agency.

GETTING STARTED

In the very first contact with a helpee, you (or someone in your agency) will need to determine the nature of the concern being presented and if you are the best one to provide the needed services. This very first encounter with the helpee will set a tone for the work that will follow, so it is a critical to get it right. In thinking about this very first communication offered to a helpee who is seeking services, David Epston's concept of **respectful welcoming** (Masterswork Productions, 2002) comes to mind. A respectful welcoming is an invitation into relationship that communicates interest in and respect for the personal stories, skills, and knowledge of the helpee. It describes what Michael White famously referred to as a *decentered* position (White, 2005), meaning that the helpee, not you, is at the center of the relationship.

Illustration 6.1   A Respectful and Warm Welcome

©Can Stock Photo Inc./cundm

A respectful welcoming begins with a warm invitation and a welcoming stance. To this end, you or whomever answers the phones, opens the doors, sits behind the reception counter, or initiates contact with the helpee should offer full attention to the helpee. For example, "Hi. Welcome! My name is Anne. How can I help you today?" or "Hi. Thanks for coming in. My name is Anne. I will be meeting with you this morning. Please come in." Its usually a good idea to err to the side of being slightly formal at these initial meetings, calling someone Mr. or Mrs., rather than by first name, and then asking the how the person would like to be addressed. In this very first encounter, it is important to communicate to the helpee that he or she will be respected, taken care of, helped, and understood.

Research indicates that high drop-out rates in therapy are associated with long wait times prior to initial contact (Carter et al., 2012) and between an initial interview and receiving services (Claus & Kindleberger, 2002). In addition to waitlists, unanswered phone calls, and experiences such as being put on hold listening to classical music do not make for a respectful and inviting welcome. These all have the potential of starting the helping relationship off in the wrong direction. If your helpee has had to wait for services, be sure to initiate contact with an apology and make a commitment to avoid delays in the future.

Once you are in a confidential location, provide the helpee with an **explanation** of the types of services you are prepared to offer and a brief **orientation** to the setting in which you will be working. This will help set the stage for appropriate expectations, establish credibility, and communicate respect—your helpee has the right to know about the services he or she is about to receive. For example, Frank introduced himself to the family members of a new resident in an elder care residence by saying, "My role here at The Manor is to meet with residents and their families. I am available for families to talk about any special concerns or requests that they have regarding their loved ones. Here is my number." He gave them his business card. "Please be in touch whenever you have questions and concerns." Then he provided them with a brief tour of the facility.

Keep in mind that when we work in the same agency or facility day after day, it is easy to forget what it might feel like for a newcomer to walk into our office. Even when helpees are familiar with one aspect or branch of services offered in an agency, they do not typically have the "bird's eye" view of agencies that employees have. So, welcomes and introductions are always important.

As you are introducing yourself and discussing the services you are available to provide, you will also want to invite the helpee to articulate what type of assistance he is looking for. This, basically, is an invitation for the helpee to articulate a **request for services**. Even when you have an idea what the helpee is looking for—when you have read a file about his history or have talked to someone in advance about him, remember to ask the helpee what, specifically, he is looking for. Doing so will help you learn more about the helpee, and it also communicates respect. As Miller and Rollnick (2013) point out, "People are the undisputed experts on themselves. No one has been with them longer, or knows them better than they do themselves" (p. 15). Our work should always be aimed at the perceived needs of the helpee—it should be helpee centered.

You can elicit the request for services by asking, "Can you tell me what brought you here?" or "I know that you have been waiting to see me. I apologize for the long wait. Can you tell me about your concern?" "What did you have in mind for our work together?" If the presenting concern has already been exposed, you should, as mentioned, still invite the helpee to articulate the concern in his own words. For example, "I know that you have been admitted into this program because of an issue with Child Protective Services. Can you tell me a little bit more about what you might be looking for in these parenting classes?"

As the helpee articulates her concern, be sure to listen carefully, express empathy, affirm her efforts to seek services, and express optimism that things will get better. For example, "It sounds like this has been a difficult time for you.

Figure 6.1 Getting Started

It must have been very hard to make the decision to come here, given how angry you were. I think that we will be able to work together to make things better for you and your family. Sometimes it seems that the first step—to just get in the door that very first time, is the hardest—and yet, here you are." Be sure that your initial contact with the helpee (and, of course, all subsequent contacts) is both **compassionate** and **professional**. Compassion refers to an empathic concern for the welfare of others. Professionalism, as discussed in Chapter 1, refers to helper behaviors that communicate competence and respect.

Of course, not all helping relationships initiate in an office. Some happen in groups, in meetings, in emergency rooms, over the phone, or in public spaces. Regardless of the particular setting of your initial contact with the helpee, it is always important to provide a respectful welcoming, offer information about the services you can provide, ask the helpee for their perspective on the issue or concern, and always act with compassion and professionalism. These components of getting started are summarized in Figure 6.1.

VIDEO LINK:
Starting the
Conversation

THE HELPING "CONTRACT"

In Chapter 1, it was pointed out that the exchange of services is a defining feature of helping relationships; it is one of the key aspects of helping relationships that make them unique from other types of relationships. The helping contract is the formal or informal agreement regarding this exchange of services. The components of helping contracts mentioned here are summarized in Table 6.2.

Formal helping contracts are written helping agreements. They are sometimes also called *consent for services* or the *treatment plan*. While formal contracts vary considerably across different helping agencies, most include specific details about the problem or concern being addressed, the intended goals for the work together, and an action plan, which is the strategies and expectations that will be used to accomplish the identified goals. Some formal contracts also include the number of meetings and the settings where the work will happen and relevant policies or laws, particularly around confidentiality and duty to warn. In some situations the contract may even include financial remuneration for the helping services. Sometimes these are drafted at the agency level, other times by the specific helper.

Informal contracts, too, are an articulation of the services that will be rendered in the helping relationship. Informal contracts are not typically drafted in writing and often don't use helping jargon such as goals, treatment plans, and reimbursement for services. However, they are an articulation of the helping work that will occur. An example of an informal contract might be a commitment by a helper to provide a helpee with a ride to her AA meeting. Or, an agreement between a helper and helpee to spend the afternoon together out in the community. Notice that these examples imply a commitment for a service that will be provided to the helpee, and they require communication regarding meeting times and dates.

Both formal and informal contracts also *clearly* communicate, explicitly or implicitly, the **boundaries** around the services that will be provided within the helping relationship. For example, the goals and helping strategies identified in a formal contract are the implied parameters of that relationship. That is, they describe what will happen in that relationship. An informal contract should do this as well. For example, an informal contract that includes transporting a client to an AA meeting does not commit the helper to also attend that meeting with the helpee. An agreement to take a helpee out in the community for social engagement because she lacks adequate social skills to go out alone does not mean that the helper will be taking the helpee to spend time with the helper and his friends in the local café. Even when the boundaries of the helping relationship are not explicitly stated, it is the helper's responsibility to be clear about the boundaries of the relationship and to monitor and structure it so that these boundaries are clear and firmly in place.

Helping relationships should never include the exchange of services that do not center on the helpee and should never include the kind of mutuality that exists in friendship and intimate relationships. In short, formal or informal, all helping relationships must be established upon a clear outline and boundary of services that will be provided. No helping relationship should be so informal that the terms of services are not discussed.

VIDEO LINK:
Negotiating
the Helping
Contract

Photo 6.1 Clear Boundaries

©iStockphoto.com/kavram

Table 6.2 The Helping Contract

The Helping Contract	Identifies the problem, issue, or concern to be addressed in the helping relationship.
	Identifies goals for the work together.
	Includes an action plan that outlines helper and helpee responsibilities and commitments.
	Is clear about the boundaries around the helping relationship.
	Includes a respect for confidentiality that is breached only in cases of duty to warn or court order.

ASSESSMENT

Work toward change begins with an understanding of that which needs to be changed. Assessment is that process; it is about learning more about the helpee and the problem he or she is bringing into the helping relationship. It also involves determining the level of investment that the helpee has in working toward change. Here we will discuss helpee assessment, problem assessment, and investment in change.

Understanding the Helpee

Learning about the helpee typically begins with some sort of an **intake** process. Intake is the professional helping term for acquiring basic information about the helpee such as name, address, phone, and emergency contact information. Often helpers also find it helpful to learn more about the helpee's family, social life, work and/or educational history, personal interests, and spiritual or faith practices. In clinical work, gathering this information is part of what is called a *psychosocial assessment*. It is also relevant in some helping situations to assess the helpee's emotional and cognitive functioning as well as interests, strengths, and resources. Additional information about developmental milestones, mental health or medical issues, substance or alcohol use, behavioral challenges, and experiences of crisis, trauma or loss may be gathered in some settings if relevant to the helping contract.

Illustration 6.2   Gathering Information About the Helpee

©iStockphoto.com/doodle machine

Of course, the specific information you will ask about in the assessment depends on the nature of the helping contract. For example, if you are working with someone to find a job, you will need to know about the helpee's work history, educational attainment, job preferences, and work-related skills. It would not be appropriate to ask for information related to the helpee's trauma history or medical conditions in this situation unless it is specifically relevant to the job placement work. If the helping work is about the helpee's substance use, however, then knowing her substance and alcohol use history clearly is relevant. In this latter case, you will also probably want to learn about the effects of the helpee's substance use on family, friends, and work situations, mental health concerns, past actions to ameliorate the problem, a history of trauma or abuse, and other variables related to use. If the helping relationship is centered around medical care, then, of course, a medical history would also be appropriate. Generally, the assessment should focus on gathering the specific information that is appropriate and relevant to the specific context of helping. A final point is that conducting an intake assessment as described here is appropriate in noncrisis situations. When helpers are in initial contact with a helpee who appears to be in crisis, initial assessment will follow the format of a harm assessment described in Chapter 9.

VIDEO LINK:
Gathering
Information

Helpers can gather psychosocial information in a variety of ways. Asking direct questions or inviting the helpee to complete a written questionnaire are often used. Asking the helpee to draw a family tree is good way to gather family history information. Drawing a timeline on a piece of paper is a tool that is used to explore one's history. Here the helpee is asked to indicate key dates in her personal history from birth to present in linear fashion along a line that is drawn

Photo 6.2 Using Art for Assessment

©iStockphoto.com/leungchopan

on a piece of paper. Pictures can also be used with youth. For example, the Kinetic Family Drawing (Kottman, 2002) is an assessment tool that asks children to draw a picture of their family doing something together. The helper later learns about the child's family by talking with the child about the picture he has drawn. Similarly, asking a child to draw a self-portrait can elicit helpful information.

Understanding the Problem

Helpees come to us with situations that have been identified as problematic by themselves or by others. They want help, for example, with parenting. Or they lack adequate personal skills for independent employment and need help with the daily tasks of their job. They may need help writing a paper for school, help managing a mental illness, or help controlling anger outbursts. Helping relationships expand numerous situations. Sometimes, too, helpees come to us for help in an area that is different from what was initially identified as the problem. For example, I once worked with a young man because the school wanted him to learn how to control his behavior. This young man's mother wanted him to be happier and to behave better at school. And when I asked this young man what he wanted help with, he said that he wanted to have friends at school. I suspected that these disparate requests were somehow related, but since the young man was the helpee I was assigned to work with, I wanted to be sure to center our work on the concern that was most pressing for him. As it turned out, the work I did with him also entailed helping the school develop clear and fair discipline policies for all of the students. And it included helping the mother be clear about her expectations and behavior management skills, and to have confidence in herself as a mother. All of these foci helped create a school climate that was better prepared to foster the development of friendships so that my work with this young man could be rooted in a situation that supported the changes he was making. The point is that helpers need to center their work on the problem or concern that is most **relevant to the helpee**.

Gathering Information About the Problem

As mentioned, in the initial contact, you will want to invite the helpee to briefly articulate what the problem, concern, or helping need is. Then you will want to gether more information about this problem so as to have a better idea of how you can help. As you gather more information, learning more about the intensity, history, background, and effects of the problem in the helpee's life will be helpful. Also, it is helpful to know how long the problem has existed, what appears to be its precipitating factors or triggers, and how the helpee make sense of the problem. Finally, it is equally helpful to know what actions or strategies the helpee has already used to address the problem and the extent to which these strategies were successful.

As briefly mentioned earlier, the initial assessment of the helpee, in some situations, may also include also **assessment of harm**. If the helpee is or appears to be in danger of hurting himself or articulates an intent to hurt someone else, than you must provide or immediately access emergency crisis response services. In this case, you should follow the harm assessment protocol discussed in Chapter 9. Also, if the helpee is not able to engage in the type of helping services you are able to provide, then you should make a referral—a warm handoff referral—to a more appropriate professional helper.

Levels of Problems

The theories mentioned in Chapter 2 offer explanatory systems that situate problems as existing within the individual, in interpersonal relationships, or external to the individual. **Intrapersonal** issues are those that we think of as being inside the individual. For example, a medical condition, a disability that handicaps a person from doing something, or a lack of education or information that limits a person in some way. **Interpersonal** issues are those that exist between people. For example: a conflict between two people, ineffective communication patterns within a family, or behaviors that happen within a group. Problems situated in the **external** environment are not related to something being wrong with a person, and they are not rooted in a specific interpersonal relationship. Externally situated problems are caused by beliefs, behaviors, or circumstances within a system (such as a particular situation, institution, community, or society) that limit or present hardships in someone's life. Experiences of overt or subtle racism, for example, are external to the individuals who are victim to these forces. Another example of an externally situated problem is a natural disaster, such as a flood, that causes problems to members of the affected community.

Notice that these three categories of intrapersonal, interpersonal, and externally situated problems are not mutually exclusive. Problems that appear to be situated intrapersonally, for example, can have effects on interpersonal relationships. When a person who has a disability finds that others treat him in inappropriate or unhelpful ways, then the problem of the disability is also situated interpersonally. And I would argue that in this case, the problem is likely due to or at least strongly exacerbated by external conditions, as it is situated in a social context with disempowering and insulting discourses about people who do not conform to conventional standards of "normal." Another example of how these categories overlap is when a person who has experienced an external event such as a natural disaster develops anxiety symptoms (intrapersonal) such as an inability to sleep, incessant worry, and general irritability. These symptoms are likely to cause disruptions in interpersonal relationships as well. So, while isolating problems into these three categories of intrapersonal, interpersonal, and external can help us better understand the challenges our helpees face, it is important to also understand how a problem at one level can affect functioning at the other levels.

Problem Domains

Problems that manifest in the **cognitive domain** are those that affect the ways in which we think or how we make sense of our experiences in the world.

Figure 6.2 Problem Levels

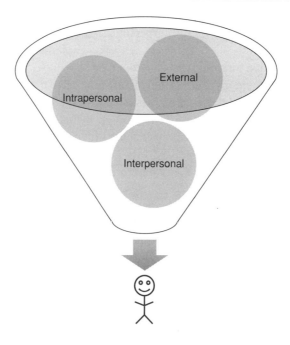

One example of this type of problem is not understanding a task, others, or a particular situation. Let's say that George is struggling at work because he can't understand how the machines work, and this, of course, makes it difficult for him to set them up at the start of his shift. This would be a situation where George probably needs more information or training. Examples of not fully understanding a social situation are when someone is inappropriately happy in a group of people who are upset or sad, or when someone asks someone a personal question that is inappropriate.

Sometimes cognitive problems appear as thinking patterns that are not particularly helpful or accurate. For example, Johannah is convinced that she is worthless, and worthless has become a lens that she uses interpret the experiences around her. When she got a B on her biology exam, she was sure that meant that she was stupid, despite evidence to the contrary. Here we see that when individuals habitually and automatically interpret their experiences through inaccurate thinking patterns, they may experience a variety of intrapersonal and interpersonal challenges. In this case, a helping approach such as cognitive behavioral therapy, mentioned in Chapter 3, might be used to help Johannah see the ways in which her assumptions shape how she interprets her experiences.

Illustration 6.3   Thinking

©iStockphoto.com/kimberrywood

Also in this category are difficulties that may be associated with neurodevelopment or processing difficulties. For example, some individuals "hear" voices that do not exist outside of their own mind. Others may be limited in their ability to make sense of complex or new and unfamiliar information. For example, a person who has difficulties following sequential directions given orally may have auditory processing challenges that require her to write down instructions so they can be better understood and remembered. These types of processing disorders refer to difficulties in interpreting information that is spoken or written, rather than impaired hearing or vision. All of these are examples of difficulties in the cognitive domain. And, as all of these examples show, having a good sense of what, exactly, the problem is, is very helpful for determining the best intervention strategy.

Problems in the **affective domain** tend to center around affect regulation. As mentioned in Chapter 5, the expression of emotion appears to involve complex

Illustration 6.4   Feeling

©iStockphoto.com/VasjaKoman

layers of neurological processes at the endocrine, autonomic, and cardiovascular levels (Siegel, 2012). As such, it is difficult to actually see emotions—we are typically cued into people's emotional state by observing their behaviors, as illustrated in the graphics included in Illustration 6.4. Emotional regulation is the management of emotional expression. Emotional regulation entails the trio processes of attending to an emotional cue, appraisal or making sense of that cue, and responding to that cue (Gross, 1998; Westphal & Bonanno, 2004). When people are well-regulated, they are able to respond to situations with appropriate emotional expressions. They are not over-controlled in their emotional expression, nor are they under-regulated. Emotional regulation also means that they are able to return to their normal, baseline homeostasis after an emotional trigger.

So, an important area of assessment is to determine the extent to which an individual is able to regulate his emotions in an appropriate and healthy way and return to normal functioning afterwards. For example, Keith was angry when a car cut him off in traffic, causing him to have to suddenly brake hard, scaring his children in the backseat. He cursed, noticed that his whole body tensed up, and then continued to drive. Within a few minutes, however, his body began to relax and he even began singing so that the youngest of his children, a baby, could go back to sleep as they continued on their journey. In this example, Keith was triggered, had an outburst of anger at being placed in a dangerous situation by another driver, and then soon calmed down. This is an example of emotional regulation. If he had continued to be angry without calming down for a long time, or if he had acted aggressively and, possibly, dangerously after being enraged by the other driver, we might say that he was having emotional regulation difficulties. Most agree that appropriate emotional self-regulation is essential for personal/individual health and interpersonal functioning (Gross, 1998; Gross & Thompson, 2007).

While the concept of a behavior problem conjures an image of someone who is out of control, acts inappropriately or, perhaps, is attempting to harm him or herself or others, here we are talking about behaviors more broadly. In this context, the **behavioural domain** actually refers to aggressive as well as passive actions. And here, too, we are referring to verbal and physical expressions. For example, talking is considered a behavior as much as walking, sitting, or cooking. Physical and physiological changes and actions are also included in this category. Let us go back to the example of Kevin above. When Kevin was triggered, his verbal behavior was to swear. Physiologically, his muscles tensed, and physically he continued to drive the car. We also see that

Photo 6.3 Doing

Jupiterimages/Creatas/Thinkstock

he soon responded by singing to his child. All of these are behaviors. And in our behavioral assessment, it is also important to take note of an inability to act at all. If a helpee inappropriately fails to respond with an expected action, and particularly if this constitutes a pattern of behavior (or, perhaps, better noted as a pattern of nonbehavior?), this observation should also be evident in our intervention planning.

Problem Levels and Domains

Many people experience problems at multiple levels and in multiple domains. For example, Adrian, age 14, is from the Navajo nation but living in a large urban area off his tribal lands. He has experienced multiple microaggressions in school that appear as "good-hearted" nicknames such as "chief," comments about his presumed habit of "spending too much time in the smoke lodge," and general diminished expectations from teachers about his academic abilities.

Let me take a moment here to explain this concept of *microaggressions*. This term refers to the everyday demeaning messages or indignations conveyed by individuals who are situated in dominant or privileged social groups toward members of nondominant social groups (Smith, Geroski, &

Figure 6.3 Problem Levels and Domains

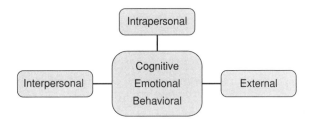

Tyler, 2014; Sue 2010). Sue et al. (2007) define microaggressions as the "brief and commonplace daily verbal, behavioral, or environmental indignities, whether intentional or unintentional, that communicate hostile, derogatory, or negative racial slights and insults toward people of color" (p. 271). Microaggressions are often subtle and they are frequently fairly invisitble. So subtle and so invisible, in fact, that perpetrators may not even be aware of committing them. This subtle quality of microaggressions often leaves recipients feeling confused. Part of this invisibility and resulting confusion is because microaggressions are an artifact of a cultural conditioning process that is permeated with bias and prejudice (Sue et al., 2007), and also because they are articulated differently than more overt forms of racism (Smith et al., 2014).

The effect of these external-level problems on Adrian, in our example here, is that he is beginning to see himself as incapable, and he is feeling alienated and lonely. In this case, we can see quite clearly that the problem of racism, which is not an intrapersonal or interpersonal deficit, affects how Adrian makes meaning of his experiences (cognitive domain), as well as his affective state. These feelings and unhelpful thoughts also sometimes manifest in behaviors that he is not proud of. Most recently, Adrian punched a peer who persisted in calling him "chief," even after Adrian asked him to stop. So, here we see that the problem with an original external source has creeped in and affected Adrian intrapersonally (feeling bad about himself) and interpersonally (striking out at others), and it seems to have taken over his thoughts, feelings, and behaviors.

Disentangling problem sources and having the ability to view the multiple and distinct manifestations of problems in thinking, feeling, and behaving domains enables us to address the different and various effects of problems in a systemic way. We will get back to Adrian's situation shortly—when we talk about goals and action plans. But first we should address the issue of the extent to which a helpee is motivated to change.

DETERMINING THE HELPEE'S INVESTMENT IN CHANGE

Embarking on a study of what enables people to make changes in their lives, Prochaska and DiClemente (1982) discovered that individuals who were engaged in smoking cessation, regardless of whether or not they were in therapy, passed through similar stages or steps in their change processes. These authors then found that these stages of change were also relevant for individuals who were involved in outpatient psychotherapy as well as those who struggled with alcohol addiction (Prochaska & DiClemente, 1986). These findings led to a model of change that is commonly known as the **stages of change** (Prochaska, Norcross, & DiClemente, 1994; also described as the *Transtheoretical Model of Change* by Norcross, Krebs, & Prochaska, 2010 and Prochaska, Johnson, & Lee, 2009).

Figure 6.4   Stages of Change

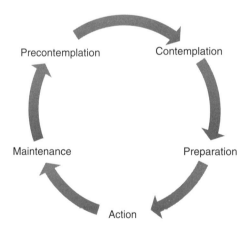

Adapted from:

Prochaska, J. O., Johnson, S., & Lee, P. (2009). The transtheoretical model of behavior change. In S. A. Shumaker, J. K., Ockene, & K. A. Riekert (Eds.), *The handbook of health behavior change* (3rd ed., pp. 59–83). New York, NY: Springer.

Prochaska, J. O., Norcross, J. C., & DiClemente, C. C. (1994). *Changing for good*. New York, NY: Harper/Collins.

Norcross, J. C., Krebs, P. M., & Prochaska, J. O. (2010). Stages of change. *Journal of Clinical Psychology: In Session, 67*(2), 143–154. doi:10.1002/jclp.20758

The concept behind this model proposes that change occurs for people as a process over time, and can be described as a series of motivational levels or stages (Norcross et al., 2010; Prochaska & DiClemente, 1986; Prochaska et al., 1994). The first and most basic stage is *precontemplation*. An individual at this level does not see that she has a problem, and thus has no motivation to change. The next stage is *contemplation*. An individual in this level acknowledges that she is having a problem and is beginning to consider the effects of that problem on her life. However, contemplative individuals often struggle to understand the causes and effects of the problem, and they are not yet committed to make change. The *preparation* stage refers to when an individual is planning to take action toward change. For example, an individual in preparation may have made a commitment to do something about the problem—perhaps she decides that she will buy a book about the problem she is struggling with. She is ready for action and may start

Figure 6.5 Stages of Change Explained

Precontemplation	• Not seeing a problem behavior or not considering change.
Contemplation	• Acknowledging that there is a problem but struggling with ambivalence. Not sure if the person wants to change.
Preparation	• Taking steps and getting ready to change.
Action	• Making changes and living with the new behaviors. At this stage the action of change requires consistent atttention and mindful action.
Maintenance	• Continuing to work on ensuring that the changes are integrated into the person's life.

Adapted from:

Prochaska, J. O., Johnson, S., & Lee, P. (2009). The transtheoretical model of behavior change. In S. A. Shumaker, J. K., Ockene, & K. A. Riekert (Eds.), *The handbook of health behavior change* (3rd ed., pp. 59–83). New York, NY: Springer.

Prochaska, J. O., Norcross, J. C., & DiClemente, C. C. (1994). *Changing for good*. New York, NY: Harper/Collins.

Norcross, J. C., Krebs, P. M., & Prochaska, J. O. (2010). Stages of change. *Journal of Clinical Psychology: In Session, 67*(2), 143–154. doi:10.1002/jclp.20758

VIDEO LINK:
Stages of
Change

outlining small steps that she might eventually take toward change. But typically, people in the preparation stage still struggle with residual ambivalence, and they are not yet taking active steps toward change. The *action* stage, as the name implies, is when an individual is actively engaged in behavior change. In this stage, the person is making choices and doing things differently. The work at this stage requires commitment and energy, however, and since change can be a difficult process, substantial results may be slow to come. The *maintenance* stage refers to the efforts an individual makes to preserve the changes that have been made. This is the work that needs to happen in order to avoid a relapse back into the problem.

The relevance of this work for helpers is that understanding the processes of change enables us to better aim our assistance in helping relationships to the helpee's level of motivation.

GOAL SETTING

Goal setting is a process of determining the direction of the helping so that meaningful, intentional work is always at the forefront. As mentioned in Chapter 1, when you work *with* a helpee to identify and establish goals for your work together (rather than identifying goals and strategies *for* him), you are more likely to develop a strong helping relationship (Gaston, 1990; Norcross, 2010) and be successful in your work (Norcross, 2010). This process begins with the **identification of the problem**, already discussed above, and moves in the direction of establishing concrete ideas about the intended outcome of the work.

Moving From the Problem to the Goal

After exploring the complexity of the problem, it is likely that you and the helpee noticed a variety of ways in which the problem is manifest. This is sometimes called a *problem list*. From this list, you will want to ask the helpee to offer a clear articulation of what problem (or what few problems) seem most important, at least initially, for your work together. You should then follow up by paraphrasing and clarifying what the helpee has said using his or her language and terminology (Chapter 7 describes paraphrasing and clarifying in detail). This will help ensure that you understand the concern that the helpee has and wants addressed in your work together.

In the above example of some of the difficulties that Adrian is having, the tutor worked with Adrian to identify the problem that he wanted most to address first. "Well it seems that you have talked about a number of challenges you have been facing these days, Adrian," the tutor said. "I heard you talk about being teased here at school and how it leaves you feeling isolated and mad. I also heard you say that you're having difficulties with your schoolwork and, especially, in believing in yourself. Am I getting this right?" This check-in invited Adrian to add to or make corrections. After Adrian nodded and said, "that's about it," the tutor went on. "Yeah, I can see how this list of things can feel overwhelming. Sometimes when it seems that the problems are big, it helps to just start with one or two small things that can be fixed. Are you with me?" Adrian nodded. "If you had to identify one or maybe two of the things on this list that we might be able to clear out of the way to start moving forward," she asked, "what might they be?" Adrian responded by saying, "This racism has got to go." And then he added, "And I really want to do better in my school work." We can see in his response that Adrian identified the need to address the external source of the problem—the racism, and also its effects on him personally, particularly in the area of his schoolwork.

Many believe that **focusing on success** is the most effective avenue for change; in fact, this is a guiding assumption of solution-focused brief therapy (Sklare, 2014), one of the therapeutic approaches in the area of positive psychology, which was described in Chapters 2 and 3. While this idea of focusing on success may seem obvious as written here now, interestingly, we as helpers often spend an extensive amount of time "helping" by talking about the problem, warning about the problem, coaxing individuals to end the problem, etc. Sometimes, the more attention we give to problems, the larger they become (Freeman, Epston, & Lobovits, 1997).

Focusing on a desired solution instead of what is not working orients the work of helping toward something that the helpee wants. Helpers can promote this positive-oriented goal thinking by inviting the helpee to consider what would be happening in her life if the problem was no longer in the way. This type of question is based on the idea of a *miracle question,* used in solution-focused brief therapy practices (Sklare, 2014). In the example with Adrian, then, the tutor asked, "Adrian, if racism was not a problem here in this school, what would your life look like here in school?" Immediately, Adrian responded that he'd have friends whom he trusted and he wouldn't feel so alone. Then the tutor asked, "And what does 'doing better in school' look like for you?" She then helped him articulate that having a solid B average in all of his classes would be a goal that he would like help to work toward. Notice that in this example, Adrian was able to articulate a fairly clear statement about his hopes. By asking the helpee what he would rather be doing, thinking, feeling, or experiencing, the goal emerges as a statement and intention that is meaningful to the helpee.

Clear Articulation of the Goal

Goals in helping relationships, then, reflect what the helpee would like to accomplish as a result of the work together. For this reason, they are typically **articulated from the perspective of the helpee**—what the helpee will think, feel, or do. They should be identified in clear and specific language as much as possible. For example, notice how Adrian's idea of "getting a B in all of my classes" is much more clear and specific than "doing better in school."

It is also helpful to **identify the domain** of the goal so that it offers more direct focus of the work that will follow. That is, is the goal about thinking differently (cognitive domain), feeling differently (affective domain), or doing something different (behavioral domain)? Notice how the goal of achieving a B average in all of the classes suggests an action—a behavior that will occur.

Goals in the affective domain typically include a feeling word and often reference an ability to regulate affect. For example, if Adrian was getting frustrated by the racism he experienced at school, which was clearly suggested in this case study, one goal for him might be to not let racism make him feel bad about himself. Another goal, this time in the behavioral domain, might be to not let racism control his behavior (i.e., cause him to lose control of his feelings and strike out at others). These are two concrete goals that Adrian can implement, because they are areas that are under his control: himself. Of course, the racism that triggers Adrian to feel and act in ways that are not helpful to him or others is a problem that exists in a realm that is external to Adrian. There is nothing wrong with him; there is a problem in the environment. While he can work to control his reaction to racism, the problem will likely continue to exist in his environment if it is not addressed by those who inhabit and, especially, those who have control over the school environment—teachers, administrators, students, and families. So, here, the goal of ending racism in the school is an appropriate goal, of course. It is one that compels the helper to be agent, meaning that she will probably need to work as an advocate for change in her school system for this goal to be realized. Helper actions related to advocacy are discussed in more detail in Chapter 8.

Two final components of effective goals are to create goals that are **realistic** and **measureable**. It makes no sense to work toward accomplishments that are not likely to happen; people tend to be motivated to continue to work toward goals when they sense that they are making progress or are able to attain those goals. In fact, Sklare (2014) reminds us that the ripple effects of change occur with small steps in the right direction. So, it is best to identify small goals (or subgoals within each goal statement) that are realistic or attainable. These, then, can set in motion a series of steps toward larger changes. For example, Adrian and the tutor will want to determine if the goal of a B average in all of his classes is reasonably attainable. If not, a goal of B's in three classes might be a better first goal, for example, and then the fourth class can be added once the first goal is attained. Goals that are realistically attainable and measureable help ensure positive outcomes.

The second goal in our case study above was identified as the goal to end racism in the school. This is a noble and important goal, but is it attainable? I, personally, would argue yes, this goal is attainable in every civil school and community. Given the insidious nature of racism and the multitude of faces that it shows, the question about measureability is also appropriate. In order to determine if there has been a change in racism, it would be helpful to think about what the school would look like if racism was not present. What would people in school be doing? Feeling? Thinking? What would an absence of racism look like, in the most concrete form possible?

Moving from the absence of racism as a goal to a smaller goal of everyone using respectful language, for example, might be a concrete first-step goal for this school. Engaging the full student body to work with teachers to identify the subtle nature of racial slurs, and to engage in, perhaps, a countdown of racialized language schoolwide, are two action steps that could be taken toward this goal. But again, I am getting ahead of myself into action plans. The point here is that when goals are defined concretely, it is much easier to determine, at a later date, if and when they have been realized.

Table 6.3 Goal Qualities

Goal Qualities	Goals should state what helpee will be doing (outside of the problem).
	Goals should be stated in simple, clear, positive, action-orienated language.
	Goals should be meaningful to the helpee.
	Goals should be articulated in domain-specific language (cognitive, affective, behavioral).
	Goals should be realistic.
	Goals should be measureable.

ACTION PLANS AND EXPECTATIONS

You may have noticed that I got a little ahead of myself a few times in the discussion about goals to talking about action steps and plans. That is because goal setting is intimately tied to action plans—what the helper and helpee will do to achieve those goals. A plan of action outlines what actions the helpee is committed to taking and what actions the helper will take to enable the accomplishment of the identified goals. Remember that in Chapter 1 it was pointed out that structure and focus in helping is more likely to lead to positive outcomes (Hubble, Duncan, Miller, & Wampold, 2010). The action plan structures the "help" that happens in helping relationships. Action plans are a key component of helping contracts.

Helping theories, such as those mentioned in Chapter 3, offer direction for helper actions. As mentioned, specific directions for action in the various helping theories are based on their underlying conceptualizations about how people grow, develop, and change, and also on the etiology of problems. Based on these underlying assumptions, helping theories inform the content of helper action plans.

For example, psychodynamic helping theories are based, very generally, on the idea that problems develop from unresolved conflicts, unconscious drives, maladaptive defense mechanisms, or the inadequate completion of various developmental tasks during childhood or the lifespan (Boyd & Bee, 2011; Goldhaber, 2000; Miller, 2002). Clinical helpers working from these perspectives develop a strong therapeutic relationship, work to promote insight, and try to uncover the meanings and motivations that cause problematic thoughts, behaviors, and affect. They promote insight as a mechanism of change.

As mentioned in Chapters 2 and 3, a number of philosophical ideas and therapeutic practices fall under the category of humanistic approaches to helping. They are united by a strong philosophical belief in people's capacity to make rational choices and reach their maximum potential. Helpers working from this perspective will honor their helpees as the authorities of their own lives and use the therapeutic relationship to create an environment that offers ideal conditions for helpees to learn and grow (Cain, 2002). Attachment theory focuses on caregiver responsiveness in the creation of parent–child attachment bonds, which become working models for future relationships (Ainsworth, 1973; Ainsworth, Blehar, Waters, & Wall, 1978; Bowlby, 1969; 1988). Action plans that are based on attachment principles typically focus on developing caregiver responsiveness and facilitating children's self-regulation and competence (Blaustein & Kinniburgh, 2010).

Behavioral theories suggest that behavior is shaped by antecedents and reinforcements in the environment (Boyd & Bee, 2011; Goldhaber, 2000). Action plans based on behavioral principles focus on variables in the environment that can be manipulated to stimulate or reinforce desired responses (Sommers-Flanagan & Sommers-Flanagan, 2004). Cognitive behavioral theory–oriented helpers attend to the cognitive processes that shape behavioral or emotional responses to environmental stimuli. Action plans oriented in this way would focus on developing helpee awareness of thought processes that limit him or her in some way (Creed, Reisweber, & Beck, 2011; Leahy, 2003; Sommers-Flanagan & Sommers-Flanagan, 2004). Finally, as discussed in Chapter 3, contemporary theories focus on external and/or socially constructed variables that affect helpees' lives, and action plans related to these theories tend to include careful examination of ideas and systems that are disempowering, and they focus on developing helpee agency. Many are also oriented toward advocacy at system levels.

These helping theories, then, inform the content of helping. They articulate what will happen to reach the identified goals. As mentioned, the coverage of these theories in this text is introductory. You will need to acquire more depth in these theories and knowledge in other help-related theories and practices that are associated with your specific practice area in order to be most effective in helping. For example, teachers use their knowledge of pedagogy to inform their work; physical therapists use their knowledge about the body musculature to develop action plans; career advisors rely on information and knowledge about work and education to inform the practices that they use in helping.

Regardless of the particular content area of helping, action plans are typically conceptualized and written as a series of steps or strategies that will be used to reach each identified goal. They should clearly and simply articulate the **strategy** that will be used to accomplish each specific **goal**. Using our case example of Adrian, notice how the action plan below lists responsibilities or strategies for the helpee (Adrian) and for the helper.

ACTION PLAN

Goal: Adrian will earn a B average in all of his classes

Adrian will

1. Attend afterschool tutoring for an hour every day after school before basketball practice from Monday through Thursday.

2. Bring all necessary books and laptop computer for completing his homework assignments to tutoring each day.

3. Be focused in tutoring on his homework assignments (i.e., he will not be walking around the room and talking to other students in the room).

4. Signal a need for help with his schoolwork during tutoring by raising his hand. If someone is working with the tutor, Adrian will list his name (as is the practice in the tutoring program).

The tutor will

1. Offer assistance to Adrian when he follows the tutoring protocols of raising his hand or listing his name.

2. Provide a homework sheet for Adrian to use for the following day.

3. Sign Adrian's tutoring attendance form when Adrian asks.

4. Enforce the rules of afterschool tutoring (quiet space, raised hands/listing name, one reminder then out).

Naming the individual responsible for each component of the action plan articulates the commitments of the work that will happen within the helping contract. It is important that the helper and the helpee not commit to actions that they not able to fulfill. Finally, action plans should be reviewed periodically, to determine if goals have been met or to determine whether the goals or strategies need to be adjusted in some way.

HELPER POSITIONING

Positioning theory was first introduced into the field of psychology by Harre and his colleagues (see Harre & Moghaddam, 2003; Harre & Van Langenhove, 1991) and is probably best described as a method of analyzing human interaction. Positioning theory attempts to describe human interaction by focusing on the ways in which individuals participate in conversations (Davies & Harre, 1999). It looks at how social interactions unfold according to local and often unspoken rules of engagement, and conventions of conduct and meaning (Harre & Moghaddam, 2003). Positioning theorists are particularly interested in the ways in which history, culture, and social context shape how individuals are invited into and maintain speaking positions when they are engaged with others. While not traditionally included in most texts on helping relationships, I include it here because it has important implications for how helpers engage in helping relationships.

Basic Tenets of Positioning Theory

Positioning theory encourages us to be aware of the ways in which invitations to speak in social interactions are governed by the rules and conventions of those social encounters (Harre & Moghaddam, 2003). The metaphor of *position*, sometimes referred to as *subject position*, refers to the relative authority or standing that one has in various social contexts. One's position is, in essence, one's role in a particular social interaction (Drewery, 2005). For example, Mr. Harvey is a probation officer assigned to Caroline. Caroline was court-ordered to meet regularly with Mr. Harvey in lieu of jail sentencing for a felony related to a drug conviction. Upon introduction, Mr. Harvey offers his hand in greeting, saying, "Hi Caroline. I am Mr. Harvey. I will be monitoring your progress according to the sentencing agreement. Should we sit down and talk about how this is going to work?" Despite the (appropriate) gesture of offering his hand and suggesting that Caroline has a choice about sitting down to meet with him, Mr. Harvey is clearly in the position of authority in this encounter. This position of authority is appropriate to the rules and conventions of this particular type of social encounter involving probation officers and convicted felons.

Subject positions dictate speaking positions. As illustrated in the above example, the individual who has the most authority in a social encounter is positioned to invite others into conversation in particular ways. Introducing himself formally with his surname (Mr. Harvey), using her first name rather than the more formal surname, and taking charge of the conversation, including the reference to his role to monitor her progress, offer evidence of his subject position relative to hers. We see that the rules of engagement in this situation relegate Caroline into a speaking position that is in response to the questions and directions of Mr. Harvey. He has the power, she doesn't.

A *position call* is a structuring statement or behavior that calls for a particular, expected response. It is an invitation to interact in a specific way in a particular social encounter. The individual who is in control of the conversation typically issues position calls for others to join in, but position calls are also structured into social encounters based on the context of the interchange. For example, it is the teacher who issues position calls in the classroom. It is the judge who has this power in the courtroom. It is the probation officer, Mr. Harvey, who issued the position call to Caroline in the example mentioned above. All of these examples are in accordance to normal rules and conventions of these particular settings.

Power dynamics, positions of privilege, hierarchical social structures, and markers of social capital invite speaking positions and influence the rules of engagement in most social encounters. Keep in mind that these rules of engagement and position calls typically occur out of active awareness of the individual participants in most social encounters. They are typically not verbally acknowledged or discussed. And this is true, as well, in most helping relationships. Helpees are often invited into conversations that are dictated by helpers. They are typically encouraged to pursue goals and take action that is recommended, required, or highly suggested by others. We see that the rules of encounter in many helping relationships are based on conventions that privilege the knowledge, insight, education or training, and skill of the helper over that of the helpee.

Individuals who have the status to dictate what happens in a social encounter are in an *agent* position. When position calls invite individuals into compromised or response positions, these are called *subjugated* or *passive* positions (Drewery, 2005). For example, the boss dictates who can speak and what topic is relevant in an office meeting. A teacher doles out speaking rights in a classroom. A coach tells her team when practice occurs, what to do during practice, and decides who gets starting positions in the next game or match. Parents also typically assume this role at home.

Van Langenhove and Harre (1994) point out, however, that position calls can be accepted, or they can be resisted or changed. Individuals can resist a position call by *repositioning* themselves in a more favorable way. For example, a bus driver participating in a strike regarding more equitable wages is repositioning himself by refusing to provide services without adequate compensation. A student who talks back to the teacher may be vying for an upper hand or more powerful position in the classroom. A woman who files for divorce due to her adulterous spouse is making a statement of agency. Most pertinent to our discussion here: a helpee who refuses to work toward a specific goal or who takes action in directions that were not discussed in the action plan is expressing agency. For this reason, it is critical that helpees be involved in making the decisions that affect their lives, that action plans be constructed *with* rather than for helpees, and that helping contracts (especially goals and action plans) are reevaluated and renegotiated after a period of time.

Discourses and Position Calls

A final important point here about positioning theory takes us back to the concept of discourse, discussed in Chapter 2. Remember that the term *discourse* was introduced by Foucault (1972) in reference to the taken-for-granted or structuring ideas in a given culture that shape everyday understandings. One way to think about a discourse is to consider a stereotype—a generalized idea about a group of individuals. Relevant here is the point that discourses offer ideas about individuals and social exchanges that prompt particular subject positions (Winslade, 2005) which, in turn, issue various position calls. That is, discourses shape how individuals interact with each other. And, because discourses shape social encounters in this way, social constructionists argue that discourses are *prescriptive* (Drewery & Winslade, 1997).

Recall that Adrian, the young man we have been discussing in the case study throughout this chapter, informed his tutor that he was experiencing racism in school. One example that he gave his tutor was that his peers were calling him "chief," and they also claimed that it was a just a "harmless" nickname. A quick check in Google images confirms that social perceptions about Native Americans are shaped by images of dark men in feather headdresses, perhaps with tomahawk in hand, and slender women with long, straight dark hair grinding corn over a stone. These images are fortified in social memory with contemporary ideas suggesting that Native Americans, across the hundreds of various Indian tribes, are alike and share common characteristics, such as alcoholism and a propensity for dancing around bonfires. For centuries, these discourses have offered deficit positioning to Native Americans, based on ideas that they are unable to function adequately in contemporary society (even as that has changed over the centuries) and are in need of being educated and taken care of by others in the dominant culture. The "nickname" given to Adrian, then, is steeped in these deficit Indian discourses; it is a mircroaggression that positions him as an "other" in his local school community. Adrian knows that being "chief" in this school context does not carry the honor bestowed upon individuals who earned this title in legitimate Indian contexts. The history of oppression of Native Americans in the United States not only renders this nickname an insult when it is imposed by someone outside of one's Indian tribe, it also reinforces still-existing systems of power and privilege.

Drewery (2005) speaks of discourses as "ways of speaking that reflect interwoven sets of power relations . . . " (p. 313). Discourses shape the way we are seen by others, and position calls are awarded accordingly. Mother discourses, for example, invite specific conventions of behavior and invite certain conversations with and about mothers. These are different than professor or doctor discourses, and with them come different expectations and conversations. Women discourses are different than men discourses. Gay, straight, Black, or White, all of these notions of identity are shaped by ideas and conventions that dictate position calls and speaking positions. And within all of these categories are embedded ideas and opportunities for social capital or power.

Of course, there are always multiple discourses on offer at any given time. But it is not hard to see the powerful and unquestioned influence that discourses have in shaping even the most ostensibly benign encounters of everyday life.

Relevance of Positioning Theory on Helping Relationships

Understanding these basic components of positioning theory is relevant to the work of helpers in two important ways. First, positioning theory helps us understand situations that may be problematic to the individuals with whom we work. It offers a language for describing the experience of being invited into subjugated positions. Talking with a helper who understands the social implications of strong and disempowering discourses and how position calls manifest in social encounters as a result of an unequal distribution of power can be liberating. When we invite examination of the discourses that position helpees unfavorably, and when we encourage helpees to resist power positions that are undesirable, space is created for an opportunity to step into agency. When we (helpers and helpees) resist the positions on offer from dominant discourses, we have an opportunity to make decisions about who we want to be in the world and how we want to live our lives. Ways in which these conversations can be initiated and carried out by helpers are discussed in Chapters 7 and 8 (see Broaching Conversations and Deconstructing Conversations).

Second, as with other social exchanges, the helping relationship also is one where position calls are made and subject positions are taken up. In fact, even before the helper and helpee meet, the helping relationship is structured by discourses and practices from which the helping is negotiated (Winslade, Crocket, & Monk, 1997). Take, for example, the agent position available to helpers who are awarded social capital for their expert knowledge and benevolent spirit (i.e., "how wonderful that they are do-good helpers"). In contrast, helpees are those in need of services, and they often arrive into the helping relationship with their named deficits in hand, positioned as needy client, patient, disabled, victim, refugee, etc. These are titles and discourses that afford little social capital and offer limited agency in the helping process.

Appropriately attending to power influences in helping relationships can have the effect of promoting helpee agency. This is a practice that enables the helpee to be in charge of his decisions and how he wants to live his life. The helping skill of immediacy, also discussed in Chapter 8, is an important tool to use in examining these types of helping relationship dynamics.

CHAPTER SUMMARY

This chapter outlines important steps to take when initiating a helping relationship. Helping should always begin with a respectful welcoming as well as a description of what services the helper can offer. The importance of establishing a helping contract is discussed, and that contract should be based on a careful examination of the problem as well as the helpee's readiness for change. The helping contract, whether formal or not, should include a clear articulation of goals that will be addressed in the helping; these goals are best when established through a collaborative process. Additionally, strategies or action steps for each goal should be identified, with clear reference to the responsibilities that will be shouldered by both the helper and the helpee. Finally, the discussion about positioning theory illuminated the importance of addressing the ways in which discourses and power dynamics affect helpees' lives and how they enter into helping relationships as well. Positioning theory offers an important caution to helpers to attend to the ways in which helping relationships should be structured to promote agency and positive change.

DISCUSSION QUESTIONS

1. Identify key components of the helping contract and good helping goals.

2. Explain the concept of microaggressions and identify some microaggressions that you have become aware of in some of the contexts of your life.

3. How does positioning theory relate to the work of nonclinical helpers, and what should helpers be mindful of when working with others?

4. How can knowledge about stages of change be used to promote success in helping relationships?

CHAPTER 7

LISTENING AND BASIC RESPONDING SKILLS IN HELPING CONVERSATIONS

LEARNING OBJECTIVES

1. Articulate the importance of and describe how to display attentive listening and empathy

2. Articulate the importance of and describe how to use reflections, paraphrases, and questions in helping conversations

3. Articulate the importance of and describe how to engage in broaching conversations

INTRODUCTION

People do not typically seek help when things are going well. They need help when things are not working—when they are stuck, confused, sad, angry, or in need of direction. Sometimes, people ask for help when they don't really seem to want it, and sometimes they seek help when they really don't want to change. Some people appear to have the expectation that helpers will solve their problems for them—as if, by magic, helpers can take the difficulties away. Others want to solve their own problems without help, and they are motivated to change. One thing we do know in the business of helping is that no two helpees and no two helping situations will be the same.

Another thing that we know about helping is that we enter into the lives of others when they are not at their best. It is hard to be in pain, and it is also difficult to sit with someone in pain. It is hard to be stuck and feel challenged; it is also very difficult to find a way to help others when their challenges seem insurmountably hearty and impermeable to change. When helpees feel ashamed that they need help and are reluctant to talk about their difficulties, helpers often feel frustrated. The challenges that helpees bring into helping relationships are challenges that are not easily solvable; if they were easy, the helpee probably would have figured them out already and would not be seeking help. Clearly, the process of helping is complex—there are no easy answers or exact formulas.

Some of the best tools of helping are attentive listening, being emotionally present and available, and offering an outside perspective—a new way of thinking or specific knowledge in the particular area. In this chapter, we will focus on the first two of these: basic listening and responding skills and being emotionally present and available. More specifically, we will discuss the helping conversation skills of listening, expressing empathy, reflecting, paraphrasing, and asking questions. I will explain how and why each of these skills is used and, when appropriate, offer a recipe for its use. Using this term, *recipe*, suggests that there is an exact procedure for these helping skills. This is not the case in helping skills; the recipe identifies key ingredients but is up to the helper to modify the recipe as needed for the given situation.

LISTENING AND BASIC RESPONDING SKILLS

Listening and responding are interconnected helping behaviors—the process of taking in information is always connected to the process of responding (even if that response is an intentional nonresponse). So, it is difficult to talk about either of these without the other. Also critical here is the concept of intentionality. In helping conversations, it is important for helpers to be able to calibrate their responses according to what they hear from the helpee. That is, helpers must first listen, then think—consider carefully—how to respond, and then, finally, respond accordingly. It may look like practiced helpers are responding automatically, but all good helpers are thoughtful about their responses.

ATTENTIVE LISTENING

Attentive or active listening are the terms used for how helpers position themselves in helping conversations. To fully understand what attentive listening means, consider the distinction between *hearing* and *listening*. Hearing refers to receiving sensory input through the ears; listening refers to a cognitive process of making sense out of what has been heard. Listening requires selective attention and focus, which is why it is called attentive listening.

In helping conversations, listening also includes the important and subtle component of being able to demonstrate that you are listening. That is, if you are listening to the helpee, he needs to know it. Our discussion here, then, begins with a review of listening postures that communicate that you are solely focused on the helpee. Then we will talk about what helpers should listen for, obstacles that get in the way of attentive listening, and how to manage multiple messages expressed by the helpee.

Listening Postures

Egan (2010) has been credited for coining the SOLER acronym (see Table 7.1) to name five helpful listening postures. As I review these postures, keep in mind that they are suggestions. Rigidly adhering to any of them could very well make the helping conversation feel strained or awkward.

- S stands for sitting **straight and squarely** facing the helpee. This also includes maintaining an appropriate physical distance. The intent is to communicate that the helpee has your undivided attention.

  To sit squarely, you may want to arrange your chair so that it is facing the helpee—perhaps at a slight angle. Be sure to sit close enough to be able to see the helpee's facial expressions and to ensure that she can talk in a comfortable speaking voice. But be careful not to crowd. It may not be appropriate to sit directly facing the helpee because doing so may seem a bit unnatural and make the helpee feel uncomfortable and unable to relax and engage in conversation. The important thing is to be aware of the nuances of the helping relationship and adjust your S posture accordingly. One way to do this is to invite the helpee to select her seat before sitting yourself. Then you can check in with her as you adjust your chair by moving closer or farther way.

  Example:

  - *Helper:* Where would you like to sit today? (pointing to the three open chairs in the room)
  - *Helpee:* Okay, I'll sit here.
  - *Helper:* Oh, it feels like I'm sitting all the way across the room! Do you mind if I pull this chair a little bit closer?

  The point is to be in a physical position that communicates full attention to the helpee without it feeling awkward.

- O stands for **open posture.**

  Openness is communicated in a number of ways in a variety of contexts, but the point is to communicate the message that you are available for listening without distractions and regardless of what the helpee has to say. Be sure to clear an appropriate space by not having a number of items in front of you and, if possible, avoid sitting behind a desk. Try to relax your body so that it is not rigid, perhaps by not crossing your arms across your chest.

  It is important to remember that some helpees may not have a clear understanding of the parameters of what helping relationships can offer. Also, some helpees enter into helping relationships because they have had experiences of mistrust and boundary crossings in other relationships in their lives. Added to this, the social meaning of physical posturing varies by context, culture, and social norms. The physical communication of openness is an area where confusion and misunderstandings can easily happen. So, be thoughtful in how you gesture the intent of openness. A particular caution should be noted when working across genders as we live in a context of sexualized and power-laden cross-gender relationships. Helpers need to be aware of how their body posture communicates listening without being distracting or confusing, and without sending potentially mixed messages.

- L stands for **leaning forward.**

  Leaning forward is helpful because it secures helper attention on the helpee and communicates that the helper is available for listening. It is not appropriate to lean forward in all contexts, however, as doing so may make some helpees uncomfortable or think that they are under scrutiny. So, you should take intensity and context into account, and use this L posture accordingly. Gently moving in one's seat during the helping conversation is very appropriate as it is natural to move around a bit, and this can have the effect of altering the intensity during the helping conversation.

- E stands for **eye contact.**

  Looking at the helpee while he is talking assures him that you are listening, but eye contact really should fluctuate between looking directly at the helpee and looking away periodically. Direct steady eye contact—a direct stare—clearly is inappropriate; eye contact should be maintained in a natural way.

  Helpers should be sensitive to the times when the helpee seems uncomfortable and be careful not to impose direct eye contact during those times. Yet, direct and confident eye contact is helpful in other situations.

So, the advice is for normal and appropriate eye contact. Most importantly, the helper's eye contact should express attentiveness, emotional connection, and empathy. The helper should never require the helpee to look back at her directly in the eyes, and she should also refrain from assuming meaning when the helpee avoids direct eye contact. The appropriateness of engaging in direct eye contact is culturally nuanced, and part of helper cross-cultural competence is to be aware of the ways in which this is perceived in the helpee's culture or family system, and in the social and discursive context of the particular helping relationship.

- R stands for assuming a **relaxed stance.**

  What constitutes being "relaxed" and how relaxed you should be is subject to the standards and practices in different contexts and cultures. Some helpees may not feel confident with helpers who appear too relaxed or casual. A high degree of formality, on the other hand, may be perceived as being emotionally unavailable. Fidgeting may communicate a lack of interest, desire to be somewhere else, or helper incompetence. Be sure to consider the norms of your work setting and communicate professionalism accordingly. Egan's point here is that the helper should assume a posture that puts the helpee at ease—that communicates that the helper is comfortable with and interested in the helpee.

In addition to the SOLER listening postures, **nonverbal gestures** and **minimal verbalizations** are also used to signal to the helpee that he has the helper's

Table 7.1 Active Listening Postures

Listening Postures
Straight and square
Open posture
Lean forward
Eye contact
Relaxed stance
Nonverbal gestures
Minimal verbalizations

VIDEO LINK:
Listening

attention. For example, smiling along with the helpee when she smiles, looking surprised when the helpee says something surprising, and expressing concern when the helpee is recounting a troubling incident are all examples of nonverbal listening gestures. Examples of minimal verbalizations include *mmmm, uh huh,* and occasional comments such as *yes, really,* and *I see.*

What to Listen For

Now that we have discussed attentive listening postures, we will now turn our attention to what kinds of things helpers should pay particular attention to. Table 7.2 outlines the major concepts we will discuss in this section.

To best understand the helpee, we are always listening for cues. **Cues** are signals—pieces of information that have a particular significance in the helping conversation. For example, when a conversation always seems to drift back to a mention of the helpee's dog, this is a cue that the dog is important to the helpee. Cues come from verbal and nonverbal messages, inconsistencies between messages, context, meaning-making, and discourse positioning. These concepts are discussed in more detail below and summarized in Tables 7.3 and 7.4.

Table 7.2 What to Listen For: Important Cues

Helpers Attend to These Cues:	
Verbal messages	The ways in which helpees understand themselves, their situation, and the problems they face
Nonverbal messages	The affect and behavioral communications of the helpee
Inconsistent messages	Discrepancies between or mixed verbal and nonverbal communications signaling multiple feelings, confusion, reluctance, or lack of awareness
Context	That which is significant in the helpee's life and situations that help us understand and/or give rise to or maintain the problem
Meaning-making processes	The ways in which helpees understand themselves, their situations, and the challenges they encounter
Discourse positions	How understandings and identity are framed by ideas and stereotypes in larger society

Cues alert us to core messages. A **core message** is the important theme that cuts across or underlies many of the helpee's stories and communications. In some cases, the theme or core message is obvious and clearly articulated. For example, Jose might come right in to the helping conversation telling the helper that he is struggling with procrastination and explain why that is a problem for him. In other cases, however, the core message may be less clear to the helpee, the helper, or both. Helpees don't always know what they need help with, and they don't always have insight into their own thinking, feeling, and behavioral processes. So, attentive listening requires helpers to attend to the multiple cues that signify a core message. For example, Gina comes to the helper in the school planning room almost daily because she never seems to have her homework completed. It is only after spending time reviewing her homework patterns with the helper that they realize that the problem is procrastination. Attending to the accumulation of multiple and sometimes varied cues is one of the important things that helpers do when they are listening in helping conversations.

Verbal Messages

Verbal messages, of course, are the words that are used to communicate. When listening to what your helpee is saying, you will want to pay attention to the **content** of her message—the subject of what is being talked about. Be particularly attentive to **word choice**. For example, when Carolina says that she *hates* her teacher, the word *hate* clearly has a different intent than if she had said that she *loves* her teacher. Strong words tend to signal an emotional intensity around a particular topic, thus cuing its significance. Notice that if Carolina had said "I like my teacher okay," our interest would not have been piqued in the same way. You will also want to attend to the **frequency** of word use. When a helpee notes that he is *sad* multiple times during a helping conversation, it is an obvious a cue that we need to pay attention to his sadness.

When we listen to the helpee's use of language, and specifically to word choice, it is important to understand the **unique meaning** of the words (and concepts and phrases) used—the ways in which the helpee uses language and understands his experiences. Words have different meanings for different people. The meanings of words and phrases are illuminated by spoken language as well as unspoken nunaces that reflect different cultures and social settings. Clearly, language usage varies across social and cultural settings. For example, a comment about *safety* for one person may refer to physical safety whereas the reference may be about emotional safety to someone else. *Hooking up* means one thing to people of middle age and something very different to contemporary youth.

We can never assume that our understandings about what others say are correct; we must always ask. For example, a helper working with a mother who comments, "My children are very religious" asks, "Can you tell me a little bit more about what you mean by 'very religious'?"

It is also important to listen to **how** words are communicated. The inflections and tone in statements offer cues about the meanings and significance of what is being said. For example, a slight inflection at the end of a word can change a statement into a question. Speaking loudly or rapidly can signal anxiety or frustration. Or not. We always want to be conservative when attempting to interpret these subtle cues; we should make no assumptions. This underscores the importance of checking out our interpretations about the meaning of what we see and hear. For example, if you wonder if the rapid speech means that the helpee is anxious, simply asking is appropriate. For example, "Frank, I notice that you're speaking very rapidly. I was wondering if that means that you're a little bit anxious about this upcoming project?"

Nonverbal Messages

Nonverbal communications include the helpee's expressions of **emotion** and **behaviors**. If a helpee suddenly looks down while speaking about a particular incident, this behavior may be a cue that the incident is significant and warrants further exploration. Similarly, an emotional response of tearing up or turning red while talking about something signals its importance. Helpee behaviors of arriving late or changing the subject frequently communicate a

Table 7.3 Verbal and Nonverbal Messages

Verbal Messages	Nonverbal Messages
Content	Posture
Word choice	Expressions of emotion
Frequency	Observable behaviors
Unique meaning	
Inflections	
Tone	

message as well. In all of these cases, attending to these nonverbal messages brings depth to understanding the helpee or the helping situation. But, again, it is important for the helper to check out interpretations since we never know what the helpee is really thinking and feeling.

Inconsistent Messages

When affect, behavior, words, or intentions are used consistently, the message typically is fairly clear. When we encounter mixed messages from helpees, however—when what they say is not what they are doing, or what they seem to be feeling—then it is difficult to fully understand the message. Consider these examples:

- Five year-old Mohammad is crying, stamping his foot, and saying that he hates his teacher. These behaviors and emotional expressions are very consistent with one another, and it seems fairly clear that he is angry about something that is happening at school. Additional cues offered later will serve to confirm this early hypothesis or shape it into a more accurate picture of the situation that is challenging for this little guy.

- Five year-old Mohammad is crying and kicking when his father opens the car door for him so he can go into preschool. But then he smiles and runs to his teacher in an open embrace when he walks in the door. These inconsistencies offer a less clear picture of what is happening for Mohammad.

It is important to pay attention to inconsistencies because they may signal helpee confusion, mixed feelings, reluctance, or a lack of awareness. They also may point to a difficulty or a core message that warrants further exploration. At the very least, inconsistencies offer nuanced details to the stories of people's complex lives. Here we will talk about a variety of inconsistencies that helpers sometimes encounter. These are also summarized in Table 7.4.

You may notice **inconsistences between verbal statements** made by the helpee. For example, the helpee assures you that she understands something you have just said, but a short time later, comments that she is somewhat "confused" about it. You may also witness **inconsistencies between verbal and nonverbal messages**. For example, a helpee says that he is very happy to be working with you but then consistently shows up late, is less than forthcoming in what he talks about, and does not follow up with assigned tasks. This represents a discrepancy between what he says and his nonverbal behavior.

Table 7.4 Types of Inconsistences

Between verbal statements
Between verbal and nonverbal messages
Between what one says and what one does
Between expressed values or beliefs and what one does

Another example of this is if a helpee says that she is *sad* but displays body language that suggests relief and smiles when talking about a recent split up with her partner.

Sometimes we witness an **inconsistency between what one says and what one does.** For example, a mother may say that she is very strict with her child but you notice that her child seems to be able to do whatever she wants. We also may see **inconsistencies between the helpee's values or beliefs and behaviors.** For example, a helpee asserts that he has strong values about treating women with respect, but you know that his girlfriend is temporarily living in a shelter for victims of domestic violence and he was the perpetrator.

Helper responses to inconsistencies are discussed under Confrontation in Chapter 8. The purpose of this discussion here is to point out the importance of noticing discrepancies and considering what they may mean to the helpee, the problem, and the helping relationship.

Context

While listening, helpers also try to understand the context of the helpee's concerns. The term *context* is used here in reference to the things that are significant in the helpee's life. Context helps us understand the helpee and it also helps us determine what might be most relevant in our work with the helpee. Depending on the particular helping contract we are working under, of course, these aspects of context often warrant particular attention: the helpee's family, community, social location, personal abilities, interests, beliefs, hopes, experiences, and developmental milestones. Context also refers to those things that may have given rise to or may maintain the problem or concern. For example, a helpee's house has burned down, so that is the context of why he needs help.

Not all of the aspects of context mentioned above are relevant for helping in every situation. The goals of the helping contract and circumstances unique to the helpee will determine what particular aspects of context are most relevant for the work that needs to be done. For example, Linda lives in a family that has many close relationships and values interconnectedness. She and many members in her family have not traveled across their own state lines, and the very idea of going across the country to attend college may be a source of concern and resistance for Linda and her family. In this case, understanding the context of Linda's family is important to the helper who is working with Linda in regard to college decision-making. Linda's classmate, Monica, also has a family that is interconnected, but her family has a strong value on independence. She has traveled with her family in and out of the country, and her decision to move far from home to attend college is met with enthusiasm in her family. In this second example, family context clearly also is important to Monica's college decision-making process. If these girls were seeking help from a math tutor, however, family context would probably be less important to the helping situations. Far more important would be the number of math classes they had taken, how they did in those classes, and what aspects of math were challenging for them.

Meaning-Making

Helpers are advised to listen carefully for how helpees understand themselves, their situations, and the problems they encounter. The ways in which understandings are constructed are what I call *meaning-making processes*. For example, what stories does the helpee tell about his experiences? What etiological frame of reference does he seem to be using to interpret or make sense of his situation? What beliefs are evident in what he says? What values seem to underlie his actions? What expectations and hopes does he have for himself and others? All of these offer insight into the ways in which helpees make sense of their world and the challenges they face.

We want to attend to the helpee's meaning-making processes because understanding how someone makes sense of her experiences provides excellent direction for how we can intervene to help. For example, if Enid believes that her daughter is not adjusting well in school because of her recent divorce, that understanding offers the teacher a direction to provide additional support to this child. If Enid approaches the teacher with concerns about her daughter being bullied in school, the teacher is cued into a very different response. In both of these examples, the ways in which Enid makes sense of her daughter's difficulties cues the teacher into how she can help.

Discourse Positions

People are influenced by larger social understandings and generalizations when creating a sense of self (identity) and also when attempting to make sense of the situations in which they find themselves. Societal or cultural ideas that influence how people think, and that offer ideas about how people should behave and how things should be done are what we called *discourses* in Chapters 2 and 6. Discourses influence how we think, how we behave, how we make sense of our world, and how we define ourselves. When our identities and our understandings about others and the world around us are based on discourses in larger society that are not relevant or that are unhelpful, they can, of course, be very destructive. For this reason, it is helpful to determine what discourses are particularly influential in the lives of our helpees.

For example, David is talking to his counselor because he has experienced depression and has had suicidal thoughts in the past. As the conversation progresses, it is clear that David is beginning to question his sexual orientation. He has never been attracted to women, and he is beginning to see that he experiences glimmers of attraction to a few male classmates at college. However, the counselor learns that in David's family, as well as the school and community where David grew up, homosexuality was considered a sin. This idea of sin is paralleled in historic and current contemporary discourses that invite us to think of homosexuality as a form of mental illness or a choice—a bad choice (e.g., Nuckolls, 2008). David, it turns out, has even witnessed verbal and physical violence perpetrated against individuals who identify as gay. With this backdrop, David struggles with making meaning of his attraction to men. It may be that the depression and suicidal gestures are indications of internalized self-hatred. In this case, it seems obvious that David's alignment with discourses of intolerance and expressions of hate influences how he is making sense of his developing awareness of his own sexual orientation.

It is important to note that in this situation, David's concerns are not imagined; the social context of people's lives have a profound influence on how they think, how they feel, and the decisions they make. As this example shows, discourses are not neutral. Discourses have very real effects on people's lives. David's concerns about emotional and physical safety in his community and, perhaps, family of origin, are valid concerns. This is true even if David is living in a local college community where sexual orientation discourses position him less harshly.

Our conversation here focuses on listening to how helpees make meanings about self and others. The use of deconstructing conversations is an important skill discussed in Chapter 8 that can be used to explore discourses that influ-ence helpees' meaning-making processes.

Obstacles to Listening

Many of us can recall a time when a helper barraged us with advice when we really just wanted someone to listen, and most of us have had the experi-ence of being in a conversation with someone who completely missed what we were saying. The seemingly simplistic skill of attentive listening is actually more challenging than it appears. Here we will discuss some common impediments to attentive listening.

When you are **tired or distracted**, your ability to stay focused on listening can be impaired. Related to this, Halstead, Wagner, Vivero, and Ferkol (2002) suggest that **feeling hurried and pressured** to get work done or to come to a solution can also be a distraction that leads to inadequate listening. Being dis-tracted by one's own thought processes, too, can pose as an impediment to listening (Hutchinson, 2012). For example, when you are working hard to make sense of what the helpee is saying, it may be that all of that mental work causes you to disengage from actually hearing in order to retreat into your own cognitive processes. It is difficult to listen to another person when you are also trying to listen to your own internal voice. So, **thinking too much or too hard** can cause you to miss important components of what the helpee is saying.

Skovholt (2005) points out that adhering too closely to a particular theo-retical orientation can sometimes cause the helper to oversimplify or shape what he is hearing so that it makes sense according to the preconceived frame-work but may not adequately reflect the helpee's intentions, situation, or needs. This can result in **filtered** or **evaluative listening.** For example, if a parent-educator who works from an attachment perspective is listening to a father talk about his child's behavioral challenges, this helper may be listening for cues about the parent–child bond and completely miss that the child is in a compro-mising situation in the day care setting. This can also happen with discourses as well. For example, you may not even realize that you are assuming that the young single mom in your office is incompetent or too stressed to adequately attend to her child if your listening is filtered by dominant single mom dis-courses that position single moms as unskilled, overwhelmed, and incapable of making wise choices. Of course, not all single moms fit these discourses. But these dominant discourses are very powerful and may lead you to miss that she is a college educated professional woman who is doing an excellent job of rais-ing her child, even if she sometimes feels stressed or makes mistakes. Or, it might lead you to miss that this single mom is underemployed, living in poverty, very stressed, and also a great mom to her child.

Rehearsing what to say next can also be an impediment to listening. For example, you are suddenly aware of needing to confront the helpee about something, and you become disengaged in the conversation and don't adequately listen to what she is saying as you practice in your head how to make the challenge. **Sympathetic listening** is another way in which listening can be impeded. If you become caught up in the helpee's story or situation and begin to feel sorry for him or overwhelmed by emotion, this emotional reaction can keep you from truly listening (Skovholt, 2005). For example, a young father who has just lost his wife to cancer and is overwhelmed with the three small children at home seeks help for resume building. His story is tragic, and his helper becomes overwhelmed with sympathy. As a result, she overfunctions by stepping outside of her role and offering to watch this man's children when he was to go for his next job interview, when all he wanted was some help editing his resume.

Listening to Two Voices

The tricky part about listening when we are in a helping conversation is that we receive input from two sources: (1) from what the helpee is communicating verbally and nonverbally, and (2) from our own internal voice—the things that we are telling ourselves; our own meaning-making processes. Both are critical. I think of these two sources of input as two voices, one sitting on either shoulder, demanding our attention. The **first voice** we listen to is that of the messages communicated verbally and nonverbally by the helpee. It is the here-and-now communication in the moment with the helper. The **second voice** is that which guides our thinking and helps us make sense of what we hear. It is the internal conversation we are having with ourselves when we sit with a helpee. This is the voice of our mind at work.

The second voice has two parts: One is the **meaning-making function.** This is the complex thinking that is happening in your brain to make sense of what the helpee is saying. As you are listening, your brain is picking up on nonverbal cues, searching its memory bank for what has been said in the past, and using your stored knowledge of development and theory to make sense of what you are hearing. For example, when the helpee says that she is confused, we may use our own thinking processes and memory functions to recall what we heard earlier about her complex situation so as to understand her current confusion. We might also consider her developmental age and then try to remember a few human development theories that we learned in the past. This second voice may also be alerting us to an inconsistency—that the helpee is saying that she is confused, but the tone in her voice suggests a lack of conviction. In short, the meaning-making function of the second voice is trying to make sense of the input received through the first voice.

The other function of the second voice is what I call **executive function**. This is the voice of self-instruction: It tells the helper when and how to intervene. For example, this inner voice might say, "The clock shows that we only have about 5 more minutes to talk and I have a meeting right after this. So, it's time to slow him down and end the conversation." Or, "Jeez, I have so many questions. Pedro seems so sad, and I'm not sure why. But it seems that he is about to talk about it, so I will just slow down, listen, reflect, and paraphrase. No questions till later."

This internal "chatter" can be overwhelming. Indeed, managing the first and second voices can be challenging. And, as a result, helpers sometimes disengage from the first voice in order to focus on their own thinking (the second voice). But both "voices," of course, are important. The following are strategies that helpers can use to manage both voices so as to be better able to listen and intervene appropriately:

1. Be aware of how the second voice can distract you from the first voice presence and remind yourself to refocus on what the helpee is telling you.

2. Consider developing a mental conceptual sorting table for the various sources of input. For example, you can organize the input into three columns as you hear it: what the helpee says, what you think (meaning-making), and three, what you should do or say (executive function). As you listen, you can train your brain to identify the category of input you are hearing.

3. Consider using a notepad during the helping conversation to briefly jot down a word or phrase—no more than that.

4. Remember that it is okay to stop the conversation in places and summarize or clarify what the helpee has said. This is a good time to note down on paper some important themes—in just one word, so as to not distract from the flow of the conversation.

5. Take a moment to think before speaking. Sometimes, starting by saying, "Okay, give me a moment here to get clear. [pause] So what I am thinking is . . ."

All of these strategies speak to the importance of being able to attend to the complex and multiple components of the listening process.

EMPATHY

In Chapter 1, we discussed the meaning of empathy and its therapeutic effect in helping relationships. Here we will briefly muddle through what empathy actually looks like in practice. From our own personal experiences most of us know what it feels like when someone really understands us, but it is a little harder to identify what exactly it is that a helper does or says that engenders this important experience of empathy. Identifying the specific components of empathy is something that has been the subject of considerable debate in medical and psychological circles for a long time (Frankel, 2009). It remains rather elusive.

Recall that empathy refers to the ability to enter into the perceptual world of the other—to understand the helpee from her own perspective (Rogers, 1951). Research suggests that this type of perspective-taking requires the cognitive abilities of comprehension, assessment, analysis, and evaluation (Neumann et al., 2009). As mentioned in Chapter 1, Wynn and Bergvik (2010) propose that empathy is actually a three-part sequence of communication that begins with an empathic opportunity—something is said that engenders the helper's empathy. To this, the helper responds—which is the second part of the empathic expression. Third, is the helpee's response to the expression of empathy. This part of the communication—the helper's expression of empathy—may include a range of responses such as a question, a feeling response, agreeing with the helpee, or answering a question (Wynn & Bergvik, 2010). I emphasize, then, that the expression of empathy requires *the ability to recognize and understand the helpee's situation or concern and the ability to communicate that understanding to the helpee.* It is not enough for you to feel empathic; the helpee must feel your empathy.

Expressing Empathy

Some suggest that empathy is not a specific skill. Instead, it is a therapeutic position—an engagement with the helpee that connotes a willingness and desire to understand and help (Halstead et al., 2002). This empathic position begins with an **acknowledgement** of the other. It also includes **warmth and caring** that are, perhaps, best captured in Breggin's (2008) suggestion to "welcome the person as . . . someone whose feelings you will treat with exquisite tenderness" (p. 43). Empathy entails watching over the emotional safety and best interests of the other. It is to extend toward the other in an emotionally available way. Empathy is communicated when the helper notices, asks, and responds to what has been said at emotional and cognitive levels.

Another component of the expression of empathy is a stance of **respectful curiosity**. This refers to being interested in the helpee's experiences and perspectives rather than centering the conversation on the helper's thoughts and theories (Neumann et al., 2009). Empathic helpers **inquire** about the helpee's experiences in an attempt to generate richer understandings, and they **follow up** on what the helpee has said. For example, Laticia says that she "feels alienated from everyone at work," and it makes her "hate" her job. The helper understands that Laticia's work environment is fairly social and that Laticia feels outside of those social circles. He responds first with an expression of warmth and caring: "Wow, that must be really hard—hard to go to work everyday when you feel so alienated." There is a moment of silence as Laticia feels the helper's communication of caring. "Did I get that right?" he asks, checking to see if his comment accurately captured what Laticia was feeling. With respectful curiosity the helper then asks, "So, can we talk about that a little more? I am wondering if you can talk about the last time that happened—when you felt alienated at work?" This is a lead question that should be followed by others to explore Laticia's experience of alienation at work.

As the example above suggests, empathy requires **patience**—giving the helpee time to communicate his story. If you move too quickly without allowing time for the helpee to fully articulate his story or to fully express his emotions, he may be left feeling misunderstood. Empathy also includes **responding appropriately to the expressed needs** of the helpee (Neumann et al., 2009). While this may seem obvious, the emphasis here is on responding to what the *helpee* expresses as a need rather than what you think is needed. Helpers are often tempted to act from what they think that others need; empathy requires us to defer to the expressed needs of the helpee.

Importantly, Norcross (2010) points out that helpers are often unable to objectively or accurately assess whether their attempts at expressing empathy are actually perceived as empathic by their helpees. That is, one's intentions to be empathic does not always translate into the helpee's felt experience of empathy. The only way to really know if an expression of empathy is accurate and appropriate is by the helpee's response (Frankel, 2009; Rogers, 1951). This means that you will need to **check in**—request feedback from the helpee—to determine if the helpee actually feels the empathy as intended. When the helper asked Laticia above, "Did I get that right?" he was checking in.

Table 7.5 Expressing Empathy

Expressions of Empathy
1. Acknowledgement, warmth, and caring
2. Respectful curiosity—inquiring and following up
3. Patience
4. Responding to expressed needs
5. Check in for accuracy

VIDEO LINK:
Empathy

All of these components of empathic positioning are listed in Table 7.5. If the helpee does not feel that the helper was empathic, a "conversational failure" (Wynn & Bergvik, 2010, p. 150) is a likely outcome. Conversational failures may look like a stop or pause in the conversation (on the part of the helpee), a helpee's attempt to reformulate what has just been said, or an abrupt change of subject. A verbal check-in helps avoid conversational failures or, at the very least, facilitates engagement and discussion if there is one. The skill of immediacy, which will be discussed in the following chapter, is an excellent tool for repairing conversational failures.

REFLECTIONS

In the practice of counseling, a reflection typically refers to the repeating back, almost verbatim, of what has been communicated by the helpee. A **content reflection** is repeating back key ideas stated by the helpee in his own words. For example, a helpee, Cameron, says, "I am so bent out of shape about this, I just don't want to go. I know that I should but I don't want to." The helper may reflect this content by saying, "You don't want to go." Here the reflection offers a condensed version of what was said, and it is stated in the helpee's exact words.

Reflections are not restricted to just repeating the helpee's words. When helpers use reflections to focus on expressed emotions, it is called a **feeling reflection**. For example, a helper might say, "You feel sad. Right?" after a helpee says that he is sad. Or, "You said you are 'stressed out.'" Notice that the verbiage in these statements is minimal—the focus is on the feeling. When you say too much, the helpee has to make sense of what you are saying and thus moves from a feeling state to a thinking state. Feeling reflections are statements that keep the focus on the feeling.

Feeling reflections are fairly complicated to use for a variety of reasons. First, because feelings are typically expressed nonverbally, it can be difficult to accurately interpret the feelings of others. We can easily get it wrong. Second, people often experience multiple feelings simultaneously, so reflecting just one feeling directs the focus on only part of the emotional message. Also, we may not know which feeling to focus on when we use a feeling reflection. Third, some people do not have a feeling vocabulary—that is, they do not label or they have difficulties accurately labeling what they are feeling. Finally, feeling reflections can make people feel uncomfortable. Helpees and helpers sometimes avoid talking about feelings because when you talk about feelings, they become more present. For many of us the expression of feeling can make us feel vulnerable, out of control, or awkward. So, avoiding a discussion about feelings keeps us more comfortable.

For these reasons, it is always appropriate to offer a feeling reflection with **appropriate tentativeness** and to **check for accuracy**. For example: Ben reports, "I don't know, I have this . . . well, I'm just . . . well, I have this upcoming nursing exam. I have to pass it." The helper offers a feeling reflection with tentativeness: "Ben, correct me if I have it wrong, but it sounds like you are a very worried about this exam. Is that right?" In this example, Ben did not directly articulate a feeling, but the way he talked about the exam suggested that he was worried. Since feeling worried was an assumption on the part of the helper, it was important for the helper to check it out. Notice how the helper used contextual cues (exams are anxiety producing) and attended to Ben's verbal and nonverbal messages to fully understand the feeling he was communicating.

Feeling reflections are used to enable helpees to become more aware of their affective states. Drawing attention to Ben's affective state in the example above can help him make sense of why he is behaving in a particular way or help provide clarity around some aspect of his situation. For example, let us say that after the helper checked in with Ben in the above example, Ben responded by saying, "Yes, I am worried, but also I'm mad that I have to go through this." This response confirms the hypothesis that he is worried, and the feeling reflection also seems to have promoted further focus and exploration, inviting Ben to identify a secondary emotion. This may then lead to a conversation about being in nursing school, his frustration with his roommate for making noise so he couldn't study, or perhaps, his alcohol problem that got in the way of him completing all of his school work. The point is that feeling reflections are used to broaden helping conversations.

Feeling reflections, as mentioned earlier, also have the tendency to arouse intensity around affect—that is, a feeling reflection sometimes can cause the helpee to become emotional. In many situations, of course, the expression of emotion is appropriate, perfectly normal, and can be very helpful. But when a helpee does not have the resources or abilities to regulate such an expression, a feeling reflection may not be an appropriate intervention. Even if the helpee is able to regulate emotion appropriately, expressing feelings may leave her feeling vulnerable. So, it is always important for helpers to have an adequate relationship with helpees when using feeling reflections, and to attend to the emotional space after the reflection. Following from the example above, Ben says, "Yes, I am worried, but also I'm mad that I have to go through this." The helper responds with another feeling reflection: "You are pretty angry." In response, Ben became agitated and pounded his fist on the arm of the chair saying, "This always happens. It just makes me so mad. I hate school. I want to be done with it. I'm only here because my parents want me to be." If Ben had stormed out of the room and indicated that he was going to hit someone, the intensity was obviously too high. This is why it is important for helpers to use feeling reflections only as appropriate and with intentionality.

VIDEO LINK:
Reflections

PARAPHRASES

A paraphrase articulates the gist of what the helpee has communicated. It is an articulation of the helper's understandings articulated in the helper's words. The difference between reflections and paraphrases is that paraphrases tend to incorporate more of the helper's ideas into the expression. Reflections, on the other hand, use the helpee's words almost exclusively.

Paraphrases are typically initiated with an **introductory phrase** such as "it seems like . . ." or "I am hearing you say . . ." They then capture a combination of **key words, phrases, feelings, or concepts that the helpee has expressed,** and are **articulated in words of the helper.** It is important to point out that because paraphrases articulate sentiments in the words of the helper, they actually entail some degree of interpretation. Paraphrases really amount to your ideas and your understanding of what the helpee has said, then. As such, paraphrases should always be articulated with **tentativeness,** and they should be followed by a **check in** for accuracy.

These components of paraphrases are listed in Table 7.6. Notice how they are used in the following example. Cameron says, "I am so bent out of shape about this, I just don't want to go. I know that I should but I don't want to." Instead of the reflection "You don't want to go," the helper paraphrases, "So,

Table 7.6 Paraphrases

Steps in Paraphrasing
1. Introduce the paraphrase. ("What I"m hearing you say is...")
2. Articulate the gist of what helpee has said, including key words, phrases, feelings, etc.
3. Speak with tentativeness.
4. Check in for accuracy.

let me get this right, Cameron. What I hear you saying is that you really don't want to go, but you feel bad about even thinking that—about not wanting to go. This is making you feel pretty worked up. Right?" Cameron listens and thinks about what the helper has proposed and responds, "Yes. That's right."

Going back to our earlier examples of reflections with Ben, who you may recall, is talking about an exam and a possible conflict about his career choice. Let us say that the helper uses information from earlier in the conversation to generate this paraphrase: "Let me see if I have this right, Ben. You are in a position where you are torn between two commitments: the commitment to yourself and the commitment to your parents. Does that make sense?" Notice how this paraphrase includes even more interpretation than the feeling reflection used earlier. This is important to point out because whenever you are responding with your own words, you are adding your own meanings into the communication. Again, paraphrases must always be based on careful attentive listening and include a statement of tentativeness or check-in. In this example, the "Does that make sense?" is the check-in used by the helper.

VIDEO LINK:
Paraphrases

THE PURPOSE OF REFLECTIONS AND PARAPHRASES

Unfortunately, the definitions of reflections and paraphrases are not consistent among those who educate helping professionals. For example, some suggest that a content reflection is the same thing as a paraphrase (Hutchinson, 2012; Ivey, Ivey, & Zalaquett, 2010). Young (2013) introduces the concept of reflection of meaning, which parallels Egan's (2010) concept of advanced empathy, and looks much like an interpretation. Brammer and MacDonald (2003) list reflections and paraphrases as separate skills, but comment that they are very similar. I agree that there is much overlap between these basic responding skills. But their differences are important: A reflection repeats back what the helper has said. It invites the helper to explain the meaning. A paraphrase interprets what has been said in the helper's words. It invites further exploration, but it really articulates the helper's understandings. And, as a result, paraphrases run the risk of being inaccurate. The two can be used interchangeably in some situations, but they are also used for slightly different purposes in others. Here we will review the different uses of reflections and paraphrases. These points are also summarized in Table 7.7.

Reflections are used in helping conversations for these purposes:

1. Reflections let the helpee know that she has been heard. They are an indication that the helper is listening. This is not insignificant, as offering one's undivided attention may be experienced by the helpee as an expression of empathy.

2. When reflections are stated concisely, they only minimally intrude in the flow of the conversation. Used this way, reflections allow you to participate and keep the pace in the conversation without changing the focus.

3. When the word or feeling reflected is one that the helpee wasn't even aware he was expressing, the reflection has the tendency to slow the conversation down and offer focus on a potentially important communication.

4. The reflection draws attention to particular aspects of what has been expressed and has the potential to prompt meaning-making. For example, Aviva says, "I thought I knew what I was doing, but apparently not." Just as she is about to go on to a new thought, the helper signals that she is going to say something by leaning in and putting her hand up gently, as if offering a stop signal. Then she reflects, "Apparently not?" with an inflection that signals a question. Aviva stops. "Well, I did know what I was doing," she starts, and then adds, "Huh, I didn't notice that I said 'apparently not.' I think it's that when I am with him, I doubt myself."

5. As illustrated in the example above, offering a reflection rather than a paraphrase allows the helpee to determine the meaning or significance of what has been said rather than relying on the helper's interpretation.

6. People sometimes talk without really listening to what they, themselves, are saying. Drawing attention to what has been said by using a reflection can promote clarity.

7. Reflections invite the helpee to stop, go back, think, or say more about what has reflected back. Here, the intent is to encourage and validate the helpee's own knowledge and experiences.

Although reflections seem to be simple, caution is advised. First, excessive use of reflections can make the helping conversation awkward. Also, reflecting on only one part of what has been said may take the conversation in a direction that the helpee has not intended or that is not helpful. Also, as mentioned, feeling reflections should be used with caution both because it is very easy to misinterpret the feeling states of others and also because focusing solely on the affective part of a message can raise the emotional intensity in the conversation. While this is often desirable, sometimes helpees are not prepared for this level of intensity.

Paraphrases are used in helping conversations for some of the same reasons that reflections are used. They communicate that you hear and understand the helpee, they focus on a particular content or emotional expression, they help to clarify what has been said, and they also are used to summarize a particular idea, theme, or intent. However, remember that paraphrases don't just repeat what they helpee has said, they also include the helper's understandings or

Table 7.7   Purpose of Reflections and Paraphrases

Reflections	Paraphrases
To communicate that the helpee has been heard	To communicate that the helpee has been heard
To keep pace in the conversation with minimal intrusion	To keep pace in the conversation with minimal intrusion
To raise helpee awareness of what he or she is saying	To raise helpee awareness of what he or she is saying
To slow down the conversation	To slow down the conversation
To bring clarity or draw attention to what the helpee has just said	To bring clarity or draw attention to what the helpee has just said
To invite the helpee to make meaning or interpret what he or she is saying	To bring clarity by summarizing key themes in the words of the helper
	To suggest new meanings or ideas
	To illuminate or point out themes

interpretations. Paraphrases are sometimes used instead of reflections to achieve these additional goals:

1. To suggest new meanings or ideas related to what the helpee has said.

2. To identify themes that appear to be an undercurrent in the conversation but, perhaps, have not been articulated directly. In this way, paraphrases are used to introduce new insights or new ways of thinking.

3. Because they include some aspect of the helper's thought processes, paraphrases can move the conversation to a new area or invite exploration at a new level. The effect of slowing down or moving forward is dependent, to a large extent, on how much interpretation is included in the paraphrase.

QUESTIONS

Questions serve a variety of purposes in helping conversations. They are used to start conversations and to gather information about the helpee and the presenting concern. Questions also provide direction and focus—they point to certain topics and invite the helpee to add information, explore, elaborate, and generate hypotheses. Questions are also used to check out helper perceptions and spark engagement. Various types of questions discussed here are summarized in Table 7.8.

Types of Questions

Closed Questions

Closed questions serve the purpose of gathering specific information in a concise manner and often begin with the words *what*, *where*, *are*, *is*, or *do*. For example, these closed questions prompt a yes/no response: "Are you feeling okay?" "Did you want to do that?" "Are you sad?" Notice how these closed questions elicit a yes or no response. Other closed questions seek specific or factual answers: "What time did you get here?" "How old are you?" "Where were you born?" These questions are focused, specific, and do not invite elaboration.

Open Questions

Open questions invite exploration rather than prompt specific responses. Typically open-ended questions must be answered in more than a few words, and they offer considerable freedom for the helpee to decide how she wants to respond. They invite what I call *paragraph responses*—responses articulated in a few or more sentences around a particular theme. Notice the open nature of these questions: "What would you like to talk about today?" "Can you say more?"

A version of the open question is the **open-ended focused probe**. This type of question is semidirectional. It is directional as it points to a particular topic or issue, but it is also open in that it prompts the helpee to respond to that topic in any way that he wants. The difference between an open-ended focused proble and a simple open-ended question is that in the former, the focus is specific, directional, and named in the question. For example, notice how the question, "What would you like to tell me about your family?" is not completely open. It invites the helpee to select what he wants to say about the named topic of his family. Similarly, "What do you like about coming here?" invites the helpee to say what she "likes" and what she wants to say about "coming here."

How, What, When, Where, and Why Questions

It is important to remember that the introductory word used to ask a question will frame its response. So, be careful what you ask for. *How, what,* and *why* questions are excellent question starts that can be used to elicit a helpee's perspective or thoughts on a particular topic or issue. They invite the helpee to offer an explanation, and thus illuminate the helpee's thinking processes. As mentioned earlier in this chapter, it can be very helpful to understand how the helpee understands or thinks about his situation. Also, these types of question communicate respect for the helpee since they invite input rather than tell.

For example, a helper asked, "What do you want to talk about today?" As the helpee began to tell a story about something that happened that day, the helper asked, "How did that happen?" The helpee's response was an explanation: "Well, I was on the way to work and . . ." Then, the helper asked, "How do you feel about that?" The helpee said, "Well, I think it is okay, but I'm not sure . . ." Then the helper asked, "Why do you think that happened?" Notice that these *how, what,* and *why* questions are open questions and open-ended focused probes, and they invite the helpee to express her ideas and perspectives.

These particular question starts are not always helpful for eliciting feelings, however. We often ask people about their feelings by using a *how* question ("How do you feel?"), and the response to this type of question typically is a *thought* about a feeling. Notice this in the example above, when the helpee responds to the feeling prompt by telling the helper that he thinks its okay but he's not sure, etc. *How, what,* and *why* questions invite thought. For this reason, it is usually better to use a feeling reflection rather than a *how* question to elicit a feeling.

When and *where* questions also are not good for eliciting feelings, and they tend to invite a much narrower focus than *how, what,* and *why* questions. *When* and *where* questions are used to elicit details, and, as you can see, they take the form of closed questions. But they are good follow up-questions for when additional information is needed. For example, a helper asks, "When did you become aware of that?" "Yesterday," responds the helpee. And when asked, "Where do you want to go with this conversation?" a helpee might say, "I want to stop talking about it."

Inflection Questions

An inflection question is one that is formed by a modulation of the intonation or pitch in the voice at the end of a statement. It is a statement offered as a question. Consider how the statement "You want to go" can change in meaning, depending on how it is articulated. When the emphasis is on the first word, *you,* it is about the subject—it is a question or statement about *you* who wants to go. The difference between whether this is a statement or a question is settled in the way in which the *you* is emphasized. Similarly, the idea of *going* is articulated as either a question or statement, depending on how it is emphasized in the articulation. It might be a question of whether you want to go, or it might be a comment that it is clear to the speaker that you are definitely ready to leave.

It can be helpful to use an inflection to make a statement into question for a variety of reasons. First, questions articulated in this way offer direction for the response. When you ask someone if she wants to go, she knows that she is expected to respond in some way about going (or not). So, this type of question directs action. Second, these questions offer an alternative to the more typical question starts (such as *how, what, when, where,* and *why*). As such, they help break the feel of interrogation when they are used sequentially with other questions (sequential questions are discussed in more detail below). Finally, inflection questions can be inserted fairly smoothly into the flow of a conversation. They often repeat what has been said, they use the language already in use in the interchange, and they have a subtle feel. They don't ask the helpee to stop and think as abruptly as other questions can have the tendency to do. Helpers should be judicious when using inflection questions, however, as if they are used too much, they can create a feel of an interview or examination. Also, inflection questions, like other questions, direct the conversation. So using them too much means that the helper is in charge of the conversation and too much control on the part of the helper may be inappropriate in some helping conversations.

Sequential Questions

We often hear the caution of not asking multiple questions in a helping conversation. This good advice is based on the observation that asking someone too many questions can make that person feel interrogated. Yet there are some good reasons for asking multiple questions. Sometimes we ask follow-up questions because our original question did not yield the information we hoped, or after asking one question, we have suddenly thought of a better question. And sometimes we ask multiple questions because we are very curious!

When questions are selected carefully and offered appropriately from a position of curiosity rather than interrogation, they can be very helpful. Sequential questions can be very effective for signaling our curiosity or interest, inviting the helpee's perspective, and for opening up or deepening the focus of a conversation. Sequential questions can lead to a very productive helping conversation when they include a variety of question types mixed with the reflections and paraphrases, and if we are careful to monitor how the helpee is responding. Borrowing the metaphor of a soccer player whose primary job

Illustration 7.1   So Many Questions

©iStockphoto.com/Hung Kuo Chun

is to kick the ball in the goal (the "striker"), I like to remind helpers to "follow their shot" when asking questions. This speaks directly to the use of sequential questions.

Going with this metaphor, in soccer, second attempt shots at goals are often the ones that score. Good strikers know that it is their job to kick the ball toward goal and then wait around until it is returned so that they can kick it in again, and sometimes again a third time, if it did not reach the intended target on the first go-around. Each kick is slightly different, of course, but all are aimed at reaching the back of the net—scoring a goal. Similarly, in helping conversations, helpers should not fire off a question and then retreat. Nor should they continue to ask the same question repeatedly. Instead, helpers should ask a question, listen carefully to the helpee's response, and then follow up with another question that invites further exploration. Used in this way, questions scaffold depth. Notice how this happens in this "following your shot" example:

Ran is working with a helper to write an essay for his college application and says, "I don't know what to write about." The helper responds, "Well, if I asked you to tell me some things about you that speak to who you are as a person and who you might be as a college student, what would you say?" (This is a focused open-ended probe.) "Well," Ran says, "One thing I know about

Illustration 7.2   Follow Your Shot

Table 7.8 Types of Questions

Type of Question	Purpose
Closed questions	Seek specific information
Open questions	Invite helpee-directed exploration
Focused, open-ended probes	Invite exploration of a particular topic or theme
How, what, when, where, and *why* questions	To invite helpee perspectives and communicate respect and interest
Inflection questions	To alter questioning format and bring focus

myself is that I am a hard worker." "What do you mean by hard worker?" the helper asks (focused open-ended probe). "When I start a project," Ran says, "I don't let it go . . . I keep at it until it's done." The helper says, "Interesting. Is that something that you think colleges would want to hear about you?" (Closed question.) "Yes," Ran replies. "I think that is something I could talk about in the essay." "Great," the helper says. "I wonder if you might want to start with a story that speaks to this idea of you being a hard worker. If you did that, what story might you tell?" (Focused open-ended probe.) As illustrated in this example, when we ask a question, we often need to follow it up with another question, and another . . . each time with new depth or a slightly different angle. We need to follow our shot.

VIDEO LINK:
Questions

BROACHING CONVERSATIONS

In Chapter 2, we discussed two critical components of work with individuals from marginalized social locations: (1) it is important to understand how heritage, culture, or group affiliation informs identity, and (2) we must also understand how systems of power and privilege in larger society influence individuals' experiences in everyday life (as well as in your helping relationship). A reluctance to address these issues—being colorblind to differences—enables helpers to enjoy a position of safety and privilege, but it may not serve the needs of helpees who identify in social groups that are marginalized (Smith, Geroski, & Tyler, 2014).

Consistent with the notion of developing cultural competence that includes awareness, knowledge, and skills, Chu (2007) speaks to the importance of helpers being able to develop a "cultural exchange" (p. 39) when working with others. This refers to engaging in an open exchange of information and questioning about cultural assumptions. Day-Vines et al. (2007), too, recommend that helpers be the one to introduce discussions about culture, race, ethnicity, and the social and political factors that affect one's experience in a particular social location into their helping conversations. They refer to this helper-initiated introduction of issues related to social location as *broaching*.

Day-Vines et al. (2007) introduce five broaching styles, ranging from complete avoidance of engaging in any conversations about race and culture (and I would expand this to include other social locations as well) to infusing notions of social justice into all of one's interactions, thoughts, and deeds. Again, remember that social location influences one's experiences in the world—both in shaping individual's values and beliefs and also affecting how individuals are perceived and treated by others. So, ignoring expressions and experiences related to social location in helping conversations means disregarding critical aspects of the helpee's everyday experiences and ignoring critical components of identity. Again, Day-Vines et al. importantly point out that it is the responsibility of the helper, not the helpee, to invite conversations about diverse identities.

There is no clear recipe for broaching conversations. However, very basically, broaching conversations typically entail:

1. **Inquiring about the individual's social location.** This may include race, culture, religion, socioeconomic status, sexual orientation, gender identification, disability status, etc., as appropriate to the helping relationship. For example, a helper asks "Chen, can you tell me a little about your cultural and racial background?"

2. **Inquiring, inviting discussion, or asking about the ways in which social location may be related to the concern or issue that is the focus of the helping conversation.** Following from the above example, the helper then says, "Chen, you indicated that you are Chinese and your family at home is very involved in the Chinese community here. I wonder if that has any connection to your worries about going off to college next year?"

3. **Respecting the direction that the helpee moves in this conversation.** For example, "Okay, so I hear you saying that you are not sure how to think about that question and would rather not talk about that right now. That makes sense. Let's go back to the college essay that we were

talking about. But I wonder if it would be okay if we checked in on this issue again some time after you have had some time to think about it. Okay?"

For another example of how broaching might be used in helping, let's go back to the case study of Mia that was used in Chapter 3. As you will recall, Mia was displaying inappropriate rest-time behaviors that included making noise when children were sleeping and running out of the room during rest time. Jorge was the teacher in that classroom who was consulting his supervisor about an appropriate course of action. Let us suppose that both of Mia's parents were born and raised in their native country of India. Mia, their youngest child, is first generation Indian, and the only child of color in her preschool classroom.

As Van Ausdale and Feagin (2001) point out, children, even at preschool ages, are aware of implicit racial dynamics in their immediate environments. Understanding this point, Jorge and his supervisor wondered how Mia was affected by being the only child of minority status in her classroom. They also wondered if this experience of minority status explained Mia's inability to fully relax during rest time. They also noticed that Mia's behaviors tended to escalate after lunch, and they wondered if the preschool meal, which was likely different than what Mia was accustomed to at home, also factored into the troubles they witnessed. They decided to broach these questions with Mia's parents.

Jorge began by asking Mia's parents if they had any reservations about their child being the only child of color in her classroom—if they had noticed any concerns. At first, the parents responded by saying that they had no concerns, commenting that everyone had been very nice to them, and they thought that children really didn't see color. Jorge's supervisor commented that even young children of minority status may feel isolated when they are the only students of color in a classroom and that they may experience subtle racism, even in preschools where staff are vigilant about these issues (Van Ausdale & Feagin, 2001). The parents nodded in agreement to this observation, still not sharing any specific concerns. Jorge then offered his hypothesis that Mia may have been having difficulties during rest time because she did not feel completely relaxed at the center. Together the parents and staff explored this issue. They also discussed their questions about Mia being accustomed to the lunch meal, as well as any home mealtime rituals that Mia may be missing at preschool. Together they came up with some ideas and a commitment to further investigate these issues. In this scenario, Jorge and his supervisor took responsibility for broaching the issue of race with Mia's parents and were gently persistent even when the parents seemed unsure about whether they could speak about race in that context.

VIDEO LINK:
Broaching

CHAPTER SUMMARY

Helping conversations require strong listening and intentional responding skills. In this chapter, we discussed the importance of careful listening and expressing empathy—both of which are insignificant if the helpee does not experience them. That is, the helpee must feel heard, and she must feel the empathy if it is to be helpful. We also talked about the use of reflections and paraphrases to bring focus in helping conversations. When these are followed by a check-in or an invitation for the helpee to clarify, they are more likely to be accurate and effective. These skills can also be used to invite the helpee to determine the direction of further conversation. We also discussed a variety of question types that are used in helping conversations. Used together in the spirit of curiosity, these different question types can bring depth and meaning to helping conversations. Finally, the concept of broaching conversations, particularly around issues related to social location, is an important helping intervention. The mix of using the different question types, reflections, paraphrases, and continued expressions of empathy and careful listening, and broaching difficult topics are the fundamental tools for facilitating helping conversations.

DISCUSSION QUESTIONS

1. The meanings of nonverbal behaviors vary widely, based on how they are expressed in one's family, community, and culture. Given this, how can you really know the meaning of your helpee's nonverbal expressions?

2. The expression of empathy is so important in helping. What do you do if you don't feel empathic toward your helpee?

3. Oftentimes individuals feel emotions but do not express them. How do we capture unexpressed feelings in reflections and how do we know if we are being accurate when we capture these unexpressed feelings in reflections?

4. What do we do when the helpee is talking about something that seems irrelevant to the helpee conversation? Do we just continue to listen attentively, or do we do something else?

CHAPTER 8

SKILLS FOR PROMOTING CHANGE

LEARNING OBJECTIVES

1. Learn how to offer psychoeducation and problem solving in helping conversations

2. Learn how to offer feedback and to challenge helpees

3. Learn how to be immediate in the helping conversation

4. Learn how to engage in deconstructing conversations

5. Learn how to advocate and motivate change

INTRODUCTION

The skills discussed in this chapter—psychoeducation/informing, problem solving, confronting, feedback, immediacy, deconstructing, motivating change, and being an advocate—are skills that are used to bring more depth into helping conversations and to move the helpee toward change. These skills, like the ones discussed in Chapter 7, can be used in a variety of helping contexts and for numerous goals or ends. In each section of this chapter, I will describe the skill and explain why and how it is used. Here, too, I will try to offer the skills in recipe form, but as with those skills reviewed in the previous chapter, you should always be attuned to the specifics of your particular helping situation to use these skills accordingly. These are powerful tools in the work of helping, so use them with intentionality and the utmost of integrity.

INFORMING/PSYCHOEDUCATION

We all can agree, I think, that having appropriate and accurate information goes a long way in solving many difficult problems. This is true in our own lives as well as in the work in helping relationships. Providing information to helpees about a topic or issue that is directly related to mental health issues is called *psychoeducation*. An example of psychoeducation would be informing a helpee about anxiety by explaining what the term *anxiety* means, what the symptoms look like, and how it is treated in therapeutic settings. Of course, information about mental health issues is not the only type of information that we offer helpees. For example, I met with the father of a new immigrant family to describe the college application process so he could better understand his son's college choices.

There is no clear recipe for how to provide information to helpees. So, let us start by taking a minute here to reflect on our own experiences of being the recipient of information when we were struggling. Many of us have had the experience of being inundated with unwanted and unasked-for information after telling someone about a challenge. Some of us have needed information, but it was delivered in overly technical jargon, with terms that we did not understand, or we were given so much information that we were left feeling overwhelmed. And sometimes, the information we are given is interesting, but we don't know exactly what to do with it.

These examples underscore some important points about using psychoeducation/informing in our work with others. First is the importance of waiting until you are asked to provide information before giving it. If you are in a situation where you believe that the helpee would really benefit from information that he has not asked for, be sure to ask if he is interested in receiving information before offering it. And, of course, honor the helpee's response. If someone is not interested in our well-intended efforts to provide information on a particular topic, then we can let him know that the information is available if and when he is interested at some time in the future.

A second guideline for informing is to limit the information that you provide to your helpees. Don't overwhelm your helpee with too much information. You want to be sure that what you give to the helpee is relevant, is at an appropriate reading level, and is written in a manner or style that is accessible. Providing complex journal articles full of professional jargon about a particular topic to a helpee with limited reading skills, for example, is obviously inappropriate. Giving your helpee too many reading materials or videos to watch can leave her wondering where to start or feeling guilty if she has not been able to read or look at all of it. Keep it simple and clear. These points are obvious, but they are easy to overlook when we are eager to help.

Finally, a third point about using informing as a helping intervention is to consider the relative benefit of instructing the helpee how to access information and resources herself rather than directly providing that information to her. There are times when it makes sense to give the helpee pertinent information, but sometimes it makes more sense to show the helpee where appropriate resources are and to remove some of the barriers so that she can access that information on her own. For example, showing someone a website with information that he can look at later may be most beneficial. You may need to help some helpees access information by, for example, creating a user name and password and bookmarking the site on their favorites bar. In short, there is power in having the knowledge and there is power in being able to help oneself. Linking helpees to information and resources is a helping skill that is often underrated and overlooked, yet it is an important component of helping.

VIDEO LINK:
Psychoeducation

DECISION-MAKING AND PROBLEM SOLVING

Some helpees come to us for assistance in making a decision or in solving a problem. Sometimes this type of request is masked in a "What should I do?" question. Solving *with* rather than *for* is the golden rule in most helping situations. Even when it is clearly appropriate for you to solve a problem for your helpee, it is always best to somehow engage the helpee in the decision-making or problem-solving process. When a person is involved in the process of creating a solution, he is more likely to be accountable for his actions, he is more likely to feel good about his successes, and the outcome has a better chance of being a good fit. Conversely, when we step in to make a decision or solve a problem for someone, we risk offering the wrong solution (because we rarely know what is really best for others) and we risk assuming the responsibility for a decision that does not directly affect us. When we resist solving problems for others, that resistance is an invitation for the other person to become empowered.

Decision-making and problem-solving models abound—they are offered in a wide range of fields from mathematics to social problem solving. These models typically unfold as a process that includes exploring the problem, assessing options, estimating potential outcomes of the various options, and making inferences about what will happen once the decision is made (Hastie, 2001). We will review these steps in more detail shortly. But first, I want to highlight that a key to decision-making and problem-solving is to be thoughtful. When we act too quickly, we risk allowing our actions to make decisions for us. When we follow a process, thought guides our choices and actions.

Below are steps for engaging in decision-making and problem solving in helping relationships. These are also summarized in Table 8.1.

1. **Identify and clarify the problem or issue.** Research suggests that people approach decision-making in a variety of ways (Galotti et al., 2006), and the way in which they view or understand the problem determines the types of solutions they will make (Fink, Boersma, MacDonald, & Linton, 2012). So, having a clear understanding of the problem is an important first step in the process. As a helper, be sure to spend time with the helpee to develop a clear sense of the problem or decision to be made. Sometimes this requires sorting out various concerns and circumstances and reducing the problem to its most basic issue.

2. **Gather appropriate information.** Next, gather as much information about the problem and the situation as possible. You can do this by asking questions about what the helpee knows already about the situation and what knowledge he may have about similar situations or the individuals involved, if relevant. Also, you can offer additional information that you think is needed for clear and sound decision-making. Sometimes the initial problem is diminished or even goes away at this stage of the process. This is because gathering information sometimes reveals obvious solutions.

3. **Be aware of the goal.** Critical to problem solving or decision-making is to be clear about what the helpee desires in terms of an outcome. So, once the problem is identified and information is available, you will want to sort out what the helpee wants in the end. For example, Janine was in conflict with her boss, and it became apparent that it didn't really matter to her if she won the argument they had; what was important was that she felt respected. In other situations, someone may hope for financial compensation as a result of a wrong, someone else may want help finding an appropriate college, and a third person may need help making a decision between two job offers. As these examples illustrate, having a sense of the outcome goal is a critical component of the decision-making process. Outcome goals should be related to helpee desires and needs.

4. **Generate alternatives or options.** With the problem clarified, a cache of information gathered, and a clear sense of what the helpee wants in the end, the next part of the process is to identify the various options that are available for moving toward the identified goal. Here you will want to encourage the helpee to consider all of the options, even if they don't seem viable or even if they seem a little odd. Knowing that one has choices, even if not all of those choices are the most optimal, is empowering. Equally important: sometimes the most creative and underutilized alternatives make for good solutions to tricky problems.

5. **Evaluate each of the options, taking into consideration their respective consequences.** After generating a list of options—and you will probably want to do this on paper—it can be extremely helpful to discuss each one, taking into consideration all of its ramifications. Some of the questions you may want to ask the helpee about each of the options are the following:

   - Will this option lead to the desired outcome or goal?
   - Are the consequences of this action likely to lead to other problems down the line?
   - Is this option consistent with your beliefs and values, and how you want to live your life or be seen by others?
   - Is this option doable?

   Keep in mind that you may have to introduce or identify potential consequences for some of the alternatives on the list if the helpee lacks awareness to do so. If this is the case, be sure to do so in a matter-of-fact way, and still encourage the helpee to weigh in on the viability of that option, considering the information you have given. For example, in a discussion with a helpee about a situation with his boss, Jamal tells the helpee, "Sure, just walking out of the room when he does that is an option. I am sure that doing that will make you feel less taken advantage of. But have you thought through what might happen if you just walked out? Do you think that might cause you to lose your job?"

6. **Select the most viable or appropriate option.** It is important to remember that what we think is best for someone is not always what they have in mind for themselves. You can respectfully promote agency and helpee accountability by encouraging the helpee to make the decision that she feels is best for the situation (as long as she is well-informed and competent to do so). For example, after discussing all of the options on their list, Jamal asked the helpee, "So, now that we've talked all of these ideas through, what do you think sounds like the best idea?"

7. **Identify the steps required for implementation.** Ambivalence, fear, or a lack of knowledge are some of the things that prohibit people from acting on the decisions that they have made. So, mapping out the sequence of actions that are needed to realize a decision is an important part of the decision-making process. Of course, not everyone will need this type of assistance, but it is always important to suggest even the most basic map for proceeding. For example, Jamal followed up with Brian's decision by asking, "Okay, Brian, that sounds like a decision you feel good about. Would it be helpful to brainstorm a few ways that you can speak up? Sometimes it can really be hard to assert ourselves when

we feel intimidated, so maybe we should spend a few minutes identifying a few first steps? We could even role-play the conversation if you want."

8. **Implement and, if appropriate, evaluate decision.** If your work with a helpee on a decision is offered in the context of an ongoing helping relationship, it is always appropriate to follow up by checking in on how things went and to continue to offer support, if needed. If the decision was not carried out or the outcome was not what the helpee expected, you can normalize the situation by reminding the helpee that things don't always go as planned and offer to brainstorm the decision-making process again with the helpee.

I realize that this process, as written, appears to be long and drawn out. But it is important to emphasize that helpees come to us for assistance because they need it. Taking the time to work through a decision-making process with a helpee—a few times, in fact—teaches decision-making or problem-solving skills that the helpee can take with her into future conflicts and problematic situations.

VIDEO LINK:
Problem-
Solving/
Decision-
Making

Table 8.1   Decision-Making Model

1. Identify and clarify the problem or issue.
2. Gather appropriate information.
3. Develop a goal.
4. Generate alternatives or options.
5. Evaluate the consequences of each of the options.
6. Select most viable or appropriate option.
7. Identify the steps required for implementation.
8. Implement and, if appropriate, evaluate decision.

CONFRONTATION

Confrontation is best thought of as offering information to the helpee so that he can be more accountable for attitudes, behaviors, and decisions that do not serve him well (Bratter, 2011). The use of confrontation and challenge in

Photo 8.1 Confrontation

©iStockphoto.com/DenGuy

clinical therapeutic helping has a long and controversial history (Strong & Zeman, 2010), yet confrontation is a powerful and effective intervention in many helping situations.

Festinger's theory that people are motivated toward consistency (Festinger, 1957)—that people are interested in behaving in ways that are consistent with their beliefs, thoughts, values, and attitudes—helps us understand why confrontation can be an helpful intervention when working with others. This inner drive toward consistency, Festinger proposed, is fueled by a desire to avoid the tension that results when there are conflicts between what we believe, hope, value, and do. When we notice that we are not doing what we say, for example, we become tense or uncomfortable, and that inner discomfort motivates us to conform or change in some way. Confrontation as an intervention, then, is to draw attention to discrepancies that appear between someone's beliefs, thoughts, values, and behaviors. The purpose is to potentially motivate people to take action in order to reduce this tension.

For many of us, however, the very word *confrontation* conjures ideas of hostility, anger, or an argument. Similarly, *challenge* suggests a competition or, perhaps, preparing oneself for opposition, difficulty, and discomfort. Weighted as such, the thought of using confrontation as a helping skill seems daunting to many helpers. And indeed, caution in using this skill is quite appropriate.

Justifying the use of confrontation in therapeutic work, Maslow (1967) said:

People are very tough, and not brittle. They can take an awful lot. The best thing to do is get right at them, and not to sneak up on them, or be delicate with them, or try to surround them from the rear. Get right smack into the middle of things right away. (p. 28)

It is an approach that he suggested calling "no crap therapy" (Maslow, 1967, p. 28). These comments may seem harsh, but Maslow was not suggesting that confrontation is an attack, nor did he endorse confrontation as an act of hostility or rage. Instead, he promoted the idea of confrontation as an intentional intervention of being honest, clear, and straightforward. Confrontation really is about giving feedback that offers a different perspective. It is giving information to the helpee so that he can better see himself as he is seen by others, and to gain better insight around his experiences in the world (Kuntze, van der Molen, & Born, 2009).

Confrontation is used widely in the substance abuse field as a way of promoting self-responsibility. The intent is for helpees to consider how their behavior affects others, and it invites them to change the way they think and behave (Polcin, 2003). Confrontation stimulates a process of self-evaluation and proactive change (Bratter, 2011) and has the potential to foster insight into the meaning and effects of one's "maladaptive interpersonal coping behavior and presenting complaint . . ." (Scaturo, 2002, p. 147). In short, confrontation is used to invite helpees to explore themselves, their interactions with others, and their situations, with the hope of evoking awareness that may lead to change.

Discrepancies

All of us have been guilty of giving mixed, confusing, inconsistent, or contradictory messages in our communication with others at one time or another. And it is these mixed messages that often create problems for us, especially in our relationships. It is easy to see how tension can manifest when we are not thoroughly consistent in our beliefs, actions, and deeds, as Festinger (1957) pointed out. Confrontation as a helping skill has to do with pointing out discrepancies with the intent of promoting insight and positive change.

Before moving into a recipe for confrontation, a few words of caution are due. Strong and Zeman (2010) emphasize that power is enacted through confrontation. They also point out that confrontation is an interactional communication. That is, what is said in a confrontation will affect the helpee and will trigger a response. In order for the outcome of a confrontation to be productive, helpers are advised to position themselves from a "power with" rather than a "power over" (Strong & Zeman, 2010, p. 333) position. Confrontations should be conducted as "dialogic" (Strong & Zeman, 2010, p. 332). If we are not careful—if we make assumptions about why the helpee is thinking, feeling, or acting in a certain way, or if we point out inconsistencies with anger or contempt, the helpee is likely to become angry, defensive, and foreclosed to conversation and exploration. The therapeutic significance of a confrontation is not the confrontation itself; what matters most is what happens after the confrontation (Strong & Zeman, 2010). So, confrontations need to be conducted in ways that open up conversation and that respect and value the ideas, actions, and feelings of the helpee.

Honoring the dialogic nature of confrontation, there is no sure recipe for successful confrontation. However, the steps below are recommended as a recipe for confronting with the intent of opening up conversations. Reasons for using confrontations as a helping skill and guidelines for their use are summarized in Table 8.2. Following are suggestions for confronting or challenging in a helping conversation:

1. **Point out the discrepancy.** This should be done in a straightforward, empathic, and nonaggressive manner. For example: "You say that you don't like to spend time with Lexi, yet you talk about her often." Sometimes the discrepancies should be pointed out with some degree of tentativeness to signal that you are open to discussion and making no assumptions about the reasons for the discrepancies. For example, "I may be wrong, so please correct me if I am. But I'm a bit confused. You say that you don't like to spend time with Lexi, yet you often talk about her in here."

2. **Invite exploration.** A simple "What do you think that means?" may be sufficient to invite discussion. Sometimes saying, "I wonder if we could talk about this a bit more?" works as well.

3. **Invite or offer a hypothesis, if appropriate.** "Why do you think that you talk about her so much in here?" invites an explanation. A comment such as "I wonder if you are worried that if you don't keep track of what Lexi is doing, then you will miss out or be less popular with your other friends?" is a hypothesis. In general, it is best to refrain from offering a hypothesis until after the helpee has had a chance to think about and articulate the meaning of the discrepancy herself. Your hypotheses

should always be offered with appropriate tentativeness—as another opinion or option to consider—since we can never know the thoughts and intentions of others.

Types of Discrepancies

Discrepancies Between Verbal Messages

Sometimes people say something and then contradict what they have said a short time later. For example, Jordan tells his mother that he completed his homework. Then, when she asks him to come help with dinner, he says that he is still finishing his homework. Another example of this type of inconsistency is when the contradictions happen within the same message. For example, Jordan tells his mother that his "challenging assignment" is "easy."

Listening carefully to the content of what the helpee says will help you hear inconsistencies that may warrant confrontation. Using the recipe above, Jordan's mother might respond by saying, "I'm confused, Jordan. You said that you were done with your homework, and now you say that you still have more to complete. Can you help me understand what you mean?" In response to the second example, she might say, "Jordan, you said that it was a 'challenging assignment,' but you also said that it was 'easy.' I'm confused." Notice that in both of these examples, the confrontation includes Jordan's words as much as possible and they do not interpret his intentions.

Discrepancies Between Verbal and Nonverbal Messages

We also may notice that the helpee's words seem inconsistent with his body language. For example, Hamish says that he is not nervous, yet his hand is squeezed tightly in a ball. Or, he may say that he is angry, yet he is smiling. Exploring these inconsistencies has the potential to unfold into interesting conversations about expressing emotion, mixed feelings, or some other relevant topic—perhaps that the helpee is uncomfortable with you. Here again, the confrontation should be clear and honest, and also delivered from a position of curiosity and not knowing. For example, you could say, "Hamish, I hear you saying that you're not nervous, but your tightly clenched hand seems to be saying something else. What do you think?" Or, "I hear that you are angry, and that makes sense in this situation. But I'm a little confused because when you talk about being angry you seem to be smiling."

Discrepancies Between Intention and Behavior

It is not unusual for us to have intentions, beliefs, or values to which we aspire, yet also have trouble putting into action. For example, we want to be studious, but the TV beckons. Or, we want to lose weight, but we love to eat ice cream. We value honesty, yet don't always tell the truth. These inconsistencies pose opportunities for further exploration, and a gentle confrontation can set that process in motion. Consider these examples: "Lequisha, I notice that even though you want to be studious, you seem to be drawn to the TV. Can we talk about how difficult it is for you to stay focused?" Or "Emelio, I know that you are worried about your weight, yet it seems difficult for you to follow through on the diet you were using." "I know that honesty is a value that is really important to you, Jude. I wonder if we can talk about why it is so difficult for you to be honest with me right now about this?"

Confrontation Cautions

As mentioned, power shapes helping relationships in overt and subtle ways, and confrontation is one of the most overt ways in which that power may be enacted (Strong & Zeman, 2010). So, take caution in the ways in which you confront others. Remember that helping relationships are based on collaborative engagement to facilitate change. In the words of Oyum (2007), "To know how to confront, and at the same time be respectful and inviting, is both necessary and difficult" (p. 42).

This brings us to an important caution around using confrontation: Be aware of the potential it has to rupture or cause problems in the helping relationship (Scaturo, 2002; Strong & Zeman, 2010). Be sensitive to and aware of how the

Table 8.2 Confrontation: Reasons and Guidelines

Reasons for Using Confrontation	Guidelines for Using Confrontation
• To draw attention to discrepancies between conflicting verbal messages, between verbal and nonverbal messages, and between intention and behavior • To create enough tension to motivate change • To encourage accountability	• Identify discrepant messages in clear, concrete, and straightforward language • Do not make assumptions about intentions • Be tentative when inviting discussion-making and meaning-making • Attend to dialogic conversation and connection

confrontation you deliver is received by the helpee. You should always work to establish a collaborative exploration of the discrepancy, and to do so in a way that honors the input of the helpee. When there is a breach in the helping relationship, this exploration must be done in a way that also repairs the relationship. This does not mean that you should rescind a confrontation or even apologize (unless your confrontation was inappropriate or delivered in a harsh or demeaning way). It does mean, however, that you must be empathic to the helpee's response, which may be embarrassment, guilt, disagreement, anger, or shame. Strong and Zeman point out that the most important component of confrontation is "what the recipient does with it" (p. 335). Working collaboratively to explore discrepancy will help assure that the helping relationship remains intact and that the helpee has learned something from the confrontation.

A second caution relates back to the concept of cognitive dissonance, which is an underlying rationale for using confrontation, according to Festinger's theory (Festinger, 1957). Recall that pointing out a discrepancy gives the helpee a cue that there might be errors in his thinking, belief system, or actions, and it calls upon him to make appropriate revisions so as to relieve the tension resulting from this revelation (Gawronski, 2012). That is, confrontations can signal the helpee to revise his beliefs or change his behavior. However, when people are called upon to learn or address something that contradicts their existing beliefs, they may resist that new knowledge or only attend to feedback that is consistent with what they want to believe (Dechawatanapaisal & Siengthai, 2006; Stone & Cooper, 2001). For example, challenging a helpee to be more independent in her decision-making may contradict the values she has for connection with family. So, be aware that even if you offer a confrontation with the utmost sensitivity and care, the helpee may not respond as you might have hoped. If the helpee does not want to engage in conversation or make a change that you think is important to make, you should continue working with the person without dwelling on the issue. Important issues that need resolve will always surface again. Also, as Dechawatanapaisal & Siengthai (2006) point out, offering a reward or otherwise increasing motivation sometimes can stimulate conformity. It can also be helpful to use the motivating change strategies described later in this chapter when there is ambivalence about change.

VIDEO LINK:
Confrontation/
Challenging

FEEDBACK

The word *feedback* reminds some of us of that awful sound that happens when a microphone gets too close to a speaker, sending an ear-biting shriek that tells us that we need to do something different.

Photo 8.2 Hearing Feedback

©iStockphoto.com/pookpiik

Indeed, receiving feedback about something that we need to change can feel like a loud obnoxious noise in the ear. But that is not the intent of feedback. Feedback is used in helping relationships to give the helpee information related to his behavior or the effects of his behavior on others (Claiborn, Goodyear, & Horner, 2001). Feedback can be descriptive (i.e., it describes what one sees or experiences), or it can be evaluative, as in the case when it is used in a performance review or final examination. The term *corrective feedback* is sometimes used synonymously with *negative feedback* and refers to identifying problems or mistakes in one's performance. *Positive feedback* focuses on what has been done well or correctly.

In some ways, feedback is much like confrontation in that it provides helpees with information about some aspect of self, behavior, or presence that affects others and of which they may not be aware. Like confrontation, the intent of offering feedback is to encourage improved performance or self-examination, or to communicate a need for change (Smith & King, 2004). It offers an opportunity for individuals to assess themselves and the effects of their behaviors on others (Morran, Stockton, Cline, & Teed, 1998). In fact, the terms *feedback* and *confrontation* are sometimes used interchangeably in the literature.

Beyond focusing on discrepancies, however, feedback often also includes a statement about how one is affected by the helpee's behavior, and it sometimes includes a direct instruction for change. For example, a childcare provider may tell a young child that his behavior is too aggressive or to stop hitting another child. A teacher may write comments on the margin of a student's paper that point out mistakes or that challenge her to think more carefully about a particular issue and that requests the student to correct and resubmit the paper. Feedback also may come in the form of telling a friend how it felt to be insulted by him in public. It comes in various forms in a variety of personal and professional settings. While there is no set recipe for giving feedback, I suggest the following:

1. **Ask if the recipient would like some feedback.** For example, "Fartun, I have some feedback for you. Would you like to hear it?" When your professional helping role *is* to provide feedback, then instead of asking, this first step would instead be to **prepare the helpee for feedback** rather than ask if she wants to hear it. For example, "Fartun, I have some feedback for you. Can you sit for a minute so we can talk?"

2. **Use the I-Message format.** This format of providing feedback speaks to your personal reaction to what has happened. Because it offers a truthful recounting of your experience with the person, I messages often circumvent arguments about whether or not the named behavior actually occurred, and can diffuse defensiveness. The I-Message format is:

   - When I heard/saw X . . . Example: "When I heard what you said about me. . . ."
   - I assumed Y. Example: "I assumed that you were criticizing me."
   - And I felt Z. Example "I was hurt and angry."
   - This message may also include instruction for what needs to happen next. For example, "I really need to talk to you about this."

3. **Clarify that the message was heard by the recipient.** Sometimes the recipient of feedback is already having a reaction to what we have told him before we have even finished talking. That reaction can cause him to misinterpret or block out what has been said. Keep in mind that as hard as it can be to hear feedback, it can also be difficult to give feedback to others—perhaps because we may be angry or uncomfortable around this level of confrontation or worried about how the person will respond. As a result, our feedback may not be as clear as we had hoped. For these reasons, it is always helpful to check that the message has been heard

correctly. For example, "Fartun, did what I said make sense?" Or you can ask the helpee, "Can you repeat back to me what you heard me saying?"

4. **Invite discussion.** Remember that the purpose of providing feedback is to invite the helpee to consider making a change. This happens most effectively when there is an opportunity to for safe and honest discussion. Discussion does not mean backing down from the feedback offered, but rather it is to better enable the helpee to make sense of what has been communicated, to clarify any misunderstandings, and to allow the recipient to respond. For example: "Fartun, let's talk a little bit about what happened here between us. Okay?"

Guidelines for Giving Feedback

Knowing that feedback typically triggers an emotional response (Ilies & Judge, 2005), it is important to think carefully about how and when to offer feedback. Research and theory in the practice of group work provides helpful information on factors that make feedback effective for promoting positive change. Morran et al. (1998) point out, for example, that corrective feedback may be more hearable when it is delivered also with positive feedback. That is, it is easier for people to accept corrective feedback when they hear positive comments about their performance as well. For example, a teacher told his student, "I like how you participated in our class discussion today—your comments were very thoughtful. Nice work. Here is your essay paper. I have asked you to redo the middle section of it because the grammar and organization are confusing. I'm happy to meet with you later to talk about the comments I wrote in the margins." Along these lines, feedback that is overly harsh, critical, negative, and that is given directly—high-intensity feedback—may actually impede task performance (Smith & King, 2004).

Dechawatanapaisal and Siengthai (2006) pointed out that experiencing cognitive dissonance for short (rather than extended) period of time may arouse movement in the direction of change. We also know, however, that too much feedback or confrontation can overwhelm the recipient. At the same time, a reluctance to give feedback or offering too little feedback can yield no change at all (Scaturo, 2002). These findings suggest that it is important to give feedback when it is needed and that the feedback we give should be clear and concise.

Smith and King (2004) also found that sensitivity to feedback influences the extent to which it is effective. Individuals who were highly sensitive to

Table 8.3 Feedback: Reasons and Guidelines

Reasons for Using Feedback	Guidelines for Using Feedback
• To provide information about one's behavior or presence • To communicate an expectation about change • To encourage improvement, self-examination, change	• Prepare the recipient to receive feedback • Include positive feedback when delivering corrective feedback • Be concrete and specific • Avoid harsh and prolonged feedback • Give corrective feedback only when the relationship is strong and secure • Adjust the feedback intensity to recipient sensitivity • Remain engaged in the relationship after the feedback is delivered • Invite discussion and meaning-making after delivering feedback

feedback, for example, performed better when they received low rather than high-intensity feedback. This finding is consistent with the point made by Morran et al. (1998) that it is important to assess the readiness and openness of the recipient to hear feedback prior to giving corrective feedback. Again, they emphasize that giving feedback to people who are not ready or willing to hear it is not likely to be effective. The depth of the helping relationship is an important consideration in feedback exchange. It is not a good idea to offer corrective feedback to someone who you do not know well or to someone with whom you do not have a good relationship. Finally, as with confrontation, it is important to remain engaged with the helpee after providing feedback. This engagement helps keep the helping relationship intact and can help the recipient make meaning from what she has heard (Morran et al., 1998). All of these suggestions are summarized in Table 8.3.

IMMEDIACY

The concept of immediacy refers to attending to what is happening in the moment. For example, a helper might say, "I notice that you stopped talking when I asked about your dog." This comment opens up and has the potential to deepen a conversation. The conversation might turn to the dog, the helper, the helpee, the relationship, or whatever has happened that has caused the helpee to stop talking. Noticing this change by using the skill of *immediacy* invites the helpee to name, explain, or make meaning about what is happening. It opens a discussion. Immediacy is typically used to give attention to and/or promote insight about a particular issue or situation, to gain deeper understanding about the helping relationship, and when the helper hopes to use communications within the helping relationship as a model for how communications can happen in other relationships in the helpee's life (Wheeler & D'Andrea, 2004). A summary of the different purposes and types of immediacy and guidelines for its use are captured in Table 8.4.

Like confrontation and feedback, immediacy can also illuminate discrepancies. For example, "You mentioned that you didn't want to lie to me anymore, yet here you admit that you haven't been truthful. I wonder if we can talk a little bit more about our work together and how we should proceed?" Notice here that while the immediacy was a confrontation, the final part of the communication reveals its intent, which was to focus on the relationship between the helper and helpee. For this reason, immediacy is an excellent way to address difficulties, ruptures, or tension in helping conversations and relationships. Immediacy can also be used to address a lack of trust or worries about a difficult or sensitive issue, it can help clarify aspects of the helping relationship, and it can be used to discuss a confrontation or feedback that has occurred.

Types of Immediacy

Three types of immediacy are typically used in helping conversations (Wheeler & D'Andrea, 2004). **Relationship immediacy**, as illustrated in the example above about being truthful, focuses on the helping relationship. The main purpose of relationship immediacy is to construct or fortify the relationship so that it is and continues to be beneficial to the helpee. It also is a good way to address discrepancies, misunderstandings, misgivings, and ruptures in the relationship. For example, a helper said: "Zahara, I can see that you look a little upset. Is that right? I have been thinking that it must have been very hard for you when I canceled our last meeting—and that was the second time I did that. I apologize—I am very sorry that I had to cancel our appointment two times. I can understand if that may have made you mad at me. I wonder if maybe we should spend a little time right now talking about this?"

Here-and-now immediacy refers to when the helper comments on something that is happening in the conversation. The example above when the helper pointed out that the helpee was silent after mentioning his dog is an example of here-and-now immediacy. The intent of here-and-now immediacy is to bring focus on something that may be particularly relevant and/or that may have otherwise gone unspoken or unnoticed. Here-and-now immediacy can open up conversations about difficult or sensitive issues or topics.

Self-involving immediacy occurs when the helper shares his personal response to something that the helpee has said or done. For example, Carlos, a helpee, tells a story about when his father died. The helper, moved by the story, says, "Oh, Carlos, I am so moved by your story. It is a story of sadness and also a story of courage." This type of immediacy comes from a genuine reaction to something that has been shared in the helping conversation (i.e., "I am so moved")—it is a genuine empathic response. Because self-involving immediacy focuses on the helper's experience, however, it is important to shift the focus back to the helpee after this type of immediacy. You will notice that the helper's comment in this example about sadness and courage begins this shift—moving the response from a personal sharing to meaning-making. The shift becomes complete when the helper adds, "I wonder if it would be helpful to talk a little bit more about what was happening for you at that time?" This final sentence directs the conversation back to the helpee.

Guidelines for Using Immediacy

Hazler and Barwick (2001) point out that using immediacy involves a certain amount of risk for the helpee. When you draw attention to difficult or uncomfortable issues, you raise the intensity in the conversation, and this elevated intensity may be more than some helpees can handle. This is particularly true if you have not first established a strong working alliance. Immediacy can also feel intense and risky for the helper, so you should not use immediacy if *you* are not willing to remain in a tense or challenging conversation with the helpee. Finally, timing is critical. If you raise an important issue without enough time to discuss it, the process will feel unfinished.

So, immediacy, like all of these change strategies, must be used with intentionality: Your helpee must be able to handle it, you must have the ability to remain in an emotionally intense situation, and there must be adequate time to engage in the important conversation that needs to happen after being immediate. This recipe for using immediacy is intended to offer immediacy in a way that respects the helpee's input and invites further discussion or exploration:

1. **Point out what you see/hear/notice.** Example: "I notice that . . ."

2. **Invite the helpee to hypothesize about what you have noticed/said.** Example: "What do you think about that?"

Table 8.4 Immediacy: Reasons, Types, and Guidelines

Reasons for Using Immediacy	Types of Immediacy	Guidelines for Using Immediacy
• To give attention to an issue or situation • To initiate discussion about a particular issue or topic • To promote insight • To illuminate discrepancies and open discussion • To address ruptures, concerns, issues in the helping relationship • To check in about the helping relationship	Relationship: • Discussion about the helping relationship Here-and-now: • Discussion about something that is happening in the moment. Self-involving: • Expressing a genuine personal response	• Be clear and direct • Monitor intensity • Be sensitive to impact • Attend to timing • Use with intentionality—only when it is therapeutically appropriate

3. **Share your hypothesis, if appropriate, and always with genuine tentativeness.** Example: "I was wondering if it means . . . ?"

4. **Invite discussion/exploration.** Example: "I was hoping that we could take a little time to talk about this."

VIDEO LINK:
Immediacy

DECONSTRUCTING CONVERSATIONS

As you will recall from Chapter 2, a discourse is a set of meanings, communicated through language, images, and other artifacts of society, that produce a particular version of events (Burr, 1995). Discourses communicate commonly accepted truths within a particular society, and they have a structuring influence in how people see or define themselves and others, and on how they live their lives. For example, the discourse of adolescence in many circles in contemporary American society suggests that youth in the teen ages are rebellious and not needing or wanting engagement with their parents. The structuring influence of this discourse invites parents to take a "hands off" approach to parenting their teenagers who otherwise might want or need more parental engagement.

Rationally, we are aware that there is no one single truth about most things in this world, and particularly about adolescence. Not all teens are rebellious, and not all parents believe that they should take a laisse-faire approach to parenting their teens. However, Foucault (1972) has helped us understand that normalized ideas about truth have immense power and structuring influence in people's lives. As mentioned in Chapter 6, one of the most profound and also one of the most disconcerting effects of powerful discourses is the positions that they offer. Discourses invite us to believe that they are truths, and many of us unwittingly adjust our behaviors and our beliefs according to discourses without question. Many parents I know worry that they are being too "hands on" or that they are falling into the dreaded category of "helicopter parents" with their teenagers. They conform to the discourse that teens need freedom, but struggle with how much freedom to offer. Many also fear that their teenagers will not like them and will rebel if they set a limit, so they avoid setting limits in an attempt avoid the dreaded conflict they anticipate will happen if they say "no." Most parents struggle with how to parent their teens amid a multiple of discourses that offer parenting ideas. And, as a result, they often forgo listening to their own wisdom, drawn from years of knowing and parenting their child. I one time had a parent, who had a very close relationship with his two healthy and very mature children, ask me what to do to help his children through a difficult period of grief. This was a parent who clearly knew how to raise his children through challenge and joy, yet he was positioned by discourses of grief or, perhaps, fathering, that invited him to give up his own expertise and, instead, rely on an "expert" to tell him how to proceed. And, of course, what his children needed most was him. They needed their connection to him and his knowledge of how to help them through thick and thin. The point is that discourses shape people's lives in subtle but powerful ways.

The practice of deconstruction, a key component of narrative therapy, entails identifying and interrogating the taken-for-granted assumptions of discourses that have influence in people's lives. It is a practice of philosophical inquiry into the meanings of language as well as one's experiences in the world (Monk, Winslade, & Sinclair, 2008), and aims to "expose the biases, flaws, and inconsistencies" (Leffert, 2010, p. 8) in one's thinking process so as to allow for multiple understandings or meanings to emerge. Deconstructing questions invite individuals to step out of their own perspective and to be aware of the ways in which they are influenced by normative ideas (i.e., ideas that we assume to be truths); it invites critical examination of ideas that have previously never been questioned (Freedman & Combs, 1996). The term *unpacking* is sometimes used for the practice of deconstruction (Freedman & Combs, 1996).

To better understand this idea of deconstructing discourses, let's talk about this idea of unpacking. Consider the metaphor of person who carries around a

Illustration 8.1 Unpacking

©iStockphoto.com/Ezrena

suitcase with a selection of outfits that he uses to dress for various occasions. We might imagine that this person guards his suitcase carefully when he is in public so that it does not disappear leaving him naked. Now think about what it would be like to sit with this individual and invite him to unpack the suitcase with us. While he is unpacking the suitcase, we ask questions about what shirt goes with which set of pants, why he wears one thing instead of another, which outfit he wears on this occasion and which one on another occasion. In this process of asking questions, we begin to learn about how he understands the contents of his suitcase; we uncover his ideas about what is right and what is wrong, and we learn something about him, too—how he understands his world and his place in it.

What would happen if we start to question this man about his outfit decisions? Suppose we ask if he ever wears shirt A with pants B? Or what it would be like to wear X outfit in some other setting? These questions that invite him to consider his outfits differently, and they invite speculation into other ideas that he has not previously considered—new ways of considering his wardrobe.

Going back, now, to the idea of deconstructing conversations: Think of the suitcase as the set of ideas that we all carry inside our heads. Deconstructing conversations are the unpacking of the suitcase of ideas that we carry around with us. When we ask someone to share his understandings about something, we learn more about him. When we invite him to look at things a different way, we open up space for critical examination of taken-for-granted practices and assumptions. We invite speculation about new possibilities. Deconstructing conversations, then, invite people to consider alternative ways of thinking and, perhaps, to take a stand against ideas and practices that do not serve them well (Freedman & Combs, 1996). Deconstruction is a process that has the potential to open up new possibilities for meaning-making (Monk et al., 2008), identity formation, and new ideas for change (McKenzie & Monk, 1997).

Deconstructing Practices

Your role as a helper in deconstructing conversations is to be **tentative, curious,** and to **avoid the position of expert,** since that position should be reserved for the helpee (Monk et al., 2008). You should assume a "deliberately naïve posture" (p. 130). The intent is not to seek specific answers to the questions that you pose, but to engage the helpee in discussion that will open up options and possibilities. Again, deconstructing conversations are particularly helpful when helpees are unaware of the influence of discourses in their lives, and these conversations also have the potential to promote agency. Again, there is no set recipe for deconstructing conversations. However, consider this basic recipe, in no particular order, for the practice of deconstructing:

1. **Briefly summarize the challenge or concern.** Example: "So you are trying out for the football team again this year, even though you hated it last year. Is that right?"

2. **Invite the helpee to consider if there is a discourse that may be influencing the concern.** Example: "Why do you think that you should try out for the team even though you don't really want to?" And then, after some discussion: "You mentioned that you think that the football team is good for your social life. What is it about football players that makes them so popular, do you think?"

3. **Ask questions that invite exploration of how the concern is related to the discourse.** Example: "So, this idea that football players are popular, you think, is related to that idea out there that, as you said, 'real men are strong and aggressive'? I am wondering if that has something to do with why you are signing up for the team even though you don't like it very

much—that idea that you want everyone here in school to think you are strong? Aggressive?"

4. **Ask questions about the validity, utility, and voracity of influence the discourse has on the person's life.** Example: "Do you think that that idea about men being strong is helpful or useful to guys here in high school?" "You mentioned how it is helpful, then, particularly in terms of girlfriends. Are there ways in which it, maybe, is not so helpful?" "Do you think that's true, that football players are strong?"

5. **Invite the helpee to decide if he wants the discourse to have such a powerful influence on his life.** Example: "So, we have been talking a bit about this idea that men need to be strong. And also that football players are tough, strong, and therefore more attractive. You mentioned that you think that maybe this is a big part of why you play football—so that you'll be perceived as strong, and it helps your popularity. What do you think about the ways in which these ideas about strength, popularity, etc. are running your life?"

6. **Invite discussion about counter discourses that may be more helpful.** Example: "I wonder if there are other ideas about men out there?" "Are there are some other ideas about men that you think are important to how *you* want to be?" "Let me reframe what I was curious about: I know that there are other ideas about how men should be—even in the Superbowl this year, there were car commercials that promoted men as caring, engaged family men. I was wondering what other ideas about how men should be are appealing to you?"

7. **Invite discussion about the helpee's own beliefs, values, and hopes that would prefer to have shaping his decisions and his life.** Example: "So now that we have talked about this a little, I wonder if any of this is relevant to the original issue that you talked about—signing up for football even if you don't like it. Is this idea about popularity important enough—and I get why it is important—for you to decide to do something you really don't like? Or is there something else you'd rather do or some other idea that you'd rather emulate?"

Case Study Example

Let us use one of our case studies in Chapter 3 as an example of how deconstructing conversations can be used in helping relationships. While the recipe above offers the major components of deconstructing conversations, this is one recipe that really cannot be rigidly followed. Deconstructing conversations are more a communication of a position and a genuine curiosity than they are a skill with specific steps.

Recall that in Case Study 2, Mrs. Morrison raised concern among staff at the senior living community because she appeared depressed and isolated. Center staff decided to consult with Mrs. Morrison's family to determine how to respond to their concerns. They learned from Mrs. Morrison's children that she had been actively involved in her community prior to entering the center and had resisted residential placement for a long time, commenting to her sons on many occasions that "old people go to those places to shrivel up and die." Mrs. Morrison's children speculated that her difficulties were likely due to initial adjustment issues and that she would soon find her niche, settle in, and become active in the residential community.

VIDEO LINK:
Deconstructing

Based on this input, Emma and the other staff decided that they could probably help Mrs. Morrison in her adjustment by talking with her about the concept of aging (i.e., the discourse of aging). By engaging in deconstructing conversations about aging, they hoped to help Mrs. Morrison begin to see her new home at the center as a place of community, opportunity for building new connections, and opportunity for being active and productive. To this end, Emma decided to broach the topic with Mrs. Morrison during her morning check-ins. Emma's plan was to ask Mrs. Morrison about her own ideas about the meaning of aging, to explore the ways in which aging is defined in larger society, and to invite Mrs. Morrison to envision how she would like to define herself amongst all of these aging discourses.

MOTIVATING CHANGE

The stages of change model discussed in Chapter 6 is based on the fundamental idea that meaningful change, regardless of what specifically is to be changed and regardless of whether an individual gets help to change, will only happen when the individual is ready (Norcross, Krebs, & Prochaska, 2010; Prochaska & DiClemente, 1982; Prochaska, Norcross, & DiClemente, 1994). Motivational interviewing (Miller & Rollnick, 2013) is a practice of helping with a dual focus on (1) respecting and supporting individuals wherever they are in the process of change, and (2) increasing helpees' motivation to change. It is the combination of empathy and relationship, and the ability to use specific techniques to evoke and reinforce change that make motivational interviewing effective (Miller & Rose, 2009). The basic principles of motivational interviewing underlie the suggestions mentioned below that can be used by helpers to motivate change. These suggestions are also summarized in Table 8.5.

Motivating change, according to Miller and Rollnick (2013), begins with empathy. In this model, **empathy** is communicated by listening carefully, working to understand the helpee's situation, and accepting the helpee's ambivalence around change. Being empathic does not mean that you necessarily agree with the helpee, however; it simply refers to accepting where the helpee is in her own process of change. For example, Maria told her social worker that she doesn't think drinking is a problem and that she really doesn't need to stop. The social worker, knowing that Maria had temporarily lost custody of her son because she was not able to protect him from harm due to chronic intoxication, expressed empathy by saying, "This is a tough spot to be in, Maria, and I hear you saying that you don't think that drinking is a huge problem for you."

Developing discrepancies, which we have already talked about in this chapter, refers to amplifying the dissonance between where the helpee is at in terms of change and where she wants to be, in terms of not having the problem (Miller & Rollnick, 2013). This entails pointing out that there is a discrepancy between one's present behavior and one's goals or desires. Back to the example above, the social worker respectfully pointed out, "You love your son very much and want to regain custody of him, Maria, but you are still not wanting to give up alcohol." This comment points out the discrepancy between Maria's decision regarding sobriety and her desire to parent her son. The helper in this example could also say, "I hear that you don't think that there is a drinking problem, Maria. But you did have that incident when you were completely blacked out from drinking, and they found little Junior walking the streets alone that night."

Developing discrepancies promotes awareness of a problem and attempts to evoke just enough dissonance to stimulate motivation. However, it is important to **avoid argumentation** (Miller & Rollnick, 2013). Arguing with a helpee about whether she has a problem or whether she should change shifts the focus away from the concern and puts it squarely in the relationship dynamic. Most importantly, arguing with the helpee about the need to change will likely evoke resistance or defensiveness. It threatens the individual's freedom to make her own choices. Helpers should resist labeling, instructing, and insisting that the helpee do something. Instead, helpers should emphasize personal choice and continue to point out discrepancies between the helpee's desires and current behaviors. Back to our example with Maria, the social worker says, "I understand that you don't think the drinking is a problem, Maria. And, of course, treatment is your choice—there is no point to sign up for treatment if you don't think you have a problem." Maria agrees. Then the social worker adds, "I do need to point out, though, that the court will probably continue to rule against custody unless there is some resolution to what happened that night when you blacked out and they found Junior alone outside."

The concept of **rolling with resistance** is a helper strategy of acknowledging helpee resistance when it presents itself (Miller & Rollnick, 2013). Here the helper can acknowledge that the helpee does not want to change at this time and also point out that not wanting to change is normal and understandable. For example, Maria says, "They are just making a big deal about the drinking incident. I'm not really an alcoholic." The social worker responds, "I hear what you are saying, Maria. It can be so hard to hear the words 'You are an alcoholic.' It doesn't sound like something that you want to be." Or he can say, "I know you've tried to give up drinking before, Maria, and it's a really hard thing to do. This is not easy."

The final principle in motivational interviewing is to **support self-efficacy** (Miller & Rollnick, 2013). This refers to highlighting the helpee's ability to carry out a desired action. It is the expression of hope or confidence in the helpee's ability to change, in whatever way and if desired. In our example, the social worker attempts to support Maria and increase motivation by saying, "I can see that you are not yet sure about the requirement to enter into treatment, Maria. You don't even see yourself as having a huge drinking problem. Stopping drinking is a very difficult thing to do—for anyone. But one thing I know about you is that you are strong and determined—you have shown that in they past when you lost your mother and when you gave up drinking for almost a year. I also know that you love your son, Junior, and you have said that you want to be a better mother to him than your mother was to you. I bet that if you decide to do it—to get into treatment and do what it takes to regain custody of Junior—you will use that strength and determination to make these things happen. It is hard, but you can be successful."

Remember that motivational interviewing is designed to respect and accept the subjective experiences of the helpee; it is not a practice of talking

Table 8.5 Motivating Change

1. Express empathy
2. Develop discrepancies
3. Avoid argumentation
4. Roll with resistance
5. Support self-efficacy

Adapted from: Miller, W. R., & Rollnick, S. (2013). *Motivational interviewing: Helping people change.* New York, NY: The Guilford Press.

individuals into something that they do not want or are not ready to do. As mentioned, the principles of motivating change are applicable across settings and for working with individuals who are challenged by a variety of problems. For this reason, motivational interviewing is an important practice for both clinical and nonclinical helpers. Clearly, this brief review is no substitute for more extensive training in motivational interviewing, so helpers using this approach should receive additional instruction in motivational interviewing principles and practice.

ADVOCACY

So far, we've discussed invoking change when the problem is situated within the individual, but a helper might take a different approach when the problem is situated externally. As mentioned throughout this book, systems of power and privilege influence the experiences of individuals in their various social locations. For those who identify in nondominant social groups, the shaping influences of discourses often result in very real experiences of marginalization, disadvantage, and discrimination. Thus, when helpers are witness to the effects of averse social forces on the lives of their helpees, advocacy may be the best intervention.

In describing advocacy, Toporek, Lewis, and Crethar (2009) emphasize the distinction between acting *with* versus acting *on behalf* of others. *Acting with* means that the helper works collaboratively with the helpee (or group) to identify the problem to be addressed, determine together the course of action to follow, and decide together who will do what toward the agreed-upon ends. Ultimately, it means that the helpee is the one who makes the decisions and takes action. *Acting on behalf* is a fundamentally different process. It means *doing for* rather than *with*. Advocates who work on behalf of others are the ones who act, typically because the helpee is unable to do so herself, for whatever reason. To clarify these two types of advocacy, consider this example of Courtney, below.

Courtney is living in a domestic violence shelter because of an abusive incident in her relationship with her husband. While clearly upset about the abuse that occurred, Courtney reports that she is committed to reuniting with her husband "after he settles down." She has some ideas for how to move forward in that relationship although, admittedly, she is not sure if her husband will comply. In the shelter, Courtney is assigned to a well-meaning helper, Amaya, who is aware of domestic violence recidivism data and has her own worries that the abuse will continue if Courtney returns home to her husband. Amaya

Illustration 8.2   Advocacy

©iStockphoto.com/jack191

tells Courtney that she really should leave the marriage and she even "helps" Courtney move in this direction by finding an alternative longer-term housing arrangement for Courtney so she can start her life anew (without the husband). Amaya advises Courtney that she can move into her new apartment within a week, using public assistance and a grant from the shelter to pay the initial deposit.

In this situation, the well-meaning but somewhat overzealous helper made a decision about what was right for Courtney without consideration of Courtney's own desires and decisions. Thus, it is an example of advocacy on *behalf* of a helpee. It is a tricky situation, but clearly we can see that Amaya made decisions for and pushed Courtney in directions that did not correspond to Courtney's own articulated desires.

Let us go back to this example but suppose, instead, that Courtney had expressed an interest in leaving her husband and wanted help finding an alternative living situation. Although more in line with Courtney's desires, we see that Amaya's action still falls within the category of acting on *behalf*. Note that while Courtney expressed a desire to leave her husband, the helper was the one who secured the housing situation without further collaboration or discussion with Courtney. As Funk, Minoletti, Drew, Taylor, and Saraceno (2005) point out, people with mental health and other disabilities are often presumed to "lack the capacity" (p. 71) to make their own decisions. In our scenario, Amaya's actions still circumnavigated Courtney; Amaya acted on behalf of Courtney without Courtney's active engagement in the process. If Amaya had taken the time to comb through various housing options with Courtney, coached Courtney on how to make initial contact with prospective landlords, and talked through the various options in decision-making, her advocacy efforts would represent advocacy *with* the helpee. These actions likely would have empowered Courtney to use her own abilities to follow through on the decisions she was making and, at the same time, offered her support and important skills (i.e., how to go about finding housing) that she may have lacked.

While acting with and acting on behalf are both appropriate advocate actions, it is important to be aware of the drawbacks of each approach to advocacy. Even in cases where there is clear consent from the helpee to work on her behalf, we should always consider the unintended consequences of such a position in terms of promoting helplessness or moving in a direction that is not desired by the helpee. For this reason, we should always endeavor to realign our work (away from a behalf position) as soon as appropriately possible to promote helpee agency. At the same time, acting *with* someone as an advocate can have adverse consequences, too, if these actions leave the helpee exposed to danger or if the helpee does not have sufficient information or ability to follow through on the identified actions.

A second dimension of the Lewis et al. (2002) model of advocacy is about the target audience or who will be addressed in the advocacy interventions. These include individual, systems, and societal levels (Toporek et al., 2009). Advocacy on the *individual level* focuses on actions that are aimed at a specific individual in a specific situation. For example, you may encourage and help your helpee to call her landlord to ask why the rent was raised (i.e., acting with her). Or you may call on behalf of the helpee, still working at the individual level. Advocacy at the *systems level* address problems in an institution, community, or a particular group. For example, let us suppose that you noticed a bias among landlords in the community against renting apartments to women who had been living in a domestic violence shelter. You could engage in a letter writing campaign to the mayor and city council members, pointing out this bias on the part of the landlords and requesting a full legal investigation into the matter. All of these actions would be acting on behalf of a helpee at a community (systems) level. Helping victims of these policies write their own letters and thinking through who they should go to would be an example of acting with helpees at a community (systems) level. Advocacy at a *political or societal level* situates concerns in the context of broader society. Efforts at this level tend to focus on public awareness and societal change and may entail engagement in legislative action and policy reform. Again, these actions can be conducted with or on behalf of members of the affected groups.

CHAPTER SUMMARY

This chapter offered a review of a number of skills that can be used in a variety of different types of helping conversations to promote change. These include informing or using psychoeducation, decision-making or problem solving, confronting, using feedback and immediacy, engaging in deconstructing conversations, and being an advocate. In addition, steps for motivating change were also reviewed. For each skill, the reason and general guidelines for its use were included. Recipes for implementation were included for many of the skills, although it is recommended that you use the recipes in creative, innovative, and intentional ways.

DISCUSSION QUESTIONS

1. What are some of the key components to remember when supporting someone in the decision-making process?

2. Giving and receiving feedback can be an intense exchange within a helping relationship. What are some things that a helper can do to minimize intensity and potential defensiveness?

3. What are the relative benefits of working *with* versus *on behalf* of someone in the role of an advocate? Give an example of working in each role.

4. How might a helper increase a helpee's motivation for change?

5. What are some appropriate ways to intervene when the helpee appears unmotivated or marginally motivated to change?

CHAPTER 9

HELPING PEOPLE IN CRISIS

LEARNING OBJECTIVES

1. Explain how natural or human-made disasters affect victims

2. Identify a number of risk factors and warning signs related to risk of harm to self and others

3. Explain initial response priorities for working with helpees who are experiencing crises or where there are concerns about harm to self or others

INTRODUCTION

The term *crisis* generally refers to an event that causes extreme stress and compromises a person's normal functioning. The experience of crisis typically results in a temporary sense of disequilibrium and a breakdown in normal coping mechanisms (Cavaiola & Colford, 2006; Collins & Collins, 2005). That is, a crisis is something that happens to someone—by surprise or not—and causes so much stress that the individual has difficulties coping.

A variety of situations—some predictable and some not—can cause this experience of disequilibrium and diminished functioning that we are talking about here in this chapter (Cavaiola & Colford, 2006; Collins & Collins, 2005). For example, normal developmental milestones or experiences are sometimes framed as crises—consider here the idea of a midlife crisis. These types of crises are referred to as *developmental* or *existential* crises. *Situational* or *traumatic* crises result from extreme or challenging events that happen in people's lives. They typically are unexpected. Situational crises may occur over a period of time or they may come and pass rather quickly. Here we are talking about events such as disasters—forest fires, storms, or floods, for example. Human-made events including school shootings, automobile accidents, or assaults are also considered to be situational crises. In this category, too, are personal crises such as divorce, loss of a job, death of a loved one, etc. All of these situational crises cause upheaval, and many victims experience them as trauma. In fact, the effects of these crises may extend beyond their immediate victims, leaving adverse effects, sometimes, on those who are witness to them—this is especially important because helpers can be affected by witnessing the trauma of others, as was mentioned in Chapter 5. Another type of crisis is a *psychiatric crisis* (Cavaiola & Colford, 2006; Collins & Collins, 2005), which is related to a psychiatric condition where a person experiences a temporary but significant loss of control over his mind or emotions, and feels or demonstrates extreme instability. Sometimes individuals in this state have a sense of being controlled by someone or something outside of themselves, and may experience hallucinations or delusions.

In this chapter, we will focus on two types of situational crises that you may encounter in your work with others: disasters (natural or human-made) and harm (to self or others). The crisis response principles that are discussed in this chapter are also relevant to other types of situational and psychiatric crisis experiences. While some might argue that nonclinical professional helpers are not the most appropriate first responders in crises unless they have had specific crisis response training, we need to remember that situational crises are equal opportunity offenders. We simply do not have the luxury of having a highly trained clinical professional available whenever crisis strikes. Having a basic understanding of what happens for individuals in crisis and how to manage these kinds of situations will help you respond with confidence if you encounter a crisis situation. The goal for nonclinical helpers responding to crises is to intervene immediately to stabilize the situation and enable the helpee to access more appropriate assistance—usually a clinical helper—as soon as possible.

We will begin with a discussion about natural or human-made disasters that includes a basic response protocol that you can use if you are working with individuals in this type of crisis. Then we will move to a discussion about crises involving harm to self or others. This discussion begins with a review of suicide and violence statistics, followed by information related to risk factors and warning signs, and concludes with strategies for responding to situations when individuals are threatening or appear likely to inflict harm to themselves or others.

NATURAL OR HUMAN-MADE DISASTERS OR CRISES

Situational crises begin with an external precipitating event (Collins & Collins; 2005). They are beyond the control of the individual, typically have a sudden onset, and pose an emergency or threat in some way (Cavaiola & Colford, 2006). As mentioned, examples of situations that can cause trauma experiences include personal victimization, accidents, and natural disasters. Typically the term *disaster* is used in situations that happen in the natural environment, such as storms, fires, etc., and *crisis* is sometimes used in reference to situational events that are human-made, such as car accidents, etc. However, these two terms are often used interchangeably.

Effects of Crisis

As discussed in Chapter 2, research has revealed that a series of neurotransmitter and neurohormonal firings initiate and regulate the body's response to stress at a neurobiological level. Basically, these neuro-firings create a state of arousal (e.g., increased heart rate, deactivation of nonessential systems, and

Photo 9.1 Natural Disasters

©iStockphoto.com/PhotoTalk

activation of threat-relevant memories) and a subsequent return to homeostasis once the threat cue is terminated (Kindsvatter & Geroski, 2014). This period of initial arousal is often referred to as a *flight-or-fight reaction* because the activation of stress hormones increases blood flow to the large muscles of the body (arms and legs), causing them to move or freeze (Cavaiola & Colford, 2006).

During a crisis event, and sometimes long afterward, victims are upset, confused, disorganized, and anxious (Cavaiola & Colford, 2006; Collins & Collins, 2005). In some cases, victims become immobilized, in a state that is often referred to as being in *shock*. They may lash out or they may retreat. People who have experienced a crisis may have difficulties performing the tasks of everyday living, difficulties regulating their emotional states (they may be over- or underregulated), and they usually feel extremely vulnerable. They also may be consumed by worry, fears of repeated trauma, and they may be isolated from their former systems of support. Many people in crisis feel these reactions so strongly, they report that they are unable to control themselves, and indeed, for some, they truly need help coping with what has happened.

These challenges often leave victims compromised in their ability to make decisions and manage everyday life tasks, and they may be particularly suggestible to the ideas and directions of others. This adds yet another layer of vulnerability and another experience of not being in control of their lives. Additionally, some people respond to situational crises with self-blame and guilt (Cavaiola & Colford, 2006). These feelings may be particularly salient in situations where the person believes that she should have been able to control the precipitating event.

Individuals who already live with stress in their lives are particularly vulnerable during acute episodes of stress, including the experience of a situational crisis. Chronic exposure to stress can lead to elevated baseline levels of stress hormones, abnormal rhythms of hormonal release, dendrite apathy, and inhibited neural growth (Siegel, 2012). Repeated exposure to stressful experiences, particularly when one is exposed to stress during the sensitive periods of early development, can have lasting effects on later emotional regulation abilities, cognitive functioning, and behavior (Kindsvatter & Geroski, 2014). According to Schreiber, Gurwitch, and Wong (2006), children who experience trauma or chronic stress may have decreased attention in school and may develop disrupted sleeping or eating behaviors. Many become disinterested in previously enjoyable activities and display mood dysregulation such as anxiety, depression, and irritability. Children often display behavioral manifestations of trauma such as increased temper tantrums or anger outbursts.

Table 9.1 Common Reactions to Situational Crises

Examples of Cognitive, Behavioral, and Affective Responses to Situational Crises	
Cognitive Tasks	• Difficulties in concentration • Disorganization • Confusion • Difficulties in decision-making (and an increased suggestability) • Sense of helplessness (that life is out of control)
Motor Behaviors	• Disrupted sleep • Disrupted eating patterns • Immobility
Affective States	• Anxiety/worry • Fear • Anger • Feeling of being out of control • Mood dysregulation • Disinterest (in previously enjoyable tasks) • Vulnerability

Adapted from:
  Cavaiola, A. A., & Colford, J. E. (2006). *A practical guide to crisis intervention.* Belmont, CA: Wadsworth.
  Collins, B. G., & Collins, T. M. (2005). *Crisis and trauma: Developmental-ecological intervention.* Boston, MA: Houghton Mifflin.

The return to equilibrium after a crisis event happens at different rates and in different ways for everyone. While some people may recover within hours, days, or weeks, others may have enduring reactions that reach many years on into the future. Many individuals who have experienced a situational crisis are subsequently triggered at times when they are reminded of the event, particularly on anniversaries or when they see photos or hear stories of the event, even many years later. Common reactions to situational crises are summarized in Table 9.1.

CRISIS RESPONSE STRATEGIES FOR HELPERS

The various models of crisis response that are offered in crisis intervention texts (e.g., Cavaiola & Colford, 2006; Collins & Collins, 2005; James & Gilliland, 2001; Roberts & Ottens, 2005) and professional organizations (e.g., American Counseling Association, National Child Traumatic Stress Network, National Center for PTSD, and the National Center for School Crisis and Bereavement) describe crisis response as a process that includes assessing the situation, determining an appropriate response/course of action, and then carrying out the appropriate response. The discussion about crisis in this chapter and summarized in Table 9.2 is loosely framed upon the *Listen, Protect, Connect* model of Psychological First Aid (Schreiber & Gurwitch, 2011; Schreiber, Gurwitch & Wong, 2006; Wong, Schreiber, & Gurwitch, 2008). The term *psychological first aid* refers to a brief, focused intervention that is used initially after a crisis occurs (Wong et al., 2008). Our discussion identifies these steps in crisis response: approaching the situation and gathering information, providing safety, and connecting the victim to appropriate resources.

Approaching the Situation

Recognizing how traumatized and disoriented victims of crisis can feel, it is a good idea to initially approach people who have been involved in a crisis with a simple introduction and brief explanation about why you are there (Cavaiola & Colford, 2006). For example, "Hi. My name is Anne. I am here to listen and help in any way I can." Helpers should try to establish a functional relationship by attending directly to the individual, offering empathy, communicating warmth, and maintaining a sense of calm. For example, use a soft and calm tone and welcoming gestures, ask the affected person for her name, allow her to dictate the terms of the conversation (i.e., tell you what they want to tell you), and be careful to respect any obvious cultural nuances (Substance Abuse and Mental Health Services Administration [SAMHSA], 2005).

Gathering Information

When you first invite someone who has experienced a crisis into a conversation about what has happened, **listen** carefully to what he wants to tell you about the incident and also to the help that he articulates that he wants or needs. Here you can use listening and attending skills discussed in Chapter 7. These simple steps, which do not need to follow this specific order, should guide this information-gathering process:

1. Ask what happened (if you do not already know). Here a simple, "Can you tell me what happened to you?" would work.

2. Appraise the victim's condition. Here you might say, "Are you hurt in any way?" "What do you need at this moment?" "What worries do you

have that need immediate attention?" While it is important to gather information from a victim, it is critically important to remember, however, that you should never pressure the individual to talk. Your role is to communicate that you are available if the victim wants help (SAMHSA, 2005).

3. Gather information about the victim's status through observation. Here again your aim is to determine the extent to which the individual is affected by the crisis. This will help you know what assistance to offer and how to proceed. These questions (to ask yourself) may guide your observations:

- What is the victim's emotional state? Is she upset, inconsolable, anxious, angry, calm, resigned, etc.? Is this what you would expect to see, given the crisis or disaster that has occurred?

- How is she behaving? Is she agitated, withdrawn, restless, etc.? Is her behavior what you might expect? Does she appear to be injured? Dangerous to herself or others?

- What cognitive functioning patterns do you notice? Are her thought processes clear and appropriate to the situation? Does she know what happened? Are her sentences cohesive? Does she seem confused? Does she have a sense of what she needs or how she wants to proceed?

- What support does she have? How is she able to access her support systems? Is there someone available that she knows who can help her? Does she seem to want the support offered by this individual?

Your observations in response to these questions will help dictate what actions you may need to take. In some cases, the victim may be hurt, and there is little time to talk as medical assistance is the priority. No two situations will be the same. Sometimes a victim may not want to talk to you. Other times, the victim may be eager to talk about what has happened and engage with you.

It is important to understand that if law enforcement personnel are involved, they will likely be the ones directing the response, including who can talk to and have access to the victim(s). In these cases, your role will probably be to serve as a support, ready to help if asked. In large-scale disaster response situations, an assessment will probably be conducted by a specific individual who is assigned to this task, and you may be asked not to intervene. However, if you are the first or sole responder to a crisis, this task of gathering information is likely yours to implement. Specific assessment issues related to harm to self and others are discussed a little later in this chapter—there is a slightly different response protocol in situations where it appears that the victim is in danger of hurting himself or hurting someone else. In nonharm situations, the purpose of the initial "interview" with the victim of a crisis is to gather as much information as appropriate to determine how to respond.

On rare occasions, a first responder may need to gather information from other people to determine the needs of the victim. This is called gathering collateral information. Gathering collateral information may be needed if you are working with someone who is significantly impaired, when you are having difficulties understanding the person, or when you are unclear about the situation. Family members and others who witnessed the event may be helpful in providing this additional information. Of course, you always want to be careful about confidentiality when talking with others. Keep in mind that this is about *gathering* information; it is not about providing information to others. We must never compromise helpee safety and integrity by offering information that is not ours to give. Helpers need to be especially vigilant about this when there is media present.

Provide Safety

The next step in this response model is to **protect** the victim. Here the goal is to attempt to reestablish a sense of emotional and physical safety after a crisis has occurred (Wong et al., 2008). Safety in this context refers to minimizing, in any way we can, the physical and psychological danger that is posed by the event (James & Gilliland, 2001). This can happen in multiple ways.

First, you can ensure safety by providing appropriate information to the victim or by taking control of the situation. This may mean letting the person know that the immediate danger has passed, accompanying her to a safe physical location, or screening her from unwanted others asking questions or taking photos. For example: "Jasmin, that was a pretty serious accident you were in. You are in the hospital now and you are safe. The doctors are monitoring you, and they are attending to others who were in the accident. I am here with you and will stay with you until your family arrives. Please let me know if there are any questions you have."

Ensuring safety may also entail addressing some of the victim's worries. For example, a victim may want a specific loved one to be contacted, may be worried about others involved in the incident, or may have lost something that he is worried about. While some of these questions are easy and appropriate for you to answer, it is important to be aware that in some cases it may not be appropriate for you to respond to some of these questions. Remember that you are not in the position to break confidentiality and disclose information about others to a victim who is asking questions. Also, you may not be the best person to convey bad news, particularly to someone who is already extremely vulnerable or alone without any personal support. And, in larger crisis response efforts, communication is almost always coordinated at a centralized level. What you always can do, however, is assure the victim that you will try to find answers to his questions as soon as possible. The emphasis here is that you should always be working in coordination with others. Your actions should always be in line with larger response efforts and protocols.

Cavaiola and Colford (2006) remind us that the experience of crisis leaves individuals feeling that they have no or limited control of their life. For this reason, they recommend intentionally inviting the victim to be in control of those things that she can and should control as much as possible and, of course, as appropriate. This invites the victim to begin to establish equilibrium. One way to facilitate a sense of control is by inviting the victim to participate in simple decision-making. For example, you can offer the victim simple choices

Photo 9.2 Listening and Providing Support

©iStockphoto.com/Yuri_Arcurs

such as, which chair she would like to sit in, what name she would prefer you use, or if she would like a blanket or a glass of water. Having said this, remember that even these simple decisions may feel overwhelming for some people when they are grappling to cope with crisis, so be careful not to overwhelm victims with too much information and too many decisions, options, or questions. Also, be sure not to invite decision-making options that are unsafe, inappropriate, or out of the control of the individual. For example, inviting an injured victim to stand up may not be medically appropriate. Again, here, it is important to work only in the area of your abilities and expertise.

Connect to Resources

A common reaction to experiences of trauma and crisis is social isolation and withdrawal. Yet, we know that maintaining connection with others and reestablishing routines promote a sense of predictability and stability in the aftermath of crisis (Wong et al., 2008). So, an important component of crisis response is to facilitate connection between the victim and key social supports and resources that are meaningful and appropriate for him.

In the immediate aftermath of a crisis event, many people will need to be with their own family, friends, or support community more than they need to be with us. Others may need us to be their support person for a time—either because others are not available or, for some reason, the victim is having difficulty (or anticipates difficulty) accessing the support that he or she needs from those in his/her immediate community. In these cases, we should do all that we can to make ourselves available to provide support, as appropriate. Some victims may need us to listen, while others may ask us to weigh in on decisions or provide service. For example, a victim may ask you if you think that he needs medical care. Another may ask to borrow your phone to call a family member. Others may ask you to accompany them to a hospital or to be present as they speak to a police officer.

Some victims will need a medical evaluation, clinical treatment, or assistance finding basic shelter—some of which you will probably not be able to provide. In these cases, your offer of support, then, is to connect the victim to others who can provide the services that they need. The availability of resources, of course, is an important variable and may limit what you are able to provide a victim. It is always best to consult with a colleague or supervisor before making any recommendations or providing any services.

Individuals who appear to be in danger of harming themselves when they are in crisis, may need to be monitored—even if they don't ask for it—until a clinical or emergency professional is available to intervene. The duty to protect individuals

Table 9.2 Crisis Response: Listen, Protect, Connect

Crisis Response: Information, Safety, Connection		
Gather Information	Invite	Introduce yourself.
	Listen	Attend; be empathic, warm, and calm.
	Assess	Determine what happened, the effects on the person, and the emotional/ physical status of the person (emotional, behavioral, thought processes); determine what is needed/wanted.
Provide Safety		Locate individual to safe location, provide information as appropriate, take control as needed, work with others, engage victim in decision-making as appropriate.
Connect to Resources		Determine what resources exist and facilitate connection to those resources as appropriate.

Adapted from: Schreiber and Gurwitch (2011); Schreiber, Gurwitch, and Wong, (2006); Wong, Schreiber, and Gurwitch (2008).

from harm should always be foremost in your mind when responding to crisis. Similarly, in situations where individuals in crisis are affected in ways that suggest potential harm to others, helpers have a duty to provide safety and, if the situation warrants, warn potential victims if there are credible threats of harm, as mentioned in the duty to warn conversation in Chapter 4. Again, I want to emphasize the importance of working with others in a crisis situation, and especially, to underscore the importance of working within the parameters of the role assigned to you by the crisis response leader if you are part of a larger crisis response situation. Do not to engage in response actions that are beyond your level of skill or ability or that put you in danger. Finally, all professional helpers, particularly those working with vulnerable populations, should be sure to acquire more in-depth and specific training in crisis response.

HARM TO SELF OR OTHERS

So far we have talked about working with people who have been victim to situational crises—external events that are extremely upsetting or traumatic. Here we will focus on situations where individuals are suicidal or who are in danger of harming another person. While clinical helpers and emergency responders clearly are the *best* responders positioned to intervene in these types of crises, nonclinical helpers may sometimes be *first* responders in these crisis situations. This is particularly true when they are working in isolated or limited-resource communities. Even as secondary responders, nonclinical helpers may play an important role in coordinated response efforts in situations involving harm to self or others (Coppens et al., 2014).

Self-Harm Statistics

According to Hoyert and Xu (2012), preliminary data from 2011 indicates that suicide is the 10th leading cause of death in the United States. This calculated to a death by suicide in the United States every 13 minutes during the year 2011 (American Foundation for Suicide Prevention, n.d.). Suicide is the second leading cause of death among children ages 15–24 (Hoyert & Xu), and older adults, particularly those between 45–65 years and over 85 years old, are some of the most vulnerable individuals to suicide (American Foundation for Suicide Prevention, n.d.). Women attempt suicide more often then men, but men are 4 times more likely to complete suicide than women (Laux, 2002) because of the lethality of the means they tend to use. The highest suicide rates in the United States are found among Whites (14.5%) and the second highest (10.6%) among American Indians and Alaska Natives (American Foundation for Suicide Prevention, n.d.). Youth who identify as gay, lesbian, and bisexual are 3 times more likely than their straight peers to attempt suicide (Centers for Disease Control and Prevention, 2011), and nearly half of all transgender youth report to have seriously thought about suicide (Grossman & D'Augelli, 2007).

Another particularly vulnerable population is military veterans. Statistics indicate that over 8,000 veterans die by suicide every year (Castro & Kintzle, 2014; National Institute of Mental Health, 2014). This adds up to an alarming approximation of 22 suicides a day within this population group. Research also suggests that children who have been exposed to stress in early life—situations in which they have experienced severe trauma or children who live in chronic aversive situations—are at risk for psychiatric disorders and suicide (due to stress response system activation and damage at a neurobiological level; Griffiths & Hunter, 2014). Sadly, these effects from early trauma can be felt later in life and, evidence suggests, even in subsequent generations (Griffiths & Hunter, 2014).

Harm to Others Statistics

According to a report prepared by the Federal Bureau of Investigation (FBI, n.d.), more than 1.2 million violent crimes were committed in the United States in the year 2012. The FBI definition of violent crime includes murder and non-negligent manslaughter (willful murder without premeditation), rape, robbery, and aggravated assault. According to these data sources, in the year 2013, the rate of domestic violence committed by intimate partners and family members was 4.2 per 1,000, the rate of sexual assault was 1.3 per 1,000 (for individuals older than 12 years), aggravated and simple assault rates were 22.0 per 1,000, and the rate of firearm violence was 1.2 per 1,000. The good news is that from 1993 to 2011, the U.S. homicide rate declined by 48% (Truman, Langton, & Planty, 2013).

In the year 2013, it was estimated that approximately 1.2% of all individuals 12 years or older in the United States, approximately 3 million people, experienced at least one violent victimization (Truman & Langton, 2014). While these rates of violent crimes decreased slightly from the previous year, men continue to be more likely than women to be the victims of violent crimes, and American Indians, Alaska Natives, and individuals who are biracial or multiracial are at high risk for becoming victims of violent crime (Truman & Langton, 2014). It is important to note that many crimes go unreported to police authorities. For example, Truman and Langton (2014) note that in 2013, it was estimated that only 46% of violent victimizations and 61% of serious violent victimizations were reported to police. A greater percentage of robbery (68%) and aggravated assault (64%) were reported to police than simple assault (38%) and rape or sexual assault (35%) (Truman & Langton, 2014).

These statistics offer a picture of the prevalence of violent crime and patterns of victimization, but they do not help us understand who is at risk of committing violent offenses. Arrest trend data collected by the FBI (n.d.), indicate that in 2012, nearly 74 percent of the persons arrested in the nation during 2012 were males. Almost 70 percent of all persons arrested were White, 28 percent were Black, and the remaining 3 percent were of other races. Reflective of nuanced issues around the criminal justice system, White juveniles under the age of 18 are more often *arrested* for property crimes compared to Black juveniles in the same age bracket who are more often arrested for violent crimes. We also know that most perpetrators of sexual violence are male and that they are often known by their victims (National Institute of Justice, 2010).

Predicting Harm

These statistics offer only a mere snapshot of who is at risk of committing self-harm and who might be at risk of harming others. Predicting who will harm themselves or others is difficult, but we do know that these types of harm rarely occur without some period of escalation. Research indicates that individuals who self-harm typically have a dispositional vulnerability which is then triggered by a current stressor (Rudd, Joiner, & Rajab, 2001). Research also shows that aggression that leads to harm against others typically follows a path that starts with a trigger, leading to increased escalation, and finally to the perpetration of aggression (Byrnes, 2002). So, there is some indication that harm to self and others sometimes can be anticipated and prevented. For this reason, we will be talking below about the triggers and escalation episodes that often precede attempts or episodes of harm. We will also discuss a harm assessment—what to look for to determine if someone is at high risk of harming self or others.

A number of caveats are worth mention here. First: Harm triggers and precipitating events are not always visible, even to those of us who are trained to look for them. Second, people with harm intentions do not always articulate or demonstrate those intentions. Third, some harm is impulsive—it is not premeditated. And finally, even when people do express intentions to harm self or others, it is not always possible stop them. The simple truth is that assessing and intervening in the case of harm to self or others is very difficult. Because of these complexities, you should never conduct a harm assessment alone, and you should never make harm intervention decisions alone. Keeping people safe is a shared responsibility. All helpers should receive advanced-level training in suicide and homicide assessment and response.

HARM TO SELF

Self-Harm Triggers

As mentioned, individuals who commit suicide often have a dispositional vulnerability that becomes triggered by an event or stressor (Laux, 2002; Rudd et al., 2001). For example, an individual may have an ongoing condition of depression, but it may be an additional stressor of, for example, a loss of a job, that triggers acute suicidal ideation. Having access to a mechanism for suicide such as a firearm could make this situation lethal.

Suicide statistics offer us some ideas about who is particularly vulnerable or at risk of committing suicide. Keep in mind, however, that a risk factor is a little like the notion of probability in statistics or odds in gambling—it gives us a likelihood that something might happen, but it doesn't offer anything conclusive. In fact, most research suggests that it is not typically any one risk factor, but rather, it is the convergence of multiple factors that can cause someone to be suicidal.

Individuals with a personal or family history of suicide may be at high risk for suicide (American Foundation for Suicide Prevention, n.d.; LeFevre, 2014). In fact, patients who have been recently discharged from psychiatric or emergency room care related to a suicide attempt are at high risk of a second suicide attempt (LeFevre, 2014), and about 20% of those who die by suicide have made precious suicide attempts (American Foundation for Suicide Prevention, n.d.). Likely related, individuals who have little social support or who are isolated (Brems, 2000) may be at high risk of suicide. As mentioned earlier, military veterans (Castro & Kintzle, 2014; National Institute of Mental Health [NIMH], 2014) are at particularly high risk of suicide. This is due, in part but not entirely, to combat and deployment experiences leaving many vets with long-term challenges related to posttraumatic stress reactions. Finally, individuals who identify as gay, lesbian, bisexual, transgender, too, are at risk (Centers for Disease Control and Prevention [CDC], 2014). This risk is typically related to their experiences coming out (in a generally hostile climate) rather than anything inherent to their gender or sexual orientation itself (Laux, 2002; LeFevre, 2014).

Some personal characteristics are also associated with suicide ideation. For example, people who have compromised coping strategies and who are highly self-critical or perfectionistic (Brems, 2000) may have an elevated risk of suicide. Additionally, individuals with impulsive or reckless behavior and who use or misuse drugs and/or alcohol are also at high risk (American Foundation for Suicide Prevention, n.d.; Brems, 2000). Mental health or psychiatric conditions such as depression, schizophrenia, and posttraumatic stress disorder (LeFevre, 2014), too, are associated with suicide ideation. Risk related to these psychiatric challenges may be due, in part, to neurochemical abnormalities involving the serotonin neurons (Stockmeier, 2006).

Again, these risk factors speak to suicide vulnerability; they alone do not indicate suicide ideation. Experiences of stress—either prolonged stress or stress related to a sudden loss or critical incident—can trigger suicidal ideation, particularly for individuals in the above-mentioned categories. Stressors such as chronic medical or mental health conditions (American Foundation for Suicide Prevention, n.d.; Brems, 2000; LeFevre, 2014), being a victim of violence or bullying (Varia, 2013), changes in employment or income status, and the loss of a loved one (LeFevre, 2014) have all been identified as triggers for suicide. These risks are summarized in Table 9.3 below.

So, clearly, we want to be aware of individuals who have experiences in any of the risk categories mentioned here. Remembering that suicide ideation is typically prompted by a triggering event, we want to be particularly attentive to triggering events when we are working with individuals in high-risk categories.

Table 9.3 A Summary of Suicide Risk Factors

Individuals who are experiencing these stressors or situations may be at greater risk for suicide:
- *Prolonged stress*: experiences of bullying, harassment, discrimination, unemployment or homelessness
- *Sudden loss*: death of a loved one, separation, job loss
- *Exposure*: witnessing others commit suicide or being exposed to graphic accounts of suicide
- *Medical condition*: cancer, HIV, lupus, traumatic brain injury, chronic pain, insomnia, adverse effects of medications

History: Individuals who have had these experiences in the past may be at greater risk of suicide:
- *Previous suicide attempts*
- *Family history of suicide attempts*
- *Mental health disorder*. Most common: major depression and other mood disorders, substance use disorders, schizophrenia and personality disorders
- *History of abuse* (physical, sexual, emotional)

Access: Individuals who have these things:
- *Access to lethal means* for committing suicide, particularly firearms and drugs
- *Access/use of alcohol and/or substances*

Other Risk Factors:
- *Gender*: greater risk for males
- *Sexual orientation*: greater risk for LGB and questioning
- *Transgender gender identity*
- *Social isolation and limited support*
- *Thoughts*: irrational thoughts, cognitive rigidity (unable to understand others' perspectives/ unable to consider new ideas), limited problem-solving abilities
- *Emotions*: emotional dysphoria (profound unease or dissatisfaction), helplessness, hopelessness, guilt, anxiety/panic, anhedonia (inability to experience pleasure), attentional difficulties.
- *Substance use/misuse*
- *Impulsive control difficulties*: aggressive behavior, risk-taking

Most Important Risk Factor:
- *Suicide ideation* (actively thinking about suicide)

This list is compiled from:

- American Foundation for Suicide Prevention (n.d.). *Understanding suicide. Facts and figures*. Retrieved from https://www.afsp.org/understanding-suicide/facts-and-figures
- Laux, J. M. (2002). A primer on suicidology: Implications for counselors. *Journal of Counseling & Development, 80*, 380–383. doi:10.1002/j.1556-6678.2002.tb00203.x
- LeFevre, M. L. (2014). Screening for suicide risk in adolescents, adults, and older adults in primary care: U.S. preventive services task force recommendation statement. *Annals of Internal Medicine, 160*(10), 719–727. doi:10.7326/M14-0589
- Rudd, M. D., Joiner, T., & Rajab, M. H. (2001). *Treating suicide behavior*. New York, NY: The Guilford Press.

Self-Harm Escalation

When individuals, particularly vulnerable individuals, experience a triggering event that leaves them feeling unable to cope, they may become suicidal. For this reason, it is important for us to be familiar with the suicide warning signs. Generally it is thought that the more warnings, the greater the risk for suicide (American Foundation for Suicide Prevention, n.d.). However, this idea can be deceptive as an individual may be displaying multiple warning signs in a variety of places, but any one onlooker may only see one or two. So, it is important for us to attend to any warning signs, even if only one is present. These are summarized in Table 9.4.

The most obvious suicide warning sign, of course, is **suicide talk** (American Foundation for Suicide Prevention, n.d.)—when a person says he wants to kill himself. The articulation of suicide intentions, however, is typically not a straight-forward "I am going to kill myself" statement. Instead, suicide ideation may be expressed in terms of not being around for long, being a burden to others, an inability to escape pain, feeling trapped, feeling revengeful, or having no reason to live. Even if we are not sure of one's history (vis-à-vis risk factors), and we don't know if there has been a triggering event, it is always important to take seriously and attend to any and all suicide talk.

Another warning sign to pay attention to is **unusual behavior.** Here we are looking at behaviors that are new, different, or extreme (American Foundation for Suicide Prevention, n.d.). Unusual or different behavior for some may include use of alcohol or substances, acting reckless, withdrawal from one's social network, restlessness, insomnia, sleeping excessively, seeking out suicidal means (i.e., tools for killing oneself), behaving in ways that suggest that one is saying good-bye (e.g., making amends or giving away prized possessions), a preoccupation with death, and occasionally we may see a written suicide note. Again, here, all unusual or uncharacteristic behavior patterns should be thoroughly examined.

Finally, an individual's **mental status** may offer indications of suicide intent. Symptoms of hopelessness, helplessness, depression, and despair are strong predictors of suicide (Brems, 2000). Additionally, when you find that an individual has symptoms of depression combined with distorted thinking about his situation—inaccurate ideas about his current emotional state, situation, or perceptions of others—it may be an indication of escalation moving to suicide crisis (Brems, 2000).

Self-Harm Crisis

The big question for all helping professionals is: How do we know if someone is suicidal? Unfortunately, the answer to this question is that we do not always know. A number of suicide assessment protocols have been developed

Table 9.4 Suicide Warning Signs

Examples of Suicide Warning Signs	
Suicide Talk	Expressions of: • Hopelessness—not having a reason to live • Not being around much longer/in the future • Being a burden to others • Feeling trapped • Feeling revengeful • Desire to escape pain
Unusual Behavior	• New, different, extreme behaviors • Use of alcohol or substances • Acting reckless • Withdrawal from one's social network • Restlessness, insomnia, sleeping excessively • Seeking out suicidal means (i.e., tools for killing oneself) • Behaving in ways that suggest that one is saying good-bye (e.g., making amends or giving away prized possessions) • Preoccupation with death • Written suicide note
Mental Status	• Symptoms of hopelessness, helplessness, depression, and despair • Distorted thinking about his or her situation—inaccurate ideas about his or her current emotional state, situation, or perceptions of others

Adapted from:
   American Foundation for Suicide Prevention (n.d.). *Understanding suicide. Facts and figures.* Retrieved November 6, 2014, from: https://www.afsp.org/understanding-suicide/facts-and-figures
   Brems, C. (2000). *Dealing with challenges in psychotherapy and counseling.* Belmont, CA: Brooks/Cole.

to assist clinical helpers and emergency responders in working with people who are suicidal. Across all suicide assessment protocols, these imminent risk indicators are important to the assessment of suicide:

1. **Ideation**: An individual who has intentions to commit suicide may follow through on these intentions. When someone is suggesting that he is contemplating suicide, clinicians typically ask: "Are you suicidal?" "Are you thinking about killing yourself?" Clinicians will often inquire about the triggering event. Empathy is a key skill used for these conversations.

2. **Plan**: If an individual has a plan for how he will commit suicide, we should assume a high level of intent—that is, that he may follow through on that plan. Generally, the more detailed the plan—such as

how, when, and where—the higher the likelihood of imminent danger. To elicit this information, clinicians typically ask, "What are your thoughts about how you might hurt/kill yourself?" Clinicians then follow up with additional questions, based on the helpee's responses.

3. **Means:** An individual who has thought about how he will kill himself and who has *access* to the identified means for doing so is in an extremely dangerous situation. To get at means and access, clinicians typically ask, "How were you thinking you would take your life?" Then they follow up by asking specific questions regarding the individual's ability to access the intended means.

4. **Risk Factors:** Determining the extent to which the individual has *hope* that his current situation will change or that his pain will go away, helps clinicians gauge the extent of suicide intent. Also, inquiring about previous suicide attempts is critical as this is one of the highest risk factors to self-harm. To get at these issues, clinicians typically ask: "Is there anything or anyone who might stop you from committing suicide?" and "Have you ever attempted suicide before?"

Responding to Self-Harm Crises

The *Listen, Protect, Connect* model of Psychological First Aid (Schreiber & Gurwitch, 2011; Schreiber, Gurwitch & Wong, 2006; Wong, Schreiber, & Gurwitch, 2008) offers a good guide for responding to subtle and overt threats of self-harm. First, according to this model, helpers should **listen** for expressed ideation, suicide risk factors, and warning signs. Helpers should take all expressions of suicide ideation seriously. Second, helpers should intervene to **protect safety.** This is done by expressing empathy, not leaving the individual alone, and getting help. And, third, regardless of the extent to which the individual is or may actively be suicidal, helpers need to **connect** the individual to support systems and clinical help as soon as possible. These actions are summarized in Table 9.5 below.

VIDEO LINK:
Harm
Assessment

When interacting with individuals who are suicidal, call for help (you can call a mental health clinician, emergency services, 911, or another colleague) or escort them to an emergency room or counseling service that is available for walk in services. If necessary, you may need to remove dangerous objects that could be used for suicide. Most importantly, if you suspect suicide ideation, you should **always consult with others. Never work alone** in these situations. All professional helpers—clinical or nonclinical—should be formally trained in suicide assessment and response procedures.

Table 9.5 Responding to a Suicide Crisis

Listen, Protect, and Connect Actions for Suicide Response	
Listen	Listen for expressions of suicide ideation.
	Listen for risk factors and warning signs.
	Take all expressions of suicide ideation seriously.
Protect	Express empathy.
	Don't leave the person alone.
	Remove (or ensure removal of) dangerous objects.
Connect	Connect individual to his support systems.
	Connect individual to emergency or mental health services.
	Call or escort the person to help.
Most Important: Always consult with others; never work alone.	

HARM TO OTHERS

In our discussion here, we are defining harm to others as aggressive, injurious, or hostile behavior that is potentially destructive to others (Siever, 2008). Most discussions of aggression make an important distinction between premeditated and impulsive aggression. **Premeditated aggression** refers to planned and intentional behavior that is not typically triggered in a moment of frustration or in response to an immediate threat or trigger (Siever, 2008). This type of aggression is not directly associated with autonomic arousal (stress response) and, in some cases, is socially sanctioned, such as in times of war. It is aggression that has been thought out in advance. **Impulsive aggression** is different. This type of aggression is associated with autonomic arousal and is precipitated by a trigger or precipitating event (Siever, 2008). Impulsive aggression is an exaggerated response to a perceived threat or stress. In our discussion, we will be focusing primarily on impulsive aggression.

Aggression Triggers

Underlying issues, conditions, or personality styles such as a prior history of violence, difficulties regulating anger, low frustration tolerance, impulsivity, poor problem-solving abilities, difficulty complying with behavioral expectations set by others (Cavaiola & Colford, 2006; Dubin & Jagarlamudi, 2010; Kaplan, 2008) and difficulties reading social cues (Siever, 2008) are potential risk factors for impulsive aggression. Impulsive aggression is also associated with a lack of social supports (Pereira, Fleischhacker, & Allen, 2007), antisocial or borderline personality disorders and substance misuse (Siever, 2008). Additionally, a history of childhood difficulties with affect expression or modulation (i.e., the ability to control one's emotions), behavior regulation (i.e, the ability to control one's behavior), deficits in social cognition (i.e., the ability to "read" others in the environment), and experiences of living in harsh home or social environments have all been identified as risk factors for later aggression and violence to others (Blake & Hamrin, 2007). Any one or some combination of these variables are typically present in individuals who are chronically aggressive. The most reliable risk factor for predicting violence, however, appears to be a past history of violent behavior (Cavaiola & Colford, 2006) or patterns of antisocial behavior and high levels of aggression (Sprague & Walker, 2000).

Photo 9.3   Aggression

©iStockphoto.com/Byrdyak

In other words, individuals who have been violent in the past may be violent again. All of these risk factors are included in Table 9.6.

Speaking most directly to school personnel, but relevant to all of us, Dwyer, Osher, and Warger (1998) recommend being alert for a constellation of the following symptoms that may suggest aggression: social withdrawal or isolation, experiences of rejection and/or victimization, low interest in school and/or poor academic performance, uncontrolled anger, patterns of impulsivity and/or aggression, history of discipline problems and/or violence, expressions of violence in writing or pictures, drug or alcohol use, intolerance of differences, gang affiliation, access to firearms, and, of course, expressed threats of violence to others. These authors caution that these factors must be understood in context and that school personnel should be careful not to misinterpret or rush to judge students based on any one of these factors alone. But nonetheless, if we are working with youth that display some of these behaviors, they warrant our attention.

At a neuorological level, Miczek et al. (2007) and Siever (2008) suggest that violence may be related to impairments in brain structures that impact moral cognition perceptions and emotional expression. Siever explains that aggressive impulses result from an imbalance in the inhibiting function or "breaks" (p. 430) in the frontal cortex in combination with the emotional responses triggered in the limbic system, particularly the amygdala and insula. So, while the frontal cortex, which normally is trying to enable the individual to appropriately read social cues and determine appropriate behavioral responses, is inhibited, the amygdala is in hyper-mode triggering a "drive" (Siever, 2008, p. 431) of emotional reactivity or aggression. These compromised functions result in reduced levels of serotonin and gamaminergic (GABA) activity, which is problematic as both are associated with regulating and suppressing aggressive behaviors.

These social and neurobiological risk variables make an individual vulnerable to difficulties in regulating aggressive impulses, but they do not cause violence. Unfortunately, we do not have a fool-proof system of predicting when someone will lash out to harm others (Sprague & Walker, 2000). Largely this is because aggression is based on situational variables that occur in an interpersonal context. That is, violence is often triggered in the heat of the moment. It is the alignment of risk factors, specific triggers, and an escalation of being out of control, that tends to result in violence (Byrnes, 2002; Pereira et al., 2007).

Aggressive impulses can be triggered by almost anything: by others in one's life, by strangers in the street, by specific events or situations, and even by objects, such as a broken-down car as one is running late for work. Triggers are the events that happen to all of us. Most of us are able to control low levels of triggered arousal

(Byrnes, 2002), but for some people who have some of the above mentioned social or neurobiological risk factors, controlling triggered emotional arousal can be more difficult. The result, sometimes, is impulsive aggression.

Table 9.6 Risk Factors Associated With Aggression and Harm to Others

Individuals who have had these experiences in the past or who fall in these categories may be at greater risk of aggression:
- *Past aggression*: A history of perpetrating violence toward others
- *Family functioning*: Individuals who experienced harsh or inconsistent parenting, who experienced violence, instability, or emotional rejection in the home environment, who experienced social isolation or lived with a serious psychiatric illness within the family
- *Instability*: Unstable history of schooling or employment
- *Rejection*: Those who experienced peer rejection or poor peer relationships during adolescence
- *Gender*: Males are more likely than females to perpetrate violence
- *Age*: Individuals between ages 15–30 are more likely to commit violence than those in other age groups
- *Thoughts*: Belief that aggression is justified, condone or encourage others to be aggressive or violent, cognitive deficits (low intelligence, limited cognitive complexity), lack of empathy or perspective-taking
- *Emotions*: Hostility, anger, irritability, fear, frustration
- *Behaviors*: Poor impulse control, low frustration tolerance, temper outbursts, recklessness, cruelty to animals, frequent fighting, truancy, oppositional behaviors, poor interpersonal skills
- *Weapons*: Individuals who have a fascination with or access to weapons
- *Stress*: Individuals who are experiencing acute or prolonged stress
- *Substance use*: Violence may be related to the ingestion of substances, may be a reaction to toxicity in ingested substances, or related to withdrawal
- *Mental health disorders*: Conduct Disorder, Antisocial Personality Disorder, Intermittent Explosive Disorder, Paranoid Schizophrenia

Most Important Risk Factor:
- Aggression or homicide ideation (i.e., admitting feeling aggressive toward someone) **and** an identified victim (i.e., naming who would be the target of these aggressive tendencies)

This list is compiled from:
- Brems, C. (2000). *Dealing with challenges in psychotherapy and counseling*. Belmont, CA: Brooks/Cole.
- Cavaiola, A. A., & Colford, J. E. (2006). *A practical guide to crisis intervention*. Belmont, CA: Wadsworth.

Aggression Escalation

As mentioned, triggers happen to all of us on an everyday basis—we all have experiences where we become emotionally aroused, upset, frustrated, or disappointed. However, when stress goes beyond one's ability to cope, then aggression may result (Byrnes, 2002). Dubin and Jagarlamudi (2010) point out that aggression may be more likely to happen when an individual feels trapped, helpless, or humiliated.

The ways in which individuals make sense of the events that occur in their lives affects how they will respond. You may recall that in the discussion about self-regulation in Chapter 5, cognitive processes are significant in transforming stimuli into perceptions and emotional and behavioral responses (Gross, 1998). So, it is important to remember that the triggering event itself may not be as evocative as how it is interpreted. Additionally, limited coping skills can lead to impulsive aggression. For example, the use (or misuse) of substances as a way of regulating one's emotions or using substances in response to an evocative trigger can be deadly. The point here is that aggression rarely occurs suddenly and unexpectedly; it escalates. The most effective management of a person who is potentially violent, then, is to prevent aggression from escalating (Dubin & Jagarlamudi, 2010). To do this, we must be aware of immediate warning signs present in the situation that suggest agitation leading to violence, including patterns of cognitive distortions (misinterpreting) and limited social skills. Warning signs for aggression are discussed here and summarized in Table 9.7 at the end of this discussion.

In the escalation phase of violence, an individual will be struggling to control his aggressive impulses (Byrnes, 2002). This may be most visible as an **increase in motor activity**, agitation, restlessness (Cavaiola & Colford, 2006; Fauteux, 2010), or **statements that are verbally abusive or combative** (Dubin & Jagarlamudi, 2010). Increased motor activity may look like agitation pacing, punching one's fist into his other hand, or even a rapid tapping of an object or one's foot on the floor. Verbally abusive statements may include intimidation or threats to or about others.

Byrnes (2002) reports a hardening that sometimes occurs in this phase of escalation. By hardening, he is referring to when an individual who is escalated responds by taking an **inflexible** stance. Consider, for example, an angry child who refuses to eat his dinner. Sometimes at this level of arousal, you may see a **hypersensitivity to criticism**, a **victim stance**, or a **mistrust of others** (Byrnes, 2002). That is, the escalated person may believe that she has been victim to slights or threats from others (James & Gilland, 2001). At this point, the individual may also deliver ultimatums or masked threats of harm (Byrnes, 2002).

In a recent incident, for example, a woman who killed a social worker believed that the social worker was unfairly "taking her child away" from her. Here the perception was that she was victim to an agency that saw her unfit to raise her child, even after repeated arrests for substance use, violence, and instances of neglect of her child. In this case, the trigger, arousal, and appraisal of victimization moved so quickly it turned into deadly violence.

As this example above suggests, a person at an initial level of arousal may appear very **defensive** (Cavaiola & Colford, 2006). Defensiveness can also manifest in aggressive **debate** with others and **attempts to establish a position of power** (Byrnes, 2002). Often, the defensive stance at this point, however, is irrational and indicative of an increase in loss of control (Cavaiola & Colford, 2006). For example, Suzie became very upset with her coworker, saying, "You don't know what you're talking about. I saw it with my own eyes. I know what she was thinking. You are wrong." As this was being articulated, she stamped her feet on the ground, pounded her hand into her thigh, and turned red. These verbal and nonverbal behaviors suggest a high level of arousal, defensiveness, and appear to be an attempt to engage the co-worker in a debate.

Table 9.7 Possible Indications of Escalated Aggression

Behaviors That May Suggest Escalated Aggression
• Increased motor activity, agitation, restlessness • Verbal abuse • Hardening • Hypersensitivity • Defensiveness • Mistrust • Statements positioning self as victim/other as enemy • Ultimatums • Masked threats This list is compiled from: • Brems, C. (2000). *Dealing with challenges in psychotherapy and counseling.* Belmont, CA: Brooks/Cole. • Cavaiola, A. A., & Colford, J. E. (2006). *A practical guide to crisis intervention.* Belmont, CA: Wadsworth. • Dubin, W. R., & Jagarlamudi, K. (2010, July). Safety in the evaluation of potentially violent patients. *Psychiatric Times, 27*(7) 15–17. • Fauteux, K. (2010). De-escalating angry and violent clients. *American Journal of Psychotherapy, 64*(2), 195–213.

Aggression Crisis

When aggressive impulses and frustration move to a point beyond the individual's ability to cope, the individual is in crisis (Byrnes, 2002) and the likelihood of aggression is high. At this stage, there is a loss of verbal, physical, and emotional control. In crisis, the individual will appear extremely agitated, will be increasingly irrational, and his or her ability to make clear judgments is severely compromised. These symptoms signal an extremely high and immediate potential for harm.

Responding to Threats or Intentions to Harm Others

You will need to intervene in some way in response to threats of harm to others when:

1. There is a threat or articulated **intention** to hurt someone. That is, the person is acting in aggressive ways or saying, in one way or another, that she is going to hurt someone.

2. The aggression has a **potential target**. The individual is expressing or implying intent to hurt an identified individual. This target may be you or someone else.

3. There is an **opportunity to attack**. The individual is able to carry out the intentions of aggression.

As with intervention in cases of harm to self, intervening with individuals who are aggressive or threatening to harm others is best handled by professionals who have been trained to manage these situations. However, here again, as a nonclinical helper, you may be the first on the ground to encounter someone who is or appears to be issuing a threat to hurt someone. When intervening in response to such threats, **your immediate attention needs to be on safety**—safety for yourself, safety for the victim, and safety for the aggressive individual who is out of control. Securing safety for self and others is the primary goal of intervention and to do this, calling for assistance is paramount whenever possible (Brems, 2000). It is also important to remember, as mentioned in Chapter 4, that helpers have a mandate to provide safety to potential victims of harm when those victims are identified as potential targets.

A number of guidelines exist for working with individuals who are agitated and potentially aggressive. The suggestions below are framed around the concepts of *Listen, Protect, Connect* (Schreiber & Gurwitch, 2011; Schreiber, Gurwitch & Wong, 2006; Wong, Schreiber, & Gurwitch, 2008).

Listen

Listening refers to attending to the warning signs of escalating tension and diminished coping abilities before aggression occurs. It also means listening to the person who is in crisis, as much as possible and if safely appropriate.

If the situation is not yet in the crisis phase, you may be able to **inquire about what is troubling the individual**. When doing this, be careful to listen to the helpee's version of events and expression of feelings –do not get into the trap of accusing and reprimanding. For example, you can ask, "What happened?" "How did you feel when she yelled at you?"

Illustration 9.1 Listening

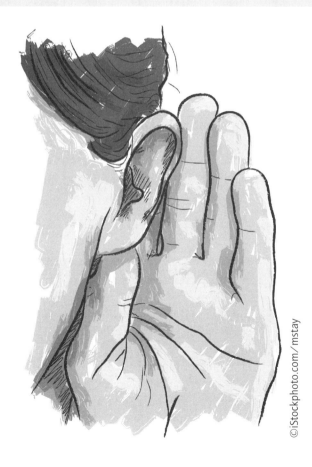

©iStockphoto.com/mstay

Do not dispute or diminish the person's experience as he tells his story. Remember that the systems of cognitive appraisal that individuals use to make meaning of the events in their lives are critical triggers of emotional reactivity. So, listening to the person's perceptions about the triggering event is important, even if you have an alternative interpretation. **Use empathy to affirm the person's experience.**

If the individual is in an advanced level of escalation, you should **avoid confrontation**, even if the helpee's interpretations do not appear to be accurate or rational. Instead, use empathy and attending skills. For example, you might say, "I see why you might be angry if you were thinking that she meant to put you down." "If you went into the situation already frustrated, it makes sense that you thought she was after you."

Be sure to **validate the person's experiences**. This entails hearing the person out and recognizing her frustration or reaction. Do not debate, argue, or criticize. For example, you can express empathy and validation by saying, "Yes, I can imagine that felt bad" even if you detect some irrational interpretations or perceptions. It is important to allow others to express their grievances and frustrations without judgment.

Finally, as you are listening, **listen for potential targets** of violence, identified or **specific plans** of violence, and indications that the individual has access to a viable **means** to harm someone. These are critical as they signal elevated risk of harm and will warrant action that includes a duty to warn. However, an important reminder here is that your most important role at this point is to listen to what the individual is saying; a full harm assessment should be conducted by a professional who has received formal training in this area.

Protect

Protecting as a crisis response refers to assuring the safety of the individual in crisis, as well as the safety of the intended target of the aggression. This begins with your ability to diffuse a tense situation before it has escalated into crisis. If that is not possible, and particularly if your own safety is threatened (either directly or by implication), you should leave the situation and/or call for help immediately. It is not appropriate to put yourself in harm's way.

If you are able to intervene before an individual has escalated beyond control, it is possible that you will be able to avert violence from occurring. This, of course, protects everyone. Byrnes (2002) says, "the more we allow an aggressor to escalate, the less opportunity we will have to diffuse him" (p. 13). Interventions, then, should first be aimed at helping the person calm down.

Second, our interventions may also enable resolution of the problem that created the crisis in the first place.

Cavaiola and Colford (2006) outline a number of suggestions for engaging with individuals who have reached the state of being in crisis. These are included in Table 9.8 below. Very generally, you should:

1. Use a **calm voice and do not to stare** directly at the individual.

2. **Be safe**. Do not allow yourself to be cornered by the other person. Position yourself in a place that has easy access to exit quickly, if needed. Also, be aware of any throwable objects.

3. **Avoid being threatening** to the person. "Telegraph" your movements by telling the person what you are doing before you do it. For example, you might say, "I am going to move this chair over now." Or "I am going to put this stick outside of the room now so it doesn't get in our way." Be sure not to tower over the other person.

4. **Talk slowly,** and **stop and breathe** with intentionality when things are tense. These efforts can have the effect of inviting the other person to slow down and also move into a calmer position.

5. If the person begins to calm down, it can be helpful to invite him to offer a solution or plan for moving toward resolve. In this conversation, be sure to **express confidence that you believe he is able to solve the problem**. Also **reinforce all of his intentions and attempts to calm himself and reach resolution.**

Notice how the suggestions above have the dual effect of calming the helpee while also protecting the helper. If the person you are working with is not calming down and, particularly, if you notice an increase in emotionality, irrationality, and aggression, physical intervention or restraint may be needed. Physical restraint should only be done by an individual trained in appropriate restraint procedures. You should never find yourself alone in a situation that requires physical restraint—that means that the aggression has tipped to a point that is volatile. **If you are threatened by someone, you should always be sure to protect your own safety, even if that means leaving the situation and calling for help. Never work alone.** I recommend that all professional helpers—clinical or nonclinical—be formally trained in violence deescalation and physical restraint procedures.

The final important function here has to do with duty to warn. Recalling the discussion on duty to warn in Chapter 4, remember that if you have information that an individual is intending to harm another person, you have a professional duty to warn that individual. You should always work in connection with others—emergency responders, law enforcement officials, supervisors—

when you have information about potential harm to others. Remember: **If others are at risk of being harmed, they must be appropriately warned.**

Connect

Connect is the third part of our intervention model. Remember that it never feels good to be in an out-of-control state. That most of us can relate to this statement is a testimony to the universality of the experience of being triggered and responding with escalated emotionality as we grapple for control. So, it is important for us to remember to be empathic to others who have been out of

Table 9.8 Responding to Crises of Harm to Others

	Responding to Aggression or Threats of Harm to Others
Listen	Listen for risk factors and warning signs.
	Listen to the person's story, feelings, and perceptions of events/others.
	Listen with empathy and attending skills.
	Validate the person's perceptions and experiences.
	Listen for information or details regarding plans, potential victims, and access to means.
Protect	Use a calm voice, talk slowly, breathe.
	Don't stare directly at the individual.
	Position yourself near the exit and be aware of dangerous objects.
	Telegraph your movements.
	Invite suggestions for solutions.
	Express confidence in the person's ability to resolve the situation and genuinely reinforce these efforts.
	Express confidence in the person's ability to cope and genuinely reinforce these efforts.
	Get help and leave a dangerous situation.
Connect	Connect with the person after the crisis has passed.
	Connect the person to emergency or mental health services.
	Protect yourself; never work alone.

control in the ways described here. As mentioned in earlier chapters of this book, empathy and respect are key to connection and relationship, and they must be firmly in place in order to help people in crisis.

Keep in mind, too, that people who have been out of control in relationships with others, often are left feeling isolated and without needed supports. So, in addition to reestablishing a connection with an individual who has been out of control, our role is also to refer helpees to appropriate professional resources and services.

CHAPTER SUMMARY

The topic of this chapter is not for the faint of heart. Working with individuals who are in crisis is stressful and depleting. The repeated message in this chapter is to listen, protect, and connect when responding to individuals who have experienced crisis or who are in a position of inflicting harm to self or others. As discussed, the assessment and intervention in the face of suicide ideation and threats of aggression or violence to others is something that is best conducted by clinical helpers and law enforcement officials who have been trained to intervene in these situations. However, you may be the first responder in a crisis situation. The important things to remember are to pay attention to the warning signs; to intervene early by listening, protecting, and connecting; and to always seek consultation and help—never work in isolation.

DISCUSSION QUESTIONS

1. What behaviors or responses might we expect to see from someone who has experienced a disaster or trauma?

2. The response model suggests that the three fundamental steps in responding to a crisis are (1) Listen, (2) Protect, and (3) Connect. Describe the function of each of these steps in responding to a crisis.

3. According to the statistics, what populations are particularly vulnerable to suicide? What factors might be impacting these statistics?

4. What behavioral or verbal signs may indicate that someone's agitation could be leading to violence?

5. What are the most important things to do when someone is presenting signs of agitation, possibly leading to harm?

CHAPTER 10
HELPING IN GROUPS

LEARNING OBJECTIVES

1. Learn about the types of groups conducted by helpers

2. Learn theories about group dynamics and stages for better understanding of what to expect when helping in a group format

3. Learn basic group leadership principles and intervention strategies

INTRODUCTION

Group work is

> a broad professional practice involving the application of knowledge and skill in group facilitation to assist an interdependent collection of people to reach their mutual goals which may be intrapersonal, interpersonal, or work-related. The goals of the group may include the accomplishment of tasks related to work, education, personal development, personal and interpersonal problem solving, or remediation of mental and emotional disorders. (Association for Specialists in Group Work, 2000, pp. 2–3)

As this definition suggests, groups can be used to address a large scope of personal, professional, and interpersonal goals. The range of services provided by clinical and nonclinical helpers working in a group format includes support and counseling, as well as meetings, workshops, and classes. Group workers tell us that the medium of group work offers a unique and powerful opportunity for growth, development, and change. This is largely because in groups, members not only learn and grow from the knowledge provided by the leader, but also from their interaction with their peers in the group. Group work is a venue where learning unfolds in front of and all around other group members. It offers opportunities to receive feedback, practice new skills, and gain valuable perspectives and knowledge from multiple others.

These great opportunities for learning that come from being in a member in a group also can present many interesting challenges for group leaders. Facilitating groups requires distinct helper knowledge and skills. In this chapter, we begin with a review of the various types of group work. We will also review theories, principles, and skills that describe and address some of the unique aspects of group work that are relevant to the development of leader competence across these various group types. As with most of the other topics mentioned in this text, additional training in group leadership, particularly if you are working in a specialty area, and regular supervision, is a must for effective group leadership.

GROUP TYPES

We will use Johnson and Johnson's definition of a group as "a number of individuals who join together to achieve a goal" (Johnson & Johnson, 2006, p. 5) to open our discussion about group types. This definition is important because it reminds us that the purpose of a group is its goal. That is, groups can be used for a variety of purposes; each specific group is designed to meet a particular and specific goal.

The way in which the group is structured to meet its goal leads to a review of various group types used in helping. The Association of Specialists in Group Work (ASGW, 2000) offers these four general categories of group types: counseling, psychotherapy, psychoeducational, and task or work groups. It is important to remember that the "edges" (Day, 2007, p. 9) between these various group types sometimes overlap. So, while we speak of these types of groups as clearly distinct phenomena, groups often shift in their nature and functions, requiring different strategies and styles of leadership at different times for changing purposes. These categories are helpful organizing principles, however, as they outline the vast scope of practice that can be addressed through group work.

Counseling and Psychotherapy Groups

Counseling and psychotherapy groups are typically used to address problems related to personal and interpersonal issues. Of these, therapy groups tend to be used with individuals who experience severe and/or chronic mental health difficulties or adjustment challenges (ASGW, 2000), and they tend to encourage a high degree of depth and self-disclosure on the part of group members. They are sometimes described as groups for "personality reconstruction" (Day, 2007, p. 9). Counseling groups tend to focus on less chronic and, perhaps, more common and less severe problems (Day, 2007) and many counseling groups are used for prevention work, particularly in schools (ASGW, 2000). For example, as a school counselor, I worked with a para-educator to facilitate a counseling group for Native American students, who were a minority population in the school. The coleader of the group was an employee from the home culture of the students, and the group was designed to offer support to some Native American students who reported feeling out of place and seemed to be misunderstood by others in the school. These students did not display problems, but they were a group of students who were at risk of failure due to issues related to their minority status in a sometimes hostile school environment. So, this counseling group would be considered a support (counseling) group. In contrast, a psychotherapy group might be used in an inpatient hospitalization program for individuals who have experienced trauma and display suicidal ideation.

In both of these group types, leaders may use one or a combination of cognitive, affective, and/or behavioral intervention strategies, and they are typically conducted by clinically trained professionals. The leaders of these types of groups typically make use of member interactions or *group process* as a helping strategy within the group. We will address this idea of using group process in more detail shortly. In some settings, particularly residential or hospital-based mental health programs, nonclinical helpers are involved in leading these types of groups, typically with and under the supervision of clinical mental health providers. Nonclinical helpers also often lead counseling groups—a group home setting is a good example of this.

Photo 10.1 Counseling and Psychotherapy Groups

© Can Stock Photo Inc./4774344sean

Psychoeducational Groups

Psychoeducational groups are designed to promote personal and interpersonal growth and development, typically with a prevention or remedial intent (ASGW, 2000). A basic assumption of psychoeducational groups is that education or information promotes change. These groups are different than support and counseling groups as the focus is largely on educational content, and they are often structured around a particular topic or predetermined activities in order to achieve a particular goal or learning objective (Chen & Rybak, 2004). They are sometimes referred to as skills training groups. Examples of psychoeducational groups that nonclinical professionals may lead include parent training, assertiveness training, conflict mediation, or informational workshops on the effects of alcohol on fetal development for parents who have a history of substance misuse. Speaking to the overlap in group types, it is not uncommon for therapeutic programs that conduct psychotherapy groups to also include psychoeducation in some of their group sessions. In fact, the therapeutic practice of Dialectical Behavior Therapy (DBT), mentioned in Chapter 3, which was developed for working with individuals with chronic and severe mental health challenges, makes extensive use of psychoeducational practices in a group format.

Photo 10.2 Psychoeducational Groups

©iStockphoto.com/SolStock

Task or Work Groups

Task groups are used to accomplish specific goals or work that needs to be completed, and they are often described as meetings, work groups, or teams. Examples of these types of groups include volunteer work groups, task force committees, discussion groups, learning groups, and meetings where members participate in discussions and assignments to address particular goals (Gladding, 2003). They tend to be time limited and goal specific (ASGW, 2000) and are designed to make use of the collaborative contributions of all members to accomplish a particular task. These groups are used to address a specific need or problem, to create and share information and knowledge, for collaborative

Photo 10.3 Task or Work Groups

©iStockphoto.com/Mark Bowden

tasks, to develop cohesion and communication, and for decision-making and problem solving (Lopez-Fresno & Savolainen, 2014). The explicit focus of these types of groups tends to be on task completion rather than individual member development, such as was the case for counseling and psychotherapy groups. Already we can see the overlap here between these task and psychoeducational groups. A careful review of the ASGW (2000) definitions of group types, however, suggests that psychoeducational groups are more focused on prevention and used with at-risk populations; task groups tend to be less therapeutically inclined. A task or work group is something you might be involved in with your colleagues, whereas a psychoeducational group is something you might offer your helpees.

Self-Help Groups

Additionally, helpers may help organize and provide material resources to members of self-help groups (Salzer, Rappaport, & Segre, 2001). Self-help groups, as the name implies, tend to be leaderless groups that develop organically among people who experience similar challenges or face a common difficulty. These may include groups for individuals who struggle with alcoholism, eating habits, weight, etc. Self-help groups often appeal to individuals who tend to avoid traditional mental health services; Salzer et al. (2001) report that approximately 10 million Americans participate in some type of self-help group annually. Because these groups are, by definition, leaderless, the role of helpers in regard to these types of groups is often ancillary—helpers may assist in organizing details, providing resources, and be available for support and consultation.

BASIC CONCEPTS IN GROUP WORK

One of the things that makes group work a unique and powerful modality for helping has to do with the way in which having multiple people interacting together in the group promotes learning. Sometimes that learning is intentional—it is what the member hoped to achieve in joining in the group. Sometimes it is not at all what the member expected but, nonetheless, still important and helpful! For example, in a psychoeducational group on getting ready for college, Jakelin learned from another member that showing up for a college tour, even when she was feeling shy about doing so, was a great way to develop a sense of which colleges were probably most appropriate for her learning needs. She also learned about a local youth center that helped college applicants from low-income families attend college tours. These were the explicit goals that the leader had hoped would be met for members of the group. Another participant in this same group, Tanya, got feedback from a group member that she frequently interrupted others and was perceived as rude. This was not the explicit goal of the group, but because of how Tanya interacted in the group and its implications on how she might be perceived in her college interviews, it was an important learning for her. The group leader helped Tanya understand that this perception did not accurately reflect Tanya's intentions, and that perhaps her anxiety about going to college added a tone to her questions that appeared overly aggressive to others—not an uncommon phenomenon when we feel that the stakes are high. As a result of this feedback, Tanya was able to learn to take a deep breath before asking questions and as the group progressed, she began to make genuine friendships with other group members.

The multiple perspectives and interactions between members within groups increases the amount of information that is potentially available for learning. However, as the example above illustrates, the group leader is an important facilitator of that learning. By attending to the interactions within the group, the leader was able to help Tanya make sense of the feedback she was receiving from the other group members. This learning had the potential to lead to changes in her behavior that would be helpful to her both within the group and, ultimately, for her later actions during the college application process. If the leader of this group had not been available to help Tanya make use of this feedback, it is possible that the learning opportunity would have been lost. This is an example of how group dynamics can facilitate learning, even in groups where personal learning is not the major focus. We will speak more about this below.

Group Process

Group process refers to the patterns of interactions and communications that happen in the group between members and also with the group leader (Yalom, 1995). Scholars of group work sometimes refer to group process as the *how* of the group: *how* members interact, *how* members work together, *how* members communicate with each other, and *how* the work of the group proceeds (Geroski & Kraus, 2010; Schwarz, 2002). Let's take a minute to examine what exactly group process may look like in a various group types. In these examples, notice how the behaviors of one or a few individuals shape the functioning of the group.

- Members of a task/work group assembled to study school climate. The group was formed as a subcommittee of a school parent-teacher organization. At their first meeting they were welcomed warmly by the school principal, thanked in advance for their commitment to the group and their work, and then asked to introduce themselves to each other, explaining why they are passionate about the topic. Initiating a meeting in this way, the group leader hoped to create an initial group process that engendered a spirit of ease and appreciation.

- A student in a classroom makes disparaging remarks to other students in the class. This dynamic inhibits other students from participating in class discussions.

- The young adults living in a residential group home notice that one of their residential counselors always greets them after school with an invitation to share a cup of tea. After making tea, the counselor asks each resident about her day and listens carefully as stories are told. Then they discuss their plans for the evening. If one resident interrupts another, the counselor gently smiles and shifts the focus back to the resident who is speaking with comments such as "I'm looking forward to hearing from you after [the current speaker] is finished." One resident reported that she "loves it" when this particular residential counselor is on duty because "she cares about us and keeps is in line."

- A child in a preschool appears to need constant teacher attention. This child always seems to be rushing to the teacher to show off her art work, jumping up quickly in front of the other children to follow instructions, and is always asking the teacher for help during activity periods. The teacher showers this child with near-constant affirmations, thinking that this will help the child feel better and become more emotionally self-sufficient. Soon, the other children in the classroom stop seeking out attention from this particular teacher and they avoid playing with this particular child.

All of these examples of group process dynamics illustrate how group member behavior influences what happens in the group. As they show, what happens between some members in a group affects what other members do, say, and whether or not the task of the group can be appropriately realized. These examples also illustrate, I believe, the important ways in which group leaders can and must intervene to influence what happens in the group. Group leader responsiveness (or nonresponsiveness) has effects on how the group functions and what group members learn from being in the group.

Group Content

Group content refers to the goals, tasks, or subject matter of the group (Geroski & Kraus, 2002); "what the group is working on" (Schwarz, 2002, p. 5). Content refers to the purpose of the group (Gladding, 2003)—what the group is about. For example, the task group mentioned above had as its goal to learn about school climate. The informal counseling group mentioned above with the tea-making counselor had as its goal to provide a time for residents to decompress after school, which was an important goal for the group's members who had difficulties with self-regulation in social situations.

As the examples mentioned so far in this chapter illustrate, the realization of the goals related to the content of a particular group is a function of the group process dynamics in that group. That is, how group participants interact and work together will affect how (or if) the intended group goals are realized. Most group researchers suggest that there must be a dual focus and balance in the amount of attention given to group process and group content in order for a group to function appropriately (Kraus & Hulse-Killacky, 1996). Achieving this balance is a critical group leader role in all group types.

Group Dynamics

It is important to remember that people act differently in groups than they do in pairs or alone. Gladding (2003) explains that this is due to the social influences within groups. That is, people adjust their behaviors, their words, their attitudes, and even their beliefs when they are in a group, based on the influence—real or perceived—of other group members. For example, you may be angry at something that your boss said to you and willing to tell a coworker about how angry you are when the two of you are alone. But when you are in a larger task group that includes your boss and others at her level, you may be more reluctant to say anything about your anger.

Perceptions about personal power, how one will be perceived by others, and concerns about the later implications of one's actions are factors that weigh into decisions regarding what one will and will not say in a group. Even discourses (i.e., normative ideas in society that shape one's behavior and how one is perceived by others) influence the positioning that members will assume in various groups. And that positioning dictates what they will say or do in that group.

Research suggests that when we are in a group with others with whom we identify, look up to, or respect, we feel more pressure and are more likely to be influenced by group dynamics than when we are in groups with people we do not know or identify with at all (Gladding, 2003). As an example of this, have you ever had the experience of being on a long plane ride sitting next to a complete stranger who tells you endless stories that include personal details of his life? The same is true in groups—members tend to be less inhibited in what they say or do when they are in a group with people they don't know or when they don't particularly care what the other group members think about them.

Bandura (1977) pointed out that individuals who are perceived to have higher status, prestige, and power are particularly influential over the behavior of others. He also suggested that individuals who have been rewarded for emulating certain behaviors, who lack self-esteem, who feel incompetent, and who are highly dependent, are more suggestible than others. Along these lines, Raghubir and Valenzuela (2010) reported that women and men are evaluated and rewarded differently in mixed-gender groups. This finding can be explained through Bandura's observation of the influential effects of perceptions of status, power, and privilege on group member behaviors. It is not difficult to see how group process dynamics are affected by the perceived social capital of various group members or by discourses around status, and how these can affect what happens within a group. These ideas call attention to why careful and intentional leadership is necessary across group types. Group leaders have the dual tasks of focusing on the accomplishment of group content goals as well as for facilitating the group process to achieve those goals. The take home message here is that group dynamics—what happens in the group—are not just a function of who is in the group, group type, and group goals, they also are a function of how the group is facilitated by the leader.

THEORIES AND MODELS OF GROUP WORK

There are a number of theories or models that help group leaders understand the complexity of group dynamics and how to facilitate groups so as to make the most of the process and content learning opportunities. The first theory we will discuss below is systems theory. The second is a stage model of group dynamics that attempts to explain general trends of group process dynamics that happen in groups over time and across group types. These discussions will be followed by general suggestions regarding leadership principles and specific skills that are used by group leaders across the various group types.

Systems Theory

Systems theory is a theoretical lens that is often used to describe and make sense of complex interactions among individuals in a variety of contexts including families, communities, and group work (Harris & Sherblom, 2005). Systems theory captures the complexity of groups by describing them as a collection of parts that interact together to function as a whole (Schwartz, 2002). The theory focuses on the interconnectedness of individuals within a social system (such as a family, a community, or a group) and emphasizes that what each member brings to the group and how it is communicated influences what happens within that group. That is, the interactional styles of group members and the group leader as well as their social and emotional needs influence how the group functions (Toseland & Rivas, 2005).

The image of a body is often used as a metaphor for this systems theory notion of parts and whole in group functioning. The first point, using this metaphor, is that we know that each organ of the body is affected by the functioning of the other body organs. For example, if the heart is not properly regulating blood flow, the extremities will be affected. In a group, individuals make decisions about their own participation in the group based on how others are functioning or behaving. If members see that their contributions or the contributions of their peers are met with scorn or insult, for example, they will be less likely to participate.

Second, the body exists as a total of all of the organs; its functioning is based on the interdependent functioning of all of the parts. In application to group work, we know that the goals of the group will more likely be achieved if all of the members work well together. In a task group, for example, if group member attention is drawn to a side issue or focuses just on one member, than the accomplishment of the group task will likely be hampered.

Third, how the body functions as a whole, all of the parts together, also influences the strength and capacities of the individual organs. A group that is working well has the potential to offer new learning opportunities and knowledge to the individual members in that group. In our earlier example of the group of students discussing college tours, we saw that both Jakelin and Tanya were able to personally learn something significant from the group experience.

Illustration 10.1   The Body as a Function of Parts That Must Work Together

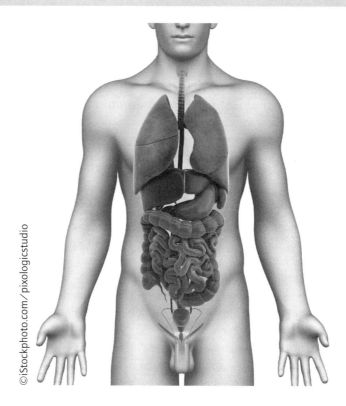

©iStockphoto.com/pixologicstudio

In summary, then, the points here in regard to group work are the following: (1) individual group members shape the functioning of the group, (2) individual group members are shaped by and have the capacity to learn from each other, and (3) the overall functioning of the group will determine the accomplishment of the group task as well as learning that happens for each individual member of the group.

In order to be effective, then, groups must be able to function more or less harmoniously (Gladding, 2003). Using this term, harmonious, however, can be misleading. This does not mean that all members in a group must get along all the time and that things should always calm and happy. Group members learn from discord as well. The point that Gladding was making, I believe, is that groups need to be managed properly for adequate functioning and learning to occur. The terms *equilibrium* or *homeostasis*, sometimes used to describe the ways in which groups as systems move toward the maintenance of order and stability (Day, 2007; Toseland & Rivas, 2005), are relevant here. There needs to be an energy in the group that favors system functioning. Let us go back to the analogy of the body to help explain this concept. When an organ in the body is injured, the body will attempt to carry on living, despite the injury. Certain resources will be sent to achieve recovery—the development of antibodies, for example, to help a particular organ fight infection—and at the same time, the body will attempt to carry on with its business of living. In groups, whatever happens in the group is significant, and the group must continue to work with the changes that are brought about with each development along the way.

For group harmony to occur, members must also buy into the purpose of the group and they must be able to adapt to the particulars and contributions of the other group members. Kraus and Hulse-Killacky (1996) talk about the important role that group leaders play in achieving this harmony in their groups. Leaders do this, according to Kraus and Hulse-Killacky, by maintaining an appropriate and flexible balance between group content goals and group process dynamics. That is, for groups to function effectively, there must be a focus on the goals or intent of the group and there must also be attention on the personal and interpersonal needs and dynamics of the various group members. Achieving this important balance is particularly critical in times of conflict in the group.

Gladding (2003) points out that group members are always in the process of assessing their own individual presence and their own needs in relation to the needs and presence of others. This is a process that Gladding refers to as *integrating* with and *differentiating* from group members. So, while the group is established to address a content-related goal, members are also making decisions about the extent to which they want to participate in and grow from the group. Gladding's point about member investment is critical to how groups function because, as mentioned earlier, each part of the system affects other parts. As we will see shortly when we review group stage theory, group conflicts may result from challenges related to member involvement and the leader's inability to manage group process and content dynamics. How group leaders help members negotiate group conflict is an important determinant of whether group goals will be met. Here the point is that group facilitation requires careful attention to the purpose of the group (content) as well as on interpersonal dynamics (process).

Group Stage Theory

Scholars of group work have long attempted to describe group process in a series of stages, and the result is a proliferation of stage models of group development. These models offer similar characterizations of what happens in groups at the start, in the middle, and at the end, and they map these out as distinct and fairly predictable processes. It should be noted that research suggests that group processes may not be as linear and foreseeable as these models would suggest. For example, research suggests that not all groups follow the identified stages and not always in the order expected (Harris & Sherblom, 2055). Others report that groups are often cyclic, moving from one stage to the next and then back again through earlier stages (Toseland & Rivas, 2005). Despite this lack of precision, however, these models do describe a group phenomenon that has been observed by many and across multiple group types, offering some degree of face validity. Importantly, knowledge about group stages can be very helpful for group leaders because having a general sense of how a group is likely to develop and grow over time can help them decide what interventions are most appropriate at different times in the lifespan of a group, and it also can help leaders anticipate and respond to challenges more effectively.

Tuckman's model (Tuckman, 1965; see also Tuckman & Jensen, 1977) of group stages is arguably the most widely used stage model in the literature on group work. In this model, four group stages are summarized in these catchy descriptive terms: *forming, storming, norming,* and *performing.* These stages are described in this section and summarized, along with suggested leader interventions, at the end of this chapter in Table 10.2. Note that the addition of a termination or *adjourning* stage was subsequently added to the Tuckman model and is included in our discussion.

Initially referred to as a stage of testing and dependence (Tuckman, 1965), *forming* is what happens when groups (of any sort) initiate. This is when members become oriented to the task at hand and its relevance, and they begin to determine what is needed for task completion. Interpersonally, members are exploring each other and seek to determine what behaviors, ideas, actions, and words are acceptable in the group.

Storming is Tuckman's term (Tuckman, 1965) for the next stage, named to describe its defining characteristic of conflict within the group. Moving from the relative comfort in the forming stage, members in this stage typically start to grapple with expressing individuality. As a result, they may resist group structure and become wary of "progression into the 'unknown' of interpersonal relations" (Tuckman, 1965, p. 386). This is where Gladding's (2003) concepts of differentiation and integration are very present in the group. Group member personal needs (differentiating) come in conflict with their competing needs of integrating—interacting with others and being part of the group. As a result, members may compete with each other to find their place or struggle for a powerful position, and they may feel anxious, defensive, or resistant, particularly to the direction and leadership of the group (Gladding, 2003). Group content goals related to the purpose and goals of the group may be difficult to achieve during this phase as conflict brews interpersonally (Tuckman, 1965).

When the conflicts that surfaced during the storming process begin to resolve, a sense of cohesion often takes place. This is what characterizes the next stage of group development referred to as *norming* (Tuckman, 1965). In this stage, members begin to accept each other and the group is able to refocus on its goals. It is a process described by Tuckman (1965) as an "open exchange of relevant interpretations" (p. 387). In therapy groups, this refers to personal sharing and openness; in nontherapy groups, it tends to manifest as an open exchange of opinions and ideas. In this norming stage, members demonstrate an investment in the group, and in doing so, they establish norms so as to preserve a sense of group harmony. Conflict is often avoided in this stage, as members become reinvested in the process and tasks of the group.

Performing is Tuckman's term for the final stage of group development (Tuckman, 1965). This is sometimes called the *working stage* of the group because it refers to when the group focuses on its intended goal (Day, 2007; Gladding, 2003). During this stage, members are invested in the tasks of the group, often with constructive action. They experience safety and freedom to try new behaviors, learn from each other, and take risks. Also at this time, members are able to negotiate disagreements with an investment and competence that was not present during the earlier stages, and as mentioned, completion of the group goals or tasks consumes the work that happens in the group.

It is important to mention that ending a group is considered an important stage of group work. This last phase, called *adjourning*, was originally overlooked in Tuckman's stage model of groups (Tuckman & Jensen, 1977). Adjourning refers to the final task of group leaders to attend to issues of separation of group members as the group comes to close. Group closure typically occurs when the tasks of the group have been adequately met, although, of course, sometimes groups end prematurely due to any number of unforeseen circumstances. For example, members may decide to drop out of the group before it is done or circumstances in the agency or setting dictate an early ending to the group.

The tasks of this final stage of the group, when the ending can be planned, center around summarizing the group experience—both process and content, and having members think about how their experience in the group will transfer into their everyday lives in the future (Gladding, 2003; Toseland & Rivas, 2005). In many groups, particularly counseling and therapy groups, termination also entails acknowledging and, perhaps, resolving any remaining concerns regarding the interpersonal relationships that were part of the group process (Toseland & Rivas, 2005). A second final task for group leaders during closure is to assess the success of the group (Toseland & Rivas, 2005). This can be accomplished by evaluating the end product of the group (this is most applicable to task groups), asking members to reflect on their learning, or inviting members to complete questionaires about their experiences in the group.

While facilitating closure among group members is particularly salient for counseling and psychotherapy groups, Keyton (1993) points out that attending to the interpersonal relationships is also important in work or task groups. Even if a task group is embedded within an organization and individuals in the group will likely continue to work with each other again in the future, attending to the interpersonal relationships and reaching resolution on difficult issues that may have arisen in the group is critical. Clearly, unresolved issues, especially in a work group, can affect future participation in group tasks and can also affect the life and climate of the organization.

GROUP LEADER PRINCIPLES

The discussions above about group dynamics, group systems theory, and group stages provide insight into the complexity and the benefits of using group work for helping. Group work provides an exciting venue for working on challenging tasks, stimulating growth, learning from others, and practicing new ways of being with others. All of these things can happen as primary or secondary outcomes of being in a group; but only if the group is led by skilled group leaders. There are volumes of information and an abundance of training opportunities for helpers who are interested in learning more about group leadership. I recommend that all helpers who work in a group format receive specific training in leading groups and actively engage in supervision or consultation throughout their group experience. Below are some general principles that are recommended for group leaders to use across group types.

1. Plan Carefully

Being well-prepared is a precursor to successful group leadership (Geroski & Kraus, 2010). It seems obvious, but still, it is important to point out that

Illustration 10.4   Plan Carefully

©iStockphoto.com/Jeff Gardnerto

planning a group begins with having a clear sense of purpose. And again, purpose refers to why the group is being established in the first place—what the group is about.

Remember the group types mentioned earlier? Sometimes groups are formed in response to an identified problem. Other groups are intended to avoid a particular problem from developing. Still others are designed to provide information, to generate understandings, or to complete a particular task. Whatever the purpose of the group may be, its intent is typically articulated as its *goal*. Group goals are an articulation of the intended outcome of the group and what members will gain from the experience of being in the group (Geroski & Kraus, 2010). Functional groups are built upon clear intentions. Without clear purpose, groups often flounder (Corey & Corey, 2006).

Being clear about what should be accomplished in the group will dictate the type of group that will be established. For example, when the purpose of the group is to accomplish a specific task rather than personal growth or development, the group will likely be a task or work group. This is not to say that personal growth and betterment may not come from participating in task groups, but only that personal growth is not typically the purpose of these particular types of groups. When the intent of a group is to teach personal or interpersonal skills, then the group type is more likely to be psychoeducational. Counseling and therapy groups typically have as their goals to ameliorate or attempt to address identified personal or interpersonal challenges.

Being clear about the intention of the group will also determine group membership. An important question to ask when determining who will be in the group is whether the individual's problem or need will be addressed appropriately in the group (Toseland & Rivas, 2005). Clearly, helpees should not be invited into groups that are not relevant to them and they should not be in groups that will not be beneficial to their specific needs and abilities. Member selection also depends on the extent to which an individual is able to bring appropriate knowledge and skill to be successful in the group (Schwarz, 2002). That is, does the member have something to contribute to the group? Finally, Schwarz (2002) points out that membership considerations should include who can make a commitment to the group. That is, members should be willing to commit to being in the group across time.

Group homogeneity, which refers to the extent to which members are alike, is also important. As mentioned, groups should be composed of members who share a common purpose and who have some common personal characteristics (Toseland & Riva, 2005). Too much homogeneity (similarity) among members, however, may stifle group creativity and the potential for change. For example, Schwarz (2002) suggests that groups should be composed of members that have the potential to offer diverse perspectives or skills, who are somewhat open to other perspectives, and who are interested in personal learning and change. But when group members are too different from each other, it may be challenging to develop common goals and to facilitate appropriate and functional interpersonal engagement in the group. So, group member selection must look at all of these variables.

When and where a group is conducted are additional details relevant to planning groups. The setting of the group—seating, space, room size, furniture, etc.—are variables that have the potential to affect the success of the group (Toseland & Riva, 2005). Groups need to be held in settings that suit their purpose. For example, a task group that will ask members to brainstorm, create lists, and write things down will likely need tables, desks, and/or white boards. Support groups may do better in settings with comfortable seats and, possibly, dim lights. Therapy groups may need to be held in a location that offers member anonymity. Each group is unique; group purpose, type, and membership needs should be large factors in determining when and where your group will meet.

Finally, the number of participants in a particular group should be based on the needs and skills of the potential members as well as practical constraints such as the size of the space, schedule, availability, etc. (Toseland & Rivas, 2005). Schwarz (2002) points out that having too many members in a group may inhibit task engagement and result in the group not being productive. For example, a grief and loss group of 20 members makes it difficult for many members to have "air time" and may also inhibit members from getting to know each other. This type of group is likely to struggle without these important components. In psychoeducational groups where interpersonal interaction is not as necessary to the functioning of the group, higher numbers may be okay.

While not all helpers will be in the position to make decisions about who, specifically, will be in their groups, member selection is important. When members are ill-suited for a particular group, they may be unfairly asked to meet inappropriate expectations, and their presence in the group may have unwanted and detrimental consequences for others in the group as well.

2. Pay Attention to Individual and Group Goals and Needs

Here I want to point to the important job that group leaders have to be able to dually focus on the needs of individual participants as well as the group as a whole. Beebe and Masterson (2006) point out that people join groups for a variety of reasons. They may be interested in the group topic, they may have personal or interpersonal needs that will be addressed in the group, they may be motivated by who else is in the group, etc. There is no simple formula for what group is best for whom, nor to explain why individuals join particular groups over others. What we can and should assume, however, is that individuals have particular reasons for signing on to a specific group experience, and it is those particular needs that must be addressed for individuals to be able to benefit from the group experience. The task of the group leader is to be able to navigate the group so that it meets the appropriate needs of individual members and also addresses the purpose or intended goal of the group.

Let us use an example to illustrate the importance of a dual focus on individual and group goals. Mr. Rivera signed up for a parenting class because he was struggling with how to help his young son grieve—his wife, the boy's mother, had recently died of cancer. The group leader intended to use a set curriculum to teach basic parenting skills in this particular group. When the leader learned of Mr. Rivera's specific needs that focused more on how to help his grieving son rather than general parenting information, he immediately determined that the group would not be a good fit, and referred Mr. Rivera to another group that was more appropriate for his needs. Mr. Heinzer, on the other hand, was a single parent struggling with basic parenting skills and was referred to the class because he hoped to learn better techniques for raising his children. This parenting group, then, appeared to be a good match for Mr. Heinzer. Even so, it would be important for the group leader to be aware of the specific struggles that Mr. Heinzer faced, so that his particular parenting needs were included in the content of this psychoeducational group.

Group goals typically transcend the specific intentions of individual group members (Beebe & Masterson, 2006), as can be seen from the example above. Of course, group goals must be congruent with the needs and hopes of individual members of the group, but they also have a life of their own. For example, the goals of the psychoeducational parenting group mentioned in the example above were to teach participants specific parenting skills. Mr. Heinzer's specific needs for parenting his young daughter were congruent with this group goal, but his individual goal to learn how to manage this particular child in his own home context would not be the central focus of the group. That is, the group is about parenting, not about Mr. Heinzer's daughter. And we can easily imagine that the questions that Mr. Heinzer raises in the group will likely be about how the skills can be applied to his own situation with his daughter—which is his individual goal for participating in the group. But it would be the job of the group leader to ensure that the group remains focused on the group goals rather than any individual member's goals (Beebe & Masterson, 2006). The tricky part and the skill required of the group leader in this group example would be to be able to address Mr. Heinzer's individual needs while also addressing the collective needs of all members, which are represented, if member screening was adequately conducted, in the group goals.

3. Maintain a Dual Focus on Content and Process

As mentioned earlier, the terms *process* and *content* identify two important components of what happens in groups. *Process* refers to the here-and-now interactions among group members, their relationships, and how they function together within the group. *Content* refers to the focus or purpose of the group—what the group is about. Across group types, Hulse-Killacky, Kraus, and Schumacher (1999)'s observation that "process facilitates content, and process needs to be balanced with content or a group will fail to attain its objectives" (p. 114) seems to hold true. That is, attending to interpersonal group process dynamics is critical for group content goals to be met. Let us go back to Mr. Heinzer and the parenting group for a quick example of this principle. Let us say that another member in the group, Ms. Duncan, is someone that Mr. Heinzer used to work with. And let us also say that the two of them had extensive conflict in the work environment before Ms. Duncan left to take another job. If this conflict between these two members surfaces in the parenting group, it could take the focus off the topic and on to whatever interpersonal issues were at the root of the initial conflict between these two members. So, in this example, the group leader would need to ensure that these two group members are able to interact at an appropriate if not productive level so that they and everyone else in the group are available for learning the parenting content.

The extent to which a leader should attend to the process versus the content of the group appears to be determined by a number of variables including group membership and interpersonal dynamics. Group type is another factor that should determine the extent to which group process dynamics should be addressed in the group (Geroski & Kraus, 2002). Group leaders conducting task and psychoeducational groups are more likely than leaders of counseling and therapy groups to attend more to group content tasks and goals than to interpersonal processes (Geroski & Kraus, 2002; Gladding, 2003). In our example above, if the parenting group was instead a counseling or therapy group focused on interpersonal behavior or anger management, than the conflict between the two members might be an excellent source of material that could be used in the group to facilitate growth and change. The effectiveness of this, of course, depends on the leader's ability to manage these issues within the group. In many settings a co-leadership model is used for groups that focus on group process dynamics for interpersonal learning. This model, which warrants more extensive explanation but is beyond the scope of our intent here in this chapter, enables leaders to help members work though difficult interpersonal challenges.

What it means to attend to group process dynamics, it turns out, is also somewhat unclear (Geroski & Kraus, 2002). Very generally, group process interventions are those that draw attention to the ways in which individuals are interacting with each other in the group (Carroll & Wiggins, 1997). Group content interventions, on the other hand, draw attention to the topic or goals of the group. For example, in a task group focused on investigating access to services in a mental health agency, the content of the group is this task. Process dynamics is how the members interact to accomplish the task. In this group, then, the leader is not likely to spend a great deal of time on having all of the group members get to know each other at great depth and reveal the personal and interpersonal challenges they have. Instead, he will likely spend more time on keeping the group focused on the task at hand. However, if this leader does not spend some time inviting members to get to know each other a little bit and if he does not address interpersonal dynamics that threaten to rupture group productivity (if that happens in the group), then the group may not be able to achieve its goals. If group process is completely ignored, even in task groups, members may miss the opportunity to know what strengths each brings to the task, they may have difficulties conversing with each other, and the level of safety within the group may prohibit the level of risk-taking needed for creative and innovative thinking. In the end, members may lose interest and commitment to the group, they may stop attending, and the group may not be able to reach its goals. Many of us have been in work groups like this—where members do not have an adequate level of comfort to fully participate or where the behavior of one or a few members stifles the authentic participation of others in the group. Attention to group process dynamics is critical for content goal attainment.

Leaders should always focus on process dynamics in the group, regardless of group type, even when there are no apparent conflicts. This is because doing so can create a climate of collaboration and trust. Leaders do this by starting with introductions, actively inviting members to speak directly to each other, linking what one member has said to another, assigning tasks, and structuring the group in other ways, as needed, to engage all members into the tasks of the group. These skills are described in more detail in the group facilitation skills below.

4. Display Social and Emotional Intelligence and Fluency

The literature suggests that fluency in social and emotional intelligence, "people skills" as Riggio and Reichard (2008, p. 181) call them, is critical to successful group leadership and functioning (Groves, 2005; Riggio, Salinas, Riggio, & Cole, 2003). Leader social intelligence refers to the ability to identify and interpret social cues and be able to adjust one's response to these cues as needed to facilitate the group effectively (Zaccaro, 2002). Mayer and Salovey (1997) define emotional intelligence as the "ability to perceive emotions, to access and generate emotions so as to assist thought, to understand emotions and emotional knowledge, and to reflectively regulate emotions so as to provide emotional and intellectual growth" (p. 5). For the group leader, this means having the ability to perceive what group members are thinking and feeling and to respond accordingly. Emotional intelligence is critical to establishing a group climate of trust (Chang, Sy, & Choi, 2012), and similarly, social intelligence enables leaders to help members feel valued, respected, and appreciated (Upadhyay, 2009).

So what does social and emotional intelligence look like in practice? Let us use an example. Maria Antonia was close to tears when she was not immediately picked to be in a small classroom activity group by some of her friends in class. Seeing this, the teacher stood near her, touching her slightly on the shoulder, and said to all of the children in the group, "Excuse me, students. I am sorry, but I'm going to ask everyone to go back to their original seats because I realized that I made a mistake—I forgot to tell you which groups you were in." And then when all of the students were seated, the teacher had the students count off by 6, thus forming groups for the activity. Later she checked in with Maria Antonia and another student who similarly had been left out, to ensure that they were fully engaged with their peers in their small group activity. The next day, the teacher initiated a discussion during morning meeting (without mentioning specific names and events) about how it feels to be left out. These teacher/leader responses, I believe, indicate that the teacher was attuned to the emotional state of the students who felt left out and was able to intervene in a way that addressed both the individual needs as well as larger classroom task. The teacher structured the activity (on the second try) so as to avoid subgrouping. In addition to addressing the problem that some of the children felt left out, this intervention also addressed the implicit goals of cooperation and respect for others that were part of the classroom rules and norms that had been established at the start of the school year.

5. Use Group Facilitation Skills

Group leaders rely on a wide repertoire of skills for intervening in groups. All of the listening, responding, and change skills discussed in Chapters 7 and 8 are used frequently by competent group leaders across group types. The skills describe here are additional intervention skills that are particularly pertinent to leading groups. These skills are also outlined in Table 10.1.

Reframing

Reframing is when the group leader offers an alternative explanation for something that has been said or that has happened in the group (Geroski & Kraus, 2010; Toseland & Rivas, 2005). Leaders often use reframing in groups to open up member thinking, to stimulate group conversations around issues related to group dynamics, or to facilitate meaning-making. For example, in a counseling group, Stewart persistently asked the leader what time it was. The leader responded by saying, "Stewart, it sounds like you're not quite sure, yet, if you want to be here. I get that. I hope you'll give this group try before giving up. I think you may find it helpful." In this example, the leader interpreted the meaning of Stewart's questions, reframing the intent by inviting him to give the group a try.

Reframing can also be used in response to aggressive statements that are made between members in the group. For example, in a psychoeducational group that was discussing rape as a form of aggression, Zelda told another member, John, that he didn't know what he was talking about since he was a guy and "clearly knows nothing about rape." The leader reframed Zelda's comments by saying, "This is a topic that generates a lot of anger. Sometimes that anger gets directed at all men, even those who are not perpetrators of violence and rape. Let's be careful in here to understand how triggering this topic can be, and let's remember not lash out at others. Also let's be patient and respectful to each other as we all learn more about rape and how it affects both men and women. Okay?" In this example, the leader reframed Zelda's comments as a way of demonstrating how the topic is triggering, and to help members remain respectful and empathetic while engaging in difficult conversations.

Blocking

Leaders can also block inappropriate comments or interactions (Gladding, 2003) by literally saying, "let me stop you for a minute," or by physically signaling a stop sign with their hand. Geroski and Kraus (2010) refer to blocking as a metaphoric "stepping in between or standing in the way" (p. 173). When member behavior is not conducive to achieving individual and group goals, blocking can be used to provide safety. It is also used when the topic or focus is leaning away from the purpose of the group. To this end, a leader can block the direction of a particular statement by introducing a new topic or group activity.

Cutting Off

Like blocking, cutting off is a technique used to limit the extent to which one member monopolizes or takes up too much space in the group (Geroski & Kraus, 2010). It can be used to prevent rambling or regulate the content of what is said in the group (Gladding, 2003). Cutting off is a highly nuanced skill—leaders need to be able to stop a member from talking or behaving in a particular way while also being respectful. If any of the group members perceive that the leader has cut off a group member unfairly or inappropriately, it is likely engender mistrust among all group members. Seeing one member being treated in a way that is perceived as unfair can cause members to assume that they, too, may be disrespected at some point in the future.

Cutting off can be accomplished through a nonverbal cue, or it can be executed more directly by politely interrupting the speaker. An example of a more direct cutting off can be seen in this example: Consuela, who was running a task group, interrupted Jeff, cutting him off, by saying "Excuse me, Jeff, I am sorry to interrupt you, but I just noticed that the time is slipping away from us in here and I hoped that we could refocus on the steps we need to take for next week." A nonverbal cutting-off gesture is exemplified a little later in the group when Consuela lifts her hand in a stop signal to Karla, who was getting ready to interrupt Jennifer.

Shifting the Focus

Shifting the focus has to do with changing the topic or inviting a different speaker to join the conversation (Gladding, 2003). For example, "Okay, now I was hoping that we could give Jamie a chance to share his thoughts." Or, "We have been talking about college applications for quite a while, and I wanted to be sure that we have time to also talk about job applications. So, please focus here while I offer some basic tips for job applicants."

Drawing Out

Drawing out refers to encouraging less verbal members to participate more by creating openings for them in the group (Geroski & Kraus, 2010). Leaders can do this by directly inviting a member to speak. For example, "Jorge, I don't think we've heard from you for a while. What do you think?" Or by asking a member to help with a particular task such as, for example, to collect everyone's papers. Leaders can also draw out members by asking a question and waiting patiently for the person's response—sometimes quieter members simply need the leader to hold a space while they formulate a response. Another way to draw out quiet members is to use rounds where everyone is asked to respond in an orderly fashion to a simple prompt. For example, the leader of a psychoeducational group on writing college essays said, "Okay, let's just check in to see where everyone is at. Let's start with Mohammad and go around the circle—everyone just mention one idea that they heard here today that seemed to make sense." In this case, starting with a member that is likely to set a good tone or be a model for the particular response set you are looking for, and not starting with the silent member, may make it easier for quiet members to respond.

Linking

Linking is an intervention that makes a connection between words, ideas, and concepts. For example, the leader can invite someone to respond to a specific proposal that one of the members has offered (Toseland & Rivas, 2005). Linking can also be used to make connections between members. Leaders can link members, for example, by asking them to speak directly to each other (Geroski & Kraus, 2010). Leaders often use linking, particularly in early stages of the group, to enhance meaning-making and to facilitate interpersonal connections. For example, in an unstructured group for elders in a senior center, the leader, Tom, said, "Is there anyone else who has experienced what Mrs. Sargent is talking about—being talked over as if they can't hear?" Or, "Mr. Amaya, this sounds like what you were talking about last week. Right? It sounds like that idea feeling disrespected."

Leveling

Leveling is an intervention that is typically used to equalize the power differential in the group, drawing out some members while also lessening the impact of others in the group. It is often used during the norming and storming stages of group development (Gladding, 2003). Leaders can use leveling to help members consider the role they play in the group, or to alter group dynamics. For example, "Frank, when you snap your gum and whisper to Sydney while others are talking, the message you are communicating, it seems, is that what others are saying isn't important. I doubt that is your intention, but remember that giving everyone a chance to be heard is something that we all agreed was important in this group. Miriam, can you please repeat what you were saying?" The point is to modify group process dynamics so that members participate equally.

Setting and Enforcing Limits

Group leaders are the ones in the group who are ultimately in charge of member safety (Geroski & Kraus, 2010). Leaders need to prohibit sarcasm, teasing, and talking for or about others—those in or outside of the group, as all of these behaviors are likely to create anxiety and interrupt the normal processes of group development. This can be done directly by stating the rule, such as "In here we have a rule that we only talk about ourselves." In some

Table 10.1	Summary of Group Leadership Skills

Skill	Description
Social and Emotional Intelligence and Fluency	Leader social and emotional intelligence is critical for determining appropriate responses to members in the group and for establishing a climate of trust. Leaders do this by attending to member and social cues and responding appropriately. This also entails reading member nonverbal cues and emotions, responding in an appropriately regulated, but also emotionally available and expressive way.
Reframing	Reframing is used to open up member thinking, group conversations, or to facilitate meaning-making. Leaders do this by offering an alternative explanation after something has been said or has happened in the group.
Blocking	Blocking is used to interfere when member behavior is not conducive to achieving individual and group goals. It is an action aimed to offer safety or direction in a group. Leaders can do this by using nonverbal signals, or verbally, by confronting a member in the group.
Cutting Off	Cutting off entails setting a limit on an individual's participation in the group. Leaders do this by offering a nonverbal cue or by respectfully interrupting the speaker.
Shifting the Focus	Shifting the focus has to do with changing the topic or inviting a different speaker to join the conversation. Leaders do this directly by inviting a particular member to respond or bringing up a new topic.
Drawing Out	Drawing out encourages less verbal members to participate in the group. The leader can prompt or ask questions, wait patiently for the person's response, use rounds, or invite a participation in a particular task.
Linking	Linking connects individuals or concepts. The leader can ask members to speak directly to one another, to voice their reactions to something that has been said or that has happened in the group, or leaders can articulate links between members or ideas.
Leveling	Leveling equalizes power in the group. Leaders can draw out quieter members, offer feedback or invite dominant and assertive members in the group to consider the impact, or use blocking.
Setting and Enforcing Limits	Limits promote safety. The leader can restate the rule, offer an explanation for the rule, or directly instruct a member.

situations, repeating the explanation for the rule may be helpful. "We just want to be careful to provide a space for everyone's own voice in here." Leaders can also offer a more direct message to the offender, such as "Sasha, please let Aisha name her feelings for herself."

Group leaders are also charged with setting and enforcing limits related to keeping the group focused on intended group goals. As we have reiterated throughout this chapter, groups are conducted for specific purposes and members are invited into groups because it is determined that the group will be beneficial to them in some way. It is not fair for members to be in a group that is not meeting its goals as advertised. For example, the leader of a student leadership training group noticed that Jonathan seemed to want to complain about his soccer coach at every opportunity. Since this did not seem appropriate to the training goals of the group, this leader invited Jonathan to talk with him at another time about his specific concerns about the coach, and he shifted the focus of the group by directing Jonathan to share with the group his response to question number 2 (from a workbook they had been using).

INTERVENTION SKILLS AND GROUP STAGE

Earlier we reviewed stages of group development. With the group facilitation skills that we just discussed in mind, along with the additional intervention skills mentioned in Chapters 7 and 8, we will now look at how these various skills can be implemented to promote group progress at various stages of the group. This discussion will be structured by the group stages of forming, storming, norming, performing, and adjourning, and key points are summarized in Table 10.2.

Forming

Forming, as you will recall, refers to the initial process in group development where members are getting to know each other, the leader, and the tasks of the group (Tuckman, 1965). At this stage, participation tends to be limited and members are often reluctant to take risks, even if they eager to seek connections with others in the group. This kind of self-censoring is typically due to concerns that new members have about how they will be perceived by others in the group.

Tasks of group leaders during this stage are to address apprehension, review goals, clarify rules, promote positive interchange among members, set limits when necessary (Gladding, 2003), and to facilitate connections among members (Toseland & Rivas, 2005). During the first group meeting, the leader should clarify the purpose of the group, perhaps asking each member to speak to their own goals as they relate to the group intent. The leader will also want to attend to ground rules so as to clarify expectations and set the stage for what will and will not happen in the first and subsequent group meetings. As an example, the leader might remind members of rules about confidentiality and ask members to please turn off their cell phones. To help members get to know each other, leaders should also attend to introductions, perhaps using a predictable round-robin structure so that members have a prompt for what to say and can anticipate their turn for speaking. This limits the unpredictability, and also sets a norm that everyone will say something. Leaders of groups at this stage need to be patient as members develop comfort, be willing to return to group goals or ground rules as much as is needed to help provide clarity, and offer structure and direction in the group as members become more comfortable and committed.

Problems may arise in early stage groups if members establish (or hold on to existing) subgroups—smaller and exclusive groups within the larger group (Gladding, 2003). For example, if all of the students from a particular neighborhood sit together in a closed circle in the back of the room, other group members may feel excluded. So, leaders need to attend to these early dynamics by inviting relationships across subgroups and by setting norms that invite inclusion. Gladding (2003) reminds us that group leaders will also need to be careful to establish norms early in the group that do not allow one or a few members to monopolize the conversation, manipulate others, or disengage/be nonparticipatory (leaving others to wonder what they are thinking or leaving them to feel outside of the group as it develops). Setting ground rules around psychological safety and participation, and actively engaging group members to engage are important early group strategies.

Storming

Storming, ironically, is what happens in groups when members begin to invest in the group and start to feel comfortable with one another. When this level of comfort is achieved, members may begin to assert themselves as they find their own place and voice in the group. It is as if group members no longer believe that they need to be overly polite with each other and thus become more honest and assertive about their opinions—it is a time when group members feel safe enough to be real with each other (Harris & Sherblom, 2005).

For some, this means being assertive and attempting to dominate or have power over others in the group. Others may be anxious, resistant, or defensive. Most members bring their past interpersonal patterns into the group; some attempt to try on new roles and ways of interacting with others. The point is that in this stage, the group grapples with control, structure, and direction; it is a time of conflict and anxiety (Gladding, 2003). Conflicts may surface around the group tasks (this is called *task conflict*), and these conflicts are often communicated by disagreeing with ideas, facts, and opinions expressed by others. Conflicts may also surface in relationships between members, which is called *relationship conflict* (Toseland & Rivas, 2005).

Most group scholars believe that the storming phase is necessary for the development of subsequent feelings of cohesion and cooperation in groups (Harris & Sherblom, 2005). However, many group leaders are uncomfortable responding to conflict and may attempt to ignore, minimize, or avoid it—none of which foster healthy resolve and movement toward group goals. It is most helpful to view conflict as a normal part of group development, and leaders can manage conflict by recognizing and naming it and assuring that group members interact in ways that are consistent with group norms of listening and being open, nonjudgmental, and respectful of others (Toseland & Rivas, 2005). The leader will need to be sure that all members are supported so that everyone feels safe (Gladding, 2003).

Leveling is an important skill that is used at this time so as to allow all members equal access and voice in the group. This means assuring that the group is not dominated by one or a small number of members, a subgroup, or by those who are loudest and most assertive, and, on the other hand, also proving a space for quieter members to have a voice (Gladding, 2003). Another strategy for navigating the group through the storming stage is to draw attention to the group dynamics by making *process comments*. These are comments that focus on group process dynamics. For example, when his task group seemed to be in conflict over the best way to proceed with the task, the leader, Suleman, commented, "It seems that we are at the place here where we are hearing a variety of perspectives and the conversation is getting heated. I think it would be a good idea if we took a minute to review the ground rules we decided on weeks ago. Also, I want to be sure that we find a space in this group for the voices of those who have been silent. Let's do a response-option round to hear from everyone on this issue. Can you start, Maeve?" It is very important for group leaders to be ready for this stage of conflict, and to respond with confidence, fairness, and actions that ensure safety of all members in the group.

Norming

During norming, the group begins to coalesce. Members extend toward each other—they cooperate and support one another, and a sense of group unity and mutuality characterize the group (Tuckman, 1965). Sometimes a sense of group boundaries against outsiders is also apparent in this stage. All of these represent a developing sense of "we" among group members. In this stage, personal self-disclosure among members happens more readily and group members are willing to take personal and interpersonal risks. As a result, it is often a period of movement and growth.

The first important leader behavior during this stage is to monitor what is happening in the group. The leader will also want to be sure that any new norms that might have emerged during the storming process are articulated as understandings that are shared by all group members (Gladding, 2003). Of course, the norm of respecting the views of others is always an important norm that should be maintained in the group.

Second, this is often a time when leaders are able introduce new content in the group (Toseland & Rivas, 2005). This is particularly true in psychoeducational groups, where leaders may also want to introduce activities or structure to engage members in content learning. Finally, in this phase when the group begins to move toward the intended group goals, the leader often assumes a more secondary role. Often leader behaviors at this stage shift to focusing largely on encouraging and reinforcing group member's efforts, whether interpersonal or task related, and the leader will also try to promote clear and direct communication between members (Gladding, 2003).

To see these ideas in action, let us use the example of Dr. Betts, who is leading a psychoeducational training group for nurse aides. Dr. Betts noticed that one of the participants, Jeb, in the training group consistently offered negative feedback to other group members—he did this rather than engage in conversation with his peers. It was as if this trainee was communicating that he knew more than others. This was a concern for Dr. Betts, as two of the training goals were to teach participants to be actively involved in collaborative practice and for trainees to develop productive communication skills. Dr. Betts also worried that allowing this member to behave in this way might create an interpersonal dynamic that would interfere with the content focus of the group. So, she decided to intervene the next time she saw this happen. Soon enough, Jeb corrected his partner, Angie, as she tried to adjust a blood pressure cuff. "You aren't doing it right," Jeb said as the partner began to struggle. "Here, do it like this . . ." he added as he reached for the cuff mechanism. "I wonder,

Jeb," Dr. Betts jumped in, "if it might be helpful for Angie to get a feel for how the pressure cuff works by manipulating it on her own? We all learn this best by doing rather than watching someone else do it. When Angie asks you for help, then that is your invitation to help her. Thanks."

Performing

The performing stage of the group, as mentioned, is sometimes referred to as the working stage. This is when the task or purpose of the group comes into focus and individual as well as group productivity is strong (Tuckman, 1965). The emphasis is on the task of the group, and interpersonal processes tend to facilitate task attainment. There is flexibility and collaboration among group members. Leaders of groups in this stage will want to maintain emphasis on teamwork by encouraging collaboration, continuing to build consensus around group tasks, promoting interpersonal engagement, and allowing members to resolve any conflicts that may arise in the group (Gladding, 2003). When the group is performing well in this phase, the leader mostly just offers support and resources as needed.

Adjourning

As mentioned, the final task of group leaders is to summarize learning and attend to the closure of interpersonal relationships that developed in the group. In some groups, the prospect of group termination may leave some members feeling sad, yet others will feel ready to be done. Ideally, group members will leave their group experience full of hope and inspiration (Gladding, 2003). It is not unusual for members of some groups to be in denial or not want to address closure, to feel abandoned, disappointed, unsure, and angry (Toseland & Rivas, 2005). This is especially true for members who took risks, were personally engaged in the group process, and especially for those who have little access to support outside the group. And, of course, group leaders too may have mixed reactions to ending the groups they have facilitated.

Toseland and Rivas (2005) emphasize the importance of group leaders assuring that what members have learned through the group experience is maintained into the future and is generalizable to other situations. This is a task that should not be left to the final group session—as Gladding says, preparation for ending a group "beings in the planning stage" (Gladding, 2003, p. 180). He emphasizes that it is the role of the leader to provide leadership to guide members through this final stage of the group.

In the final stages of the group, then, the tasks of the leader are twofold: to help members focus more intently on planning how to take their new knowledge and skills into the future and to bring closure to the relationships that

Table 10.2 Group Stages and Leader Interventions

Group Stage	Description of Stage	Leader Tasks
Forming	The initial process of group development where members are getting to know each other, the leader, and the tasks of the group	• Address apprehension review goals • Clarify rules • Promote positive interchanges • Set limits when necessary • Facilitate connections
Storming	Group conflict emerges as members express individuality; members grapple with integration versus differentiation and seek a place in the group identity.	• Ensure that all members are supported and feel safe • Ensure that all members have equal access and voice in the group • Draw attention to the group dynamics
Norming	A sense of group unity and mutuality develops as members cooperate and support one another.	• Allow group members to renegotiate rules and norms, if appropriate • Ensure and monitor member commitment to norms • Begin to introduce new content related to group goals • Encourage and reinforce group members' efforts and contributions
Performing	The task or purpose of the group comes into focus and productivity is strong.	• Maintain emphasis on teamwork • Encourage collaboration and consensus building around group tasks • Promoting interpersonal engagement • Offer support and resources as needed • Engage members to resolve conflicts, if necessary
Adjourning	Learning is summarized, closure is reached, and consideration is given to the transfer of learning.	• Help members summarize and reflect on what they have learned • Address any unresolved issues among group members • Lead the group in a process for expressing farewells

Adapted from: Tuckman, B. W. (1965). Developmental sequence in small groups. *Psychological Bulletin, 63*(6), 384–399.

developed during the course of the group. To promote this first goal regarding the transfer of learning, leaders can engage group members to reflect on and summarize the various aspects of their group experience (Gladding, 2003). This may include asking members to recall critical incidents or important experiences they had in the group, assess and discuss the changes they have made as a result of the group experience, address any unresolved issues with other group members, and if possible, rehearse what they have learned (Gladding, 2003). To guide closure around the interpersonal relationships that were formed in the group, Gladding emphasizes the importance of including a process (formal or informal) for saying good-bye or in some way expressing farewell in the final group meeting.

CHAPTER SUMMARY

Group work offers a powerful and effective venue for addressing a variety of helping goals. One of the unique aspects of group work is the ways in which interpersonal engagement can facilitate learning across a variety of different group situations. Understanding group structure and development can help leaders anticipate group process dynamics and intervene in ways that promote group content goals. The group leader principles and skills identified in this chapter can be implemented in a variety of group venues and in all group types.

DISCUSSION QUESTIONS

1. What types of groups are primarily aimed to help individuals address personal and interpersonal challenges, and how might these group types differ from other groups?

2. What interventions might a group leader need to employ if a few group members tend to speak up and be quite lengthy with their responses monopolizing group time, while others rarely speak?

3. Why do group's often experience a stage called "storming," when conflict begins to emerge, and how might a group leader respond?

4. Why is social and emotional intelligence so important for group leadership?

5. In thinking about your class as a group experience, what group dynamics do you notice?

Appendix A: Clinical, Nonclinical, and Other Helping Roles

Counselors

Clinical counselors receive extensive clinical training at the master's level, have participated in a clinical internship in their specialty area, and must be licensed (and pass a licensure exam) prior to working in the field. Licensure in many of these specialty areas vary from state to state, but may require approximately 2 years of postdegree practice experience under supervision. Clinical counseling specialty areas include the following:

- **Clinical mental health counselors** are professionals who provide counseling and psychotherapy for individuals facing a variety of personal, emotional, and interpersonal issues and mental illness. They work in a variety of private and community practice settings.

- **Marriage and family counselors/therapists** also work in private and agency settings and provide services to couples and families.

- **Rehabilitation counselors** provide services to individuals with disabilities, and their work often focuses on supporting independent living and job attainment.

- **Career and vocational counselors** work with individuals in the area of career or job training and placement.

- **School counselors** provide a variety of prevention and responsive services to youth in schools, K–12.

Medical Professionals

The list of different types of helpers in the medical fields is extensive, and the training requirements for all of them vary. Medical mental health related specialty areas include the following:

- **Psychiatrists** have a medical doctorate degree and residency training in the diagnosis and treatment of mental health disorders. They must complete 4 years of medical school, finish a 3-year residency in psychiatry, take a medical board examination, and be licensed in their state of practice. While some psychiatrists conduct counseling sessions, most provide diagnostic and evaluation services, prescribe psychotropic medications, and provide consultation services with others who are providing direct care.

- **Advanced-level psychiatric mental health nurses** or **psychiatric nurses** are registered nurses with additional training in the provision of mental health assessment and planning, and counseling. Some are licensed to prescribe medications. All nurses must also pass licensure exams and be licensed in their state of practice; advanced level psychiatric nurses also receive specialty training in this particular practice area.

Psychologists

Clinical psychologists are licensed professionals that must have attained a doctoral degree (PhD, PsyD, or EdD) in psychology (in most states) that includes a clinical internship and a licensure examination, and many states require a postdoctoral clinical internship. Some states license master's level psychologists for clinical practice. Clinical psychology specialty areas include the following:

- **Clinical psychologists** provide counseling or psychotherapy and diagnostic assessment services for individuals facing a variety of personal, emotional, and interpersonal issues, and they also work with those struggling with mental illness. In two states and in some very specific situations psychologists with appropriate training are allowed to prescribe medications.

- **Educational psychologists** and school psychologists specialize in educational-related assessment and related counseling services.

- **Health psychologists** work with patients to cope with medical issues.

- **Neuropsychologists** work in the diagnosis and assessment of cognitive and behavioral issues related to brain functioning and brain injury.

- **Sports psychologists** work with athletes and athletic teams to enhance performance.

Social Workers

Clinical social workers receive extensive clinical training at the master's level, have participated in a clinical internship in their specialty area, and must be licensed by the state to be able to provide counseling services to individuals with personal or interpersonal difficulties. Clinical social workers work in a variety of settings including community mental health agencies, schools, child welfare, family services, and child protective services agencies, and they work in the areas of medical or public health settings.

NONCLINICAL HELPERS

Nonclinical helpers typically work in tandem with and under the supervision of clinical and/or other professional helpers in multidisciplinary settings. Their roles are probably best described as generalists. They tend to have knowledge and training in human development or a related area, and they have good communication skills and experience working in helping roles. Some of the more common nonclinical helper roles are listed below.

Advocates

Advocates typically work in a role that is aimed at supporting an individual, cause, or group. They also may focus on promoting policy or societal change. An advocate may not need specific education or other credentials to be actively working with individuals or promoting change. Advocates may be self-employed or employed in a variety of community, governmental, and nongovernmental agencies and settings. Some advocates have advanced-level education or training that prepares them for their particular area of specialty. Those working in the relatively new profession of health advocacy, assisting people in navigating service delivery systems, fall in this latter category.

Ancillary Health Providers

Ancillary health providers may have an undergraduate or graduate college degree and work in health care settings providing patient care or administrative assistance. Ancillary health provider specialties include the following:

- **Nursing assistants** typically must complete a specialty training program that includes basic information related to nursing principles and includes supervised practice.

- **Medical assistants** work in a variety of administrative or patient care roles, depending on the practice setting. They typically have an undergraduate degree, and some may have completed a postsecondary certificate training program. Medical assistants usually receive on-the-job training for their specific job expectations.

- **Psychiatric technicians** or **aides** work in psychiatric hospitals, residential mental health facilities, and related health care settings, providing care or assisting in tasks of daily living for people who challenges related to mental health challenges or developmental disabilities. Both positions require on-the-job training, and some postsecondary education may be required for some psychiatric technician positions.

- **Patient advocates** provide pre- or post-medical care, assistance or advocacy. Their work is aimed at supporting an individual who is in need of additional assistance related to a health problem.

Behavioral Interventionists

Behavioral interventionists work with individuals who have difficulties regulating their behavior. The goal of their work is to help eliminate disruptive, harmful, or negative behaviors and replace them with positive actions. Behavioral intervention draws on multiple disciplines, including community health, social work, psychology, counseling, and education, and practitioners work in a wide variety of occupational settings and with varied client populations. A high school diploma is generally the minimum educational requirement for this position, and most behavioral interventionists receive behavior management training. Some behavioral interventionists receive advanced training and education, and they typically work in roles that require more knowledge and specific skills or as supervisors.

Case Managers

Case managers work in a variety of governmental or nongovernmental agencies including social services, juvenile court, rehabilitation, substance abuse treatment, and residential programs such as psychiatric hospitals, group homes, or elder care, etc. Case managers typically have associate or bachelor's level degrees in human development, human services, psychology, social work, and other areas. Case managers with master's level training typically work in roles that require more knowledge and specific skills such as clinical counseling or supervisors.

Counselors

Nonclinically trained counselors work a variety of roles and settings including substance abuse treatment, elder care, crisis response, benefits or eligibility determination, family support, residential housing, prisons, psychiatric hospitals, camp or group home settings, etc. Residential counselors who work in residential high school or university settings are sometimes also called residential advisors. Most of the helpers mentioned here have associate or bachelor's level degrees in a human development, human services, psychology, social work, and other areas, but their positions do not require master's level clinical training in counseling.

Early Childhood Educators/Interventionists

Early childhood educators or interventionists provide direct services to infants, toddlers, young children, and their families in a variety of settings. They work with children who have sensory or physical impairments, cognitive delays, emotional challenges, and/or individuals who have experiences of trauma or neglect. Working in classroom, home, or center-based programs, they often provide technical/medical interventions, developmentally appropriate learning activities, and caregiver support and training. At least a bachelor's degree with an endorsement for working as an early interventionist or teaching early childhood special education is typically required for these positions and many early interventionists have master's level education and training as well.

Intake Workers

Intake workers work in a variety of settings including governmental or nongovernmental agencies, social services, juvenile court, rehabilitation, substance abuse treatment, and residential programs such as psychiatric hospitals, group homes, or elder care, etc. Intake workers typically have associate or bachelor's level degrees in a human development, human services, psychology, social work, and other areas. Intake workers who have clinical or master's level degrees and training often take on additional clinical counseling or supervisory roles in their work settings.

Para-Educators (Teacher Assistants)

Para-educators (also called teacher assistants, teacher's aides, or instructional assistants) work in a variety of roles in school or day care settings. They often have roles and responsibilities related to providing special education services to students who have behavioral, mental health, or learning difficulties or other special needs. Some may also deliver lessons to individual students, assist in small groups, grade papers, supervise students in recreational activities, and help prepare lessons. Para-educators often have an undergraduate degree, although this is not a requirement for some positions, and they typically work under the supervision of a classroom teacher, special educator, or other educational specialist.

Probation Officers

Probation officers often have bachelor's level training, and many are required by their employers to pass oral, written, and psychological exams. They work in various criminal justice facilities with criminal offenders or in the monitoring of offenders to prevent them from committing new crimes.

Social Workers

Nonclinical social workers may have a bachelor's or master's level training. They work in a variety of settings including community mental health agencies, schools, child welfare, family services, child protective services agencies, and medical or public health settings. They are often hired in intake, advocate, case management, and administrative or managerial roles in a variety of governmental and nongovernmental agencies.

OTHER NONCLINICAL HELPING PROFESSIONALS

There are many professional helpers who have special training to work in particular roles in particular settings. These include ministers, coaches, teachers, behavioral assistants, lawyers, etc. While all of these professionals have obtained training and/or experience to work in these roles, many of these professions also require advanced educational degrees and state licenses for practice.

There are many professional helpers who work in service industries such as waiters, waitresses, hostesses, concierge personnel, clerks, and customer service representatives offer important help to others as required by their role. These professionals may or may not have educational degrees and their positions vary in regard to the specific training requirements needed for employment.

This information was compiled from the following sources:

- American Counseling Association. (n.d.-b). *What is professional counseling?* Retrieved November 6, 2014, from http://www.counseling.org/ aca-community/learn-about-counseling/what-is-counseling/overview

- American Psychiatric Association. (n.d.). *What is a psychiatrist?* Retrieved November 6, 2014, from http://www.psychiatry.org/medical-students/ what-is-a-psychiatrist

- American Psychiatric Nurses Association. (n.d.). *About Psychiatric-Mental Health Nurses (PMHNs).* Retrieved November 6, 2014, from http://www.apna.org/i4a/pages/index.cfm?pageid=3292#1

- American Psychological Association. (n.d.). *Therapy.* Retrieved November 6, 2014, from http://apa.org/topics/therapy/index.aspx

- National Association of Social Workers. (n.d.). *Practice.* Retrieved November 6, 2014, from http://www.naswdc.org/pdev/default.asp

- Personnel Improvement Center. (n.d.). *Career Exploration.* Retrieved July 7, 2015, from http://www.personnelcenter.org/ear_chil.cfm

- Psychology Resource Information System. (n.d.). *What do Psychologists do?* Retrieved November 6, 2014, from http://psyris.com/pages/text/a6 .html

- United States Department of Labor. (2014). *Occupational Outlook Handbook.* Retrieved on November 6, 2014, from http://www.bls.gov/ ooh/

Appendix B:
Helping Professional
Organizations

ALLIANCE OF PROFESSIONAL HEALTH ADVOCATES (APHA)

http://aphadvocates.org

The Alliance of Professional Health Advocates (APHA) serves as a marketing and business service for early career and seasoned patient health advocates from a variety of disciplines in the United States and abroad. It also provides resources for patients and their caregivers in need of services.

AMERICAN ACADEMY OF CLINICAL NEUROPSYCHOLOGY (AACN)

http://www.theaacn.org

The American Academy of Clinical Neuropsychology (AACN) is a professional network for neuropsychologists. AACN disseminates research and practice information and promotes ethical practice. Membership is offered to neuropsychologists and students looking to enter the field.

AMERICAN ACADEMY OF CLINICAL PSYCHOLOGY (AACPSY)

http://www.aacpsy.org

The American Academy of Clinical Psychology (AACPSY) is an organization of certified clinical psychologists with the mission of promoting high quality clinical services and ethical practice. AACPSY also provides member services, promotes the value and recognition of certification in clinical psychology, and encourages those qualified by training and experience to become candidates for Board certification.

AMERICAN ASSOCIATION OF PSYCHIATRIC TECHNICIANS (AAPT)

http://www.psychtechs.org

The American Association of Psychiatric Technicians (AAPT) is a nonprofit organization that provides certification to professionals who work as psychiatric technicians. AAPT uses the term "Psychiatric Technician" to include a variety of bachelor or pre-bachelor level health care providers who offer direct care to individuals with mental illness and/or developmental disabilities. Some examples of job titles are words such as psychiatric, mental health, or behavioral health followed by technician, aide, worker, counselor, assistant, or associate.

AMERICAN BOARD OF PROFESSIONAL PSYCHOLOGY (ABPP)

http://www.abpp.org/i4a/pages/index.cfm?pageid=3289
The American Board of Professional Psychology (ABPP) is an organization that aims to increase consumer protection through the examination and certification of psychologists. Board certification assures the public that specialists designated by the ABPP have successfully completed the educational, training, and experience requirements of the specialty, including an examination designed to assess competency.

AMERICAN CAMP ASSOCIATION

http://www.acacamps.org
The American Camp Association is a professional organization aimed at providing education, support, and accreditation to camp professionals (adults who work in camps for children) and programs.

AMERICAN CASE MANAGEMENT ASSOCIATION (ACMA)

http://acmaweb.org/section.aspx?sID=4
The American Case Management Association (ACMA) aims to provide professional development services including mentoring, education, career, and practice information and other resources to professional case managers who work in medical and related health care organizations. ACMA also attempts to create networking opportunities for case managers and to influence the policies, laws, and other issues related to case management services.

AMERICAN COUNSELING ASSOCIATION (ACA)

http://www.counseling.org
The American Counseling Association (ACA) is a not-for-profit professional organization dedicated to the counseling profession. There are 20 chartered divisions within the American Counseling Association aimed at providing leadership, resources, and information unique to specialized areas and/or principles of counseling. ACA provides professional development; ethical, training, and practice standards; and resources and publications to

members. It also conducts public policy advocacy at a national level for the profession of counseling.

AMERICAN MENTAL HEALTH COUNSELORS ASSOCIATION (AMHCA)

http://www.amhca.org
The mission of the American Mental Health Counselors Association (AMHCA) is to engage in advocacy, provide education, and foster collaboration in order to advance the field of mental health counseling. The organization serves mental health counselors working in a variety of settings.

AMERICAN PROBATION AND PAROLE ASSOCIATION (APPA)

http://www.appa-net.org/eweb/
The American Probation and Parole Association (APPA) is an international association composed of professionals who are actively involved with pretrial, probation, parole, and community-based corrections, in both criminal and juvenile justice arenas. Its mission focuses on education, communication, and training for members and enhancing collaboration among professionals working in criminal and juvenile justice roles. APPA also is engaged in developing standards for the profession, is involved in advocacy for the profession, and serves as a resource for various community corrections professionals, government officials, researchers, and others invested in the field of corrections.

AMERICAN PSYCHIATRIC ASSOCIATION (APA)

http://psychiatry.org/
The American Psychiatric Association (APA) aims to progress the field of psychiatry by fostering psychiatric research, providing professional development opportunities, and promoting the best care guidelines to ensure appropriate and effective treatment for people with mental disorders, including intellectual disabilities and substance use disorders. The mission of APA also includes promoting education, collaboration, and research within the field; serving the needs of its members; and advocating for the profession. Membership is available to psychiatrists from the United States and abroad as well as medical students and medical residents.

AMERICAN PSYCHIATRIC NURSES ASSOCIATION (APNA)

http://www.apna.org/i4a/pages/index.cfm?pageid=3277
The mission of American Psychiatric Nurses Association (APNA) is to recognize mental health issues, promote patient well-being, and progress the

field of psychiatric mental health nursing through education and science. APNA provides continuing education and resources to members. It also advocates for mental health care at a national level and collaborates with other professional organizations to disseminate information related to mental health and substance use disorders. Professional membership is open to registered nurses (RN) including associate degree (ADN), baccalaureate (BSN), and advanced practice (APN), clinical nurse specialists (CNS), psychiatric nurse practitioners (NP), and nurse scientists and academicians (PhD).

AMERICAN PSYCHOLOGICAL ASSOCIATION (APA)

http://www.apa.org
American Psychological Association (APA) is a scientific and professional organization representing the field of psychology in the United States. APA's mission is to advance the information and practice of psychology so as to improve people's lives and benefit society, more generally. APA provides professional development; ethical, training, and practice standards; and resources and publications to members. It also is engaged in public policy advocacy and offers resources and information to the general public. Membership is open to researchers, educators, clinicians, consultants, and students in the field of psychology, and the organization has 54 divisions or interest groups/sub-disciplines of psychology that focus on a range of psychology-related issues.

AMERICAN REHABILITATION COUNSELING ASSOCIATION (ARCA)

http://www.arcaweb.org
The American Rehabilitation Counseling Association (ARCA) brings together practicing counselors, students, and educators who work specifically for people with disabilities. ARCA has multiple foci, including professional development, advocacy and outreach, research, and consultation.

AMERICAN SCHOOL COUNSELOR ASSOCIATION (ASCA)

http://schoolcounselor.org/
The American School Counselor Association (ASCA) is a professional organization aimed at providing leadership, resources, and information to school counselors working in schools K–12. ASCA provides professional development; ethical, training, and practice standards; and resources and publications

to members. It also conducts public policy advocacy at a national level for the profession of school counseling.

ASSOCIATION FOR ADDICTION SPECIALISTS (NAADAC)

http://www.naadac.org

The mission of the Association for Addiction Specialists (NAADAC) is to offer education, advocacy, knowledge, practice standards, ethics, professional development, and research-informed information to professionals working in the field of addictions. NAADAC also conducts public policy advocacy at a national level. Membership is open to professionals in the addictions fields and to those who are working toward qualification, licensure, or certification in addictions and have less than five years of experience.

ASSOCIATION FOR APPLIED SPORT PSYCHOLOGY (AASP)

https://www.appliedsportpsych.org

The mission of the Association for Applied Sport Psychology (AASP) is to promote the development of science and ethical practice in the field of sport psychology. AASP offers certification to qualified professionals in the field of sport, exercise, and health psychology. AASP also offers a platform for sharing research, promoting ethical practice, and encouraging best practices in client care. It aims to extend theory and research in order to benefit coaches, athletes, parents, exercisers, fitness professionals, and athletic trainers about the psychological aspects of their sport or activity.

ASSOCIATION FOR CHILDHOOD EDUCATION INTERNATIONAL (ACEI)

http://acei.org

The mission of the Association for Childhood Education International (ACEI) is to promote and support education, development, and well-being of children worldwide. This organization holds consultation status with the United Nations.

BEHAVIOR ANALYST CERTIFICATION BOARD®, INC. (BACB®)

http://www.bacb.com/index.php

The Behavior Analyst Certification Board®, Inc. (BACB®) is a nonprofit corporation that provides professional credentialing to behavior analysts, and information to consumers of behavior analysis services.

COUNCIL FOR EXCEPTIONAL CHILDREN (CEC)

http://www.dec-sped.org

The Council for Exceptional Children (CEC) is an international organization dedicated to improving educational outcomes for students who have disabilities and/or those who are gifted. CEC provides professional development; ethical, training, and practice standards; and resources and publications to members. It also advocates globally for issues related to the education of exceptional children. CEC has a number of special interest divisions aimed at meeting the professional development and advocacy needs of professionals working in various areas of specialization.

DISABILITY ADVOCATES OF AMERICA

http://disability-advocate.com

Disability Advocates of America is a client-centered advocacy/service organization focusing on providing services to individuals who are having difficulties with their Social Security Disability Insurance (SSDI) and Supplemental Security Income (SSI) claims.

HEALTH PSYCHOLOGY

http://www.apa.org/about/division/div38.aspx

Health Psychology is the 38th division of the American Psychological Association (APA). This organization is made up of doctors, psychologists, mental health professionals, and students interested in the field of health psychology. The goal of the 38th division of the APA is to advance the field by promoting and disseminating research that integrates biomedicine and psychology, by advancing healthcare and health policy, and by providing educational resources to its members.

INTERNATIONAL ASSOCIATION OF ADDICTIONS AND OFFENDER COUNSELORS (IAAOC)

http://www.iaaoc.org

The International Association of Addictions and Offender Counselors (IAAOC) is a division of the American Counseling Association. IAAOC addresses the professional development needs of counselors working in the field of addictions or in the criminal justice system. IAAOC also aims to advocate and provide various resources for clients who are involved with the criminal justice system and/or who are grappling with addiction.

NATIONAL ASSOCIATION FOR THE EDUCATION OF YOUNG CHILDREN (NAEYC)

http://www.naeyc.org
The National Association for the Education of Young Children (NAEYC) is a professional organization that works to promote high-quality early learning experiences for children, birth through age 8. NAEYC aims to connect early childhood practice, policy, and research and offer support to educators, caretakers, and others who work with children in this age group.

NATIONAL ASSOCIATION OF EMERGENCY MEDICAL TECHNICIANS (NAEMT)

http://www.naemt.org
The National Association of Emergency Medical Technicians (NAEMT) works for emergency medical providers, emergency medical technicians, and paramedics to ensure that their needs within the healthcare field are met. NAEMT also provides educational resources, guidelines for safe patient care, and career assistance for current and aspiring EMT practitioners.

NATIONAL ASSOCIATION OF HEALTH CARE ASSISTANTS (NAHCA)

http://nahcacareforce.org
The National Association of Health Care Assistants (NAHCA) supports certified nursing assistants by providing professional development opportunities, education, and other support services. An important mission of NAHCA is to elevate the professional standing of nursing assistants through recognition, motivation, and building professional alliances with other health care providers.

NATIONAL ASSOCIATION OF SCHOOL PSYCHOLOGISTS (NASP)

http://www.nasponline.org/index.aspx
The National Association of School Psychologists (NASP) provides professional development; ethical, training, and practice standards; and resources and publications to school psychologists. It also conducts public policy advocacy at a national level for the profession of school psychology.

NATIONAL ASSOCIATION OF SOCIAL WORKERS (NASW)

http://www.socialworkers.org

The mission of the National Association of Social Workers (NASW) is to enhance the professional growth and development of social workers. NASW also maintains ethical, training, and practice standards and offers resources and publications to members. NASW engages in advocacy for the profession and encourages research in order to progress the field of social work. Additionally, the NASW Credentialing Center administers professional and advanced practice credentials to appropriately trained members. Membership is offered to bachelors, masters, and doctoral level-trained social workers and students in social work.

NATIONAL ASSOCIATION OF THERAPEUTIC SCHOOLS AND PROGRAMS (NATSAP)

http://natsap.org

The National Association of Therapeutic Schools and Programs (NATSAP) serves a variety therapeutic schools and wilderness or residential programs whose focus is on working with children and adolescents facing significant mental health issues. The mission of NTASAP is to provide resources including ethical and practice standards, continuing education, and advocacy for their member programs, so these member programs can provide quality services to their clients.

NATIONAL BEHAVIORAL INTERVENTION TEAM ASSOCIATION

https://nabita.org

The National Behavioral Intervention Team Association (NaBITA) is an organization that provides support and professional development to behavioral intervention team members who work in schools and other work environments.

NATIONAL BLACK CHILD DEVELOPMENT INSTITUTE (NBCDI)

http://www.nbcdi.org

The mission of the National Black Child Development Institute (NBCDI) is to improve and advance the quality of life for Black children and their families. NBCDI works in the areas of education and advocacy by engaging leaders, policymakers, professionals, and parents around critical and timely issues that directly impact Black children and their families. NBCDI offers resources that are relevant to the unique strengths and needs of Black children around issues including early childhood education, health, child welfare, literacy, and family engagement.

NATIONAL BOARD FOR CERTIFIED COUNSELORS (NBCC)

http://www.nbcc.org

The National Board for Certified Counselors (NBCC) provides career guidance, education, certification, and other resources to mental health counselors. NBCC is also involved in advocacy for the profession of counseling and supports research and international counseling development projects.

NATIONAL EDUCATION ASSOCIATION (NEA)

http://www.nea.org

The mission of the National Education Association (NEA) is to advocate for educators and their students with the intention of promoting academic success and diversity in public schools. NEA provides professional development, information about current trends in education, and resources and publications to members and the general public. NEA also conducts public policy advocacy at a national level for the profession of teaching. Membership is open to professional educators, education support staff, and students entering into the field at or above the undergraduate level.

NATIONAL EMPLOYMENT COUNSELING ASSOCIATION (NECA)

http://employmentcounseling.org/

The National Employment Counseling Association is a division of the American Counseling Association and provides education opportunities and other resources for counseling professionals whose work increases employment opportunities for clients. NECA also provides information for anyone in need of employment resources.

NATIONAL HEAD START ASSOCIATION

http://www.nhsa.org

Head Start was first launched in 1965, with the idea of providing comprehensive health, nutrition, and education services to children in poverty. Its mission is to provide every child, regardless of circumstances at birth, an opportunity to succeed in school and in life. The four major components to Head Start are education, health services, parental involvement, and social services. The mission of the National Head Start Association is to work with policy makers and funders and to bring voice to the staff, teachers, parents, and alumni who work in Head Start centers.

NATIONAL NETWORK OF CAREER NURSING ASSISTANTS

http://cna-network.org/home-national-network-of-career-nursing-assistants/
The National Network of Career Nursing Assistants is a nonprofit educational organization promoting recognition, education, research, advocacy, and peer support for nursing assistants who work in nursing homes and other long-term care settings. The National Network of Career Nursing Assistants also advocates for nursing assistants in the national arena.

NATIONAL ORGANIZATION FOR VICTIM ASSISTANCE (NOVA)

http://www.trynova.org
National Organization for Victim Assistance (NOVA) is a private, nonprofit victim assistance organization that offers educational information to the general public about crisis and crime, promotes public policy, and offers education and training to individuals interested in working in the field of crisis response or victim assistance.

PROFESSIONAL CRISIS MANAGEMENT ASSOCIATION (PCMA)

http://www.pcma.com
The Professional Crisis Management Association (PCMA) provides crisis management and behavior analysis training, certification, and consultation to individuals and organizations.

ZERO TO THREE

http://www.zerotothree.org
Zero to Three is a national nonprofit organization that provides advocacy, education, and support to parents, professionals, and policymakers working with babies and toddlers. Key issues of interest to Zero to Three are childcare, infant mental health, early language and literacy development, early intervention, and the impact of culture on early childhood development. The emphasis is on multidisciplinary service delivery.

REFERENCES

Ainsworth, M. D. S. (1973). The development of infant-mother attachment. In B. M. Caldwell & H. N. Ricciuti (Eds.), *Review of child development research* (Vol. 3). Chicago, IL: University of Chicago Press.

Ainsworth, M. D. S., Blehar, M. C., Waters, E., & Wall, S. (1978). *Patterns of attachment*. Hillsdale, NJ: Lawrence Earlbaum.

American Counseling Association. (n.d.-a). *Vicarious trauma* [Fact sheet]. Retrieved from http://www.counseling.org/docs/trauma-disaster/fact-sheet-9---vicarious-trauma.pdf?sfvrsn=2

American Counseling Association. (n.d.-b). *What is professional counseling?* Retrieved November 6, 2014, from http://www.counseling.org/aca-community/learn-about-counseling/what-is-counseling/overview

American Counseling Association. (2014). *ACA Code of Ethics*. Alexandria, VA: Author. Retrieved from http://www.counseling.org/docs/ethics/2014-aca-code-of-ethics.pdf?sfvrsn=4

American Foundation for Suicide Prevention. (n.d.). *Understanding suicide. Facts and figures*. Retrieved November 3, 2014, from https://www.afsp.org/understanding-suicide/facts-and-figures

American Psychiatric Association. (n.d.). *What is a psychiatrist?* Retrieved November 6, 2014, from http://www.psychiatry.org/medical-students/what-is-a-psychiatrist

American Psychiatric Nurses Association. (n.d.). *About Psychiatric-Mental Health Nurses (PMHNs)*. Retrieved November 6, 2014, from http://www.apna.org/i4a/pages/index.cfm?pageid=3292#1

American Psychological Association. (n.d.). *Therapy*. Retrieved November 6, 2014, from http://apa.org/topics/therapy/index.aspx

American Psychological Association. (2002). *American Psychological Association ethical principles of psychologists and code of conduct*. Retrieved July 17, 2013, from http://www.apa.org/ethics/code/index.aspx

Anderson, M. L., & Collins, P. H. (2004). *Race, class, and gender: An anthology* (5th ed.). Belmont, CA: Wadsworth/Thompson Learning.

Anderson, T., Lunnen, K. M., & Ogles, B. M. (2010). Putting models and techniques in context. In B. L. Duncan, B. E. Wampold, & M. A. Hubble (Eds.), *The heart and soul of change* (2nd ed., pp. 143–166). Washington, DC: American Psychological Association.

Arredondo, P., Toporek, R., Brown, S. P., Jones, J., Locke, D. C., Sanchez, J., & Stadler, H. (1996). Operationalization of the multicultural counseling competencies. *Journal of Multicultural Counseling and Development, 24*(1), 42–78. doi:10.1002/j.2161-1912.1996.tb00288.x

Association for Specialists in Group Work. (2000). *Professional standards for the training of group workers*. Retrieved January 9, 2015, from Association for Specialists in Group Work website: http://www.asgw.org/pdf/training_standards.pdf

Bandura, A. (1965). Influence of models' reinforcement contingencies on the acquisition of imitative responses. *Journal of Personality and Social Psychology 1*(6), 589–595. doi:10.1037/h0022070

Bandura, A. (1977). *Social learning theory.* Englewood Cliffs, NJ: Prentice Hall.

Bardeen, J. R., Fergus, T. A., & Orcutt, H. K. (2013). Testing a hierarchical model of distress tolerance. *Journal of Psychopathology and Behavioral Assessment, 35*(4), 495–505. doi:10.1007/s10862-013-9359-0

Baum, A. C., & King, M. A. (2006). Creating a climate of self-awareness in early childhood teacher preparation programs. *Early Childhood Education Journal, 33*(4), 217–222. doi:10.1007/s10643-005-0050-2

Beauchamp, T. L. (2007). The "four principles" approach to health care ethics. In R. Ashcroft, A. Dawson, H. Draper, & J. McMillan (Eds.), *Principles of health care ethics* (2nd ed., pp. 3–10). Hoboken, NJ: John Wiley & Sons.

Beebe, S. A., & Masterson, J. T. (2006). *Communicating in small groups* (8th ed.). Boston, MA: Pearson Education.

Beer, J. S., & Lombardo, M. V. (2007). Insights into emotion regulation from neuropsychology. In J. J. Gross (Ed.), *Handbook of emotion regulation* (pp. 69–86). New York, NY: The Guilford Press.

Bergman, S. J. (1995). Men's psychological development: A relational perspective. In R. F. Levant & W. S. Pollack (Eds.), *A new psychology of men* (pp. 68–90). New York, NY: Basic Books.

Bernard, J. M. (1979). Supervision training: A discrimination model. *Counselor Education and Supervision, 19*(1), 60–68. doi:10.1002/j.1556-6978.1979.tb00906.x

Bernard, J. M., & Goodyear, R. K. (1998). *Fundamentals of clinical supervision* (2nd ed.). Boston, MA: Allyn & Bacon.

Bernstein, D. A., & Borkovec, T. D. (1973). *Progressive relaxation training: A manual for the helping professions.* Champaign, IL: Research Press.

Bertrand, B., & Mullainathan, S. (2004). Are Emily and Greg more employable than Lakisha and Jamal? A field experiment on labor market discrimination. *American Economic Review, 94*(4), 991–1013. doi:10.3386/w9873

Blake, C., & Hamrin, V. (2007). Current approaches to the assessment and management of anger and aggression in youth: A review. *Journal of Child and Adolescent Psychiatric Nursing, 20*(4), 209–221. doi:10.1111/j.1744-6171.2007.00102.x

Blaustein, M. E., & Kinniburgh, K. M. (2010). *Treating traumatic stress in children and adolescents.* New York, NY: The Guilford Press.

Bohart A. C., & Tallman, K. (2010). Clients: The neglected common factor in psychotherapy. In B. L. Duncan, B. E. Wampold, & M. A. Hubble (Eds.), *The heart and soul of change* (2nd ed., pp. 83–112). Washington, DC: American Psychological Association.

Borrell-Carrio, F., & Epstein, R. M. (2004). Preventing errors in clinical practice: A call for self-awareness. *Annals of Family Medicine, 2(*4), 310–316. doi:10.1370/afm.80

Bowlby, J. (1969). *Attachment and loss: Vol. 1. Attachment.* New York, NY: Basic Books.

Bowlby, J. (1988). *A secure base.* New York, NY: Basic Books.

Boyd, D. G., & Bee, H. L. (2011). *Lifespan development* (6th ed.). Boston, MA: Pearson.

Boysen, G. A. (2010). Integrating implicit bias into counselor education. *Counselor Education and Supervision, 49*(4), 210–227. doi:10.1002/j.1556-6978.2010.tb00099.x

Brammer, L. M., & MacDonald, G. (2003). *The helping relationship: Process and skills* (8th ed.). Boston, MA: Pearson.

Bratter, T. E. (2011). Compassionate confrontation psychotherapy: An effective and humanistic alternative to biological psychiatry for adolescents in crisis. *Ethical Human Psychology and Psychiatry, 13*(2), 115–133. doi:10.1891/1559-4343.13.2.115

Breggin, P. R. (2008). Practical applications: 22 guidelines for counseling and psychotherapy. *Ethical Human Psychology and Psychiatry, 10*(1), 43–57. doi:10.1891/1559-4343.10.1.43

Brems, C. (2000). *Dealing with challenges in psychotherapy and counseling.* Belmont, CA: Brooks/Cole.

Bronfenbrenner, U. (1979). *The ecology of human development.* Cambridge, MA: Harvard University Press.

Brown, B. (2010, June). *Brene Brown: The power of vulnerability.* Retrieved from http://www.ted.com/talks/brene_brown_on_vulnerability?language=en#t-338058

Brown, B. (2013, December, 10). *Brene Brown on empathy.* Retrieved from https://www.youtube.com/watch?v=1Evwgu369Jw

Brown, K. W., & Ryan, R. M. (2003). The benefits of being present: Mindfulness and its role in psychological well-being. *Journal of Personality and Social Psychology, 84*(4), 822–848. doi:10.1037/0022-3514.84.4.822

Bruner, J. (1986). *Actual minds, possible worlds.* Cambridge, MA: Harvard University Press.

Bruner, J. (1990). *Acts of meaning.* Cambridge, MA: Harvard University Press.

Burman, E. (1994). *Deconstructing developmental psychology.* London: Routledge.

Burr, V. (1995). *An introduction to social constructionism.* London: Routledge.

Byrnes, J. D. (2002). *Before conflict: Preventing aggressive behavior.* Lanham, MD: Scarecrow Press.

Cain, D. J. (2002). Defining characteristics, history, and evolution of humanistic psychotherapy. In D. J. Cain (Ed.), *Humanistic psychotherapies: Handbook of research and practice* (pp. 3–54). Washington, DC: American Psychological Association.

Cain, D. J. (2010). *Person-centered psychotherapies.* Washington, DC: American Psychological Association.

Calkins, S. D., & Hill, A. (2007). Caregiver influences on emerging emotion regulation. In J. J. Gross (Ed.), *Handbook of emotion regulation* (pp. 229–248). NY: The Guilford Press.

Cammaert, L. P. & Larsen, C. C. (1996). Feminist frameworks of psychotherapy. In M. A. Dutton-Douglas & L. E. Walker (Eds.), *Feminist psychotherapies: Integration of therapeutic and feminist systems* (pp. 12–36). Norwood, NJ: Ablex Pub Corp.

Carroll, M. R., & Wiggins, J. D. (1997). *Elements of group counseling: Back to the basics.* Denver, CO: Love.

Carter, O., Pannekoek, L., Fursland, A., Allen, K. L., Lampard, A. M., & Byrne, S. M. (2012). Increased wait-list time predicts dropout from outpatient enhanced cognitive behaviour therapy (CBT-E) for eating disorders. *Behaviour Research and Therapy, 50*(1), 487–492. doi:10.1016/j.brat.2012.03.003

Castro, C. A., & Kintzle, S. (2014). Suicides in the military: The post-modern combat veteran and the Hemingway effect. *Current Psychiatry Reports, 16*(8), 1–9. doi:10.1007/s11920-014-0460-1

Cavaiola, A. A., & Colford, J. E. (2006). *A practical guide to crisis intervention.* Belmont, CA: Wadsworth.

Centers for Disease Control and Prevention [CDC]. (2011). *Sexual identity, age of sexual contacts, and health-risk behaviors among students in grades 9–12: Youth risk behavior surveillance.* Atlanta, GA: United States Department of Health and Human Services.

Centers for Disease Control and Prevention [CDC]. (2014). *Lesbian, gay, bisexual and transgender health: Youth.* Retrieved from http://www.cdc.gov/lgbthealth/youth.htm

Champe, J., Okech, J. E. A., & Rubel, D. J. (2013). Emotion regulation: Processes, strategies, and applications to group work training and supervision. *The Journal for Specialists in Group Work, 38*(4), 349–368. doi:10.1080/01933922.2013.834403

Chang, J. W., Sy, T., & Choi, J. N. (2012). Team emotional intelligence and performance: Interactive dynamics between leaders and members. *Small Group Research, 43*(1), 75–104. doi:10.1177/1046496411415692

Chen, M., & Rybak, C. J. (2004). *Group leadership skills.* Belmont, CA: Brooks/Cole.

Chu, (2007). Considering culture one client at a time: Maximizing the cultural exchange. *Pragmatic Case Studies in Psychotherapy, 3*(3), 34–43. doi:10.14713/pcsp.v3i3.905

Claiborn, C. D., Goodyear, R. K., & Horner, P. A. (2001). Feedback. *Psychotherapy, 38*(4), 401–408. doi:10.1002/jclp.20112

Claus, R. E., & Kindleberger, L. R. (2002). Engaging substance abusers after centralized assessment: Predictors of treatment entry and dropout. *Journal of Psychoactive Drugs, 34*(1), 25–31. doi:10.1080/02791072.2002.10399933

Coan, J. A. (2008). Toward a neuroscience of attachment. In J. Cassidy & P. R. Shaver (Eds.), *Handbook of attachment* (2nd ed., pp. 3–54). New York, NY: The Guilford Press.

Collins, B. G., & Collins, T. M. (2005). *Crisis and trauma: Developmental-ecological intervention.* Boston, MA: Houghton Mifflin.

Collins, S., & Arthur, N. (2010a). Culture-infused counselling: A fresh look at a classic framework of multicultural counselling competencies. *Counselling Psychology Quarterly, 23*(2), 203–216. doi:10.1080/09515071003798204

Collins, S., & Arthur, N. (2010b). Culture-infused counselling: A model for developing multicultural competence. *Counselling Psychology Quarterly, 23*(2), 217–233. doi:10.1080/09515071003798212

Conarton, S., & Silverman, L. K. (1996). Feminine development through the life cycle. In M. A. Dutton-Douglas & L. E. Walker (Eds.), *Feminist psychotherapies: Integration of therapeutic and feminist systems* (pp. 37–67). Norwood, NJ: Ablex Publishing Corporation.

Coppens, E., Van Audenhove, C., Iddi, S., Arensman, E., Gottlebe, K., Koburger, N., . . . Hegerl, U. (2014). Effectiveness of community facilitator training in improving knowledge, attitudes, and confidence in relation to depression and suicidal behavior: Results of the OSPI-Europe intervention in four European countries. *Journal of Affective Disorders, 165*, 142–150. doi:10.1016/j.jad.2014.04.052

Corey, G., Corey, M. S., & Callanan, P. (2003). *Issues and ethics in the helping professions* (6th ed.). Pacific Grove, CA: Brooks/Cole.

Corey, M. S., & Corey, G. (2006). *Process and practice groups* (7th ed.). Belmont, CA: Thompson Brooks/Cole.

Costa, L., & Altekruse, M. (1994). Duty to warn guidelines for mental health counselors. *Journal of Counseling and Development, 72*(4), 646–350. doi:10.1002/j.1556-6676.1994.tb00947.x

Courtois, C. A., & Ford, J. D. (2013). *Treatment of complex trauma: A sequenced, relationship-based approach.* New York, NY: The Guilford Press.

Cozolino, L. (2010). *The neuroscience of psychotherapy* (2nd ed.). New York, NY: W. W. Norton & Co.

Crain, W. (2011). *Theories of development. Concepts and applications* (6th ed.). Upper Saddle River, NJ: Pearson Education.

Creed, T. A., Reisweber, J., & Beck, A. T. (2011). *Cognitive therapy for adolescents in school settings.* New York, NY: The Guilford Press.

Davies, B., & Harre, R. (1999). Positioning: The discursive production of selves. *Journal for the Theory of Social Behaviour, 20*(1), 43–63. doi:10.1111/j.1468-5914.1990.tb00174.x

Davis, T. & Ritchie, M. (2003). Confidentiality and the school counselor: A challenge for the 1990s. In T. P. Remley, M. A. Hermann, & W. C. Huey (Eds.) *Ethical & legal issues in school counseling* (pp. 197–207). Alexandria, VA: ASCA.

Day, S. X. (2004). *Theory and design in counseling and psychotherapy.* Boston, MA: Lahaska/Houghton Mifflin.

Day, S. X. (2007). *Groups in practice.* Boston, MA: Houghton Mifflin.

Day-Vines, N. L., Wood, S. M., Grothaus, T., Craigen, L., Holman, A., Dotson-Blake, K., & Douglass, M. J. (2007). Broaching the subjects of race, ethnicity, and culture during the counseling process. *Journal of Counseling & Development, 85*(4), 401–409. doi:10.1002/j.1556-6678.2007.tb00608.x

Dechawatanapaisal, D., & Siengthai, S. (2006). The impact of cognitive dissonance on learning work behavior. *Journal of Workplace Learning, 18*(1), 42–54. doi:10.1108/13665620610641300

Diller, J. V. (2007). *Cultural diversity* (3rd ed.). Belmont, CA: Thompson Brooks/Cole.

Doidge, N. (2007). *The brain that changes itself: Stories of personal triumph from the frontiers of brain science.* New York, NY: Penguin.

Donati, M., & Watts, M. (2005). Personal development in counselor training: Towards a clarification of inter-related concepts. *British Journal of Guidance and Counselling, 33*(4), 475–484. doi:10.1080/03069880500327553

Dooley, C., & Fedele, N. M. (2004). Mothers and sons: Raising relational boys. In J. V. Jordan, M. Walker, & L. M. Hartling (Eds.), *The complexity of connection* (pp. 220–249). New York, NY: The Guilford Press.

Douthit, K. (2008). Cognition, culture, and society: Understanding cognitive development in the tradition of Vygotsky. In K. L. Kraus (Ed.), *Lenses: Applying lifespan development theories in counseling* (pp. 83–118). Boston, MA: Lahaska/Houghton Mifflin.

Drewery, W. (2005). Why we should watch what we say: Position calls, everyday speech and the production of relational subjectivity. *Theory & Psychology, 15*(3), 305–324. doi:10.1177/0959354305053217

Drewery, W., & Winslade, J. (1997). The theoretical story of narrative therapy. In G. Monk, J. Winslade, K. Crocket, K. & D. Epston (Eds.), *Narrative therapy in practice: The archaeology of hope* (pp. 32–52). San Francisco, CA: Jossey-Bass.

Dubin, W. R., & Jagarlamudi, K. (2010, July). Safety in the evaluation of potentially violent patients. *Psychiatric Times, 27*(7), 15–17.

Dwyer, K., Osher, D., & Warger, C. (1998). *Early warning, timely response: A guide to safe schools.* Washington, DC: United States Department of Education.

Egan, G. (2010). *The skilled helper* (9th ed.). Pacific Grove, CA: Brooks/Cole Publishing.

Eisenberg, N., Hofer, C., & Vaughan, J. (2007). Effortful control and its socioemotional consequences. In J. J. Gross (Ed.), *Handbook of emotion regulation* (pp. 287–306). New York, NY: The Guilford Press.

Eliot, J. A. (2013). Hope-lore and the compassionate clinician. *Journal of Pain and Symptom Management, 45*(3), 628–634. doi:10.1016/j.jpainsymman.2012.10.233

Family Education Rights and Privacy Act [FERPA], 20 U.S.C. § 1232g; 34 CFR Part 99, 1974

Fauteux, K. (2010). De-escalating angry and violent clients. *American Journal of Psychotherapy, 64*(2), 195–213.

Federal Bureau of Investigation [FBI]. (n.d.). *Crime in the U.S.* Retrieved from http://www.fbi.gov/about-us/cjis/ucr/crime-in-the-u.s/2012/crime-in-the-u.s.-2012/violent-crime/violent-crime

Festinger, L. (1957). *A theory of cognitive dissonance.* Stanford, CA: Stanford University Press.

Fields, A. J. (2010). Multicultural research and practice: Theoretical issues and maximizing cultural exchange. *Professional Psychology: Research and Practice, 41*(3), 196–201. doi:10.1037/a0017938

Fink, I. K., Boersma, K., MacDonald, S., & Linton, S. J. (2012). Understanding catastrophizing from a misdirected problem solving perspective. *British Journal of Health Psychology, 17*(2), 408–419. doi:10.1111/j.2044-8287.2011.02044.x

Forester-Miller, H., & Davis, T. E. (1995). *A practitioner's guide to ethical decision making.* Retrieved from American Counseling Association website: http://www.counseling.org/docs/default-source/ethics/practitioner's-guide-to-ethical-decision-making.pdf?sfvrsn=0

Foucault, M. (1972). *The order of things: An arcaeology of the human sciences.* New York, NY: Pantheon.

Francis, R. D. (2002). The need for a professional ethic: International perspectives. *Educational and Child Psychology, 19*(1), 7–15.

Frankel, R. M. (2009). Empathy research: A complex challenge. *Patient Education and Counseling, 75*(1), 1–2. doi:10.1016/j.pec.2009.02.008

Frankl, V. E. (1963). *Man's search for meaning.* New York, NY: Simon & Schuster.

Freedman, J., & Combs, G. (1996). *Narrative therapy: The social construction of preferred realities.* New York, NY: W. W. Norton & Co.

Freeman, J., Epston, D., & Lobovits, D. (1997). *Playful approaches to serious problems.* New York, NY: W. W. Norton & Co.

Funk, M., Minoletti, A., Drew, N., Taylor, J., & Saraceno, B. (2005). Advocacy for mental health: Roles for consumer and family organizations and governments. *Health Promotion International, 21*(1), 70–75. doi:10.1093/heapro/dai031

Galotti, K. M., Ciner, E., Altenbaumer, H. E., Geerts, H. J., Rupp, A., & Woulfe, J. (2006). Decision-making styles in a real life decision: Choosing a college major.

Personality and Individual Differences, 41(4), 629–639. doi:10.1016/j.paid.2006.03.003

Gaston, L. (1990). The concept of the alliance and its role in psychotherapy: Theoretical and empirical considerations. *Psychotherapy*, 27(2), 143–153. doi:10.1037/0033-3204.27.2.143

Gawronski, B. (2012). Back to the future of dissonance theory: Cognitive consistency as a core motive. *Social Cognition*, 30(6), 652–668. doi:10.1521/soco.2012.30.6.652

Geroski, A., & Kraus, K. (2002). Process and content in school psychoeducational groups. *Journal for Specialists in Group Work*, 27(2), 233–245. doi:10.1080/742848694

Geroski, A., & Kraus, K. (2010). *Groups in schools: Preparing, leading, and responding*. Boston, MA: Pearson.

Gert, B. (2012). The definition of morality. In E. N. Zalta (Ed.), *The Stanford Encyclopedia of Philosophy* (Fall ed.). Retrieved from http://plato.stanford.edu/archives/fall2012/entries/morality-definition/

Gladding, S. (2003). *Group work* (4th ed.). Upper Saddle River, NJ: Merrill Prentice Hall.

Goldhaber, D. (2000). *Theories of human development: Integrative perspectives*. Mountain View, CA: Mayfield Pub Co.

Gresham, F. M., Watson, T. S., & Skinner, C. H. (2001). Functional behavioral assessment: Principles, procedures, and future directions. *School Psychology Review*, 30(2), 156–172.

Griffiths, B. B., & Hunter, R. G. (2014). Neuroepigenetics of stress. *Neuroscience*, 275, 420–435. doi:10.1016/j.neuroscience.2014.06.041

Gross, J. J. (1998). The emerging field of emotional regulation: An integrative review. *Review of General Psychology*, 2(3), 271–299. doi:10.1037/1089-2680.2.3.271

Gross, J. J. (2008). Emotion regulation. In M. Lewis, J. M. Haviland-Jones, & L. F. Barrett (Eds.), *Handbook of emotions* (3rd ed., pp. 497–512). New York, NY: The Guilford Press.

Gross, J. J., & Thompson, R. A. (2007). Emotion regulation: Conceptual foundations. In J. J. Gross (Ed.), *Handbook of emotion regulation* (pp. 3–24). New York, NY: The Guilford Press.

Grossman, A. H., & D'Augelli, A. R. (2007). Transgender youth and life-threatening behaviors. *Suicide and Life-Threatening Behaviors*, 37(5), 527–537. doi:10.1521/suli.2007.37.5.527

Groves, K. (2005). Linking leader skills, follower attitudes, and contextual variables via an integrated model of charismatic leadership. *Journal of Management*, 31(2), 255–277. doi:10.1177/0149206304271765

Halstead, R. W., Wagner, L. D., Vivero, M., & Ferkol, W. (2002). Counselors' conceptualizations of caring in the counseling relationship. *Counseling and Values*, 47(1), 34–48. doi:10.1002/j.2161-007X.2002.tb00222.x

Harre, R., & Moghaddam, F. (2003). Introduction: The self and others in traditional psychology and in positioning theory. In R. Harre & F. Moghaddam (Eds.), *The self and others: Positioning individuals and groups in personal, political, and cultural contexts*. Westport, CT: Praeger.

Harre, R., & Van Langenhove, L. (1991). Varieties of positioning. *Journal for the Theory of Social Behaviour*, 21(4), 393–407. doi:10.1111/j.1468-5914.1991.tb00203.x

Harris, T. E., & Sherblom, J. C. (2005). *Small group and team communication* (3rd ed.). Boston, MA: Pearson.

Hastie, R. (2001). Problems for judgment and decision making. *Annual Review of Psychology, 52*(1), 653–683. doi:10.1146/annurev.psych.52.1.653

Hazler, R. J., & Banvick, N. (2001). *The therapeutic environment: Core conditions for facilitating therapy.* Philadelphia, PA: Open University Press.

Health Insurance Portability and Accountability Act of 1996 [HIPAA], Pub. L. No. 104-191, § 264, 110 Stat. 1936.

Hedtke, L., & Windslade, J. (2004). *Re-membering lives: Conversations with the dying and the bereaved.* Amityville, NY: Baywood Pub.

Hess, S. A., & Schultz, J. M. (2008). Bronfenbrenner's ecological model. In K. L. Kraus (Ed.), *Lenses: Applying lifespan development theories in counseling* (pp. 52–82). Boston, MA: Lahaska/Houghton Mifflin.

Hogan-Garcia, M. (1999). *The four skills of cultural diversity competence: A process for understanding and practice.* Belmont, CA: Brooks/Cole.

Hoyert, D. L., & Xu, J. (2012). Deaths: Preliminary data for 2011. *National Vital Statistics Reports, 61*(6), 1–34. Retrieved from http://www.cdc.gov/nchs/data/nvsr/nvsr61/nvsr61_06.pdf

Hubble, M. A., Duncan, B. L., Miller, S. D., & Wampold, B. E. (2010). Introduction. In B. L. Duncan, B. E. Wampold, & M. A. Hubble (Eds.), *The heart and soul of change* (2nd ed., pp. 23–46). Washington, DC: American Psychological Association.

Hulse-Killacky, D., Kraus, K. L., & Schumacher, R. A. (1999). Visual conceptualizations of meetings: A group work design. *Journal for Specialists in Group Work, 24*(1), 113–124. doi:10.1080/01933929908411423

Hutchinson, D. (2012). *The essential counselor* (2nd ed.). Los Angeles, CA: Sage.

Ilies, R., & Judge, T. A. (2005). Goal regulation across time: The effects of feedback and affect. *Journal of Applied Psychology, 90*(3), 453–467. doi:10.1037/0021-9010.90.3.453

Isaacs, M. L. (2003). The duty to warn and protect: Tarasoff and the elementary school teacher. In T. P. Remley, M. A. Hermann, & W. C. Huey (Eds.) *Ethical & legal issues in school counseling* (pp. 111–129). Alexandria, VA: ASCA.

Ivey, A. E., Ivey, M. B., & Zalaquett, C. P. (2010). *Intentional interviewing and counseling* (7th ed.). Belmont, CA: Brooks/Cole.

James, R. K., & Gilliland, B. E. (2001). *Crisis intervention strategies* (4th ed.). Belmont, CA: Wadsworth/Thompson.

Johnson, D. W., & Johnson, F. P. (2006). *Joining together: Group theory and group skills* (9th ed.). Boston, MA: Pearson.

Johnson, M. H. (2005). Sensitive periods in functional brain development: Problems and prospects. *Developmental Psychobiology, 46*(3), 287–292. doi:10.1002/dev.20057

Jordan, J. (1991). Empathy and self-boundaries. In J. V. Jordan, A. G. Kaplan, J. B. Miller, I. P. Stiver, & J. E. Surrey (Eds.), *Women's growth in connection* (pp. 67–80). New York, NY: The Guilford Press.

Jordan, J. (2004). *Toward competence and connection.* In J. V. Jordan, M. Walker, & L. M. Hartling (Eds.), *The complexity of connection* (pp. 11–27). New York, NY: The Guilford Press.

Jordan, J. (2010). *Relational-cultural therapy.* Washington, DC: American Psychological Association.

Jordan, J. V., & Walker, M. (2004). Introduction. In J. V. Jordan, M. Walker, & L. M. Hartling (Eds.), *The complexity of connection* (pp. 1–88). New York, NY: The Guilford Press.

Joseph, S. & Linley, P. A. (2006). *Positive therapy. A meta-theory for positive psychological practice.* NY: Routledge.

Kaplan, A. (2008). Violent attack by patients: Prevention and self-protection. *Psychiatric Times, 25*(7), pp. 1–9.

Kennedy, A. C., Adams, A., Bybee, D., Campbell, R., Kubiak, S. P., & Sullivan, C. (2012). A model of sexually and physically victimized women's process of attaining effective formal help over time: The role of social location, context, and intervention. *American Journal of Community Psychology, 50*(1–2), 217–228. doi:10.1007/s10464-012-9494-x

Keyton, J. (1993). Group termination. Completing the study of group development. *Small Group Research, 24*(1), 84–100.

Kindsvatter, A., & Geroski, A. (2014). The impact of early life stress on the neurodevelopment of the stress response system. *Journal of Counseling & Development, 92*(4), 472–480. doi:10.1002/j.1556-6676.2014.00173.x

Kitchener, K. S. (1984). Intuition, critical evaluation and ethical principles: The foundation for ethical decisions in counseling psychology. *The Counseling Psychologist, 12*(3), 43–55. doi:10.1177/0011000084123005

Kottler, J. A. (1991). *The compleat therapist.* San Francisco, CA: Jossey-Bass.

Kottman, T. (2002). *Partners in play* (2nd ed.). Alexandria, VA: American Counseling Association.

Kraus, K., & Hulse-Killacky, D. (1996). Balancing process and content in groups: A metaphor. *Journal for Specialists in Group Work, 21(2),* 90–93. doi:10.1080/01933929608412236

Kubiak, S. P. (2005). Trauma and cumulative adversity in women of a disadvantaged social location. *American Journal of Orthopsychiatry, 75*(4), 451. doi:10.1037/0002-9432.75.4.451

Kuntze, J., van der Molen, H. T., & Born, M. P. (2009). Increase in counselling communication skills after basic and advanced microskills training. *British Journal of Educational Psychology, 79*(1), 175–188. doi:10.1348/000709908X313758

Lambert, M. J. (2013). The efficacy and effectiveness of psychotherapy. In M. J. Lambert (Ed.), *Bergin and Garfield's handbook of psychotherapy and behavior change* (6th ed., pp. 169–207). New York, NY: John Wiley & Sons.

Larsen, D. J., & Stege, R. (2010). Hope-focused practices during early psychotherapy sessions: Part II: Explicit approaches. *Journal of Psychotherapy Integration, 20*(3), 293–311. doi:10.1037/a0020821

Laux, J. M. (2002). A primer on suicidology: Implications for counselors. *Journal of Counseling and Development, 80*(3), 380–383. doi:10.1002/j.1556-6678.2002.tb00203.x

Leahy, R. L. (2003). *Cognitive therapy techniques: A practitioners guide.* New York, NY: The Guilford Press.

LeFevre, M. L. (2014). Screening for suicide risk in adolescents, adults, and older adults in primary care: U.S. preventive services task force recommendation statement. *Annals of Internal Medicine, 160*(10), 719–727. doi:10.7326/M14-0589

Leffert, M. (2010). *Contemporary psychoanalytic foundations. Postmodernism, complexity, and neuroscience.* New York, NY: Routledge.

Levenson, H. (2010). *Brief dynamic therapy.* Washington, DC: American Psychological Association.

Lewis, J. A., Arnold, M. S., House, R., & Toporek, R. L. (2002). *ACA advocacy competencies*. Retrieved July 17, 2014, from http://www.counseling.org/Publications/

Lewis, J. A., Lewis, M. D., Daniels, J. A., & D'Andrea, M. J. (1998). *Community counseling: Empowerment strategies for a diverse society* (2nd ed). Pacific Grove, CA: Brooks/Cole.

Linehan, M. (1993). *Cognitive-behavioral treatment of borderline personality disorder.* New York, NY: The Guilford Press.

Linehan, M. M. (2015). *DBT Skills training manual* (2nd ed.). NY: Guilford Press.

Linehan, M. M., Armstrong, H. E., Suarez, A., Allmon, D., & Heard, H. L. (1991). Cognitive-behavioral treatment of chronically parasuicidal borderline patients. *Archives of General Psychiatry, 48*(12), 1060–1064. doi:10.1001/archpsyc.1991.01810360024003.

Linehan, M. M., Heard, H. L., & Armstrong, H. E. (1993). Naturalistic follow up of a behavioral treatment for chronically parasuicidal borderline patients. *Archives of General Psychiatry, 50*(12), 971–974. doi:10.1001/archpsyc.1993.01820240055007

Loganbill, C., Hardy, E., & Delworth, U. (1982). Supervision: A conceptual model. *The Counseling Psychologist, 10*(1), 3–42. doi:10.1177/0011000082101002

Lopez-Fresno, P., & Savolainen, T. (2014). Working meetings: A tool for building or destroying trust in knowledge creation and sharing. *Journal of Knowledge Management, 12*(2), 137–143.

Luborsky, E. B., O'Reilly-Landry, M. & Arlow, J. A. (2008). Psychoanalysis. In R. J. Corsini & D. Wedding (Eds.), *Current psychotherapies* (8th ed., pp. 15–62). Belmont, CA: Thompson Brooks/Cole.

Mareck, J. (2002). Unfinished business. Postmodern feminism in personality psychology. In M. Ballou & L. S. Brown (Eds.), *Rethinking mental helath and disorder: Feminist Perspectives* (pp. 3–28). New York, NY: The Guilford Press.

Maslow, A. H. (1967). Synanon and Eupsychia. *Journal of Humanistic Psychology, 7*(1), 28–35. doi:101177/002216786700700104

Masterswork Productions (Producer). (2002). *Narrative therapy with a young boy* [Motion picture]. Retrieved from http://masterswork.com/david-epston-individual/david-epston-dvd-narrative-therapy-with-a-young-boy

Mayer, J. D., & Salovey, P. (1997). In D. Sluyter & P. Salovey (Eds.), *Emotional development and emotional intelligence: Implications for educators* (pp. 3–31). New York, NY: Basic Books.

McKenzie, W., & Monk, G. (1997). Learning and teaching narrative ideas. In Monk, G., Winslade, J., Crocket, K., & Epston, D. (Eds.), *Narrative therapy in practice: The archaeology of hope* (pp. 82–117). San Francisco, CA: Jossey-Bass.

Medelowitz, E., & Schneider, K. (2008) Existential psychotherapy. In R. J. Corsini & D. Wedding (Eds.), *Current psychotherapies* (8th ed., pp. 295–327). Belmont, CA: Thompson Brooks/Cole.

Melbourne Academic Mindfulness Interest Group. (2006). Mindfulness-based psychotherapies: A review of conceptual foundations, empirical evidence and practical considerations. *Australian and New Zealand Journal of Psychiatry, 40,* 285–294. doi:10.1080/j.1440-1614.2006.01794.x

Merecek, J. (2002). Unfinished business. Postmodern feminism in personality psychology. In M. Ballou & L. S. Brown (Eds.), *Rethinking mental health and disorder: Feminist perspectives* (pp. 3–28). New York, NY: The Guilford Press.

Miczek, K. A., de Almeida, R. M., Kravitz, E. A., Rissman, E. F., de Boer, S. F., & Raine, A. (2007). Neurobiology of escalated aggression and violence. *The Journal of Neuroscience, 27*(44), 11803–11806. doi:10.1523/JNEUROSCI.3500-07.2007

Miller, A. L., Rathus, J. H., Linehan, M. M., Wetzler, S., & Leigh, E. (1997). Dialectical Behavior Therapy adapted for suicidal adolescents. *Journal of Practical Psychiatry and Behavioral Health, 3,* 78–86.

Miller, J. B. (1991). The development of women's sense of self. In J. V. Jordan, A. G. Kaplan, J. B. Miller, I. P. Stiver, & J. L. Surrey (Eds.), *Women's growth in connection* (pp. 11–26). New York, NY: The Guildford Press.

Miller, P. A. (2002). *Theories of developmental psychology* (4th ed.). New York, NY: Worth/Macmillan.

Miller, W. R., & Rollnick, S. (2013). *Motivational interviewing: Helping people change.* New York, NY: The Guilford Press.

Miller, W. R., & Rose, G. S. (2009). Toward a theory of motivational interviewing. *American Psychologist, 64*(6), 527–537. doi:10.1037/a0016830

Monk, G. (1997). How narrative therapy works. In G. Monk, J. Winslade, K. Crocket, & D. Epston (Eds.), *Narrative therapy in practice: The archaeology of hope* (pp. 3–31). San Francisco, CA: Jossey-Bass.

Monk, G., Winslade, J., & Sinclair, S. (2008). *New horizons in multicultural counseling.* Thousands Oaks, CA: Sage.

Morran, D. K., Stockton, R., Cline, R. J., & Teed, C. (1998). Facilitating feedback exchange in groups: Leader interventions. *The Journal for Specialists in Group Work, 23*(3), 257–268. doi:10.1080/01933929808411399

Mosak, H. H., & Maniacci, M. (2008). Adlerian psychotherapy. In R. J. Corsini & D. Wedding (Eds.) *Current psychotherapies* (9th ed., pp. 67–112). Belmont, CA: Brooks/Cole.

Myerhoff, B. (1979). *Number our days.* New York, NY: Penguin Books.

National Association of Social Workers (n.d.). *Practice.* Retrieved November 6, 2014, from http://www.naswdc.org/practice/default.asp

National Institute of Justice [NIJ]. (2010). *Victims and perpetrators.* Retrieved from http://www.nij.gov/topics/crime/rape-sexual-violence/Pages/victims-perpetrators.aspx

National Institute of Mental Health [NIMH]. (2014). *Suicide in the military: Army-NIH funded study points to risk and protective factor.* Retrieved from http://www.nimh.nih.gov/news/science-news/2014/suicide-in-the-military-army-nih-funded-study-points-to-risk-and-protective-factors.shtml

National Organization for Human Services. (1996). *Ethical standards for human service professionals.* Retrieved June 18, 2014, from http://www.nationalhuman-services.org/ethical-standards-for-hs-professionals

Nelson, M. L., & Neufeldt, S. A. (1998). The pedogogy of counseling: A critical examination. *Counselor Education and Supervision, 38*(2), 70–88. doi:10.1002/j.1556-6978.1998.tb00560.x

Neumann, M., Bensing, J., Mercer, S., Ernstmann, N., Ommen, O., & Pfaff, H. (2009). Analyzing the "nature" and "specific effectiveness" of clinical empathy: A theoretical overview and contribution towards a theory-based research agenda. *Patient Education and Counseling, 74*(3), 339–346. doi:10.1016/j.pec.2008.11.013

Noddings, N. (2002). *Starting at home: Caring and social policy.* Berkeley, CA: University of California Press.

Norcross, J. C. (2010). The therapeutic relationship. In B. L. Duncan, B. E. Wampold, & M. A. Hubble (Eds.), *The heart and soul of change* (2nd ed., pp. 113–142). Washington, DC: American Psychological Association.

Norcross, J. C., Krebs, P. M., & Prochaska, J. O. (2010). Stages of Change. *Journal of Clinical Psychology: In Session, 67*(2), 143–154. doi:10.1002/jclp.20758

Nuckolls, T., & Baker, C. (2003, November 9). Watch these straight people answer a question gay people have been asked for years. Retrieved from http://www.upworthy.com/watch-these-straight-people-answer-a-question-gay-people-have-been-asked-for-years-6?c=ufb3

Oyum, L. (2007). Dilemmas of confrontation: Challenging the participants while keeping the process going. *Systemic Practice and Action Research, 20*(1), 41–52. doi:10.1007/s11213-006-9048-y

Pearlin, L. I. (1989). The sociological study of stress. *The Journal of Health and Social Behavior, 30*(3), 241–256. Retrieved from http://search.proquest.com.ezproxy.uvm.edu/docview/201659323?accountid=14679

Pereira, S., Fleischhacker, W., & Allen, M. (2007). Management of behavioural emergencies. *Journal of Psychiatric Intensive Care, 2*(2), 71–83. doi:10.1017/S1742646407000325

Perry, B. D., & Szalavitz, M. (2006). *The boy who was raised as a dog.* New York, NY: Basic Books.

Personnel Improvement Center (n.d.). *Career Exploration.* Retrieved July 7, 2015, from http://www.personnelcenter.org/ear_chil.cfm

Pieterse, A. L., Lee, M., Ritmeester, A., & Collins, N. M. (2013). Towards a model of self-awareness development for counselling and psychotherapy training. *Counselling Psychology Quarterly, 26*(2), 190–207. doi:10.1080/09515070.2013.793451

Polcin, D. L. (2003). Rethinking confrontation in alcohol and drug treatment: Consideration of the clinical context. *Substance Use and Misuse, 38*(2), 165–184. doi:10.1081/JA-120017243

Poppen, R. (1998). *Behavioral relaxation training and assessment* (2nd ed.). Thousand Oaks, CA: Sage.

Prochaska, J. O., & DiClemente, C. C. (1982). Transtheoretical therapy: Toward a more integrative model of change. *Psychotherapy: Theory, Research and Practice, 19*(3), 276–278. doi:10.1037/h0088437

Prochaska, J. O., & DiClemente, C. C. (1986). Toward a comprehensive model of change. In W. E. Miller & N. Heather (Eds.), *Treating addictive behaviors: Processes of change* (pp. 3–27). New York, NY: Plenum Press.

Prochaska, J. O., Johnson, S., & Lee, P. (2009). The transtheoretical model of behavior change. In S. A. Shumaker, J. K., Ockene, & K. A. Riekert (Eds.), *The handbook of health behavior change* (3rd ed., pp. 59–83). New York, NY: Springer.

Prochaska, J. O., & Norcross, J. C. (2007). *Systems of psychotherapy: A transtheoretical analysis* (6th ed.). Belmont, CA: Thompson Brooks/Cole.

Prochaska, J. O., Norcross, J. C., & DiClemente, C. C. (1994). *Changing for good.* New York, NY: Harper/Collins.

Psychology Resource Information System (n.d.). *What do psychologists do?* Retrieved November 6, 2014, from http://psyris.com/pages/text/a6.html

Purkey, W. W., & Stanley, P. H. (2002). The self in psychotherapy. In D. J. Cain (Ed.), *Humanistic psychotherapies: Handbook of research and practice* (pp. 473–498). Washington, DC: American Psychological Association.

Raghubir, P., & Valenzuela, A. (2010). Male-female dynamics in groups: A field study of the weakest link. *Small Group Research, 41*(1), 41–70. doi:10.1177/1046496409352509

Raskin, N. J., Rogers, C., & Witty, M. C. (2008). Client-centered therapy. In R. J. Corsini & D. Wedding (Eds.), *Current psychotherapies* (8th ed., pp. 141–186). Belmont, CA: Brooks/Cole.

Rathus, J. H., & Miller, A. L. (2015). *DBT skills manual for adolescents.* New York, NY: The Guilford Press.

Riggio, R. E., & Reichard, R. J. (2008). The emotional and social intelligences of effective leadership. *Journal of Managerial Psychology, 23*(2), 169–185. doi:10.1108/02683940810850808

Riggio, R. E., Salinas, C., Riggio, H. R., & Cole, E. J. (2003). The role of social and emotional communication skills in leader emergence and effectiveness. *Group Dynamics: Theory, Research, and Practice, 7*(2), 83–103. doi:10.1037/1089-2699.7.2.83

Roberts, A. R., & Ottens, A. J. (2005). *The seven-stage crisis intervention model: A road map to goal attainment, problem solving, and crisis resolution.* Advance Access Publication/Oxford University Press. doi:10.1093/brief-treatment/mhi030

Rogers, C. R. (1951). *Client-centered therapy: Current practice implications, and theory.* Boston, MA: Houghton Mifflin.

Rogers, C. (1957). The necessary and sufficient conditions of therapeutic change. *Journal of Consulting Psychology, 21*, 95–103. doi:10.1037/h0045357

Rogers, C. (1975). Empathic: An unappreciated way of being. *The Counseling Psychologist, 5*(2), 2–10. doi:10.1177/001100007500500202

Roth, M. (2012, July 3). Recession has taken a toll on black families. Retrieved from http://www.post-gazette.com/stories/local/neighborhoods-city/recession-has-taken-hidden-toll-on-black-families-300882/?p=0

Rudd, M. D., Joiner, T., & Rajab, M. H. (2001). *Treating suicide behavior.* New York, NY: The Guilford Press.

Russell, S., & Carey, M. (2002). Remembering: Responding to commonly asked questions. *The International Journal of Narrative Therapy and Community Work, 3*, 1–13. Retrieved from http://search.informit.com.au/documentSummary;dn=66155 1679355288;res=IELHEA

Safran, J. D. (2012). *Psychoanalysis and psychoanalytic therapies.* Washington, DC: American Psychological Association.

Salovey, P., Rothman, A. J., Detweiler, J. B., & Steward, W. T. (2000). Emotional states and physical health. *American Psychologist, 55*, 110–121. doi:10A037//0003-O66X.55.1.110

Salzer, M. S., Rappaport, J., & Segre, L. (2001). Mental health professionals' support of self-help groups. *Journal of Community & Applied Social Psychology, 11*(1), 1–10. doi:10.1002/casp.606

Scaturo, D. J. (2002). Fundamental dilemmas in contemporary psychodynamic and insight-oriented psychotherapy. *Journal of Contemporary Psychotherapy, 32*(2–3), 145–165. doi:10.1023/A:1020540909172

Schreiber, M., & Gurwitch, R. (2011). *Listen, protect, connect. Family to family, neighbor to neighbor.* Retrieved from http://www.ready.gov/sites/default/files/documents/files/LPC_Booklet.pdf

Schreiber, M., Gurwitch, R., & Wong, M. (2006). *Listen, protect, connect—model & teach: Psychological first aid (PFA) for students and teachers.* US Department of Homeland Security. Retrieved from ERIC database. (ED496719)

Schwarz, R. (2002). *The skilled facilitator: A comprehensive resource for consultants, facilitators, managers, trainers, and coaches.* New York, NY: John Wiley & Sons.

Seligman, M. E. P. (2002). *Authentic happiness.* New York, NY: Free Press.

Seligman, M. E. P., & Csikszentmihalyi, M. (2000). Positive psychology: An introduction. *American Psychologist, 55*(1), 5–14. doi:10.1037//0003-066X.55.1.5

Seligman, M. E. P., & Csikszentmihalyi, M. (2001). Positive psychology: An introduction: Reply. *American Psychologist, 56*(1), 89–90. doi:10.1037//0003-066X.56.1.89

Seligman, M. E. P., Linley, P. A., Joseph, S., & Boniwell, I. (2003). Positive psychology: Fundamental assumptions. *Psychologist, 16*(3), 126–127.

Seligman, M. E. P., Rashid, T., & Parks, A. C. (2006). Positive psychotherapy. *American Psychologist, 61*(8), 774–788.

Shearin, E. N., & Linehan, M. M. (1994). Dialectical behavior therapy for borderline personality disorder: Theoretical and empirical foundations. *Acta Psychiatrica Scandinavica, 89* (suppl. 379), 61–68. doi:10.1111/j.1600-0447.1994.tb05820.x

Siegel, D. J. (2012). *The developing mind* (2nd ed.). New York, NY: The Guilford Press.

Siegel, R. D. (2010). *The mindfulness solution: Everyday practices for everyday problems.* New York, NY: The Guilford Press.

Siever, L. J. (2008). Neurobiology of aggression and violence. *The American Journal of Psychiatry, 165*(4), 429–442. doi:10.1176/appi.ajp.2008.07111774

Skinner, B. F. (1971). *Beyond freedom and dignity.* New York, NY: Alfred Knoph/ Bantom/Vintage.

Sklare, G. B. (2014). *Brief counseling that works: A solution-focused therapy approach for school counselors and other mental health professionals.* Thousand Oaks, CA: Corwin.

Skovholt, T. M. (2001). *The resilient practitioner.* Boston, MA: Allyn & Bacon.

Skovholt, T. (2005). The cycle of caring: A model of expertise in the helping professions. *Journal of Mental Health Counseling, 27*(1), 82–93. Retrieved from http://search.proquest.com.ezproxy.uvm.edu/docview/198720018?accountid=14679

Smith, C. D., & King, P. E. (2004). Student feedback sensitivity and the efficacy of feedback interventions in public speaking performance improvement. *Communication Education, 53*(3), 203–216. doi:10.1080/0363452042000265152

Smith, J. C. (2001). Review of ABC relaxation research: Implications for practice. In J. C. Smith (Ed.), *Advances in ABC relaxation: Applications and inventories* (pp. 33–58). New York, NY: Springer.

Smith, L. C., Geroski, A. M., & Tyler, K. B. (2014). Abandoning colorblind practice in school counseling. *Journal of School Counseling, 12*(16). Retrieved from http://www.jsc.montana.edu/articles/v12n16.pdf

Sommers-Flanagan, J., & Sommers-Flanagan, R. (2004). *Counseling and psychotherapy theories in context and practice.* Hoboken, NJ: John Wiley & Sons.

Sprague, J., & Walker, H. (2000). Early identification and intervention for youth with antisocial and violent behavior. *Exceptional Children, 66*(3), 367–379. doi:10.1177/001440290006600307

Stasiewicz, P. R., Bradizza, C. M., Schlauch, R. C., Coffey, S. F., Gulliver, S. B., Gudteski, G. D., & Bole, C. W. (2013). Affect regulation training (ART) for alcohol use disorders: Development of a novel intervention for negative affect drinkers. *Journal of Substance Abuse Treatment, 45*(5), 433–443. doi:10.1016/j.jsat.2013.05.012

Stegge, H., & Terwogt, M. M. (2007). Awareness and regulation of emotion in typical and atypical development. In J. J. Gross (Ed.), *Handbook of emotion regulation* (pp. 269–286). New York, NY: The Guilford Press.

Stockmeier, C. A. (2006). Neurobiology of serotonin in depression and suicide. *Annals of the New York Academy of Sciences, 836*(1), 220–232. doi:10.1111/j.1749-6632.1997.tb52362.x

Stone, J., & Cooper, J. (2001). A self-standards model of cognitive dissonance. *Journal of Experimental Social Psychology, 37*(3), 228–243. doi:10.1006/jesp.2000.1446

Strong, T., & Zeman, D. (2010). Dialogic consideration of confrontation as a counseling activity: An examination of Allen Ivey's use of confronting as a microskill. *Journal of Counseling & Development, 88*(3), 332–339. doi:10.1002/j.1556-6678.2010.tb00030.x

Strumpfel, U., & Goldman, R. (2002). Contacting gestalt therapy. In D. J. Cain (Ed.), *Humanistic psychotherapies: Handbook of research and practice* (pp. 189–219). Washington, DC: American Psychological Association.

Sturdivant, S. (1980). *Therapy with women.* New York, NY: Springer.

Substance Abuse and Mental Health Services Administration [SAMHSA]. (2005). *Psychological first aid for first responders: Managing intense emotions.* Retrieved from http://store.samhsa.gov/shin/content//NMH05-0210/NMH05-0210.pdf

Sue, D. W. (2010). Microaggressions, marginality, and oppression: An introduction. In D. W. Sue (Ed.), *Microaggressions and marginality. Manifestation, dynamics, and impact* (pp. 3–22). Hoboken, MH: John Wiley & Sons.

Sue, D. W., Arredondo, P., & McDavis, R. J. (1992). Multicultural counseling competencies and standards: A call to the profession. *Journal of Multicultural Counseling and Development, 20*(2), 64–88. doi:10.1002/j.2161-1912.1992.tb00563.x

Sue, D. W., Capodilupo, C. M., Torino, G. C., Bucceri, J. M., Holder, A. M. B., Nadal, K. L., & Esquilin, M. (2007). Racial microaggressions in everyday life: Implications for clinical practice. *American Psychologist, 62*(4), 271–286. doi:10.1037/0003-066X.62.4.271

Sue, D. W., & Sue, D. (2003). *Counseling the culturally diverse: Theory and practice* (4th ed.). New York, NY: John Wiley & Sons.

Sue, D. W., & Sue, D. M. (2008). *Foundations of counseling and psychotherapy.* Hoboken, NJ: John Wiley & Sons.

Surrey, J. (1991). Relationship and empowerment. In J. V. Jordan, A. G. Kaplan, J. B. Miller, I. P. Stiver, & J. E. Surrey (Eds.), *Women's growth in connection.* (pp. 162–180). New York, NY: The Guilford Press.

Theory. (n.d.). In Dictionary.com online. Retrieved March 15, 2014, from http://dictionary.reference.com/browse/theory?s=t

Thompson, R. A. (2008). Early attachment and later development. In J. Cassidy & P. R. Shaver (Eds.), *Handbook of attachment* (2nd ed., pp. 348–365). New York, NY: The Guilford Press.

Toporek, R. L., Lewis, J. A., & Crethar, H. C. (2009). Promoting systemic change through the ACA advocacy competencies. *Journal of Counseling and Development, 87*(3), 260–268. doi:10.1002/j.1556-6678.2009.tb00105.x

Toseland, R. W., & Rivas, R. F. (2005). *An introduction to group work practice* (5th ed.). Boston, MA: Pearson.

Trippany, R. L., White Kress, V. E., & Wilcoxon, S. A. (2004). Preventing vicarious trauma: What counselors should know when working with trauma survivors. *Journal of Counseling and Development, 82*(1), 31–37. doi:10.1002/j.1556-6678 .2004.tb00283.x

Truman, J. L., & Langton, L. (2014). *Criminal victimization, 2013.* Retrieved from http://www.bjs.gov/index.cfm?ty=tp&tid=31

Truman, J. L., Langton, L. & Planty, M. (2013). *Criminal victimization, 2012.* Bureau of Justice Statistics, U.S. Department of Justice. Retrieved from http://www.bjs.gov/ index.cfm?ty=tp&tid=942

Tuckman, B. W. (1965). Developmental sequence in small groups. *Psychological Bulletin, 63*(6), 384–399. doi:10.1037/h0022100

Tuckman, B. W., & Jensen, M. A. (1977). Stages of small group development revisited. *Group and Organizational Studies, 2*(4), 419–427. doi:10.1177/10596011 7700200404

United States Department of Labor (2014). *Occupational Outlook Handbook.* Retrieved from http://www.bls.gov/ooh/

Upadhyay, D. (2009). Concept of social intelligence: A needed skill for leaders. *Social Science International, 25*(2), 75–79.

Values. (n.d.). In Dictionary.com online. Retrieved June 18, 2014, from http:// dictionary.reference.com/browse/values

Varia, S. (2013). *Bullying and suicide.* Retrieved from http://www.suicideprevention-colorado.org/uploads/8/7/8/4/8784346/bullying_and_suicide_-_smita_varia.pdf

Van Ausdale, D., & Feagin, J. R. (2001). *The first R: How children learn race and racism.* Lanham, MD: Rowman & Littlefield Publishers.

Van Langenhove, L., & Harre, R. (1994). Cultural stereotypes and positioning theory. *Journal for the Theory of Social Behaviour, 24*(4), 359–372. doi:10.1111/j.1468-5914.1994.tb00260.x

Vygotsky, L. S. (1997). *Educational psychology* (R. Silverman, Trans.). Boca Raton, FL: St Lucie Press. (Original work published 1926)

Walsh, D. (2004). *Why do they act that way?* New York, NY: Free Press.

Walsh, R. A., & McElwain, B. (2002). Existential psychotherapies. In D. J. Cain (Eds.), *Humanistic psychotherapies: Handbook of research and practice* (pp. 253–278). Washington, DC: American Psychological Association.

Wampold, B. E. (2010). The research evidence for common factors models: A histori-cally situated perspective. In B. L. Duncan, B. E. Wampold, & M. A. Hubble (Eds.), *The heart and soul of change* (2nd ed., pp. 49–82). Washington, DC: American Psychological Association.

Weiner, I. B., & Bornstein, R. F. (2009). *Principles of psychotherapy: Promoting evidence-based psychodynamic practice.* Hoboken, NJ: John Wiley & Sons.

Weinfield, N. S., Sroufe, L. A., Egeland, B., & Carlson, E. (2008). Individual differences in infant-caregiver attachment. In J. Cassidy & P. R. Shaver (Eds.), *Handbook of attachment* (2nd ed., pp. 78–101). New York, NY: The Guilford Press.

Westphal, M., & Bonanno, G. A. (2004). Emotion self-regulation. In M. Beauregard (Ed.), *Consciousness, emotional self-regulation and the brain* (pp. 1–34). Philadelphia, PA: John Benjamins North America.

Wheeler, C. D., & D'Andrea, L. M. (2004). Teaching counseling students to understand immediacy. *The Journal of Humanistic Counseling, Education and Development, 43*(2), 117–128. doi:10.1002/j.2164-490X.2004.tb00012.x

White, M. (1989). Saying hullo again. In M. White, *Selected papers*. Adelaide, Australia: Dulwich Centre Publications.

White, M. (2005). *Workshop notes*. Retrieved from http://www.dulwichcentre.com.au/articles-about-narrative-therapy.html

Winslade, J. M. (2005). Utilising discursive positioning in counselling. *British Journal of Guidance & Counseling, 33*(3), 351–364. doi:10.1080/03069880500179541

Winslade, J., Crocket, K., & Monk, G. (1997). The therapeutic relationship. In G. Monk, J. Winslade, K. Crocket, & D. Epston (Eds.), *Narrative therapy in practice: The archaeology of hope* (pp. 53–81). San Francisco, CA: Jossey-Bass.

Winslade, J., & Geroski, A. (2008). A social constructionist view of development. In K. L. Kraus (Ed.), *Lenses: Applying lifespan development theories in counseling* (pp. 7–51). Boston, MA: Lahaska/Houghton Mifflin.

Wiseman, T. (1996). A concept analysis of empathy. *Journal of Advanced Nursing, 23*(6), 1162–1167. doi:10.1046/j.1365-2648.1996.12213.x

Wong, M., Schreiber, M., & Gurwitch, R. (2008). Psychological first aid (PFA) for students and teachers: Listen, protect, connect—model and teach. Helpful hints for school emergency management. *U.S. Department of Education-Readiness and Emergency Management for Schools (REMS) Technical Assistance Center, 3*(3), 1–11.

Wynn, R., & Bergvik, S. (2010). Studying empathy as an interactional three-part sequence. *Patient Education and Counseling, 80*(1), 150. doi:10.1016/j.pec.2009.05.007

Yalom, I. (1980). *Existential psychotherapy*. New York, NY: Basic Books.

Yalom, I. D. (1995). *The theory and practice of group psychotherapy* (4th ed.). New York, NY: Basic Books.

Yontef, Gary M. (1993). *Awareness, dialogue & process: Essays on Gestalt therapy*. Gouldsboro, ME: The Gestalt Journal Press.

Yontef, G., & Jacobs, L. (2008). Gestalt therapy. In R. J. Corsini & D. Wedding (Eds.), *Current psychotherapies* (8th ed., pp. 328–367). Belmont, CA: Thompson Brooks/Cole.

Young, M. E. (2013). *Learning the art of helping*. Boston, MA: Pearson.

Zaccaro, S. J. (2002). Organizational leadership and social intelligence. In R. E. Riggio, S. E., Murphy, & F. J. Pirozzolo (Eds.), *Multiple intelligences and leadership* (pp. 29–54). New York, NY: Lawrence Erlbaum.

INDEX

relational development and
competence elements of, 88
social contexts elements of, 88, 93
systems change focus of, 88
See also Feminist theory
Feminist theory
centrality of connection in women's
lives and, 42, 45 (table)
developmental theories *vs.*, 42
feminist personality theory (Mareck)
and, 42
gender equity focus of, 42
growth-fostering relationships concept
and, 43
as helping theory, 42
interpersonal experiences and
relationships (Jordan) and, 42–43
masculine privilege issue and, 42
meaning systems and, 42–43
relational competence and, 43
Relational Cultural Theory (CRT,
Miller) and, 43
relational gender differences
and, 42
separation and individuation elements
of, 42
See also Feminist helping approaches
FERPA. *See* Family Educational Rights
and Privacy Act of 1974 (FERPA)
Festinger, L., 209, 210, 214
Fidelity, 102, 103 (table)
burnout and, 120
confidentiality and, 105–106
ethical decision-making and, 110
Fight or flight reaction, 53–54, 122–123,
130–131, 235–236
Flexibility, as competence element, 12
Forester-Miller, H., 110, 112 (table)
Formal helping relationship, 6
formal helping contract and,
144, 145 (table)
Forming intervention skill, 292–293,
297 (table)
Forming stage of group
development, 278
Foucault, M., 49–50
Frankl, Victor, 17

Freud, Sigmund
deterministic models of development
and, 26
psychoanalytic theory of, 24–25, 44
(table)
superego *vs.* values and, 47
See also Psychoanalytic theory
(Freud); Psychodynamic helping
approaches and theories
Frontal cortex, 131, 254
Frontal lobe, 121
Functional behavioral analysis (FBA),
of behavioral and learning helping
approaches, 82
Functional Behavioral Assessment (FBA),
of behavioral and learning helping
approach, 85–86
Funk, M., 231

Gender equity, feminist theory and, 42
Generate potential decisions step, in
ethical decision-making, 111, 112
(table)
Geroski, A., 288
Gestalt therapy
contact concept and, 29–30, 44
(table), 77
mindfulness approach, of humanistic
helping, 77–78, 80
one with environment concept and, 30
self-awareness and boundaries issue
and, 30, 77
styles of contact and, 30, 77
Gilliland, B. E., 120
Gladding, S., 273, 276, 277, 278,
293, 296
Goal consensus, 13
See also Goal setting
Goal setting
action plans and expectations and,
162–164
affective domain of, 160
behavioral domain of, 160
clear articulation of goal and, 140
(table), 145 (table), 160–161
goal qualities and, 161 (table)
identification of the problem and, 158